The World Comes Under Islam

The World Comes Under Islam

Transformation of Civilizations

Dr. Gangadhar Nanda

Kaveri Books
New Delhi - 110 002

First Published in 2006

ISBN-13: 978-81-7479-070-5

Published by

Kaveri Books

4832/24, Ansari Road

New Delhi-110002 (India)

Tel: 011-23288140, 4707 2321

E-mail : info@kaveribooks.com

kaveribooks@gmail.com

Website: www.kaveribooks.com

PRINTED IN INDIA

Dedication

Dedicated to memory of the unarmed innocent men and women who faced an unprecedented death in the World Trade Centre on 11th September, 2001 unwittingly as an instrument to open the eyes of Euro-American Christians and their non-Muslim allies to witness the dreadful consequences of Islamic Jehad, sponsored by Global Islamic Movement, (misnomered as terrorists' attack) while setting its first step in the United States of America for the escalation of 'Transformation of Civilizations'.

And

Dedicated to memory of those orthodox men, women and children of Bosnia and Herzegovina who suffered a cruel death and extreme humility in millions for five hundred years challenging it for a national gain for their next generations in the face of the gun and taught the world that only a determined will can generate a power structure which is more powerful than the gun and pen to win over their enemy backed by the strongest world power and accelerate in their favour the great 'Transformation of Civilizations'.

Author

Preface

In a report heading "Asia 2025" with a concerted conclusion made by some keen observers of the USA stated that the Third World War might occur on the Asian soil, probably towards 2025 A.D.

On the other hand, some social thinkers say that if there would be a Third World War, it would be between two civilizations.

Both the above statements seem to be erroneous and evasive. These statements give rise to three questions– (a) shall there be a Third World War as it had occurred earlier on a certain land among some rival nations confined to a fixed period? (b) If there shall be a Third World War, what would be its infrastructure? (c) Which two civilizations would confront in the ensuing Third World War?

The USA is certain that the occurrence of the future World War would be somewhere in Asia. Some speculate that the Third World war may be a star war or a war in the space. It would consume the least time from the beginning to the end.

This simply means that a nation should attack on another using the space as it was done in the last World War or that X dropped a bomb or launched a missile on Y to retaliate it with out any precaution.

This is impossible on two grounds. First, X has its own men (men of similar blood, skin, race, language and culture) in the land of Y. On the face of imminent war and animosity it is untenable for X to repatriate its men from the land of Y. It so happened in the case of the USA who surrendered before Iran to repatriate its own men. It brought unpopularity to the then President Jimmy Carter. Secondly if X drops a bomb or launches a missile against Y, the men of Y who constitute a strong minority in the land of X must oppose and pressurize X to refrain from its attempt.

Secondly the chance of occurrence of a Third World War similar to that of last World War is very slim. The Second World War took place 20 years after the First World War. Present difference between the Second and expected Third World War is an uncertain period plus past 60 years.

Sixty years back the USA was the only atomic powerful country. But presently production of nuclear weapons, its testing and simultaneously threatening through it now has become an old fashion. Use of bomb for mass destruction as was done in the last World War would be impossible.

Research reveals that if there will be a Third World War, its debute will be in a new shape. It will get converted in to a constellation of civil wars, which is more dangerous, more horrendous and more extensive than before. The expected Third World War will take the shape of a Global Civil War that does not mean a war between two strong nations or countries, which keep other countries in tandem. Global Civil War here means the struggle between people or group of people of two or more different civilizations in thousands of different places in different countries until one civilization wins over all other adversary civilizations. In other words the world war will take the shape of civil wars fought in almost all the countries of the world between the people or groups of people of different races, societies or civilizations with a retaliatory motive of one against the other that leads to the ethnic cleansing of the weaker sections or groups or civilizations

Regarding the places of occurrence, it shall be in those countries where Islam has formed a strong minority, approximately forming 25 to 40 percent of the total national population or where the minorities, although proportionately less are strong enough to encounter the majority on account of their unity and defensive strength. From this point of view the most affected countries in the expected Third World War turned

Global Civil War would be the U.S.A, all the European countries, African countries, India Nepal and Sri Lanka etc in Asia and all other countries that come under this category. By that time the pre-armageddon death toll of non-Muslim minorities that is counted in millions reaching up to their extinction in Islamic countries like Pakistan, Bangladesh, Algeria and some African countries will not come to light

The characteristics of the 3rd World War would be almost similar to the previous two wars if it occurs before 2020. After the year 2020, ratio of religious population of the Western countries and the U.S.A would have changed to an effective extent, giving rise to a strong Islamic vigour with a formidable shape of offensive population in the Western soil. . Hence, if there will be an extensive war after 2020, the war would be a Global Civil War. The war between two civilizations would have no particular starting point of place, date or time. One can easily see the glimpse of a Global Civil War in modern Bosnia, Chechnya, Lebanon, Palestine, Kosovo and in the Kashmir part of India. Whether it would be a usual world war or a global civil war, the Great War is inevitable with in 2020 to 2025. Contrary to the notion of the U.S.A, the future world war will be more severe in Western countries and in the U.S.A than anywhere in the world. The rest of the world has tasted earlier the pungency of the civil wars related to Transformation of Civilizations. All the Islamic countries would come out to participate in their holy war of jehad, the last great war of Transformation of Civilizations.

There is reason to describe 2020 to 2025 as the interim period for the great Transformation of Civilizations. Millions of babies born out of human cloning and artificial insemination could be best used as an instrument of war during this interim period. It is learnt that the scientists defying the world opinion have already impregnated many women through this process. A cloned baby born in the year 2005 would be 15 years old towards 2020. This could be best used as an instrument of war in this transitory period. Boys at an average of 15 years were used in thousands in 1990 in the Iran USA war. They were used as front line guards to protect the soldiers who were at the rear and were blasted in hundreds. In many Afro Asian countries the boys and girls at this tender age are handling lethal weapons. Towards 2020-25 they would be used as vote banks in the popular elections and bring victory to their respective political parties. Islamic countries would produce millions of such babies to train them as terrorists towards 2020.These unidentified and rejected productions would act as the best weapons by the Islamic countries to fight against anti Islamic forces in general and against their arc enemy Euro Americans in particular.

Although majority of European countries and the U.S.A differ in many points they are almost concordant in cultural and religious affinities. Majority of the people of Europe and the U.S.A are the followers and preachers of Christianity and great adherents of Western civilization, widely known as modern civilization. Christian culture diffused over all the aspects of life of both European and American Christians either expressedly or impliedly. The word "Euro America" is used here in this respect.

Now is the question of "Global Islamic Movement". Before 1980 Islam was confined with in its society with all its paraphernalia in different countries of the world. As a natural process of Islam the society was gradually expanding with its increasing influence in harmony with the increase of its population. Islamic revolution in Iran gave rise to Islamic renaissance, which diffused, over all the countries of the world where there are Muslims whether in the majority or in the minority form of population. Muslims round world are interlinked with the knitting of their unstinted culture that elevates Islamic brotherhood. Though Muslims everywhere in the world are equal in their socio-religious sphere of life, they could feel as a universal entity after the Islamic renaissance that took place during the last eighties.

After the Second World War was over, communist USSR and capitalist USA continued the cold war to topple each other. Mean while they pocketed different Islamic countries of the world in tandem to maintain their balance of power. During this period the Islamic countries unprecedently began to flourish with the natural source of oil and with the help of supporting world powers. USSR died down and it took rebirth in the shape of many new Islamic countries on its land. The encumbrance of oil reserves under the U.S.S.R soil now became the unprecedented wealth of Islamic countries. Emergence of new Islamic states, oil enrichment, technical development, hasty enhancement in Islamic population throughout the world and the religious scripture Quran with its extraordinary deliverance of Islamic communal expansionism spurred the Islamic countries to form a consolidated entity with a new spirit of adventure to fight and take vengeance against the capitalist master mind U.S.A to crush its spirit of modern civilization and finally to convert the whole world in to a kingdom Allah, the only God with Mohammed the only messenger who codified the only religion Islam which is defined by the only religious scripture Quran. This tendency of Muslims gave rise to the "Global Islamic Movement." U.S.A which once used Pakistan and Afghanistan as its claw to pounce over U.S.S.R would gradually realize that Pakistan is no other than a bear whose warmth had given him the pleasure of a blanket.

Islamic virus has almost oxidized the ancient societies or civilizations of whole of Asian secular countries and the African countries. The administrative policy of the largest democratic state India is fully under its directives. Jehad has been already intruded in to the USA and Europe flanked by terrorism. Osama bin Laden, the most favourite man in the Islamic world next to Prophet Mohammed has dreamt to hoist the flag of crescent on the American soil during his lifetime. Unambiguously we can say that Islam has been deep rooted in America with all its accessories and weapons. Can the President of the USA cancel the celebration of Eid-ul-Fitr in the White House which is a devotional function of Muslim Mujahids or the so called terrorists who are the pioneers of crescent and followers of Jehad which is an inevitable part of Islam, the religion of Muslims? As long as Euro- America could remain aloof or secluded from the track of Islamic influence there would be the maintenance of balance of power between the cross and the crescent. Nobody can deny that the scale-pan of Islam had been lowered on September11, 2001 to the extent of touching the ground. It was a sheer escape but the terrorism and Jehad, which has galvanized the whole of Europe, particularly England, the heart of Europe and the USA, would make the people escapists. There must be an equilibrium maintained between the two super powers to save the national life of different states. Let the garden of the world get embellished with varieties of social flowers and tribal buds to be more pleasant ant charming.

Every nation must find out the ways that would restrain its citizens from the clutch of its civil enemies. The whole of Europe and the USA must innovate ways to save its majority people (who are the torch bearers of Western Civilization) from carnage, to save the culture from obliteration, to save the society from anarchy and destabilization and to save the Western Civilization from extinction. Euro Americans concentrate their plans on issues related to present but Islam concentrates its pans and issues that relates to future.

It is very convenient to get a child from a forcible copulation or rape than to get a revolver or a gun or even a knife. When a rapist's vigor, virility and vengeance is reflected as a human baby and this weapon is cheaply and easily available on forcible marriage and rape, unobstructed production of children from a wife or wives is the best means to win over a land by victory in the war field or in the field of popular election. People of keen observation on future prospects and belonged to an organized and offensive race, can better use this method for a global victory. This process helped Islam to win a large number of countries in the world and to devastate a lot of ancient civilizations. Presently this weapon has become policy oriented as "Grow and Get" (grow your population and get the kingdom) by Islam like the policy of "Divide and Rule" by the British. The Muslim soldiers of Pakistan raped and impregnated Bengali women in 1971. This was the result of the production of thousands of ruthless, barbaric youths, who were used as human weapons against USSR by Afghanistan and against India by Pakistan. Global Islamism has implemented this Grow and Get policy very carefully on the soil of Europe and U.S.A to win over this land and to wave the flag of crescent.

Because a Muslim (with few exceptions) is above all nationalisms or national interests other than Islamic nationalism, he is in general an international citizen. He is a part and parcel of Global Islamic Nationalism. Islam is adversary to Euro American interest, culture and civilization. Global Islamic Movement exclusively meant for the pulverization of all non-Islamic civilizations of the world in general and Euro American civilization in particular. So let the Euro Americans feel the fervour of Islamic nationalism and realize how the consolidated strength of Islam with its intensive measures of Islamic celebrity is extensively stretched in different countries of the world including their own.

As a part of strategy the USA and NATO countries have deployed their naval, air and army forces in different countries of the world to extend their power of control over those countries to which they want to subdue. Similarly, as a strategy of war, a global civil war, which is under process, the Islamic countries under the Global Islamic Movement have set their war instruments (mostly human beings with an Islamic bent of mind) in different countries of the world to extend their power of control over the non-Islamic countries, which are presently under the process of Islamization. This has been elaborated in the IInd and IIIrd chapter of this book.

Everybody meticulously knows about the Western civilization. But very few people, hardly one in a million are aware of the charactreristics of Islam. Islam changed the notion of the Westerners about what really it is. Nevertheless the larger part of it is still unearthed or undetected by the Westerners. The Europeans particularly the Western politicians do not have the clear concept of Islam. Their actions and reactions against Saddam Hussain and Bin Laden etc prove its veracity. They think that suppression of Husseins and Ladens is the only way of solution of the tragedy of terrorism. This is not a correct idea. Very few people know that Quran, the religious scripture of Islam is the chief instigator of jehad, which, according to Western terminology is called "Terrorism". Mohammed is the first Prophet who introduced jehad as an inevitable part of Islam, the religion he propounded according to the will of Allah, the only God. Hence 'Terrorism' according to Western ideology or jehad according to Islamic ideology is a part and parcel of Islam. Where there is no jehad there is no Islam. But the word 'terrorism' is not sufficient to explain jehad. It only describes a narrow view or a side view of jehad. Hence jehad is briefly described in chaptrer I.

Out of more than one billion Muslims who constitute the Islamic population, a third of them live in 35 states where Muslims are in a minority as in India, Britain, France and Germany. Interestingly in the Muslim majority countries they kill, convert and expell the non-Muslim minorities. On the contrary they demand, fight and get the superclass citizenship status as minority race in non-Muslim majority countries.

Majority of politicians and bureaucrats of many non-Muslim countries pose themselves to be very wise. But they lack comparative analytical studies of different religions and cultures. Hence they cannot correctly access the on going incidents of their societies and act foolishly. They lead the nation towards anarchy and destabilization. I have elaborated the ideas, sentiments, aspirations, conditions, actions, reactions and catastrophic conditions of the people of some "affected naions" (defined in chapter IV) of the world who are suffeing heinously for the crimes committed by their national leaders. Almost all the Euro-American and Afro-Asian countries of the world are put in the Islamic cauldron and as a result, the civilizations of those countries are under serious threat giving rise to a civil war, a global civil war. I have given the indications of the Global Civil War and future prospects of affected countries of the world in chapter IV.

In this book I want to draw the attention of dear readers and social thinkers on the following points

1. Terrorism is incomprehensible with out the knowledge of Jehad.
2. The anticipated Third World War would be a Global Civil War, if it occurs after 2020.
3. Human beings would be used as the best weapon in this Global Civil War.

4. The war would be more severe in the European countries and in the USA than any other flourishing countries of the world.
5. Non-proliferation of human beings or "Global Human Birth Control" is more essential than non-proliferation of weapons.
6. The present social system of Euro America having its constitution given equal or special privileges to non-Christian minorities would bring Euro-America entirely in the name of secularism under the shadow of Islam.
7. Islamic civil invasion on Euro-America relevant to Transformation of Civilizations is under process. Pre indications of the third world war or the Global Civil War are in the offing.
8. The first decade of twenty first century would signify the division of World power into Christianity and Islam instead of the previously held capitalism and communism. Towards the year 2015 the world population would be divided into two entities– (a) The Islamic entity and (b) non–Islamic entity.
9. A single civilization that symbolizes either of the power would be dominant over all the civilizations according to the theory of "Transformation of Civilizations".
10. All political slowgans and promises of different political parties of different nations of the world will be rebounded against the invincible wall of Islamic communalism saturating the second phase of the Transformation of Civilizations. All quotatioins, morales, moral precepts and cermons would prove foolish and futile soon after the ethnic population of a non-Islamic country comes down to an average of 75% of the total population abdicating the rest 25% to Islamic minority.
11. A race or civilization with out warring perspective or retaliatory spirit is subject to dissolution with in the second decade of this century.

12. Communal questions would be more dominant than all other questions in the Parliament houses of all the secular democratic nations.
13. Towards the year 2015, all the secular countries of the world would discard their secular characteristics to identify themselves through a particular religion, the religion of their strongest community,
14. Disintegration of European countries, communist countries and the U S A giving rise to Islamic states would be a common phenomenon after 2015.
15. Presently the world powers are identified by their economic strength. In the next decade the world powers will be identified by the strength of their defensive religious population.
16. A mutiny would sweep the defence force of secular countries on communal grounds resulting the division of military into two groups, one group supporting the national interest and the other committing treachery to the nation.
17. The past two World Wars were fought between two power groups for colonial expansion. But the third World War or the Global Civil War would be fought among the people under religious divisions for the victory of one civilization over other civilizations.
18. Religion plays the vital role after the discoveries and inventions to shorten the distance between the nations around the globe.

Let the politicians and great thinkers of the world draw their attention on the above points. These give rise to many serious questions – Whether the world civilizations would entirely extinct by the greatest Islamic fanatic blow gradually and systematically in a planning manner?

If a concerted attempt will not be initiated from today to counteract the dragonish assault of fanaticism and stop the proliferation of human weapons then no powerful force on the surface of the earth would be able to stop the process of the great Transformation of Civilizations. Absorption of civilizations by the strongest civilization is no different than the extermination of civilizations. It is high time for the European and American Christians to be alert for their social and civil security.

I thank Sri Tripurari Rath, my venerable uncle who taught me Islam and Christianity. I owe to Mr. A Ghosh, Houston, Texas, U.S.A whose thrilling literature prodded me to study the future aspects in connection with practical application of religious precepts over the world affairs.

I thank my *Dharm Patni* (wife) Smt. Saudamini Devi for her service and devotion that helped me to concentrate in my study.

I am grateful to Sri Sarat Chandra Panda, a great scientist of Odisha, Bhubaneswar, for his timely suggestions and needful guidance to enrich the brilliance of this book.

Last but not the least is my homage to Shri Rakesh Goel, honourable publisher of this book. His timely attempt could bring this book to light.

Gangadhar Nanda

Bidya Bhusan Nagar, Jaypur,
Pin-764 001, District : Koraput
Odisha, INDIA

Contents

CHAPTER 2 : EURO-AMERICA UNDER GLOBAL ISLAMIC MOVEMENT 94-167

1

Islam and Jehad

While the state was exhausted by the Persian war and the Church was distracted by the Nestorian and Monophysite sects, Mohammed, with the sword in one hand and with the Koran in the other, erected his throne on the ruins of Christianity and Rome.

— *Edward Gibbon*

1. Islam and its Aspects

"Islam came into this world in the bosom of one of the most backward of the peoples. In a very short time it has raised them to pre-eminence in every field. Now the Muslims make 25 per cent of the world population and are now 1.5 billion strong Ummah. The Muslims' sincerity, honesty, integrity and truthfulness are the forces of the Islamic world and the purpose of the Islam is to lead mankind to live as Allah wills".

(a) Some Fundamental Concepts of Islam

Islam has some fundamental concepts. The first of all is:

(i) Hazrat Mohammed is the last Prophet of Allah, the God of Muslims (There is no God but Allah and Mohammed is his Prophet).

(ii) The message of the Quran, the religious scripture of Islam, is the last and immutable message of Allah (delivered by Him to none but Mohammed).

(iii) To honour Mohammed as the last Prophet, to honour the Quran as the religious scripture and to worship Allah as the only God is absolutely necessary for every Muslim.

(iv) Those (Muslims) who honour and accept all these principles are collectively called the "Millat" who are only authorized to stay in this world and to enjoy it. Those who do not obey these principles are Kafirs and have no right to live in this world. They are subject to be tortured and killed.

According to these principles, unity and co-existence of humanity or universal brotherhood is anti-Islamic and is not acceptable. To finish these Kafirs or non-Muslims, to assimilate them by conversion into Millat or Islamic brotherhood is the religious duty of every Muslim.

Secondly Islam divides this world into two parts- a) Dar-ul-Islam or the land of Muslims and (b) Dar-ul-Harab or the land of non-Muslims. It is the religious duty of Muslims to convert the non-Islamic land or Dar-ul-Harab into Islamic land or Dar-ul-Islam.

The third fundamental concept of Islam is Jehad. Jehad is the name of that religious war which is meant to kill the non-Muslims and to convert their land into Islamic land. To die in this religious war or to die for Islam is the most sacred duty of a Muslim. Every Muslim cherishes to die as a religious fighter or Mujahid, because the attainment of Jannat or Islamic heaven is definite only for them.

The five pillars of Islam : (i) Shahada (professing of the faith), (ii) Salat (Prayer), (iii) Soum (fasting), (iv) Zakat (alms for the poor Muslims) and, (v) Hajj (Pilgrimage to Mecca) are a must for every Muslim. Religiously a Muslim is duty-bound to say Namaz five times a day.

There is a definite process to work out these Islamic principles. This process is called Jehad which is an inevitable part of Islam. Mohammed himself implemented this Jehad for the expansion of Islam and his followers have been following this process throughout the last 1400 years.

(b) Islamic Concept of Nationalism

Islam is a military religion. It possesses a full-fledged definition of a Muslim's birth, behaviour, marriage, language, culture, system of worship, etc. The Quran is the religious scripture of Islam. Allah (There is no God but Allah) is said to have dictated all the precepts and rules of action to Mohammed. No more can be added to the Quran or deducted from it as it is absolutely defined by Allah. As a soldier works out the order of his general instantaneously without thinking anything, so a person who has faith in the Quran and Islam performs religious observances without waiting for the consequence. Islam has some specific rules. It means to an Islamic nation entrusted with some special working policies, which ordains the Islamic reality with its equality, honesty and jurisprudence. Islamic jurisprudence, police force, diplomacy and every branch of an Islamic nation signify the differences between an Islamic nation and a non-Islamic nation.

Islam does not recognize any nationalism

According to Islam, nationalism is the narrow-minded and sectarian thought of the administrative infrastructure of a country. Islam wants to launch a World Islamic Movement in the name of Hizbullah movements in all parts of the world and Iran is likely to take its leadership. Interest in nation-building is weird thinking for Islam. As quoted by M.R.Beg-"If a Muslim is true to the Quran he cannot be a nationalist, nor an internationalist and never a humanist. It is only communalism, which breeds in his mind. Such persons cannot be expected to work for national interest."

Generally nationalism means the unit of language, birthplace, race, tradition, culture, etc. Nationalism in Islam means only to an Islamic discipline "Deen." Quran opposes all nationalism but Islam. It believes only in one theory that is "Global Islamization".

According to Prophet Mohammed "No person or group which serves Western political, cultural or economic interest can claim the leadership of the Islamic Ummah or even a part of it. If they are faithful in mobilizing the whole Islamic Ummah against the Non-Islamic forces, which is mentioned as their enemy, there will be no room left for nationalistic or sectarian sentiment".

"People would converge from different countries and from four corners to one point (Mecca). They belong to varieties of language, colour, race and creed. But when they come into a particular circumference they take off their national robes of their own lands and wear a uniform dress and all become one. Those are the army of the great Emperor of the whole world and the heaven and chained into the loyalty of one Lord and led into procession towards one capital. Here they would express their unquestioning obedience."

"This is what we call Islamic nationalism. They are the citizens of an international group. No colour or creed, language, birthplace, etc., can create any barrier for such a group. According to them the words like Turkish nationalism, Iranian nationalism, and Arbian nationalism are the enigmatic thoughts of Western rudiments. People of Islam have specific principles and destinations which are described in the Quran". Islam is to Muslims what Nationalism is to all the non-Muslims of the World. Nationalism is a meaningless word in the Islamic dictionary.

Assertions of Maulana Maududi on Islam

Maulana Abul Ala Maududi, the founder of Jamat - e- Islami says – "Nowhere the Quran recognizes a nationalism that is founded on the combination of Muslims and Kafirs. The Quran has divided the whole world into two groups, i.e. one is the group of Allah or Hijb-e-Allah and the other is Hijb-ul-Satan or the group of Satans. All non-Muslims belong to the latter group (Hijb-ul-Satans).

Some liberalists profess that a nation can be formed with the coalition of Muslims and Non-Muslims as it was done possible in Medina in the time of Mohammed by the union of Jews and Mohammedans. But regarding the falsehood and impropriety of such kind of concerted nationalism Maududi asserts – "The concerted nationalism that had once occurred at the time of Mohammed by Jews and Mohammedans can be said to be a military alliance. Afterwards the Muslims expelled many Jews and exterminated the rest. This is the last result of concerted nationalism".

There is a religious advice given in the system of Islamic administration not to accept or obey any other kind of political rule except the sovereignty of Allah. In short, an Islamic nation is a missionary nation, which aims at establishing in the whole world the empire of Allah.

"Where there are Muslims in majority and are organized, it is their religious duty to enforce Islamic rule. To support or favour an anti-Islamic rule remaining outside of that party is anti-Islamic. It does not suffice to express our willingness to the Quran. Practically we have to introduce ourselves as honest Muslims and to do this we have to introduce Islamic rule in this country".

"It is not an ordinary thing to introduce Islamic rule by canceling the present administration. Remaining under a non-Islamic (false) government and enjoying all sorts of advantages from it if we only hope for a true Islamic rule it is nothing but a fool's Paradise. Discard all sorts of advantages you avail from the false (Non-Islamic) Government and face the danger with courage. You can't obtain a good Government at your convenience".

According to the Islamic term what the Muslims want to establish is "Din-i-Haq". It means to obey Allah as the only ruler and to dedicate out personal and congregational life in His service. "Before the formation of an Islamic country the Muslim multitude must be made a strong unit. A national feeling would be created in them. A strong man having strong leadership qualities must direct them. This man would unite the Muslims and a national military unit would be made. Where there are Muslims in majority they would form the Islamic rule according to the Islamic democratic policy. When Muslims are in minority, they should try to safeguard all their rights and protect their Islamic personality in accordance with the special right of minorities. Muslims must protect their Islamic identity in all the employment and political fields of representation. Muslim representatives having been elected by their voters must get their due job in the Ministry".

"Those Muslims who are at the helm of affairs, must always think that they are invested with a serious responsibility to work out the orders of the Quran. If they shrink to do so, they shall certainly be punished on the Day of Judgment. A society which cherishes such a religious thought is not a minority society. It is a nation within a nation. The name of its constitution is Shariat, which is above all the man made constitutions. It is not amendable like all other constitutions".

(c) Islamic Concept of War

The Islamic concept of war is called Jehad. It is fought either in the battlefield or is door-to-door attack on the basis of communal bigotry. Islamic war or Jehad doesn't recognize any prescribed time or place of war, any agreement or treaty of war or any international law.

The adversary wing or the opponent party of an Islamic war of Jehad is the non-Muslim entity. All the non-Muslims are considered as the true enemies of Islam. In an Islamic majority province or in an Islamic country the non-Muslims are treated as the enemies of Islam. Islamic war or Jehad is meant to wage against them.

Islam does not recognize the citizenship of a native as described in geography. It recognizes only one's citizenship, the Islamic citizenship. Hence all the non-Muslims of the world are treated as their enemies and they are subject to be killed in the religious war termed as Jehad.

The Jehad or Islamic religious war is waged in three terms, (a) internal war or civil war based on communal grounds as it is in vogue in Israel, Bosnia and Kashmir between Muslims and non-Muslims, (b) external war in the form of Islamic invasion against a non-Islamic country as is made presently by Pakistan against India.(c) Global war, the war between nations of the world with a division of two entities, the Islamic entity and the non-Islamic entity. This Global war is the last Transformation of Civilization, which seems to take place towards 2020 A.D.

(d) Islamic Concept of Peace

Islam itself means peace or surrender. One cannot detect from the definition the presence of war or violence. Really Islam means complete surrender to Allah and his Prophet

Mohammed. There is no peace in the heart of a non-Muslim as long as he has not surrendered to Allah and his Prophet.

In his book "The Quranic Concept of War," the author says that there are three steps to bring peace and justice in the world. They are:

(a) To convince the non-Muslims that they should accept Islam without any question.

(b) To create puzzle and despair psychologically in the minds of non-Muslims.

(c) To inflict a military attack on non-Muslims.

Out of the above steps, particularly 'b' is applied against those communities who don't prepare to surrender before Islam. This step 'b' is the beginning stage of militant attacks against the non-Muslims. If the psychological war is fought successfully, then victory comes without the second step. If the situation forces Islam to wage war, the psychological depression that has been applied over the enemy through terrorism would help to get victory in the war with a complete surrender to Islam. This is the Islamic concept of peace.

(e) Some Peculiarities of Islam and Characteristics of a Muslim

> *"Islam is not like Christianity. It is not a religion of private conscience and private practice. Islam comes with some legal concepts. These concepts have civic significance and create a kind of social order. The religious ideal of Islam cannot be separated from the social order. Therefore the construction of a polity on national lines, if it means a displacement of the principle of solidarity is simply unthinkable to Muslims." – Md. Iqbal*

Islam is comprehensible through its distinctions. Unless its peculiar characteristics are not analyzed it would be difficult to accurately assess Islam. Some of its key characteristics are described below.

Islam never tolerates any nationalism except Islam. Every Muslim is asked to rot in Madrassas. "First I am a Muslim, than who so ever". A Muslim in Europe is first a Muslim and next he is a British or American or French. A Muslim is very conscious about his Islamic identity than any other non-Islamic civilian.

Muslims, by dint of their unity and strength, give their helping hand to a country's majority society to expel the foreign rule, particularly the Euro-American colonialism from that country. Soon after the success, they demand the price of their labour in kind of a separate Islamic homeland. In European countries they took part in the rebuilding of the nation after the Second World War as wage-earning migrants from African and Asian countries. But now they claim their justified price by strangle-holding the majorities with the strength of their unity and population of global Islamic bigotry.

Azan, the Challenging Call of Islamic Victory

One of the most important characteristics of Islam is the performance of Azan. Every Muslim is required to pray five times a day at particular intervals. Before the commencement of the prayer a call is given to the Muslims to congregate in the mosque for prayer. This is called Azan or call to prayer. This is the inevitable part of Islam in the whole of Islamic infrastructure. The commencement of Azan in a non- Islamic or secular country is the first sign of Islamic suzerainty over that country challenging the authenticity and ethnicity of the cultural and religious heritage of that land. Once the regular call for prayer or Azan is established in a non-Islamic nation, it is confirmed that the religion and culture of the land, which constitutes its national civilization, is under challenge of Islam. The call to prayer (Azan) is as follows:

Allah Ho Akber, Allah Ho Akber, Allah Ho Akber, Allah Ho Akber. Ashhado Allah Illaha Illallaha Ashado Allah Illaha Illallaha. Ashhado Rana Mohammed Ar Rasululla. Ashhado Anna Mohammed Ar Rasululla. Haya Allah-Sa-Salah. Haya Allah-Sa-Salah Haya Allah-La-Falah.Haya Allah Li Falah Allah Ho Akber, Allah Ho Akber. La Illah Illalah.

Meaning of Azan

"Allah is the greatest. Allah is the greatest. Allah is the greatest. Allah is the greatest. I swear that no body is worthy to be worshipped but Allah. (There is no God but Allah). I swear that Mohammed is the only messenger of Allah. I swear that Mohammed is the only messenger of Allah. Come to prayer. Come to prayer. Get success. Allah is the greatest. Allah is the greatest. Nobody is to be worshipped but Allah."

Muslims are very sensitive towards their collective interests. Whenever and wherever they feel that there is a non-Islamic touch to their Islamic sentiment, they immediately react and revolt in unison against it with a concerted slogan- "Islam is in danger. Allah! Ho Akbar". They are not compatible with any other people except Islam. No race in the world is so reactionary as Islam. Such kind of reactionary motives not only terrifies others but also gives impetus to Islam to proceed ahead in the midst of oppositions, impediments and conflicts as a formidable and victorious race.

Muslims belong to the category of a mobile race. They are tenacious travellers and are ambulant from the very root of their civilization. Though the Europeans did not recognize them as good discoverers during the sweeping period of navigation, they were skillful mariners and expert rovers. Apart from this they were hard-core cavaliers, merciless invaders and successful conquerors. This made them to overlord a large part of land on the earth.

By nature Islam is an invading race. Such a race always poses a sense of contempt to others. Even a slight deviation in its internal discipline creates havoc and holocaust that leads the society to utter misery.

An invading race with a distinct code of conduct always poses a dreadful appearance, gesture and gait. The people of this race always go in uniform like the army from their headgear to foot wears. Their clipping of moustache and trimming of beard, etc., are cared for under prescription. The observation of sunnat (Religious system) is a must for a Muslim. A Muslim male to whichever country he belongs, must undergo the circumcision of his penis as an inevitable part of Islamic religious rite.

Islamic tenets and rules are codified and uniformed in such a manner that it create civilians most disciplined but limited to

Islam. "Muslims, wherever they are in any part of the world, they never dissolve themselves in the main stream of that nation. Maintaining their Islamic identity and Islamic character untainted, they go on multiplying their population and prepare for a great Transformation of Civilizations.

Hence according to the definition of Islam one must conceive that a Muslim born either in the USA, England or in France is a friend and follower of Pakistan, Afghanistan, Palestine, Iran and Iraq. He is an international citizen of all the above countries. He would concentrate and care more for the benefit and welfare of all the above countries than his own homeland. He thinks and acts himself as a member of the Islamic world and a partner of the Global Islamic Movement. He least bothers about his own homeland and promulgates attempts to convert his homeland into an Islamic homeland.

As long as Muslims feel that their compatriots are not strong enough to crush them in a rise of revolt, they remain silent and perpetuate proliferating their population and strength. Whenever they sense that their non-Islamic neighbours are unequal in strength and are not capable to fight against them, they immediately declare Jehad against them.

Muslims take pride to have their nomenclature with the family members of Mohammed in general and prophet Mohammed in particular. They prefix, suffix or interpose the name Mohammed to glorify their personal life style. Mohammed was a great conqueror, a ruthless killer of nonbelievers (i.e., non-Muslims), a lustful sexy Prophet, a Prophet of polygamy with religious over-lordship over the womenfolk and blessed by Allah as a husband of unrestricted number of wives, a master of plundering wealth and slave women, a great instigator to provoke his followers to kill non followers of Islam (particularly Christians and Jews) world wide and a great proponent of a wonderful Paradise with unending opportunities for coition with the most beautiful women of one's choice for an infinite period. Naming oneself as Mohammed, one aspires to be a man like him, to be wealthy, sexy, rude to others and a religious zealot.

Islam is male-dominating with their women treated as half the man in the matter of jurisprudence. In case of divorce, maintenance and inheritance, etc., women are left alienated compared to man.

Islam never believes in democracy, which it spurns as a Western form of government system. Islam has its own form of democratic system of government where there is no place for non-Muslims.

The sword is the religious emblem of Islam. Islam stands by sword and expands by sword. It harbours civil war religiously inherent in itself.

Muslims cannot pull on together with any other race or nationals even though they seem very humble, simple or obedient. They are the most incompatible race engrossed with xenophobia. Hence they try to expel, kill or convert other non-Islamic compatriots. When a non-Muslim population comes to a decaying position either mentally or physically, it faces one of the three factors - it has to (a) flee from that country as refugees or (b) stay there embracing Islam or (c) be killed by the people of Islam.

Muslims belong to the most migratory race in the world. One can find them in every nook and corner of the world with undeviated and uniformed Islamic social tradition and Islamic cultural affinity. One can hardly find in a Muslim the exterior deviations as an exception to suit the situation. Mohammed emboldened them to go and preach his message, the message of Allah to convert the whole world to Islam.

Individual freedom is sanctioned to a Muslim male but not to a female in Islam. Strict religious discipline is imposed in the case of a Muslim woman. When the British Princess Diana was roaming with the Arabian Amir Dodi Fahd and was entertaining herself with Arabian tycoons, it was not a point of objection. But when the Bahraini princess Mariam al Khalifa eloped with her American lover Lieutenant captain Johnson in the guise of an American marine, they did not accept it and challenged their marriage. If the princess would not have asked for political asylum soon after her arrival at Chicago and get a positive response from the Government she would have faced prosecution for breaking an Islamic taboo and it would have created danger to her life. This peculiarity of Islam restrains their womenfolk from their reciprocal marriage outside Islam and protects Islam from ethnic cleansing.

Islam does not believe in secularism, cultural, religious or national pluralism. It believes in one culture and one religion. In no sphere is the pluralism accepted in Islam except in polygamy. To accept cultural, religious and national pluralism is anti-Islamic and strictly prohibited in the Islamic circle. This pluralistic co-existence is replaced by the holy war Jehad.

Lack of cultural and religious pluralism leads to a lack of linguistic pluralism in Islam. Allah is sympathetic to only one language, Arabic. Hence a Muslim is compulsorily taught Arabic. Twenty-two countries of the world have accepted Arabic as their national language and main source of communication. One billion Muslims in the world recite Quran in its original language, Arabic.

Muslims are as much defensive to their own religion as they are averse and offensive to the religions of others. A Muslim living in an alien non-Islamic country never feels himself a fish out of water. He never feels that he is an immigrant or an outsider of that country. Soon after his arrival on a new soil he confirms it as its own and thinks its non-Islamic natives as its opponent.

Wherever in the world there is a single Muslim, he is an Islamic entity. He is the pivot and founder of Islamic nation on that soil. The nation building process starts from the same one man through Islamic Jehad without deviating from the Islamic identity.

Islam is adheres to monotheism. Mecca being the only abode of Allah, Muslims all over the world concentrate their religious journey to this particular place. A confluence of two million people at a place creates international brotherhood limited to their co-religionists.

The word "enemy" has a peculiar definition in Islam. All those who are not devoted to Islam are considered as enemies of Islam. Although all non-Muslims are emphasized as enemies of Islam in general, Christians and Jews are in particular enemies of Islam.

The holy war or Jehad against non-Muslims is a must for a true Muslim. Because it is a sacred duty, the precepts of the Quran provoke every Muslim to resort to Jehad to be praised by Allah and go to Paradise. This inspires a married young man of 29 Mustafa Mozeh (1968–97) to leave his motherland with a determination to kill Salman Rushdie in London. The same inspiration impelled the British youth Belal to go to India and got exploded in Kashmir. Both died unsuccessful but with the spirit of Islam.

Muslims are well trained to be merciless and less averse for killing any animal. As a part of religious duty every Muslim is obliged to sacrifice an animal on the occasion of Id-ul-Zuha by cutting the throat of the sacrificial animal. Hence Muslims comparatively are less sensitive and least serious about the killing of any sort of creature whether it is a man or an animal. A man with less barbarity can kill a man by shooting him at a distance. But it is not easy in the case of killing a man by slitting his throat or killing him/her by hard torture. One must have unflinching rudeness, brutish ferocity to face a man or an animal to cut his throat or a major organ of the body. Mohammed gave unreserved praise to his fellow men for killing a man. This made them courageous to slit the throat of US soldiers in Iraq.

A Muslim is always addicted to sex and violence. Sex at home emboldens him to resort to polygamy. Relating to violence his act knows no bound. In a collision he cuts the throat of his rival or sets fire to his house or rapes his rival's females. He is more interested to test his weapon on Kafir. Hence to exterminate a non-Muslim from the occupied land and declare the land a sacred one, Dar-ul-Islam is a dream of his life. Even the corpse of a Muslim is distinguished from that of a non-Muslim as Anjahani and Marhoom respectively.

Islam believes only in one religion, Islam. According to it, it is the only religion of mankind. Non-Muslims are irreligious or Kafirs. According to Islam Kafirs are not privileged to sustain in this world.

Christianity's doctrines have evolved the course of history, continuing to change as compromises made with current cultural standard. Thus one finds women ordained as priests in the

Church of England and homosexuality condoned in some American churches even though traditional Christian teachings would not have permitted such things. Such things don't occur in Islam. The basic teachings of Islam are wreathed on the foundation of the Quran revealed by Allah to Prophet Mohammed while the central teachings of Christianity are based on the Bible and the decisions arrived at in various councils. The teachings of the Quran cannot be amended or deciphered. Islam demands its people never to accept another as their God except Allah.

It calls to the Muslims to resort to divine legislation wherever any problem or dispute arises.

Islam wants the Muslims to be strong against their enemies i.e. non-Muslims and compassionate to each other.

It orders the Muslims never to consider the enemies of Islam as their friends. The holy Quran says "Let not the believers take the unbelievers as friends rather than believers, and whoever does this, he shall have nothing of Allah". (Al Imran 27)

Islam wants the rulers to do their best for the welfare of their community, to protect and safeguard Muslim property and dignity. Rulers should defend the Muslims, borders of Muslim countries and never give up an inch of the Muslims' land to the enemies. The Prophetic narration says – "Invaded nation suffers humiliation".

This religion is like a trap where access is very easy but it has no way for exit. A man without any restraint can embrace Islam but a Muslim cannot opt for an apostate, nor can remain in the society independent of religion. A renegade is considered anti-Islamic and declared as an enemy of Islam. Islam permits a Muslim to marry a non-Muslim woman whether she is a spinster or a widow but forbids a Muslim girl to marry outside.

Islam indulges in polygamy for man and monogamy for women. A Muslim can keep four wives at a time. In the Muta system he can keep concubines apart from these four wives. Exogamy is exclusively reserved for Muslim males.

Divorce is highly flexible in Islam. It takes as much time for a man to divorce a wife as he takes to spell "Talaq"(Islamic religious system of divorce) thrice. A man is privileged to divorce his wife at his will and pleasure. No decree of a judicial court is sought to empower a man to divorce his wife. But a Muslim woman is forbidden the right to divorce her husband.

Islam condemns birth control. On the contrary it strictly adheres to birth proliferation, which is considered as the best and the most successful weapon to be used for demographic attack. Excessive growth rate of population in Islam helps it to infiltrate and invade non-Islamic countries through internal conflict and popular election. There are hundreds of instances of Octogenarian Arabic Sheikhs having matrimonial alliances with teenaged Muslim girls from South India the Philippines, etc. Slave women proliferate innumerable children to their Muslim masters. An infertile woman becomes an easy prey to divorce.

Disintegration of a non-Islamic country is a must if there is an Islamic community in the term of minority. An Islamic society in a democratic or communist country is a troop of Islamic persons who always confine themselves to a 'ghetto' preparing themselves as a religious army to protect their socio-cultural and religious value and simultaneously to convert the country into an Islamic state. The former USSR may be quoted as an instance, which was segregated into many Islamic states. The rest- of the disintegrated part also apprehends division into some Muslim countries. Today's affected nations of the world including Euro-America may also be quoted as best examples of such kind of planned division in the near future.

Muslims always want to see their country populated exclusively with Muslims. In no way can non-Muslims become men of importance in a Muslim country and particularly in a country fully islamised and ruled under the Islamic law of Shariat. There are some Islamic countries like Afghanistan, Bahrain, Brunei, Djibouti, Gambia, Iran, Mali, Mauritania, Niger, Sahrawi, Somalia, Saudi Arabia, Maldives, Yemen, etc., where Islamic population is 99 per cent. Gradually all other Islamic countries are leading their population to reach the highest level of percentage by systematically dispelling the non-Muslims from their respective lands. Such peculiarity cannot be found in any non-Muslim European, Christian countries. On the contrary Western

Christian countries have become the target of Ethnic Cleansing and are put on the wheel of conversion into Islam.

Wherever there is a democratic country in the world with an Islamic entity in it having given to it constitutional special protective measures as a religious minority, the segregation of that country is inevitable including Euro-America. Euro-America is under an exact and accurate process of Islamisation and probably the Islamic world expects to reach its destination within 2015.

Islam is completely centralized as regards sexual matters and the sword. It permits a man to have sex with any of his co-wives in any manner and at any time. The Quran impels men to use the women captured in war for their sexual amusement (S 33:50). One can use a woman as a farmer uses his land at any time and in any manner he likes. Women can also be bought and sold (S 4:25). Mohammed received two slave girls as gifts from the Governor of Egypt.

According to Islam mankind is divided into two parts. One is believer of the faith, or the 'Momin' and the other is the 'Kafir' who does not accept Islam. The Kafir is defined as the enemy of Islam who is liable to be killed mercilessly. It is the pious duty of every Muslim to obey the order of the Quran. The enemy of Islam does not mean to a single person or society. It covers the whole of the non-Islamic world.

It is an infallible truth found in the course of history that where there are Muslims in majority in any part of the world, they pose a threat and feeling of hatred towards their non-Muslim compatriots. Their feeling of despise towards non-Muslims even in a non-Muslim majority country is a consensus.

The followers of Islam have three excellent characteristics i.e. (a) Unquestioning faith in one God, Allah (b) Equality among Muslims and (c) Incessant struggle or Jihad against their common enemy, the non-Muslims, in the name of Islam and Allah. They do not accept any other God exept Allah. Allah has no partner.

They don't compromise on any sort of political solution and bilateral agreement with non-Islamic people, group, government or nation in the matter of war, justice and conquest. Whatever agreement done in this regard is only temporary. They would repudiate the agreement made with non-Islamic government whenever they avail the opportunity and prepare for Jihad against their non-Islamic counterpart.

Islam defies everything, every argument that is un-Islamic. So when a Westerner questions about the divorce of a Muslim woman without a moment's hesitation only by uttering Talaq thrice and about the system of polygamy where a Muslim can marry and maintain up to four wives at a time and about the maintenance of the divorcee women, its Islamic reply does not satisfy him. But a true Muslim does not bother about it because he least wants to concern with the non-Islamic or anti-Islamic comments. He is concerned only about his own society.

Islam opposes birth control and family planning. On the contrary it favours growth of population. Islam advocates this policy since its inception. Mohammed, the founder of Islam encouraged polygamy and birth proliferation. He says, "My religious community (Umma) will increase its number more rapidly than other communities." Mr. Abdul Aziz, Editor, Pak weekly "Insaaf" told, "*Muslims reproduce children at a faster rate as compared to other nations*". This encouragement of birth proliferation and growth of population help Islam to win the war in the battlefield and popular election by securing majority of vote. In the Western countries decrease in the population of Europeans by birth control is being compensated by increasing number of Muslim settlers, infiltrators and proliferated Muslim children. This policy of birth proliferation can be identified as the poky of "Grow and Get" like the British policy of "Divide and Rule". "Grow and Get" policy advocated by Islam has the direct result of creating Islamic homelands everywhere on the surface of the earth. Literally "Grow and Get" means – "grow your population and get the land for you".

Islam is opposed to celibacy. Mohammed condemned ascetism and renouncement of worldly pleasures. According to him to embrace ascetism is cowardice. Renouncement of worldly pleasure is anti-Islamic. To observe celibacy is to go against Allah. A man reluctant to marry and enjoy women is not appreciable and not praiseworthy of Mohammed and Allah.

According to Islam, the Quran has been pure from its origin to this day. No human hand can replace or add any word written in the Quran. Many amendments have been made in Biblical precepts but the Quran is such a holy scripture, which is never amendable. According to the Quran to die for Islam is the best possible glory. A martyr in Islam is the direct itinerant to Paradise.

The characteristics of a Muslim can best be illustrated from the views made by Muslim scholars on Dr.A.P.J.Abdul Kalam, the President – elected nuclear scientist of India. In the Indian sense he is a Brahmachari, a bachelor of purest mind and body, who remains above all the worldly pleasures. He is so widely popular among the 800 million Hindus for his dedication to the national interest and personal character that he ranked the position of the first President of India, Dr.Rajendra Prasad.

But this noble man is felicitated neither by the Muslim community of India nor by the Muslim communities of the rest of the world. On the contrary there are the list of charges against him by the Muslim bigwigs.-"Dr Abdul Kalam never fought for the Muslims or Muslim causes. He never identified himself with the Muslim community." This is the statement made by a national level Muslim leader and an Ex-Muslim M.P. Syed Shahabuddin.

According to a sober Muslim thinker Rafiq Zakaria, "Dr. Kalam is a vegetarian, a bachelor and recites the Bhagavat Geeta. He has no Muslim friends. How could he be regarded as a Muslim President like Dr. Zakir Hussain and F. A. Ahmed"? According to the Islamic school Tabligi Jamat, simply having an Islamic name does not make a Muslim a Muslim. To be a Muslim he must become a Muslim. To become a Muslim he must disown all links of Pre-Islamic traditions of the convert.

Islam has a constitution of its own named the Quran. Its significance is that it cannot be amended. It asserts a code of law named Shariat. It defines a code of conduct for the Muslims, which is one and the same for 1400 years.

You mark a Muslim. You can find in him all the characteristics of a Muslim of the past 1400 years. You can find in him a Muslim who represents the feelings of the present Muslim community of the World. You can find in him the spirit of a Muslim who is destined to be born some day after some hundreds of years in the future.

(f) Mohammed Bin Osama Bin Laden, A Knitting Personality of Islamic Character

"The West's occupation of our country is old, but takes new forms. The struggle between them and us began centuries ago, and will continue. There can be no dialogue with occupiers."

> *"The Christian-Jewish alliance will not, God willing, be safe from attacks by the Mujahideen (Muslim warriors)...The alliance's installations and facilities everywhere will be subject to attacks. The enemy should not feel safe whether on land, sea or air,"*
>
> – Osama bin Laden.

Osama Bin Mohammed Bin Laden is a typical Islamic character. Though he is a versatile genius of Islamic sentiment, he leads a very ordinary life, rather the hardcore life of a cave dweller in the hilly tract of Afghanistan. He was born in the city of Riyadh in Saudi Arabia in the year 1957 and was one of the 53 children of his father, a building contractor. He studied in the High School and in the College of Jedda with management and economics as his favourite subjects and accomplished his career as a computer engineer.

The study of the Quran and the civil war in Beirut brought about a great change in his life. He could have been a good building contractor in Saudi Arabia and also a billionaire. But he chose a thorny path for his own way of life by abandoning a good career and comfortable life-style. However his source of income is no less than that of the richest person in the world. He married four wives, the first wife being a Saudi Arabian, the second a Syrian and the third probably an Indian. As to his fourth wife, he married a Pustu girl of Afghanistan who was most probably the niece of the Governor of the NWFP of Pakistan. He is related to the Pustu clan by blood as a protective measure by the terrific Pustu tribe. With all his wives and fifteen children he chose to remain in Afghanistan after he was banished from Saudi Arabia for his anti-American stance and extremist attitude of Islamism.

Laden has only one dream– to paint the whole world green, the colour of Islam. He wants that the non-Islamic countries should be Islamised and the Islamic countries should be ruled by the law of shariat. He is extremely dedicated to the cause of Islam. He could not tolerate the presence of the USA army force in the Gulf countries. He is against the oil extraction managed by the foreign companies in Saudi Arabia. The uprising of the Jews and the formation of a Jewish state in the middle of Palestine is not to his liking. Moreover the support given to Israel by the USA and NATO countries is also beyond his capacity to tolerate. He made a strong objection against the deployment of American warships in the Gulf. He raised a strong protest against the lifting of the naval blockade imposed by the U.N around the Arabian Peninsula and the withdrawal of warships. He is a staunch anti-Western only because the Westerners are non-Muslims. Their cultural, educational and civil entity spoils the Islamic radicalism and detracts the minds of Muslim youths.

He tried to persuade king Fahd of Saudi Arabia to intercept the intervention of America and to expel the foreign power from the Islamic soil. The king was unhurried in his own decision for the safety and security of his country. As a result the Saudi Government cancelled Osama's citizenship in the year 1994 when it was found that he had been entangled in some subversive activities and explosions on American embassies.

He left Saudi Arabia for Khartum, the capital of Sudan, and raised a formidable militant force for Jehad against the non-Muslims, particularly the USA. His militant military force is the largest international force next to the UNO. In his army there are Palestinians, Pakistanis, Bangladeshis, Taziks, Uzbeks, Chechens, Arabs, Iranians and members of many other countries. They are all extremely loyal to bin Laden. It is estimated that there are half a million Islamic terrorists in the world out of which 50,000 are controlled by Osama bin Laden.

After his migration from Sudan to Afghanistan he expanded his Islamic terrorist activities all over the world. One can feel the invisible hand of Osama Bin Laden in the explosions made everywhere from Kenya to Calcutta and from the World Trade Centre of the USA to the Assembly hall of Kashmir.

Mohammed defined the principles of establishing an international religious society without any deviation of its ethical principles. One basic principle among it is to exterminate the adversary society on the point of sex and sword. Osama, as a staunch follower of Mohammed, was steeped in the latter to activate and escalate the principles to realize the goal. By the way, he became the initiator of international terrorism.

Osama had his miraculous hand in the explosion detonated in the basement of the World Trade Centre on February 26, 1993 killing 6 and injuring around 100 people. His plan was triggered in a car bomb explosion in Riyadh on November 13, 1995 killing 5 US soldiers and injuring more than 60 people. His plan of demolishing a building at the US Military base in Khobar in Saudi Arabia on June 25, 1996 killed 19 Americans and injured 386 persons. He had his hand in devastating simultaneously US embassies in Nairobi and Dar-es-Salam in East Africa with a death toll of 224 and injury to more than 5000 people in August 7, 1998. In the Yemen port of Aden one of the most modern ships of the USA fleet "USS Cole" was destroyed by Osama bin Laden in October 2000. It caused a death toll of 17 American sailors with injury of 38. Osama did not spare even the Islamic Leaders like Ahmad Shah Masood who did the UnIslamic deeds by giving a helping hand to the USA in September 9, 2001. His suicide bombers killed Masood in the guise of Arab journalists. Planes were used notably for the first time as a war instrument when it crashed into the twin towers of the World Trade Centre in September 11, 2001. This incident raised a billow of death from 3000 to 30000 people.

Osama gets pleasure by killing his targeted enemies. A suicide bomber dropped on a US Navy vessel and killed 17 Americans off the coast of Yemen in October 2000. This incident was given a poetic charm, which described how the U.S. mole was destroyed slowly by a bomber, an Islamic terrorist. Bin Laden took pleasure in reading a poem in Arabic at the wedding ceremony of his son in the South Afghanistan town of Kandahar.

Referring to the USA and Israel Osama Bin Laden has enlisted them as the foremost enemies of Islam and has declared that as long as he is alive there would be no rest for the enemies of Islam.

Thus spoke Osama-"I have enough riches to enjoy myself like an Arab Seikh.. But I decided to fight against those infidel forces that want to sever us from our Islamic roots. For that cause the Arabs, Taliban and my family have been martyred."

Bin Laden's subversive terrorist organizations have been working in 36 countries of the world. Beginning from Al Sayef of the Philippines to Gama Islamia of Egypt and from the Laskar-e-Toiba of India to Harket-e-Mujahiddin of Pakistan – all organizations indicate the all-pervading hand of bin Laden.

2. Jehad and its Aspects

> *"The totalitarian nature of Islam is nowhere more apparent than in the concept of Jehad, the holy war, whose ultimate aim is to conquer the entire world and submit it to the one true faith, to the law of Allah. To Islam alone has been granted the truth, there is no possibility of salvation outside it. It is the sacred duty, an incumbent religious duty, established in the Koran and the traditions of all Muslims to bring Islam to all humanity. Jehad is a divine institution enjoined specially for the purpose of advancing Islam. Muslims must thrive, fight and kill in the name of God."*
>
> –*(Dictionary of Islam, p. 243).*

Jehad literally means religious war against non-Muslims. To persecute and kill a man who is reluctant to embrace Islam and the process to establish an Islamic state by reducing the number of non-Islamic people of a non-Islamic country is called Jehad. "Jehad" is the Islamic concept of war.

When the World Trade Centre was bombarded in the year 1993 it was perceived to be the mischief of some miscreants of America. Then it was thought to be an individual action like other crimes perpetrated by criminals. Action against them was taken like other indicted convicts.

When the World Trade Centre was air-crashed on September 11, 2001 the same supposition was disseminated that terrorists attacked the World Trade Centre. This also followed with the launching of a war against Afghanistan, but the government of America did not conceive that both destructive attempts against the World Trade Centre were nothing but the call for a Jehad or an Islamic religious war against America. The same attacks on American embassies in Tanzania, etc., are nothing but a call for Jehad. The majority of the people of the whole world in general and Euro-America in particular misunderstood this Jehad as a terrorist attack. "Jehad is waged in Islam for Allah. Hence the war or Jehad of the Muslims is always justified, ideal and humane" says Islam.

(a) Jehad Misnomered

Jehad does not require any particular place, person or time of action. To set fire to the houses of non-Muslims, to kill Kafirs by throwing them into the flames of fire, to exterminate them without any discrimination of age, sex and race, to sack women, to keep them as slaves in the harem, etc., are all included as acts of Jehad.

By destroying all other religions and faiths and by completely crushing the non-Islamic countries to establish an Islamic rule over the land Jehad is the only way. Jehad is a fundamental element and an inevitable part of Islam like Azan (call to prayer), Namaz (Prayer), Haj (pilgrimage to Mecca), etc. It is a religious fight, which can be launched, in different spheres of life i.e. in social, cultural, matrimonial, linguistic spheres, etc. But its most important part is mortal war against the enemy. This is a war that the Muslims of the world like to wage to bring the whole world under the banner of Islam. "Islam wishes to destroy all nations, Governments, States anywhere on the surface of the earth which are opposed to the ideology of Islam regardless of the country or the nation that rules it. The purpose of Islam is to set up a state on the basis of its own ideology". "The objective of Jehad is to eliminate the rule of an un-Islamic system and establish in its place an Islamic system of state rule".

Jehad is often misnomered by the people of different countries in different times. It was called as a "terrorist attack" on the World Trade Centre by the USA on September 11, 2001. But it was stark Jehad against America by the Global Islamic Movement, which was precedent to the first attack on W.T.C. in the year 1993. But its inception on American soil dates back to that unknown period, when the first Muslim stepped down in the U.S.A.

Jehad is very often misquoted as war against the enigmatic desires of man. These are the verdicts of pseudo secularists. Such persons speak it out of fear, out of their ignorance and out of pretension and joke. A Sufi saint was killed by Aurangzeb, a Muslim ruler of mediaeval India when the Muslim saint professed the definition of Jehad to be a war against ignorance. After the Pakistans' attack on India and its defeat was over, Jeffrey Goldberk, Journalist of "New York Times" had an interview with the General-turned President of Pakistan Parvez Musharaff. Enunciating to the terrorist groups of Harkat-ul-Mujahideen of Fazlur Rehman Khalil which is now waging back door war in India, Mushrraf said to Mr Goldberk-"These people are not terrorists, they are fighting a Jehad which is a tolerant concept."

Jehad is misquoted as the "Direct Action Day" in Indian history when Mohammed Ali Jinnah ordered Muslim youths, police and army men to kill mercilessly the non-Muslim Hindus. More than half a million unarmed and helpless Hindus were assassinated just before the partition of India. Jehad has been misinterpreted in Bangladesh in the Year 1971 as "Pakistan's barbarous attack on Bangladesh" when 3 million unarmed Hindus drenched the soil with their ceaseless blood dripping.

Jehad brings immeasurable booty to Muslims besides vast land and innumerable women. Last century saw the emergence of a large number of Islamic countries in East Europe, Central Asia and Africa. The formation of Pakistan is the result of 700 years of Jehad against India by Islam. The formation of Tajikistan, Turkmenistan etc. are simply the results of the demographic attack by Muslims on the Ex-U.S.S.R. It is interesting to note that the European Christians discovered many lands in the world and made their cultural and monitory expansions. But Muslims simply got large portions of land in different parts of the world by birth proliferation, conversion and religious war.

(b) Jehad, the Root of Terrorism

Terrorism is derived from terror, which is a religious part of Jehad. Jehad is always flanked by terrorism. The creation of terror in the minds of non-Muslims is an inevitable part of Islam. Terror precautions death and causes half death. The fearful and cruel appearance of a combatant Muslim and his merciless slaughtering mentality in an Islamic majority area terrifies the people who immediately start to flee. The Prophet himself has quoted in the order of Allah: - *I will throw fear in the hearts of those who disbelieve. Then smite their necks and smite off each of their fingers (VIII/12 Quran).*

By the decree of a court martial of a Taliban in Afghanistan, the throat of a man Mohammed Daud was slit in a public place. In retaliation, the mother of the victim licked the bloodstained knife. Such sights would certainly impress a profound sense of terror in the minds of the audience. In the same year a woman in Afghanistan was stoned to death in a public place for her committing adultery. Stoning to death is a very common phenomenon in Pakistan even today.

Beheading the Hindus by Islamic religious fighters in the Kashmir part of India is still rampant. This incident carries India to the dark age savagery and compels the minority non-Muslims to flee from that land.

Terror is applied to degrade the personality of a man (or any animal) by creating fear in his mind. So fear is a sentiment, which is created by certain means in the mind of the victim to suppress his ego or self-existence. After one's ego is suppressed it becomes very easy to exploit him. When one hears the roaring of a tiger or sees its fearful appearance in a leaping position he becomes half dead, gets fainted or faded. Then it becomes very easy for the animal to use the victim according to its own pleasure.

Non-Muslims are the enemies of Islam. Hence as a policy of Islam the Muslims create terror among the non-Muslims of the locality where they have the upper hand, dominance or majority. At first they create a psychic depression and destroy the self-respect of their victims. Then the victims are turned into chicken-hearted cowards and come down to the lowest level of life's existence. Life is the most valuable thing of every animal in creation. They forget their every possession and simply want to escape from the situation to save their lives. To avoid death they prepare either to become refugees or converts. In his book "The Quranic Concept of War" S.K. Malik, former Brigadier of Pakistan says – "Terror struck into the heart of the enemies is not only a means, it is the end in itself.... It is not a means of imposing decision upon the enemy, it is the decision we wish to impose upon them".

Terrorism is the outrider of jehad. The main instrument to attain success in this "God determined strategy" is to spread terror. The martial law as spoken about in the Quran orders the Muslims not to be terrified by the enemy and on the contrary they should either consciously or unconsciously create terror in the minds of the enemies, the non-Muslims.

An example of such a strategy was manifested by Pakistan soldiers by killing six Indian army men in a most barbaric way by hacking their penis, testicles, gouging out their eyes and stabbing their entire body violently, disfiguring their limbs, leaving them to die in excruciating pain. Such kind of cruel killing is considered as the most sacred duty of a Muslim. The demolition of the World Trade Centre, the attack on the Pentagon and the attempt to smash the White House, etc., belongs to this category of Islamic strategy. Malik's book describes, "Force the enemy to live in terror". "As one attacks in the name of self-defence, so as we must defy the agreement and treaties in the name of Jehad."

So when the U.S authority reiterates that it launched cruise missiles against the terrorist objectives in Afghanistan or Sudan to crush terrorism, the statement seems enigmatic. Islamic terrorism is not an individual oriented interest or a group reaction. Launching missiles on a warring group or on a particular region cannot subdue it. It is a religious concept of Islam that constitutes the psych of Islamic youth. Government of India also reiterates like a parrot that it would suppress terrorism with a stern and stiff hand. But it is only a false firing to give periodical relief to the affected people. But it should be remembered that as long as there is a single man on the surface of the earth being identified as a non-Muslim, terrorism is going to be a part of Jehad waiting against him.

According to the Muslims Jehad is not terrorism. Rather it is the guarantee of peace in the world. Jews and Christians have been imposing worst persecutions on the Muslims. Jehad is the only solution to solve all these problems.

All the past achievements, which Allah made obligatory for the Muslims, were attained through Jehad. So Jehad is the only means and the best means to attain all the requirements of the Muslims. Whenever they apprehend any danger or inconvenience they take resort to Jehad which outrides the terrorists.

It is an unhealthy obsession in the minds of all that terrorists attacked the Parliament in India, the World Trade Centre in America, the Embassy in Tanzania, hijacked the plane of Israel and were trained in England, etc. In a real sense they are not terrorists. They are the holy Mujahids, the Islamic religious fighters. They have launched Jehad, the religious war worldwide to islamise that particular nation where these casualties are happening. At the end all the countries will shun their distinct nationalism as a snake casts off its slough and will be one nation, one kingdom, the nation of Islam and the kingdom of Allah. There is no God but Allah. (*La Illah Illalah*).

So these subversive activities like the bombardment of the embassies, the explosion in the train, the gunning down in Parliament, which we see, feel, read about and realize, are parts of Jehad.

(c) Jehad, an Inevitable Part of Islam

It is an inevitable part of Islam and an instrument of Islamic expansionism. Allah has ordained through the Prophet abundant pleasure and infinite enjoyment to his devotees or the believers i.e. the Muslims. So the rich Muslims enjoy a heaven on this earth with a number of wives, children and special privileges as a minority in the Muslim minority states but those Muslims owing to their large families, unemployment and lack of proper education seek for a heaven which they can't possibly attain on this earth. The Quran promises them a safe and extremely enjoyable heaven after death with the assurance that death would cause them very little pain or no pain at all. The description of Paradise allures every Muslim male to go there. Jehad is the best conveyor through which one can attain this Paradise. Jehad is to be fought against anti-Islamic forces termed as "the enemy". To kill an enemy and own its property is a religious duty or a part of Jehad. Muslims say that the term 'fundamentalist', 'terrorists' etc., as used by non Muslims is a term that emerged in the context of the U.S. society, has no meaning whatsoever for the Arab world and is quite alien to Islamic terminology.

'Terrorism' is the Western version of the Islamic word 'Jehad'. Those who are called as terrorists are the Mujahids or Jehadi fighters. A true Muslim is entitled as a fundamentalist by the West. The Muslim population in the world is more than one billion. They form 15% of the world population. In Europe the Muslim population is more than 14 million of which 5 million reside in France and 3 million in Germany. Out of 60 million people of England the Muslims constitute a considerable proportion. Presently they are the second largest ethnic race in almost all the developed nations of Europe. Despite having a handful of Muslims in England Margaret Thatcher, the former British Prime Minister, once said in 1991 after the fall of communism – "The biggest danger for us is Islamic fundamentalism".

The comment made by Margaret Thatcher is not far from the truth. There are some basic points that provocate Muslims to launch Jehad against the European Christians. Religious war is inevitable for a Muslim against a Non-Muslim as it is considered to be the major part of a Muslim's life. Growth of population is an objective in a Muslim society, which leads to poverty and obstructs a nation's development. It forces the Muslim youths to take asylum in another world, the Paradise, which is easily attainable only if they face a war against their immediate enemy, a Non-Muslim, who is at his vicinity. Hence if a Paradise on earth is beyond the reach of a Muslim, he is impelled to reach the other world which he can attain in his after-life though Jehad. So Jehad, frequently quoted as terrorism, is a must for the Asian Islamic countries like Afghanistan, Pakistan, Bangladesh, Indonesia and Islamic countries of Africa and India.

The Westerners are misunderstood and misquoted about Islamic history and practices. Majority of them have neither studied the Islamic history of a country thoroughly nor have gone deeply through Quranic verses. British historians have written hundreds of books on Islamic aggression and expansion of Jehad or holy war but practically they did not have the experience of Islamic aggression in their homeland. For the first time of course they felt the Islamic brunt in Salman Russdie's case.

The idea and action of Jehad is deeply rooted in Islamic thoughts and Islamic philosophy. It can be well defined by the following aspects:

Denial of chanting the National song of a Non-Islamic country by the Muslim students is also a call for Jehad against that nation. Islamic religious leaders frequently pass Fatwas or religious orders denying singing the national song in India, the largest democratic country of the world. According to the Muftis of Dar-ul-Ulema, Deoband - "There is no importance of prayer to anybody except Allah. Because the Indian national Anthem is meant to pray to Mother India, it is against the Islamic religious sentiment. Hence Indian Muslims are denied religiously not to chant the national song".

To lay upper hand in the administration of an alien country is also a symbol of Islamic Jehad against the nation. Although Sunday is generally accepted as weekly holiday for State Bank of India throughout India it is not so in Muslim majority areas like Karim Nagar District in Assam where the State Bank of India remains closed on every Friday, the day of Juma when the Bank's of Islamic countries remain closed.

Growth of Islamic population in contrast to the national demand is an undeclared Jehad against that country by Muslims.

Such kind of Jehad is current in almost all non-Islamic countries of the World where Muslims are in minority. Take for example the case of India. In the difference of twenty years of census between 1971 and 1991 the population of Muslims in the district of Malda, Murshidabad, Nadia, Dinajpur, Purulia and Bardhaman has almost doubled which is beyond one's imagination. This threatens the national security of West Bengal as well as life security of the local civilians who are forced to leave their home lands and go to seek asylum somewhere else when they felt that their existence as a non-Muslim minority in that area was threatened.

To infiltrate into a non-Islamic country and enhance their subversive activities is a type of Jehad. The militant infiltrators at the time of Kargil war (when Pakistan attacked India at the border District of Kargil, Kashmir) announced that this was Jehad and hence all the Muslims of India should unite and fight for their victory against India. When a Shia leader of Kashmir (India), was asked to express his willingness whether to support Pakistan or to India in this war, he replied that they are waiting for the order of their spiritual leader Bali Umr of Iran. They will act according to his suggestion. Here the man keeps his religion far above the national interest.

Internal Jehad is a distinct feature of Islamic holy war. Here a Muslim fights against the Non-Islamic Government of that country with or without the co-operation of a foreign Islamic compatriot. In the recent Indo-Pak war, the Pakistani missiles were dropped on the accurate point in the Kargil sector. It signifies the activities of insurgency or the Internal Jehad conducted by Pakistan supporters in India who sent the messages to Pakistan soldiers accurately. The undeclared war in Kashmir between the Government military force and separatist Muslim militants who attempt to seize the state is the same as the war rampant in Algeria between the Government army and Muslim militants who try to bring the power under their control. This is an instance of internal Jehad.

Psychic Jehad is another type of religious war which is fought to create terror and psychological depression in the minds of Non-Muslims and give them a clear idea about Islamic ideology. However great, glorious and magnificent may be an un-Islamic construction or achievement like the World Trade Centre or the Statue of Liberty of America or the statue of Bamiyan Buddha of Afghanistan or the Sphinx of Egypt or the World famous libraries of Alexandria and Nalanda, they are no more than the value of dust particle in the eyes of Islam. The attack on the W.T.C was the show of strength, solidarity and formidability of Global Islamic Movement. Psychic Jehad is also imposed by forceful verbal threatening by Islamic leaders to create terror, gloom, disappointment and mental tension in the minds of Non-Muslims. Inspite of the super status and special privileges conceded to Muslims as a minority community in India, Maulana Ali Nadbi, the former President of Muslim Personal Law Board and the Chief of Nabatul Ulema University had printed and published a manifesto in Urdu where he had stated- "I want to tell you that we have to stay in this country with our full dignity and Islamic identity. We are not prepared to stay here like a beast who is satisfied only with food and security. We are Muslims and we will stay here with full Islamic characteristics and Islamic identity. This is our concluding statement".

Muslims always hanker to quench their own thirst. They never bother about others' needs. Here the statement made by Nadbi spurns the interest of Non-Muslims who are majority and national citizens of that country.

As long as Muslims feel that their rivals are strong enough to crush them in a rise of revolt they remain silent and perpetuate increasing their population and strengthen Islamic fundamentalism in their society. Whenever they sense that their non-Islamic neighbours are unequal in strength and are not capable to fight against them, they immediately declare Jehad against them.

(d) Jehad, an Instrument of Civil War

Civil war is an inevitable part of that country where there are Muslims in minority or Muslims are recognized as a minority group by the constitution. The civil war is waged for an indefinite period. There are many instances in history, which denotes that when Muslims constitute a minority population of 10 to 20% they inflict heavy burden on the nation by terrorist activities or perpetuating religious war (Jehad) against non-Muslims. This is the primary civil war, oft quoted as communal riots, between Islamic minority and non-Islamic majority. When the Muslims form 25% of a population there starts the civil war against the majority community. When they come to 40% of a population there starts the decisive civil war between the Muslim minority and non-Muslim majority. During this chaotic situation the Islamic population grows to 60% and then they terribly attack non-Muslim civilians until the minority-turned non-Muslim civilians become completely exterminated. The Non-Muslims then become bound to choose any of the three conditions. They either (a) get converted to Islam (b) leave the country to take refuge elsewhere or c) killed by the majority Muslims. This is the fundamental process of Transformation of Civilizations.

Jehad is not only confined to Islamic war against non-Muslims. It is also fought against those Muslims and Muslim rulers who are in favour of non-Islamic regimes, although it is for the security of their Government. That is why Islamic militant forces are against the rulers of Saudi Arabia, Turkey, Egypt, etc., for their allegiance to the US. This view of Islam emboldened a Muslim youth to assassinate Anwar Sadat. The life of Hosney Mubarak, the present Egyptian President, is also hanging on a thread.

In short, Islam can be defined as a religion and Jehad as an inevitable part of Islamic expansionism. But in fact there is no holy war without Islam and there is no Islam without Jehad or holy war. Both are inseparable like the two sharp edges of a sword. Islam and Jehad can be felt simultaneously.

In an Islamic religious conference held in Sudan in the year 1993 a fatwa was issued declaring the Muslims of a non-Muslim state who fight against the Islamic government as apostates and all the Non-Muslims as Kafirs thus justifying to kill both the categories without any hesitation as a religious duty of true Muslims or Mujahids. Another Islamic thinker of Egypt, Mohammed Qutb, has identified the modern state as Jahiliyah or barbaric. This has affected all the secular and non-Islamic states of the world, which are framed according to Western democratic principles or non-Islamic principles. Muslims are obliged to fight against the governments of all such barbaric regimes as a matter of Islamic religious principles. This verdict of Qutb has also been supported by most Islamic countries who proclaim in harmony with the verdict of Qutb that Muslims should not compromise with non-Muslims in a non-Muslim majority country as the true followers of Allah and his prescribed way of life. According to Islam there is no question of mutual understanding with Islam and Jahiliyehs or co-existence between Muslims and non-Muslims. This clearly indicates an all-out armed struggle.

(e) Jehad, a Proselytizing Weapon and the Ground Work of Islamic Education System

Islamic education system in many Islamic countries is gradually craned towards Jehad in such a way that at one point both become one and inseparable. This Islamic education system makes them remain aloof from the non-Islamic social life style. In a non Islamic country whenever and wherever they get a chance to lead a life free from non-Islamic attachment, instantaneously they come out exposing their Islamic identity, as a part of universal Islamic brotherhood.

Mulla and Maulvi— These two are the two sides of a coin. One directs the religion and the other, the Islamic education system. Both carry the flow of the two streams to the climax of Islamic politics. Education is a prime medium to bring about changes in the society. These two are the chief controllers of an Islamic country and the starting point of the Islamic thought fountain. Mullas look after the mosques and the Moulvis run madrassas or Islamic religious schools. As a hotelier supplies food ingredients according to the demand and the need of the customers, the Madrassas (Islamic religious institutes) similarly act by supplying the Mujahids according to the need and demand of Jehad.

Many plans and programmes have been set to attract the natives of African countries and maintain their Islamic solidarity under the banner of Jehad. Charitable hospitals and educational institutions have come up in thousands in the name of Jehad or as a pattern of holy war to conquer the whole of African nations. In Tanzania some 14 thousand people annually treated in Iranian "Jehadi clinics". Jehadi educational institutions or the Islamic Madrassas preach the tenets of Islam in Africa.

Mujahid, the Jehadi fighter : Those Jehadi fighters or the militants as quoted by the Westerners, who are in the field of Jehad are called as the Mujahids. They develop certain characteristics for their safety and success to reach the goal.

- They change their hide-outs only after dusk and don't emerge from there till the next evening.
- They demand the Muslim inhabitants of Muslim populated streets to extend hospitality for the night.
- Almost all of them are below 30 years of age. Having undergone rigorous training in military camps they are strong enough both mentally and physically and are immunized to face all sorts of hurdles in life.
- They are trained in seditious activities and professionally are also very skilful.
- All of them are well equipped with lethal weapons and competent enough to handle them.
- As all of them are orthodox Muslims they used to have pocket size Quran with each of them, which they read daily, at regular intervals.
- They are ready to kill non-Muslims as the sacred duty of a Muslim and as a part of holy war, according to Quran, by the order of Allah, the Islamic Almighty.
- Whatever they do is only for Allah. They fight with the confidence and determination that they lay down their lives for the holy cause. Martyrdom according to them is the real purpose of the life of a Muslim.
- They seldom listen to Radio or watch Television, as it is un-Islamic. They don't want to keep in touch with anything that is worldly because it tends to make them harm the spirit of Jehad in them. Because they are absolutely devoted to Islam, their unquestioning obedience to Allah and their strong faith in holy war

promise a Mujahid or a holy fighter an enjoyable paradise where they remain engaged for an indefinite period.

- The cult of suicide bomber is something different from that of the ordinary militants. Nearby 68% of suicide bombers come from the Gaza Strip. Almost 47% of them are singles and 64% of them are between the age group of 18 to 23. An essential qualification for a prospective single bomber is his intense interest and belief in Islam.

Though the suicide bombers are selected within days, the Muslim youths are brainwashed from their very childhood and primary stage of education. In Hams run kindergarten schools sign boards on the wall read- "Children of the Kindergarten are the shahids (holy martyrs) of tomorrow", "Israel has nuclear bombs but we have human bombs". The suicide bombers are indoctrinated for months. They are made to believe that Allah sends them on their missions. They are set in a hypnotic state by the time they are ready to be strapped with explosives. They believe that by blowing themselves in a crowd they are forging their gateway to Islamic Paradise. Before they are set up on their missions, the bombers are taken to a cemetery and made to lie between graves for hours. This is to prepare them mentally to face immenent death. They are then made to wear a white hooded shroud normally used to cover the dead bodies for burial. The bomber is later taken to a safe house and made to proclaim his devotion to Islam and express his willingness to undertake the mission. As maintenance of secrecy is paramount, suicide bombers are not allowed to say goodbye to their family or reveal their plans to their family or others.

The extremists or Jehadi fighters are trained at Army facilities in the camps of Pakistan, Afghanistan, Sudan, Algeria and in the Senai-desert of Egypt. Their training includes plane hijacking, manufacturing and explosion of bombs, use of rocket launchers and clandestine penetration of international boundaries.

Apart from these training camps there are Jehadi Organisations (often quoted as terrorist organisations) flourishing in all the Islamic countries of the world and even in Non-Islamic countries like India, Nepal, Sri Lanka, Philippines, etc. Whitemen's countries like America, England, France, Germany and Turkey are no exceptions from Islamic militants or Jehadi fighters' groups. Ikhwan-Ul-Muslimeen of Egypt is considered as a well-organized Jehadi organization, which has spread a large militant net all over the world. Anwar Sadat, the Egyptian President, was assassinated by this national organization. The blind men that held responsible for the W.T.C bombardment in 1993 is supposed to be a member of this Organisation. The militants who attempted to dethrone Hajid Assad's government in Syria, Laila Kahlid the first lady haijacker of an Israeli plane and most of the militants who kill unarmed people everyday in the Kashmir province of India belong to this organization. Moulana-Abul-Ala Maududi, one great Islamic zealot, established Jamat-e-Islami in India, Bangladesh and Pakistan in the line of Ikhwan-ul-Mulk. There are 72 terrorist organizations working in Kashmir, out of which 28 organisations have foreign mercenaries from Afghanistan, Sudan, Iran, Bahrain, Chechniya, etc. Similarly 46 training camps and Jehadi centres are identified in Pakistan.

There are almost 10 thousand madrassas in Pakistan, which impart Jehadi education to the students coming from Afghanistan, Kazakstan, Tazikistan, Uzbekistan, and Chechnya besides Pakistani students. In Pakistan the madrassas are the factories of Jehadi fighters and that there is at any time a stock of one million trained Jehadis willing to die at the call of their faith in its battle against any other religion. "These madrassas in Pakistan, Afghanistan and one or two other countries admit children at a young stage. Added to the curriculum in such madrassas is the concept of "Mujahiddin" or the holy warrior. They are brainwashed to believe that their salvation lies in indulging in the so-called "Jehad". In this way, such madrassas breed a new kind of battle-hardened youngmen ready to kill others, destroy property, cause havoc and, if needed, give up their own lives."

In the 16th conference of "Academy of Muslim World League" held in Mecca the king of Saudi Arabia Shah Fahd at the outset proclaimed that Islamic experts would tour round the world and convince the non-Muslims that Islam is not a religion of intolerance. He asserted that there is no question of terrorism in Islam. Islamic education must be imparted for the character development of every student.

The General-turned President P.Musharaff of Pakistan has been defending these terrorist Jehadis and is taking every care for the enrichment of Jehadi training centres in the whole of Pakistan. To escalate the Islamic Global Movements for the Transformation of Civilizations Pakistani Brigadier S.K.Malik has written a book "The Quranic concept of War". Its foreword has been written by General Mohammed Zia-Ul-Haq, Ex-Military dictator of Pakistan. In this book both the writers of the book and the foreword have mentioned their view about how and why to fight against non-Muslilms. This has been treated as the best book to give guidelines to Muslims including both civilians and soldiers to fight against those who are non-Muslims. According to this book terrorism should be made use of as a firsthand weapon to win over the non-Muslim opponents.

The main stream of thought of this book is derived from the Quran and the history of military expeditions of Mohammed. The full concept of Islamic war is spontaneously described in this book. Mohammed had set an example by waging war against non-Muslims and it is alone the "Holy Message" of Mohammed that the religious duty of a Muslim is to fight against non-Muslims and war should continue on the land of non-Muslims until they are vanquished and killed and completely wiped out from that land.

The war waged by Mohammed was a full-fledged war, a war of Jehad. This war was internal and external, financial and military, fought from every corner of society. The planning and projection of the war of Pakistan against India is the same as that which Mohammed did against non-Muslim Arabians. So Jehad is an endless perpetual process of war, which is imposed by Pakistan against India and by Mujahids or Islamic religious fighters in America, Britain and France. Because the Civil war is under process, its brunt has not yet been severely felt in the above-mentioned European countries including the USA. Jehad, as defined by Zia is the most important and splendid word in the dictionary of Islam, which means a full-fledged war.

Malik has also narrated "we have to fight against the enemy only in his soil and kill him there". He also explains Jehad as "a war of defence". According to him, the main intention of a war is to carry out the order of Allah. First, it is their religious duty to fight. Hereafter a Muslim is religiously ordered to fight in the way of Islam, to convert an unholy state (Dar-ul-Harab) to a state of Allah (Dar-ul-Islam). Consequently he who opposes it becomes the invader and then war is waged against him and to kill him on his own land through this defensive war." In this way the war of Jehad has been promulgated in every corner of the world, to liberate Muslims from the oppression of non-Islamic majority people.

Malik begins his verdict by paying due homage to the policy of agreement or treaty of war. But he says: "whenever we smell the hypocrisy or defrauding we soon spurn the treaty. According to him "any treaty or agreement can be denied according to our sweet will".

This Islamic psyche is the source of animation for Jehad that constitutes the Islamic Organisations to lead Muslims for a global victory.

(f) Jehad, a War of Reprisal against Non-Islamic States

The West is aware of the fact that there is no other ideology, which can unite all Muslims except pure Islamic beliefs, which they call Islamic fundamentalism. Following this attitude Western pressure on all Muslim countries has grown to such a magnitude that they want to control all their resources, talent, potentials, especially the military power in order to restrict the growth of Muslim power, which could imperil the Western interest. Islam is a religion, which invokes its followers better to die but not to remain suppressed or oppressed. Hence they express their reaction through their arms and ammunitions.

There is an unwritten division of people into class structure prevailing in the West. The first consists of Western Christians and Jews. The second-class group is East European Christians, who form half of the world population. Muslims and other deprived nations belong to the category of 3rd Class. This last group is called the third world group.

Killing the people of the first class is a great crime; killing the people of the second category is a half crime and the killing of the 3rd class is no crime. Genocide is considered a common occurrence in the third class.

After the downfall of the communist empire people developed a craze to follow the Western style of democracy as the only alternative. Accordingly Bosnian Muslims have been deeply attracted to Western values. They had completely adapted themselves to Western life style. Nevertheless they failed to become an integral part of Europe because they are neither Christians, nor Jews. In the eyes of the Westerners they belong to the group of the 2nd world race. When they fought for an Islamic homeland, they anticipated every form of help from Europe, which would have prevented Serbian aggression. Now they could realize the fact that Europe is more disposed to the Christian Serbian objectives than to Muslim Bosnian interests.

Europe repudiated Bosnian Muslims. Bosnians had accepted Western values and a democratic system. Now they collected the divine rules of the holy Quran: - "And the Jews and Christians will not be pleased with you until you follow their religion".

Bosnia is the testing ground of Islamic misery in the midst of Christian environment. Muslims already have one problem, Palestine. Now Bosnia was the next to Palestine. Although the Bosnian problem was solved to some extent, the wound that was carved on them left a profound mark that made Muslims ever revengeful against Europeans in general and Americans in particular. The Muslim community is not prepared to believe the steps taken by the UNO, nor the Europeans civil rights group's demand to punish the Serbs who committed inhuman and monstrous acts against Bosnian Muslims.

Syrians are also waiting to give a lesson to the USA and its allies. Hence they talk in terms of Jehad. Most Syrians are Arab descendants and the country's official language is Arabic. Christians make roughly 10% of the population. It has a glorious history extending to 2000 B.C. The Amorites who came from Arabian Peninsula first settled on it. Later it came under the subjugation of Alexander of Greece in 333 B.C. After the manifestation of Jesus, Christianity began to spread in Syria and

Syrian Christians shouldered the responsibility to propagate Christianity and came up to India in East Asia. Even a Roman Emperor who was crowned as Caesar in Italy was an Arabian born in Syria. After the debut of Islam in Syria the Byzantine rule was over and Syria was completely Islamised. From the late 18th century Western powers intervened in Syrian affairs. During the Ist world war the British incited the Syrian nationalists to fight against the Ottoman Empire. The French played the 'divide and rule' policy and divided Syria into 3 administrative districts on the pretext that political decentralization would safeguard the rights of minorities.

When it was found that Syrian airfields were used by Germans en route to Iraq, British and French forces invaded and occupied Syria. The country got its independence in January 1944.

In 1967 the Arab Israel war broke out and the Israelis captured the Golan Height, 19 km deep into Syria. In 1973, during the 4th Arab Israeli war the Syrian troops dislodged the Israeli occupiers from the 1967-cease fire line, liberating several kms. of occupied Golan Height. But after the intervention of the United States of America, Israel spoiled the initiative of Syria and pushed it out of Golan Height.

In the year 1982 when Israel invaded Lebanon, Syrian troops joined their hands with Lebanon against Israel as a principle of Islamic brotherhood. Then Israeli Prime Minister Menachem Begin announced the annexation of Golan Height with Israel and settled the Jews from other countries in the Golan Heights. The secret of the great success of Israel, a landless nation of 1950, who could defeat the Arab at the end, lies in the fact that the USA and its allies patronized it.

In 1967 Israel captured East Bayt-ul-Muqaddas in the Middle-East war and later annexed it. To add fuel to fire the US President Bill Clinton declared to move the U.S. embassy from Tel Aviv to Bait-ul-Muqaddas, which is famous for Al Aqsa Mosque. It is the most sacred place of Islam next to Kaaba. Hence by admitting the place to be part of Israel territory the USA became the target of 1.2 billion irate Muslims of the world.

The Jews are considered the archenemies of Muslims since the beginning of Islamic history. Prophet Mohammed had killed hundreds and thousand of Jews during his Islamic conquest. These Jews exert influence in all the decision-making fields of the American administration. Beginning from Disraeli the one time Prime Minister of England to Henry Kissinger, the former-Secretary and principal political advisor of the State to the President of America were all Jews. That was the momentous period in the fortune of Jews conquering the Palestine lands and expelling the local Muslims into exile. This Jewish diplomat of America Henry Kissinger, decades after his hibernation, again reappeared in American politics and was sent as a political agent of the U.S and an advisor to the Prime Minister of Indonesia. This is a Muslim country where the majority of Islamic groups are engaged in cleansing the ethnic Christians from the Indonesian soil. During Jimmy Carter some U.S state officials were Jews. Nowadays Jews influence the U.S policies even in areas other than the Middle East. There were many Jews in the Clinton and Bush administration. Besides the Jews having their influence in the American government many of them are working in managerial popular anchor posts. A large member of reporters, Editors-in-Chief of Newspapers, reviewers, academicians, movie industrialists and littérateurs are devout Jews.

In their outlook, behaviour, and action some Jews don't differ from the natural Americans. In every sphere they resemble ethnic Americans. Their originality is identified only when their corpses are carried to a Jewish cemetery.

So the scrupulous Muslims don't differentiate Americans from their dreaded enemy Jews, the Israelis, the occupiers of Qods, the usurpers of Bait-ul-Muqaddars, the killers of thousands of Palestinians and the conquerors of Arabia.

Muslims are well aware of the fact that 85% of the World's wealth belongs to 15% of the world's population, the Americans and the Europeans. Unless a revolutionary change occurs, it is probable that in the next 20 years this ratio may change to 90% and 10% respectively.

To minimize this difference between the rich and the poor, i.e. the difference between man and man, communism was expected to be the only solution, which advocated mass war against the rich by the poor. But this great expectation from communism proved to be a fool's errand. After the Bedouins, as quoted by Europeans, became the oil kings now found the solution of this discrimination religiously as advocated by the Quran. According to the Quran, the challenge by Islam to world oppression must start in the name of Allah and continue in the name of Jehad.

To materialize this solution there are terms in the Quran like Jehad, resistance, forbearance and justice, vis-à-vis the enemies of Allah and the human kind. Such are the terms which make up the components of a challenge against them who have been domineering against God's servants. The holy Quran contains many verses to the effect that the Prophet waged Jehad for ten years in terms of primary wars, defensive wars, liberating wars and armed struggle against despots and despotic rules. A majority of Muslim juries have decreed armed uprisings in the name of Allah against unjust and cruel exploiters as a duty of the believers in the case that no alternative to it remains. Jehad is the only alternative to solve the problem of discrimination of wealth distribution in the world. So Islamic Jehad is destined to launch against the 15% of world capitalists who have procured 85% of the world's wealth. Almost all those capitalists belong to America and European countries. They are now the targets of Islamic Jehad for the equilibrium of global wealth.

Islamic critics conclude-"Islam provides a good government. A prosperous, justifiable and peaceful government is possible only by observing the tenets of Islam as quoted in the Quran. All the aspects of life, all about the daily activities from dawn to dusk are defined in a vivid description, which has not yet been amended or deflected for over 1400 years. Islam advocates a special type of administration, the Islamic Government "Din", which is quite different from democracy. Democracy is said to be the invention and contribution of Westerners. According to them without a democratic system of government there is no peace and prosperity in any country. But in this regard the

Muslim world tried to prove that democracy as a gift of the West is an utter failure to bring peace of mind and to cherish any such development as was expected. Hence Islamic rule is the only solution for global peace which is possible only by Jehad against the opponents of Islam."

(g) Jehad, an Islamic Mission for World Conquest

Great Muslim thinkers have devised some points for the acceleration of Jehad in different non-Islamic countries to proselytize and evangelize the non-Muslims into Islam. The points for the implementation of Jehad to fulfil their achievements are as follows:

(1) Cultural Islamic centres should be set up in different countries to arrange and sponsor lectures, symposiums and dialogues according to a clear-cut plan to meet the ends.

(2) Institutes for Islamic studies with selected discourse and qualified scholars should be set up. Those scholars and lecturers should have scientific experiences besides morals and intellect.

(3) Institutions with vocal and vision facilities should be set up to present Islamic injunctions through interesting video tapes, using current modern language, art and technology.

(4) Voluntary missions of Muslim activists from Muslim countries should make seasonal trips to those non-Muslim countries, to hold conferences, symposiums and to hold lectures, teach and discuss the above-mentioned topics.

(5) Islamic book exhibitions should be arranged to present Islam in written literature through books, booklets and pamphlets.

(6) Effort should be made to contact the Churches, the cultural clubs and other institutions to exchange views.

(7) Attention should be focused on Western civilization and the secularist ideology with all its evils and ills that created hell in Western communities, spreading fear, decease and concerned factors.

The sphere of Jehad is unlimited. It includes all sorts of learning, discoveries, inventions, wars, arts, architectures, science, cloning, famines etc. to saturate Islam. Though Crusade is meant for the spread of Christianity, it has a limited sphere of action compared to Jehad. For instance Christianity invented aeroplane. Aeroplane may have been utilized for the spread of Christianity. But it was never used for the spread of terrorism. But Islam could use this as an instrument of terror in 11/9. The last World Wars were the wars of power show. But the coming world war would be a war of Civilizations. Christian nations develop cloned bodies to show their skill in cloning. But Islam would develop cloned bodies to use it in Jehad.

3. Islamic Paradise, the Key Source of Jehad

The description of Islamic Paradise imposed a profound influence on the minds of Muslim followers. It allures them with an assurance of getting bountiful of amenities, the means of enjoyment and entertainment in their after-life, which is nothing but a dream, with the condition of performing some particular activities and following a particular life style which is exclusively Islamic.

Mohammed was born in the midst of hot desert, brought up in the desert and died in the same deserted land. As an itinerant he had travelled the vicinity of Mecca. He felt the dearth of everything enjoyable in one's life. He had also a feeling of hatred for Christians and Jews.

When he accumulated power he made the projection of such a Paradise that imbibed the Arabians indiscrimination of race, sex (both heterosex and homosex) and age to attain that perfectly conditioned Paradise. The condition was that one must embrace Islam and follow the tenets of Islam strictly. Life in the desert was a burden but the after-iife, Paradise, was extremely alluring and dreamful. Hence to escape from a burgeoning life with a hope to saturate the dream, the followers of the Quran preferred even instant death to reach that Paradise. In the passage of time this attraction of Paradise created most sacrifices and formidable warriors who fought and died for Islam. People indiscrimination of age preferred death with a smiling face as if it is a wreath waiting to be thrust on one's crown.

The world is a combination of contradictions and is conditioned to contradictories. Mohammed was a perfect veteran of these contradictions, particularly as regards to war and sex. Mohammed divided the Islamic life into two parts i.e. one earthly and the other heavenly or after death. He made the Islamic life on earth filled with war. Hence Islam emerged as a religion of military discipline. For the stimulation of a warring life he added it with sex and booty. In addition he projected the Paradise for the aggravation of that stimulation to construe courage in the Muslims to remain ever ready for war. In this projected Paradise sex was converted into "houries" and young men with silk robes and the booty into luxurious amenities of Paradise. Hell was projected for non-Muslims as a place to stay with a tortured and tormented life. As to the law of the religion accepting the world as a combination of adversaries, women were left on the other side utterly neglected, hated, languished and limited to a despicable life.

A frame of mind was envisaged for the Muslim community, which naturally regarded plunder and homicide as the purest of human acts. It was considered to be a merit of Islam. It is not necessary for a Muslim to be a spiritual person in the sense that he must follow austerity, celibacy, nonviolence, veracity, sympathy to other beings, etc. Spirituality in general in Islam only means to exterminate a particular class of human beings who are the non-followers of Islam. This act is sufficient for him to have an access to Islamic heaven, the Paradise.

The chief attration of Islamic Paradise is the most beautiful nubile women who are ever neat and clean. This Paradise is ever thronged with these beautiful fairies with transparent bodies. The young women or the houries are always smiling, amusing and entertaining with a dedicated mind. Their marrows of bones are transparent like pearls. A "houri" is a woman of chastity and modesty. She never thinks of any other person except that Muslim hero to whom she is betrothed. The spinster always feels grateful for being the woman of that particular man who instantly chose her and enjoyed the heavenly joyous moments with her for an endless period. She is never indifferent and distasteful to his call and is ever attentive to his will and pleasure. The heavenly maidens of Islam are entirely free from routinely physical feminine disabilities like menstruation and all other offal discharges. She is also free from the childbearing phenomena.

She looks even young. Her remarkable peculiarity is her agelessness. She is free from the bondage of age limitation, which is subject to senility. She speaks in a very sweet and soft voice with accent that suits most to her beloved paramour. These angels of Islamic Paradise always dwell in the ever-luxurious palaces embellished with all entertaining amenities. They are ever young and most enjoyable.

Amazingly seventy-two houries are kept reserved for each Muslim who has access to the Islamic Paradise. Another provision for a Muslim-turned earthly man in the attainment of such a hourifiul Paradise is that it is not counted at what age he died. A man, whether he is an octogenarian or an eight year old boy, soon after his entry into this Islamic Paradise, becomes a vigorous virile man of 30 years with the strength of one hundred men!

Apart from these attractive virgins there are a large number of handsome young men reserved for the carnal gratification of different tastes of men who have reached the Islamic performances in this terrestrial world. These young men, like the houries, are also liberated from the bondage of age. They are also as pretty as pearls. They are embellished with silver bracelets and are dressed in transparent clothes of silk. These young men are, as the critics say, meant for those who simply want gratification outside heterosexuals.

This Paradise is situated on a vast air-conditioned mountain. There flows a cold spring named Salsabil. Its water tastes as sweet as nectar. Comfortable cushion chairs are stretched on two sides of the spring with its carpeted banks. The worthy lovers of Allah dressed with silken robes wander freely and amusingly in the shade of innumerable outstretched trees, which are evergreen and ever fruitful. The delicacy of the fruits is inexplicable. The trees are so pliable that the fruits can be plucked without any hard attempt.

An ever flowing river of milk free from pollution, a river of wine extremely tasty and a river of sweet honey are found in this Paradise.

Contrary to the Paradise is the description of hell in the Quran, which is meant for not only non-Muslims but also for Muslims who are not fully surrendered to Allah or Islam or to the dictates of Mohammed verbatim. The heart-ripping descriptions of the torment of hell horrify a man and pressurize him to be more inclined to Islam. The description of hell provokes a Muslim to long for Paradise. Every Muslim deserves to follow a specific code of conduct.

4. Islamic Renaissance and its Consequences

(a) First Phase of Islamic Renaissance

The first face of Islamic renaissance began towards 1950 after the detection of oil reserves stretched over a vast area under the whole of the Arabian Peninsula. Muslims own the world's largest oil wealth which has brought them prosperity and strength to fight in the name of Allah. In addition to their present consumption of oil from the reservoirs they have been blessed with many other sealed reservoirs, which are preserved exclusively for them. The oil reservoirs beneath the Caspian Sea are one such example which, if exploited in the near future, will supply 60 billion barrels of oil and 57 trillion cubic metres of gas. The Caspian Sea is the third largest petroleum reservoir. However it was the belonging of the U.S.S.R. After its disintegration the newly emerged Islamic countries were lucky to be the owners of these reservoirs. The sealed repository under the Caspian Sea is the largest of its kind that belongs to the Muslims. Export of oil, nature's gift, is the principal wealth of the gulf countries. They spend a large portion of it to feed Mujahids and to spread Islam through Jehad.

Their introductory nomenclature changed from camel drivers to oil merchants and later as oil kings. Their fortune smiled on them with an enriched and flourished life. A new type of trade unprecedented since the beginning of world civilization flourished on the surface of the earth. Arabian oil exporting countries bartered oil for European modern technology and armaments of war. They used oil as a weapon to control the world business and power politics. They could get whatever they wanted in exchange of oil.

After the Second World War was over, a large-scale construction programme was launched in European countries, which required a large number of manual labourers. This again helped the needy Muslims to continue a flow of migration and penetration into the European countries and America. Islam is always escorted in its itinerary with high birth proliferation. Muslims from East Asian and African countries migrated to Europe in millions to make their fortune. Under their democratic system of government the Muslims could avail all sorts of facilities which they could not obtain had they been in their Islamic home land. They settled there as manual labourers. Their key characteristics, the religious intolerance, that led to cultural alienation inspired them and compelled them to enhance their population which is a peculiarity of Islam. It strengthened their ever-alerted community life. The use of the sword was a bygone weapon and no more effective to win a country and confirmed one's settlement in a country which is quite alien to one's culture. Hence the Muslims resorted to demographic expansion in Europe by birth proliferation, infiltration, immigration and conversion of native people.

This not only helped them to settle in the Western developed countries but their participation in popular elections also made their position strong enough to represent the people of that country and raise their strong voice in the parliament to give special protection to their rights of citizenship as a minority. The democratic system of government in European countries enhanced their fortune and position. On the contrary, it is quite impossible for a non-Muslim to lead a free and prosperous life in an Islamic country.

Muslims are doubly benefited by this migration. They got the means for their livelihood and in course of time a homeland. Europeans got satisfied having the vast land of America and Australia as their new homeland, and Africa and Asia as their feeding land. Synchronomously Islam found the USA and the Western land as its home land and feeding land.

Present Asia became irrevocably a Muslim continent except for a few countries like China, Japan, Korea and Myanmar. Africa has become a testing ground of operation for both the European Christians and Arabian Muslims. Islamic Jehad and Christian crusade are collaterally competing to acquire this vast continent. But pan Islamism plays a dominant role in all the countries of the world. It has three distinct wings (1) Politicization of Islam (to spur the Islamic societies of different nations to fight against their non-Muslim majority compatriots to achieve their political goal, (2) to Islamize through oil (to spend a large portion of their oil product for the upliftment of Islam), (3) To harness the Islamic countries and societies of non-Islamic countries with atomic weapons. Islam fought and won the battles and could acquire more than fifty countries of the world during a span of 1400 years. Now the rest of the non-Islamic lands are to be acquired by the use of lethal weapons.

(b) Second Phase of Islamic Renaissance

It started with the Islamic revolution of Iran in the year 1979. It threw away the monarchial regime of Shah-en-Shah Rezah Pallavi Arya Meher of Iran who was supported by the Western countries. After the religious leader Ayatollah Ruholla Khomeini came to prominence there rose a great billow of inspiration among the Muslims of the whole world. They vowed to establish Islamic rule in their respective homelands. Iran shouldered the leadership to escalate the Islamic revolution throughout the world. As a result Russia bowed before the great Islamic upsurge, merged itself in the Islamic ocean. Islamic youths formed Islamic groups to establish an Islamic empire the world over to make the world Dar-ul-Islam. The flow of petrodollars from the Gulf countries played a great role to ignite and hasten this phenomenon.

Impact of Islamic Revolution of Iran

Uptill a quarter century after the Second World War people concentrated on events like the French Revolution, the American War of Independence, the rise and fall of communist socialism, etc. But during the last 20 years discussions have been concentrated on the influence of Islamic revolution on the regional administrations and in the international arena. The following changes and events took place to signify the Islamic renaissance and create an opportunity for a rethinking of the value of traditional Islamic history.

The success of the revolution in Iran escalated the Islamic movement throughout the world. It was like a ray of hope to the Muslims in the dark of despair. The French Revolution in the present day is a subject of study in the classrooms but the influence of Islamic revolution is highly palpitated everywhere in the world. Muslims residing in different countries were inspired to fight for their right and to turn their respective homelands in to Muslim countries.

In the past, just before the last decade, every discussion, debate, thinking and teaching was concentrated on American capitalism and communist socialism. Nobody bothered about Islam which has a totally different system of its own. The beginning of the last decade of the last millennium is an epoch-making period, which totally changed the pattern and way of international thinking. Islamic Afganistan that turned the world attention towards it pulverized the great communist empire. New dimensions are presented and new horizons are opened in the field of information and analysis. The emergence of Islamic republics in the disintegrated erstwhile USSR, all the policies, bilateral relations, cultural transactions, financial speculations and monetary agreements, the bombardment on the World Trade Centre of America, the continuation of un-obstructed terrorism for an indefinite period in the Kashmir valley to segregate India, the ceaseless fighting of Islamic combatants against the military force in Algeria, the national level plans of Iran for the financial improvement of the African countries, the unprecedented Millennium March in the USA defying its policy of apartheid, an emergence of the Islamic parliament in England, the decision of the French Government to change the outlook of French Christian traditions, Englands' best effort to give protection to its citizens from the wrath of world Islamic community, the serial attempts to murder the greatest traditional Christian leader Pope John Paul-II, the demolition of Bamiyan Buddhist statue in Afghanistan defying the world opinion, free covariation of Muslim Youth with the princess of the British royal family, lastly the exhibition of the super brain power of Islamic intelligentsia in pulverizing the formidable 107 storied WTC Building, one of the finest illustrations of American Architecture and pride of the USA – all these are the various aspects of a new perspective that raised a great wave to terrify and warn the whole world to be alert about global Islamism.

The Islamic revolution in Iran mobilized the Muslims at the regional and international level. Islamic Jehadi fighters (misnomered as Islamic terrorists) sprouted everywhere in the world where Muslims are fighting for their justice, i.e. for a separate homeland. Although terrorism is a part and parcel of Islam for its imperial expansion in the name of Jehad, it multiplied in all the Islamic and non-Islamic countries after the Islamic revolution in Iran.

The development of financial administration and increase in the number of scientific, vocational and artistic institutions, the development of Islamic libraries and foundations of Islamic Universities and the opening up of innumerable Madrassas or Islamic educational institutions throughout the world, the raising of thousands of Mosques in different countries in the world are some significances of Islamic revolution.

Another great significance of the Islamic revolution in Iran is that it emboldened the Islamic youths of the world to sacrifice their lives for the cause of Islam. This inspiration was so vigorous and violent that thousands of young men rushed out to be used as suicidal weapons. As a result, the greatest accidents of the world like the demolition of W.T.C. could be possible.

Islamic revolution produced global Jehadi fighters. An Islamic fighter is not limited to the geographical, constitutional or territorial limits. A British Muslim can explode suicidal bombs in an Army camp in India though of India's political relation with England remains cordial. An Algerian Jehadi fighter joins with an Afghan Taliban in war against Russia and after the victory of Afghanistan he may join with the Pakistan militant Islamic fighters at Kashmir valley to separate it from India. A Jehadi fighter is always above geographical boundaries. He is an international entity.

Another noticeable significance of Islamic revolution is the emergence of new Islamic countries, particularly in Eastern Europe and other parts of the world. Perpetual fighting in the name of Jehad has been hastened.

A young Islamic generation emerged in the past 20 years in Muslim countries that are more ardent, more adventurous and more dedicated to Islam. This armed struggle in Iran generated the Islamic youths who are well versed with international issues and more independent in belief and experiments. Ideologically they are stronger than their preceding generations. They rejected westernized thoughts and compromising life, subservience to the West. They are ever ready to protect Islamic laws, which they think divine, against man-made laws, promulgated in different democratic, secular and Islamic countries.

The Islamic revolution in Iran exhibited a new version of political Islamic system, which is different from the Christian system of secularism. Politics in Islam has been envisaged as an indispensable part of religion. Religion can be separated in European politics but it is beyond imagination in Islam. A true Muslim is a political Muslim and the politics of a Muslim is always religious. Hence a Muslim always fights for his political existence and political extension of his surrounding and political administration for his religious and cultural benefit, which automatically leads to an Islamic nation. Such a tendency was multiplied after the Islamic revolution.

After the Islamic revolution the idea of democratic nationalism has almost ceased to exist in Islamic countries and this significance gave rise to ideal Islamic community life which is an invincible force to set up a unifying Government that leads to global Islamism.

Islamic revolution is embedded in Islamic culture. So it was a cultural revolution that questions the validity of the global Western culture and its credibility.

Islamic revolution raised a serious question, which is quite above all the wordy altercation. That is, "If Iran could be able to topple a monarchy 2500 years old, why can't we the Islamic fighters or Mujahids conquer the existing non-Islamic

Governments ruling in different countries?" The spirit of this question gave much impetus to the Islamic youths to initiate a global Jehad.

The Islamic revolutions in Iran led to Eastern Islamic revolution in the Old Russian Empire that perturbed its Christian Imperialism. Octogenarian Pope John Paul–II rushed out to bring different Christian denominations under one roof. He started his campaign from the old Church in Greece and not only did he visit the Saint's tomb but also kissed his relics.

Islamic revolution envisaged a promising future for Muslim youths. The civilization that was worldwide, acquainted and dominated was Western civilization. It covered the whole of Europe, America, Australia and large parts of Asian countries. But another old civilization, which hibernated for 400 years emerged vigorously in the name of Islamic civilization with a clear-cut view on all aspects of life. Moreover this civilization is based undisputedly on Islamic religion. It identified the people of the whole world in two parts, i.e., a) Muslim, the Momin or holy and allied b) Non-Muslim, the kafir or unholy and enemical who is subject to be looted, prosecuted and killed.

Islamic revolution generated self-confidence among the Muslims. It emboldened Iran to take bipolar leadership and usurp the position of the former USSR to stand as a rival to the U.S.A for the maintenance of balance of power.

After the Knesset of Israel approved a plan for the expansion of Israeli territory, the Jews settlement in Western Bait Ul Muqaddas was extended and accordingly 30,000 more Jews were settled there. Iran, as the current head of the OIC called for the meeting of the OIC's foreign ministers to discuss the matter and take appropriate action. 50 Islamic countries requested the OIC to take action against Israel's occupation of Qods. On the pressure of the Islamic countries the Security Council of the UNO also was compelled to ask Israel to withdraw its people from the last occupied area. It was perhaps for the first time that Islamic organization could pressurize the UNO to work out its own interest.

The Westerners, after their discovery of the dense forest of Africa, penetrated into it with their conversion instruments. They made the people poor, plundered their natural wealth, enslaved their generation, became their Lord and colonized the whole of Africa. In course of time the situation was subject to change. After the Islamic revolution, Iran approached the African people. They found in Iran a true friend who is thriving to extricate them from the clutches of the slave lords. In the International conference of Human Rights held in Vienna, Iran had many common positions which the African countries appreciated and welcomed Iran's activities to bring the third world countries together to confront the west.

History does not answer those who don't have necessary tools for historic changes. One of those tools is power. Getting control over a historic situation is an important and basic principle in Islam and without this crucial historic denomination nothing can be achieved.

The Islamic revolution in Iran once again enhanced Islam's significance over history. The best way of delivering the message of Islam is to establish a world Islamic movement, which is able to foil and thwart all Satanic plots all over the world. The Islamic movement needs to let the Islamic Government's power be felt everywhere. Such a thing has come into being somewhat in Lebanon as the Hizbullah force backed by Iran could be able to defeat American, British and French forces as well as the Zionist army. In Afganistan also Mujahiddins dealt a deadly blow to the great enemy of Islam.

Many changes have been witnessed recently. For instance 30 /40 years ago only old men used to go to the Mosques. Today Mosques all over the world are thronged with young men and women who are very active in different Islamic movements. The present Islamic generation is more religious than the old ones. These changes show that a big internal change is taking place in the Islamic Ummah, something which indicates that a change in the balance of power is happening in the Islamic world. The most important part of this change and development is that revolution has already taken place among the young generation as far as what they expect to happen in future. They believe that during their lifetime Islam will be victorious everywhere. They have the notion that Western civilization is a tool in the hands of infidelity, which spread sedition and corruption on the surface of the earth.

After the collapse of communist imperialism and the emergence of a new world order with the growing popularity of Islam in the global social-cultural scenario, it is the turn of civilization to play the most important role and set the standard of international relation.

Islam has appeared before the Europeans and Americans as a hydra-headed snake. The great World Trade Centre was (WTC) pulverized with the twinge of its poisonous sting. It wants to retain its lost empire, which has now been usurped by Western Powers. The history of the world starts with the history of Europeans and ends with the history of Europeans. Now the Muslims will create a distinct history equal to that of Euro-American Christian history. The Islamic history begins from a historical Prophet and torpedoes ahead with Imam Ali Hussain, Taimurlang, Nadirsaha, Allauddin Khilliji, Mohamed Ali Jinnah, Idi Amin, Ayatullah Ruholla Khomeini, Mohammed Farra Khan, Osama Bin Laden and Saddam Hussain.

Just four decades ago Islam was introduced as the religion of Bedouins, the Cattle tenders, the camel drivers. The camel was their symbol of civilization, means of transportation and livelihood. The camel, sword, mirage and tent were every thing to them. So Islam is often represented in the West as a loveless religion, and the religion of the sword.

Soon after the Islamic Renaissance it was expected that the West should treat Islam as its equal partner in the field of politics, religion and culture. It exerted the Non-Islamic countries to reshape their perspectives towards Islam. The West as the confronting force with its culture and as a new threat considers the once underestimated Islam after the demise of the U.S.S.R.

After the Islamic nations had grown suddenly and fabulously rich owing to the discovery of the oil reservoirs under their sandy desert they needed to start an independent technological process in their countries in order to fill up the gap between the technologically developed states and the Muslim world.

Islam was known as a tenacious political entity in the year 1990. The contradiction between Islam and Western perspective has become one of the major issues of the contemporary world. In the last three decades the western states have voiced their concern over the spread of a political brand of Islam in the West. That is why Western statesmen expressed dissatisfaction and concern over issues such as wearing Islamic dress (Hijab, Burka etc) for women in their society. Western leaders gradually realized that the native Muslims along with the immigrant Muslims are second largest religious groups in all the secular European countries. Therefore they have no other alternative but to come to terms with the Muslims.

Today the South European countries feel that they are the neighbours of North African countries and that any change in these countries will inevitably affect tnem. Presently the main problem is to preserve the socio-economic and cultural stability in the African countries. There are numerous issues such as petroleum, the flow of immigrants, population growth, etc. All the African countries don't have political and economic stability, especially after the events, which occurred in Algeria. The main factor, which can preserve the stability in a state, is its socio-cultural significance. Lack of this significance has spurred constant holocaust and carnage, which seem to have no end. Islam has taken steps to rely and confirm the current ruling Governments by providing ideal opportunities to preserve Islamic and religious identity in those African countries. It is obvious that today Europeans can't ignore the presence of Islamic culture in Southern states.

From this standpoint, immediately after the victory of the Islamic revolution in Iran, the West considered the new practical developments as a threat. Even though European countries do not openly declare about their internal fear it is obvious that they are quite desperate and terrified observing the violent rise of Islamic nationalism with great unexpected and unprecedented integrity with their revengeful attitudes towards the Europeans' cultural expansion heading with crusade. The International Herald Tribune of July 28, 1994 edition carried a headline on its front page saying "West fears a new wave of Islamic

Terrorism" a reference to the acts of terrorism being perpetrated against Jews, Europeans and Americans.

The revival of Islamic culture is the main factor behind the disintegration of the USSR. Europeans and Americans have been attempting for long to retaliate the communists. But to their surprise they found that the dismantling of communism in Russia exclusively gave rise to Islam. At this juncture the Westerners were not prepared to face the ideological rivalry. Meanwhile Islamic ideology emerged forcefully and worldwide once again, especially in the heart of European countries. The revival of Islamic movement in Egypt, the major victory of Islamic movement in Algeria in 1992 democratic elections, the demolition of an apartment complex in Oklahoma all exemplify that political Islam again comes to the scene. Muslims are determined to capture power worldwide in this period. The flourishing Islamic tendency rose upto challenging the West's interests. The West could not show any resistance, as the Muslims were strong in their struggle. During this period the Muslims demonstrated their long-standing aspiration for implementing Islamic laws in total in the contemporary era. The destruction of the WTC is nothing but a signal of Islamic brunt to Western Civilization.

In the new world order, which has been created in recent years, those enjoying abundant wealth, industry and high economic might, unlike the past, cannot dictate their opinion or be indifferent to others. In the present day situation mutual dependency has reached in Europe to the extent that it has even restricted the initiatives of mighty powers and in some cases silenced their voice to be heard. In the USSR the Government was forced to recall its army from Afghanistan due to the reluctance of its Muslim soldiers to fight against their co-religionists in Afghanistan. One day Europe ruled over Africa without any concern and denied the rights of its immigrants. It was indifferent to the minorities. But nowadays one cannot do so. The Europeans cannot impose their will on others. It has to be receptive to the new ideas put forward by the opposition.

Now the Europeans came to the conclusion that they cannot change the Islamic thoughts, ideas and ideology by suppression or by criticism. The strong presence of Muslims and their steadfastness to defend their religion laid the foundation for a better understanding of the realities by the Europeans. This positive process in the right direction will further continue in the years to come.

Islamic countries are also greatly influenced by the Iranian revolution. This impelled Lebanan to undergo a great change to harmonise with the Israeli invasion in the year 1982. This incidence gave way to the emergence of a fundamentalist Islamic group Hizbullah. It confronted the Israeli Army supported by the USA and earned global fame.

The Islamic Tawhid movement has also turned into a fundamentalist movement and has enhanced Islamic strength.

In Algeria the Islamic movement was stabilized in the early 1980s. But when the victorious Islamic salvation party (FIS) of Algeria in 1990 was denied its privileged right to rule the country, the situation paved the way to Islamic fundamentalism and religious militancy to continue its fighting against the military government supported by the Western countries.

The Persian Gulf regions also did not remain untouched with this impact. Although the riot of 1979 (Seizure of the holy shrine at Mecca by the Islamic militants) ended by firing and beheading its leaders, it made the Saudi rulers aware of the importance of the Islamic forces.

In Kuwait political and religious groups enjoy a noticeable base. The victory of Islamists in Jordan in the Parliamentary election is a salient instance of the fact that Islamic forces gained power under the leadership of Ikhwan-ul-Muslimee (Islamic brotherhood).

Yemen is also another country that has witnessed extensive growth of Islamic movement in recent years particularly following the union of the two Yemens. Yemen's presidential council in a statement rejected the existence of any form of law that contradicts the Islamic law "Shariat".

Islamic renaissance thrust self-confidence and indomitable courage in the minds of one billion Muslim community of the world. This spurred even the most disgraceful Saddam Hussain behind the bar to assert that still he is the ruler of Iraq. Noticeably Islam has become the strongest minority in almost all the non-Islamic democratic countries of the world and wants to capture power of these countries through popular election.

5. Polarization of Iran Against Euro-America

(A Counter-balance of Islamic Power Structure Against Christianity)

Islam has extended its space from the Atlantic to the Pacific Ocean and from South India and Africa to Siberia, Albania and Bosnia. In addition there are a considerable number of Muslims in parts of Europe, America, Central and the Southern region of Africa. Today, close to a billion Muslims live in Islamic lands and as minorities in other countries. It was reticent for some centuries like the proverbial bottled genie but was awakened towards the end of 2nd millennium. The beginning of the third millennium of the Christian era saw its manifestation which not only put Euro America but the whole Un-Islamic world in a quandary. Now Iran has shouldered the responsibility to unite all the Islamic nations and dreams of a world totally Islamised.

After the collapse of the USSR Iran plays the role of the principal rival of the USA. It leads other Muslim majority nations to stand up for Jehad and global Islamisation. As the primary step to achieve the goal, Iran now attempts to consolidate the Islamic countries behind it in tandem.

Regarding Iran's relation with the East and South African countries the ex- monarch of Iran had started diplomatic ties with the republic of Kenya in the year 1971. After the imperial rule was overthrown, relationship between Kenya and Iran was again renewed in 1982.

Iran has been maintaining good relationship with other African countries like Cameroon, Ghana, the Ivory Coast, Mauritania, Comoros, Madagaskar, the Upper Volta, Tanzania, Seychelles, Zaire, Abidijan, Republic of South Africa, Mozambic, etc.

The African countries have attracted the European nations since its discovery. Its rich mineral resources like gold mines, copper mines, platinum reservoirs, large quantities of precious stones, coal, aluminum, uranium, iron and oil reservoirs, its fertile land with abundant water facility, etc., are the sources of its allurement for the Europeans. But Iran has its eye for the Islamic populous Africa. Africa is the only continent with a Muslim majority of 55% of its total population. The African countries like Sudan, Algeria, Nigeria, and Egypt are Muslim dominated countries. The growth rate of Islamic population in Africa is higher than that of other Islamic countries and exceeds that of Christianity. The dominating languages of African countries are Islamic rooted Arabic the language of the Quran and the official language of many Muslim countries. In view of all these features Iran attaches special importance to Africa. The African countries contain one third of the members of the United Nations.

Hamas, the Islamic extremist group of Palestine is becoming more powerful day by day. It seems to enjoy greater support in the occupied territories than in the Palestine Liberation Organization. On the other hand, despite the Palestine Liberation Organization's recognition by Israel, Iran's indirect persuasion to the Arab countries not to extend their diplomatic recognition to Israel encourages the Muslims to fight against Israel and keep hold of Palestine.

Relation between Iran and Saudi Arabia has been improving since 1995. Today Iran considers Saudi Arabia as an important state in the Persian Gulf region. Unlike in the past, Saudi Arabia is not showing any green signal to the Jews in connection with the Middle East peace process.

Another positive sign of closeness between Saudi Arabia and Iran is the Saudi Government's rejection of the United State's pressure to make it declare Iran as responsible for the bomb blast in the U.S military base in the town of "Khubbar". The Saudi Government realized that it was an unfortunate claim and was part of an evil conspiracy against Iran, which could have grave consequences in the region. So the Saudi Government categorically denied Iran's involvement in this bombing.

To strengthen the Islamic tie ISAFA (Iran Saudi Arabia Friendship Association) has been formed in the middle of 1999.

Accordingly Saudi Arabia is drawn closer to Iran for the development of its Islamic global outlook and give strength to the anti-American stances of Iran.

Iran is trying to retain its previous Islamic friendship with Iraq. Syria, an Islamic state, is mediating in resolving the dispute between Iran and Iraq. On the other hand, Iran has in all circumstances defended Syria against Israeli persecution.

World Muslim community was first dissatisfied with the dictatorial activities of Saddam Hussain. But when they saw the unobstructed killing of the people of Iraq by the USA and the NATO group, their Muslim sentiment got hurt and it turned to Iran to be sympathetic towards Saddam Hussain. The downfall of Saddam Hussain and his imprisonment by the USA created a wave of sympathy among the Muslims of the world. The disrespect towards Saddam Hussain by launching a criminal trial against him is now conceived by Muslims as disrespect to the Islamic multitude. Moreover the assertion of Saddam Hussain from behind the bar that he is still the ruler of Iraq and the action taken by the USA is illegal and inhuman ranged the Islamic community against the Christian world. Even those countries, which had given a helping hand to the USA to fight and win over Iraq, also raised a voice of protest against the aggression. Iran, which had launched a war for 10 long years, sympathized with Iraq with limited assistance. The countries like Algeria, Tunisia, Morocco, Mauritania, Sudan, Libya; Egypt, etc., launched rallies against the USA.

Iran is also tilting towards Iraq forgetting completely its past bitter relations. Iran wants to resolve the problems connected with Iraq imposed war. Exchanging the prisoners of war currently in captivity in both the countries is one of the main problems. However Iraq participated in the 8th OIC summit held in Tehran which was a sign of improvement of relations between the two countries.

The policy that 'enemy's enemy is my friend' brought the Hizbulla of Iran and the Al-Qaeda of Bin Laden close together. Both have now joined their hands to fight against their common enemy the USA. Bin Laden finds a strategic place in Iran to fight against their common enemy. It is not Iraq but Iran that is developing the 'weapons of mass destruction' for the last 18 years and aiming against its last but not the least target.

Egypt had a long-time cordial relation with Iran. But at the time of Islamic revolution in Iran the Shah of Iran took asylum in Egypt and hence the rift between the two countries widened. In course of time Egypt's leaning towards Islam has pleased Iran to come closer to Egypt.

Iran and Egypt coordinated their position on the nuclear issue at the Nuclear Proliferation Treaty Conference's review in August'1995. There has been growing co-operation between the Iranian religious leadership and Egyptian clergy to enhance the status of Al Ajhar. Qatar too normalized its position with Iran. Prince Khalid bin Sultan who was the commander of the Saudi forces during the Persian Gulf War against Iraq had publicly urged the West not to equate Iran with Iraq. Despite the animosity and differences between Tehran and Bagdad, relations between the two neighbours are also showing a marked improvement.

The scientific representations of Syria, Egypt and Saudi Arabia met in a conference in December 1994 in Cairo organized by the al-Ahram Institute of strategic studies. There they publicly urged the building of an Arabian nuclear option to counter the Israeli bomb.

Iran also gradually brought Egypt into its clutch. Stressing the importance of the Palestinian issue Iran itself was secluded from Egypt as it signed the Camp David Peace Treaty with Israel. But today Egypt is distancing itself from Israel and keeping its relation close to Iran. Amar Musa, the foreign minister of Egypt in 1996, made fairly positive moves in supporting Syria, Lebanon and Palestine. He also stated that the West's desire in having Israel armed with nuclear weapons and banning the Islamic states from using nuclear energy for humanitarian purposes is unacceptable. Recently in a statement the Egyptian President Hosni Mubaraq said that his country would not take part in any US led military action against International terrorism.

Iran wants that the two million pilgrims who go for Haj every year to Mecca should be informed about the global Islamic problems and aggressive Islamic Jehad under the Global Islamic Movement. They should follow the Bara'a (disavowal, it means that Muslims urge the Muslims to come together and take a stand against criminals who savagely kill the Muslims and against those who support the rivals of Muslims and those who decide in their favour in the international organizations). Haj cannot be complete without this. Iran asserts that a Haj without Bara in true sense is not a Haj. Bara is an essential part of it. Presence or congregation of Muslims in the Haj must be a meaningful presence and meaningful congregation. Mohammed wished that every Muslim must come together to a particular place and at a particular time. The congregation at a particular time and place must be meaningful.

If a Muslim, although he is poor and illiterate, gets a chance to go for Haj, there appears before his minds eye a global society of Islam where he is one among it. He gets a geographical knowledge of the world. He feels the persecution of a co-Muslim. He feels that he is not alone in his vast global society. So, to utilize the expendability of Haj pilgrimage Iran is trying its level best to politicize the Haj. If the politicalization of Haj succeeds, Iran will get in every corner of the world not only its mere sympathizers, but also its own strong men.

Being propped by Iranian revolution, a half a century's Pakistan could developed a diplomatic policy of its own. Backed by the largest imperialist country, the USA and the largest communist country China, Pakistan, without having any elemental technological incentives dares to face India for a nuclear war. Diplomatically India faces all sorts of failure to keep Pakistan under its cordial clutch as a good neighbour. Despite its several attempt to create a friendly atmosphere with Pakistan by opening multilateral friendly gates India fails to bring Pakistan to the position of a good friend. Having strangled the Indian border, Pakistan denies for a shake of India's unilateral rising hand and continues its insurgency in India through its agencies. It became a good war practitioner keeping India as its adversary and the United States of America and China as its diplomatic friends. Global Islamic Movement has stung India with its fang of Pakistan and crunching it from Himalayan side, leaving India to flutter with excruciating pain. After the Movement digests India with a population of more than one billion it would be very easy for the Movement to declare its supremacy as a civil svictor of the Armageddon.

Iran's Significance in Charity

Iran, like all other Euro-American nations, also concentrates its programme of religious expansion in the African countries. The programmes implemented by Iran to meet its destination are Jihad-e-Sazandegi, a part of administration under its ministry.

The Jihad-e-Sazandegi ministry has carried out many welfare-based programmes for the all round enrichment of the Muslims in different nations. These programmes are related to agriculture, animal husbandry, fisheries, forests, pastures, rural development and rural industries. The ministry of Jihad-e-Sazandegi has spread out its work in rural areas of Tanzania, Ghana, Sierra, Leone and Sudan.

Over the years through activities in many African countries the ministry has afforded the people the spirit of self-reliance and self-confidence. The ministry has also given direct aid to the needy by erecting various clinics, which provide health education and treatment to patients. Annually ten thousand people in Tanzania enjoy the services rendered by Jehad clinics. All these activities are carried out free of charge.

As the Christian community preaches and advertises its generosity through the medical services under the banner of the Red Cross society, Iran has also expanded free medical service under the religious emblem of the Red Crescent. The Red Crescent's humanitarian aids to the needy African countries especially when they are afflicted by famine, draught and natural disasters, the establishment of various clinics and donation of medicines bring high esteem to Iran.

Like the Multinational Corporations having spread their spider net of economic profiteering business in different countries of the world, Iran has also implemented many plans and programmes to gratify its important requirements from Africa's potential resources. Africa, in view of its consumption pattern, can serve as a good market for Iran's non-oil exports. Iran's private sector is inclined to greater participation in economic ventures in Africa.

Iran's presence has been culturally accepted in Africa and the Africans think well of Iran. Giving educational scholarship to African youths, the establishment of Islamic schools and health centres in the deprived countries in Africa are among the cultural and social activities of Iran.

Iran Encounters USA

Iran with its oil productive strength and Islamic vigour is now able to stand as a challenge to the USA as a rival superpower after the disintegration of the USSR.

It enhanced its naval operation efficiency over long distances. It has also gained access to the naval facilities in Mozambique. Iran has the ability to maintain submarine patrols in the Arabian Sea. It is also a great threat to the USA. It is already capable of threatening the shipping lanes along the Red Sea from its base.

Iran wants to extend its military and territorial power to the Gulf countries. It wants its warplanes to accommodate in the Persian Gulf which is not possible as long as there is U.S. military intervention in the Gulf countries. Its supreme goal is to expel America from the Gulf countries and to crush the Christian infrastructure of the USA.

The USA has threatened to retaliate with a US law to punish the non US farms that invest more than 40 million dollars in the energy sector of Iran and Libya. The American bid to isolate Iran has failed not only in the Arab world but also among the Western allies. Russia and China also take a favourable position towards Iran.

The extension of economic sanctions by the USA on Iran and Libya on August 5, 1996 did not affect Iran. The USA's prohibition of non-USA companies from investing in these countries' oil and gas sector was ridiculed when, to the utter disappointment of America, 3 international companies from France, Russia and Malaysia signed on 2 billion dollar contracts with the National Iranian oil company (NIOC). A year after

Pakistan and East Asian countries were in the queue to contact Iran for a contract to buy liquidated natural gas from Iran.

The former-President of America Bill Clinton imposed sanctions against 7 Russian enterprises barring them from trading with, and receiving assistance from, the US for allegedly selling weapons technology to Iran. But on the contrary Iran developed a lot in the arms manufacturing technology and became self-reliant defying America's under estimation.

The USA's attempt at the prevention of Iran's access to nuclear technology for peaceful purposes had met with the disapproval of the member countries of the Nuclear Non-proliferation Treaty. The International Atomic Energy Agency (IAEA) had concluded that Iran had secretly made nuclear material.

Iran displayed its defiant tendency when it cut off its cordial relationship with Germany in the year 1991 after a German court verdict indicted 8 Iranians in the charge of attempting to murder in Germany. The religious leader of Iran Ayatullah R.Khomeini also passed Fatwa against a British national Salman Rushdie for his reputed writing "Satanic Verses" and remains heedless towards the reactions and comments passed by the irate viewers of European countries.

In a recent earthquake occurring in December 2001 in Iran that caused a death toll of more than 20000 people, the US offered its sympathetic hand for relief distribution. Iran, out of its Islamic dignity, rebuffed the US offer.

One of the largest refineries of the world and the 8th refinery of Iran was opened as a result of which Iran became a member of Oil Producing and Exporting Countries (OPEC). All the technicians of the refinery were Iranians and the value of daily production is about 5.5 million dollars. Iran had a plan to double its oil capacity to 8 million BPD (Barrel Per Day) by 2000 A.D.

Being substantiated by its infinite natural resources and impelled by all the Islamic countries Iran has stood consistently by the force of its religious impetus. In the language of the Israeli Prime Minster it is the Chief instigator of religious war

Jehad. In a summit held in Cairo, Egypt, in March 96, the Israeli Prime Minister Simon Peres told at the conference to raise a unilateral voice against terrorism. It was an insinuation against Iran.

"Terrorism knows no borders. So borders must not restrain action to smash a terrorist snake. This terrorism is not anonymous. It has a name. It has an address. It has bank accounts. It has an infrastructure. It has net works camouflaged as charity organizations. It is spearheaded by Iran. It is a regime, which initiates, promotes and exports violence and terror. A conclusion must be drawn on how to contain it. Terror threatens peace and stability in the whole world." This comment is made by no other man than the Prime Minister of Israel. The USA unbottled this terrorism through the ISI of Pakistan.

6. Islam and Euro-America in Their Reciprocal Perspectives

(a) Islam, in the Eyes of the West

According to some thinkers of Western ideology Mohammed was a warmonger and a victorious tyrant over innocent and unarmed tribes averse to war. He propounded Islam to lord over all the people of the world who do not accept his ideology perceiving him as the only Prophet and Allah, his creation, the only God. He carved in Islam such principles that would suit to his carnal desires. The foundation of Islam is booty and beauty, the two basic human instincts propped by Paradise, which promises infinite sexual enjoyment with all its necessary accessories after an 'Islamic death'.

There are more than one billion Muslims living in more than 55 countries of the world. Islam is the basis of their culture, a culture that not only affects its individual life, but penetrates all the aspects of their social life. Europe is also the home of millions of Muslims: There are more than two million Muslims in France, 3 million in Germany and more than two million in England. It is very unkindly that Muslims of these countries adhere to Islamic customs and norms forcibly. A Muslim father who has been residing in a small city in France cannot accept the fact that his daughter studies at a co-educational school or walks in the city with make-up. The Turks living in Germany still uphold their old customs and ceremonies. Muslims believe in the relationship between religion and politics. As staunch Islamic zealots Muslims are always against the present system of democratic government, which is prevailing in almost all the Euro-American countries. They want to replace it by the implementation of Islamic system of government in this land of Crusade. This is the prime cause of resentment among the Westerners. They unsuccessfully express their feeling of resentment against the aggressive attitude of Muslims.

According to some Western thinkers Islam is basically an Arabic religion. Every one who is not an Arab is a convert. Muslims are the people laden with hatred and rancore feelings against other people and nations.

An Western orientalist in his book has described some important points on Islam. First, recent changes in Islamic nations from Afganisthan to Morocco and from the Iranian revolution to other movements have been repeated in the past centuries. They are the consequences of centuries of opposition between the West and Islam. Secondly he confirms that the credit of winning position will go to the West. According to him the reason for this is connected to the defeat of Ottoman Muslims in Vienna in 1683 and Carlouse Agreement in 1969 that led to European domination.

Westerners have an obsession that Muslims are inferior intellectuals. Under-developed brains are less averse to fighting, quarreling and interested for nuclear games. Such views of Westerners may not be correct. There are numerous Muslim scientists, skillful artists; eminent poets and writers, as well as there are brave fighters, bombardiers, ruthless killers and extremist millitants. When a skilled Westerner gets converted into Islam one must confess that he is still skillful as he was before his conversion.

Muslims are both physically strong and mentally skillful. Their marriage in many occasions takes place in alien races. The Quran allows Muslim males to marry outside of their society. This provokes them to kidnap the girls of non-Islamic societies where Muslims are predominantly stronger and/or the adversary is a minority.

Majority of Western thinkers have very feeble idea about Islam. They always think ill of Islam. Many of them do not want to admit that the revolution in Iran and the movements in Algeria, Palestine, Kashmir, Turkey, Egypt, Chechnya or Bosnia show the vigilance and animation of Islamic nation. They always want that Islam and Islamic nations must harmonize themselves with the West and Western civilization and not the vice-versa.

Because they belong to the white race family of European ancestry they are pround of their Western magnificance and European bigotry. One should not forget to note the observation that the art of conquering war by using missiles or explosives is a tial of bygone days. Use of missile had a value or weight of success in wars only upto 1980. The war of third millennium never needs any battlefield, missile to attack or cannon to boom or plane to bomb. Some manual weapons like sword, machete, and gun and fertile womb for child proliferation is sufficient to conquer a country.

The effects of Islamic population explosion in the Middle Eastern countries are quite tangible in Europe in the form of refugees and immigrants. The mass migration of job seeking youths to the West in the next twenty yeas, would probably endanger European cultural and welfare systems and such issues have alarmed the West.

According to some Western thinkers, Muslims are part of the danger threatening the West from Asia, Africa and Latin America. According to him not only the Islamic terrorists are the ones who pose the threat but Islam is extremely dangerous for Christianity. He also describes that the 14 hundred years history of Islam itself manifests that Islam has been dangerous for every civilization it has encountered, particularly for Christianity. One must be sure that as long as Islam is Islam and as long as the West remains the West, without changing into East, the never ending battle between them will go on steadily as it has been over the past 14 centuries. Mr. Huntington describes the following remarkable points that create a sense of fear in the minds of Westerners towards Islam.

(a) Remarkable growth of world Islamic population.

(b) Emergence of a phenomenon known as the Islamic vigilance and its confrontation with the Western Cultural values.

(c) Usurpation of Soviet balance of power by world Islamic force.

Muslims in the West form a minority and simultaneously it holds the same truth for the Christians living in the Islamic countries. This situation calls for a specific condition of its own. Even both Muslims and Christians are in a quandary. When a confrontation occurs among the Christians and Muslim nations what will be the fate of the minority race of both the nations is a question.

Christians who are good history writers are confirmed about the fate of a minor Christian community in an Islamic nation. They know how Muslims wiped out three million unarmed men and women of Hindu minority community in Bangladesh, formerly East Pakistan in 1971, blocking their ways to escape. Europeans are well aware of the fact that whereever and whenever an Islamic warring community has obtained a chance to fight, it leaves no stone unturned to occupy the land to declare it an Islamic nation. Their strong faith in Islam is the chief weapon that makes them victorious everywhere on the surface of the earth, simultaneously creating in their mind a feeling of contempt towards non-Muslims. A Muslim is impelled to kill his enemies blindly wherever he avails a chance.

After the downfall of the communist empire in Russia, the USA and its allies took a sigh of relief. But all their hopes again were dispelled when they found a great genie has appeared before them who is more terrific and more ferocious than their previous rival in Russia and China. Moreover communism as inimical to imperialism fought against the U.S.A standing outside of its courtyard. But this great indomitable enemy of the USA has stood as a dreadful and incurable disease in its own precincts.

There are two factors that reflect Islamic strength and vigour to confer Islam global victory. They are Islamic fundamentalism and the growth of Islamic population in Euro American countries. These two are frequently mentioned as sources of threat to Western interests, Growth of Islamic population and Islamic revival are the two sides of a coin. More than half of Iran's population is under 20. Turkey having a population of 20 million in the year 1950 became 60 million towards the end of 2000. In 1960 the population of Algeria was 10 million. But in 1995 it reached 25 million. In the year 1951 the Muslim population of India was 30 million but presently it is almost 160 million, five times more than what it was 50 years ago.

The scarcity of comfortable living in Islamic countries due to this heavy population compelled the Muslims to migrate and penetrate into non-Islamic European countries. But surprisingly it was found that Muuslims have formed the strongest minority community in almost all the non-Islamic European countries and presently they are in an attempt to capture the central power in Europe.

Christians as a whole were greatly proud of the World Trade Centre as the highest and noblest tower with its architectural and commercial fame. It was also used as center of exhibition and entertainment mostly for converted Christians who were told about the unilateral prosperity of Christian world in connection with the World Trade Centre and Statute of Liberty as a symbol of Christian civilization compared to the rest of civilizations. Demolition of World Trade Centre not only shock the financial backbone of the USA but it also demolished the lofty tower of pride and prestige of Christian world. On the other hand Muslims are going to reserve the pride of ownership of the highest building in the world with Dubai as its point of admiration. An international consortium led by a South Korean company won a deal with $850 million to build the world's tallest building in Dubai with a height of 800 meters and 160 floors above the ground. Jehadi terror has mitigated the indomitable spirit of Euro-Americans to rethink for the construction of such a lofty tower.

In a public opinion survey in France, 75% of the respondents positively answered to the question "Can Islam be described as a religion of intolerance?"

In a public opinion survey in Germany, 47% of the respondents expressed their apprehension of Islamic fundamentalism by considering it as a threat to the Western interest.

In a German magazine the writer Borkhein Heebler writes– "Islam is more hostile than all other religions. Its 1.2 billion believers possess a revolutionary zeal. They are fundamentalists who carry the banner of the prophet of God and keep the flame of disgust of Western values burning. They consider themselves as the pioneers for the establishment of the world of Islamic system. Europe will soon witness the formation of intolerant religious government at its back door." He further says – "The potential power and force of Muslims has exposed the West to a holy war, a war which Islam will force on the United States".

According to the President of the USA George W. Bush the Islamic countries like Iran, Iraq, etc., are the "axes of evils". The states like Syria, Cuba and Libya, etc., are the rogue states. Bush confessed the USA led war against Afganistan is a Crusade. The Crusades were Christian military expeditions from 11th to 14 th century aimed at recapturing the holy land from the Muslims. By invoking that memory for the current fightings against terrorism he simply renewed the old tradition again by conquering Iraq in the month of March 2003.

The whole of Euro-America has a sense of fear for Osama bin Laden and his Jehadi army structure Al Qaeda. This terrorist network of Osama bin Laden is the most formidable organization in running militant activities worldwide. Its spokesman Suleiman Ghaith threatened the U S and Britain with more suicide attacks and cautioned Muslims against traveling by air and staying in high-rise buildings. Their key claims in the guise of warning to Euro- America were to :

1. To retreat from Afghanistan and Iraq
2. To stop assistance to Jews in Palestine
3. To relinquish their imperialism in Iraq
4. To leave their overlordship in the Arabian Peninsulla.
5. To cease their support to Hindus against the Muslims engaged for separation of Jammu and Kashmir from India.

"Terrorism (Jehad, in Islamic sense) and Islam are two sides of a coin. As soon as Ayatullah Khemeini took over charge in Iran and announced the necessity of a holy war, Muslims in most part of the world got excited. The war was in fact directed towards the West and stemmed from Jehad. Intolerant Muslims formed a united front against Westernization".

A feeling of animosity towards Islam has conquered the minds of both Europeans and Americans. Words like the Muslims, terrorists, militants, fundamentalists, the third world, Arabs and similar ones have formed a horrible image in the minds of Westerners and inflamed fear in their hearts. Western foreign policies especially those of the USA, are based on this fear. It has become a good excuse for political, economic and cultural intervention in Islamic countries.

Islamic fundamentalism and population growth in Muslim states as well as in Western countries are frequently mentioned as sources of threat to Western interests.

After the incident of 11/9 Islamophobia is gradually developing among the Euro-Americans. The anti-terrorist law has enhanced its 'stop and search policy' which is gradually alienating young Muslims. Fear of an Al Qaeda attack is always troubling Euro-Americans.

(b) Euro-America in the Eyes of Islam

> *"I will throw out all Jews and Christians from this Arab peninsula and will not allow any one to live there except us"*
>
> *– Prophet Mohammed*

Definition of terrorism and the role the USA according to Islam–

Responses differ if seen from different perspectives since, in modern international law, terrorism is a largely undefined term. One country's terrorist is another country's freedom fighter.

> "The lexical meaning of terrorism is the use of violence and threats, especially for political ends. Politically suppressed but ideologically conscious groups in many Third World countries have no

other option but to take up arms for the sake of regaining their birthrights and removing injustice which colonialism has imposed upon them. Ironically, Uncle Sam is calling these groups, which run full-fledged liberation movements, as 'terrorists'. Of course, no one in his right mind would ever agree with the views of the White House that spiritually strong and morally upright groups like the Islamic Jehad and the Hamas of Palestine or the Hizbulah of Lebanon are terrorists. To call them terrorists is to act like the blind person who picks up a spotless white cloth and calls it black. As a matter of fact these groups with their lofty humanitarian ideals have exposed for the world public opinion the identity of the real terrorists and the forms of terrorism they practise including military, economic, cultural, biological and cyber, not to mention media terrorism."

"With world people bewildered by the idea of cyber-terrorism and media-terrorism exploding in their own living rooms, and with world governments-for a variety of reasons ranging from absence of clarity of vision to over-dependence on master terrorist USA, unable to tackle the roots of terrorism, we say as a parting word that jihad for the lofty goals of Islam should not be confused with terrorism, nor should the violent acts of Talibans, Bin Laden and like-minded groups in the name of religion, be mistaken for an Islamic campaign."

The USA is the most powerful nation. It is not accountable to anyone, at least to the U.N.O. It applies sanctions against any country, which crosses its path and expects all other nations to follow suit. Whenever it cannot satiate its purpose, it starts terrorism and dictatorship without the slightest compunction. The only two countries where it has come a cropper is Iran and Iraq. The current

> charge against these countries is that they have developed the capacity to produce weapons of mass destructions (W.M.D). Hence Khomeini and Saddam Hussain are made out to be monsters that have to be destroyed. The simple reason is that they can come in the way of Western powers that are exploiting Middle East oil on which their very existence depends. The United States is in the Gulf only because of oil. Muslims are not prepared to admit that the attack on World Trade Centre is a terrorist attack. According to them "it is an act of self defence in an undeclared way by a group driven to despair by the USA's domineering policies and his support for state sponsored terrorism."

Justifying the pulverization of the World Trade Centre Muslims say that "In a state war, including civil discontent, such acts are justifiable, especially in view of the fact that the targets selected were not residential areas or public places picked at random for mere sadistic pleasure, but the main financial and military centres of the enemy."

USA, the chief creator of state terrorism

The Muslim world alleges the USA as the creator of State terrorism. According to some Ismalic thinkers USA's attack on Vietnam, Iran, Iraq and Afghanistan etc are the instances of state terrorism.

"Before listing some of the acts of state terrorism committed by the super-terrorists of our times, it would not be inappropriate to find out why some people or groups turn radically violent, commit destructive acts, and are quickly labelled as "terrorists" by the real advocates of international terrorism. A list of instances of state terrorism, especially by the United States and Israel, could be long and exhausting."

"In the event of the Boston Tea Party, when a group of rebellious colonists disguised themselves as American Indians to board His Majesty's ship and dump crates of tea into the sea is too remote an incident, although it was a prelude to the use of force and intimidation to declare the 13 New England colonies independent in 1776 and then embark on a police of westward expansion and occupation of extensive lands by terrorizing and almost exterminating the indigenous America-Indian race. The second phase of terrorism was the enslavement of the black people who were kidnapped from Africa and forced to foil for the benefit of the white Anglo-Saxon man in the New World."

"U.S' state terrorism in its present form started during the Second World War with the dropping of atom bombs on the cities of Hiroshima and Nagasaki at a time when the Japanese were on full retreat from all fronts and the war was almost over. Hundreds and thousands of innocent people died merely because President Harry S.Truman was eager to test a new and devastatingly explosive toy. The next stage of state terrorism was set in Vietnam where for twenty years the U.S bombed cities, massacred civilians and used toxic chemicals to destroy the environment. Simultaneously CIA agents fanned out across the globe to play cloak and dagger games in order to terrorize and subvert popular governments such as the coup in Iran in 1953 to topple Prime Minister Mohammad Mosaddeq and the killing of Chile's President Salvador Allende by the henchman General Pinochet. At the same time military dictatorships that assumed power with U.S backing in Latin American, Asian and African countries and the crimes they committed against their people, were in fact an extension of the terrorist policies of Washington."

"However, the most profound example of U.S state terrorism was seen in the post-Islamic Revolution Iran, where group lets such as the MKO were used by the Yankees to eliminate some of the top Muslim thinkers including Ayatollah Morteza Motahhari, Ayatollah Mofatteh, President Mohammad Ali Raja'ie, Prime Minister Hojjatoleslam Mohammad Javad Bahonar and Chief Justice Ayatollah Seyyed Mohammad Hosseini Beheshti and 72 senior officials who died along with him in a blast. For 8 long years Iran was subjected to the worst form of terrorism. It included the bombardment of cities, the targeting of oil tankers, the chemical holocaust and finally the downing of the Iranian passenger plane with 298 persons on board by the U.S.A. Vincennes on July 3, 1988. Vincennes' commander, Captain Will Rogers, was even felicitated by President Ronald Reagan for this blatant act of terrorism."

In the year 1975 civil war started in Lebanon among the Muslims, Christians and Palestinians. This continued up to 1977. During this two years of war an estimated 50,000 civilians were killed and twice that number were wounded. In 1978 Israel occupied Southern Lebanon and in 1981 Christians fought against Syrian Muslims. In 1982, Palestine guerillas encamped in Lebanon and instituted their war programmes against Israel. Israel, to take vengeanc on Lebanon vigorously attacked and devastated the country, evacuated 7000 Palestinian guerrillas from Lebanon under the patronage of the U.S.A and European allied troops. Lebanon's Phalangist Christians with the collaboration of Jews attacked the refugee camps of Sabra and Shatile and killed thousands of civilians including women and children.

Sources say that America was a provocateur to Iraq in 1990 and encouraged Baghdad's military adventurism in the neighbouring Kuwait.

The U.S.A and Britain want the Arab State to remain as puppets. Saddam Hussain refused to be one such. His attempt to take over Kuwait gave the Western powers a chance to hit at him viciously on the spurious excuse that Saddam was invading an independent nation. Iraq was literally pulverized and it had been isolated for its courage. Though the Iraqi position is on the verge of starvation, 6,00,000 children died for want of medicine, but the Iraqis are a proud people. So in spite of the great loss that Iraq suffered without committing any such severe sin as compared to its attempt of annexation of Kuwait, Iraq did not bow before the U.S. The U.S could not topple Saddam Hussain even after lodging a package of $97 million to Iraqi opposition group to topple Saddam.

As a step against the military might the U.N. as an agent of the USA virtually eliminated Iraq's capability to develop missiles in terms of the U.N's special commission appointed for this purpose. Electronic equipments were installed in 30 different Iraqi industrial and other plants, which were engaged in developing such capabilities. A full time team of 80 men constantly monitored this effort. Even then USA swooped on Iraq, usurped the Islamic Umma of Iraq by dislodging Saddam Hussain. Probably never before in contemporary history has a country, which is not under foreign occupation being subjected to so much international control as Iraq is in spite of its lacking military capability.

Frequently made bombardments by the adversaries on Iraq infuriate it to take vengeance. The explosion made more than two years after operation Desert Fox, had ended in December 98. President of USA called it a routine mission. The strikes were in response to recent and more sophisticated Iraqi efforts surface to air missile attacks against the U.S and British aircraft in southern Iraq. The USA and British Government want to degrade, disrupt the ability of the Iraqi air defence. This made Iraq more inflamed against America.

Iraq is an unstinted Muslim populous country of the world since its emergence as an Islamic country, with Islam as its national religion and culture. But soon after the subjugation of Iraq by the USA and its allied force, the missionaries of its most fundamentalist Christian outfit in the USA, "Southern Baptist" publicly declared Islam as evil and distributed food packets labelled " Truth was realized through Jesus Christ".

Taking advantage of people in distress will do no good to Jesus Christ but it is a cherished tradition of American Evangelists. Between exploiters of oil and peddlers of Christianity, the Americans will establish themselves as an occuping force in Iraq. Their enemies will be legion. From these enemy ranks will rise new Osama bin Ladens. The USA will never again know peace.

Muslims are now confirmed that Euro-Ameericans are the most opportunistic and they can go to any extreme end to obtain their requirement. In the case of Iraq "Saddam Hussain's only sin was that he did not bow before the Euro-American supremacy. This made the USA to attack Iraq in a plea to find out the 'Weapons of Mass Destruction' restored by Saddam. The USA did not count the Islamic blood that has been spilled in

Iraq since its invasion which has formed a parallel stream of the Tigris." This impelled the Islamic movement to preserve the weapons of mass destruction, the suiucide bombers, in every nook and corner of Euro-America.

Handling of Saddam Hussain like an animal raised a sense of utter humiliation by the USA and its allies against the Muslim world. In addition, their ill treatment of the prisoners of War globally multiplied Islamic anger that resulted in serial bomb blasts over army camps, taking hostage of peace-keeping force and their conditional killing.

Even America has gone to the extent of creating an international tribunal to try Iraqi President Saddam Hussain and his entourage for war crimes against humanity. This indicates the highhandedness of a nation to punish the ruler of a sovereign Islamic country alleging him as a culprit. This reveals how they are acting in a vindictive manner. It also indicates America's intransigence in fighting Islam. In spite of the self willing imposition of Saddam Hussain's despotic power terrified the people, the majority of the Iraqis are strong and blind supporters of Saddam. They have sworn to launch an unending Jehad against the USA and its allies.

After Iraq, Afghanistan became the next target of the USA. Afghanistan served a lot as a mercenary of the USA. It offered its land to be used as the battleground and men as soldiers to fight against the USSR. USSR defeated the USA which retained its pride of victory. Afghanistan lost its 105000 people in the war. One in eight Afghan became disabled as war victims.

"It could therefore be said that terrorism is a synonym for the government of the United States of America. What Bush is currently carrying out in Afghanistan is without doubt state terrorism, especially when one sees the bombing of the UN food warehouses, residential areas, farmlands and the showering of cluster bombs whose yellow-coloured unexploded explosives bear a striking resemblance to the food packages mischievously dropped by the U.S aircraft to kill and maim innocent and hungry Afghan children. Last decade we saw carpet bombing on Iraq and the economic destruction of that country by President George Bush Sr., and what we are witnessing now in

Afghanistan by his son is part of the same elaborately hatched terrorist plot."

The crippled Afghanistan was again crushed by the USA after the demolition of WTC on the ground of harbouring bin Laden, the suspected mastermind behind this tragedy. But Muslims are not yet prepared to confess to having any Islamic link behind the demolition. Nevertheless after the November 11 issue the number of deaths, maimed and refugees again doubled. This infuriated the Islamic community more than ever. So they are in quest of a ripe time to blow the Jehadi cyclone over Euro-America.

The Muslim world has emphasized that the USA is a terrorist country. The USA's missile attack on Afganisthan is nothing but the launching of a crusade against the Muslims. Iran persists that Osama bin Laden is innocent. There is no evidence of any Islamic attack or attack by bin Laden on the World Trade Centre. Hence the USA's attack on Afghanistan is a terrorist attack. "The innocent people of Afghanistan have committed no crime. Are the lives of those who died in the World Trade Centre more precious than those of the people of Afghanistan? Is it because their colours are dirty?" questions Iran. "Hence to fight against the USA is to fight against terrorism. It is obligatory. It is Jehad. Any one who can take part in this fight must do so."

"Islamic governments shoulder a heavy burden of responsibility. They must enter the arena as a global movement against terrorism, against the violation of people's lives. The Organization of the Islamic Conference is duty bound to enter the arena as a great humanitarian movement. Afghanistan is a Muslim nation. It is a part of the Islamic Umma."

According to an Iranian monthly the "American President's call for a crusade against Muslims and his indiscriminate shedding of Afghan blood on the pretext of retaliation for the 11\9 attacks is far more terrorising than the events in New York and Washington."

The USA'S marketing policy of war weapons in Muslim countries creates a sense of hatred in the Muslim mind against it. An instance of such policy can be best quoted in the case of

Kurdish Democratic Party (K.D.P.) and Patriotic Union of Kurdistan (P.U.K.) which are the two Kurdist fractions which have been fighting over the control of Iraqi Kurdistan. America is supplying weapons to both the factions and simultaneously acting as the mediator between the two. Both the parties have had their rations of American weapons.

The USA interfered in Algeria to dislodge the Islamic government under the leadership of Islamic Salvation Front (F.I.S). The U.S.A started negotiations in order to prevent disastrous conditions in this country and materially it made an attempt to subdue the Islamic movement and thereby it helped to hasten the civil war among the Muslim civilians favoured by military rule and the Jehadi fighters. Next came France hand in hand with America to poke into the Algerian civil war. France is contemptuous of many Algerians. It was once the oppressive colonial power over Algeria.

USA, the killer of Islamic Democracy

Muslims are very fond of democracy i.e, Islamic democracy. Unlike the Western system of secular democracy the democratic government professed by the Muslims is perfectely based on the foundation of Islam. But to their utter agony the Islamic democratic infrastructure formed in different Islamic countries encounter a Western backlash and immediately gets demolished. In 1981 the Egyptian nationalist movement succeeded in convening an elected Parliament but this was aborted only a year later by British occupation. Tunisia had promulgated a constitution in 1860 setting up the Supreme Council to limit the power of the monarchy. But this was suspended in 1964 when the French discovered that it interfered with their ambitions.

Iran had formed an elected Parliament in the year 1906. But in the next year the British and Russians carved it out for their spheres of interest and the Parliament was dissolved in 1910. Amidst a perpetual attempt to reinstate a Parliamentary form of Government in Iran, on the contrary the Pehlavi dynasty was brought to power in the year 1931 by the British. These factors make Muslims revengeful against the West.

Wheresoever and whenever happens an incidence of outbreak of national revolution for an Islamic freedom movement, the USA stands in favour of the opposition. Relevant to the disintegration of the USSR both the USA and Moscow were fully aware that hegemony in the Russian federation suffers from linguistic, cultural and political conflicts and challenges. Chechnya is but an example of the struggle for independence like other republics such as Tartaristan and Karelia. 63 provinces are more or less asking for administrative, economic, banking and custom self-rule. Islamic culture and civilization is the common denomination in the present independent movements in Tajikistan, Azerbaijan, Bosnia, Albania, and other regions have given form and organization to the struggle. But the U.S.A. stands hard and fast against all these Islamic countries seeking freedom from the Russian clutch and make their path of revolution most miserable and the bloodiest. Hence the USA has been remaining as the enemy No.1, in the memory of the Muslim world.

Even the Islamic community has no faith in the UNO's activities. They are disinterested in the UNO for its inclination towards Western culture. According to them the "Universal Declaration of Human Right" could be nothing more than words and expressions to fool the people of the world and solace the millions of suffering hearts of the world.

Euro-America, the Millenium's arch enemy of Islam

According to the statement of Muslim scholars, before the emergence of Islam in Arabia, Christians were engaged in infighting between the two denominations Monophysistes and Trinitarians. After Islam emerged as a great reformatory religious force the people of Jerusalem, Bethlehem, Nazareth, Damascus and Antioch, etc., welcomed and embraced Islam and threw the yoke of Byzantine, or the Eastern Roman empire. The majority of Monophysites embraced Islam and found in the Quran the monotheistic message of Jesus, Abraham, Moses and all the Prophets.

In the year 1095 the Crusaders seized the city of Jerusalem. They occupied Bait ul Muqaddas in July 15, 1099 after putting 70000 Muslims to sword. In the 15th century king Ferdinand of Spain extinguished the light of the last Muslim stronghold of

Granada and forced tens of thousands of Muslims to embrace Christianity.

After the fall of the Roman Empire the Teutonic knights launched a bloody crusade to convert the Poles, Slavs and Nordic people to Christianity. But the end of the Crusade marked the beginning of the colonial era. The Portuguese seafarer Vasco Da Gama díscovered the route to India by skirting the Cape of Good Hope in the Suthern tip of Africa with the help of Muslim navigators. Then he killed his Muslim guides to wipe out their credit in the way of these historical discoveries soon after he landed in Goa. There he massacred the whole of the Muslim population, which included many Muslim merchants from Arabia and Persia.

The Spanish for their part destroyed the Aztech and Inca civilizations of Central and South America and burnt to death the indigenous people for refusing to accept the cross. In the Phillipines the Spanish resisted the Islamic enrichment, converted the Muslim population into Christianity and confined the Moros to the Southern Mindanao Island.

Muslims had their dominance over India five hundred years before the Europeans discovered the land route to it. Mohammed Ghazni and Mohammed Ghori, the Afghan cavaliers pillaged enormous wealth from India during their coveted invasions. Mohammed Jahiruddin Khan, nicknamed as Babur, a tribal leader from Afghanistan, could establish his dynastic rule in India up to his sixth generation. Here also the Muslims had to encounter the British who systematically looted enormous property in this land. A classic example in this pillage was the seizure of jewels and wealth from the Mughals of India. The Kohinoor, once the proud possession of the Mughals is now a part of England's crown jewels. What the Muslims snatched away from the Hindus in India was surrendered to the British by force. In the year 1947 the British had to relinquish the power of Indian administration and grant full independence to the Indians who consisted of Hindus, Muslims, Christians, Jains, Buddhists, Parsis, etc. As a result of the consultations and talks among the various political parties and religious denominations, the majority Hindus, in the power struggle, took up the reins of governing the country which displeased the second majority, the Muslims. The British did have a hand in splitting the parties and in creating a big division between the Hindus and Muslims. This fact made the Muslims at large furious.

The downfall of the Roman Empire brought disaster to the Muslims. There generated the disintegration of Arab states and the creation of Muslim states like Lebanan, Syria, Tunisia, Iraq, Algeria etc. Khilaphat kept the Muslims united and organized. But the West destroyed it in the year 1922. The Muslims are now in search of an opportunity to revive the Khilaphat, which, they hope, would dissolve Israel. For this achievement of theirs Euro-America is the key barrier.

British, the worst conspirator against Muslims

The British played the most important role to keep the Muslim world ever crippled by consecrating a Jewish homeland in the midst of the Muslim world. According to Islam, the formation of a Jewish homeland in the pit of Palestine is the root of all the troubles and turmoils because it debilitates the global Islamic spirit to turn the whole world into an Islamic kingdom. Israel is only the tip of an iceberg whose greater part is hidden spreading through the whole of the Western Christian hemisphere.

One can imagine how amazingly a statement of British Prime Minister Sir Henry Campbell Bannerman given in the year1902 for the necessity of formation of a non-Islamic home land in the midst of an Islamic country to suit the interest of the British to keep the Islamic nation ever crawling in its own soil reflected long after almost 46 years, in the year 1948, in the present form of Israel. "There are people who control spacious territories teeming with manifest and hidden resources. They dominate the inter sections of world routes. Their lands were the cradle of human civilizations and religions. These people have one faith, one language, one history and the same aspirations. No natural barriers can isolate these people from one another. If perchance this nation were to be united into one state, it would then take the fate of the world into its own hand and would separate Europe from the rest of the world.

Taking these considerations seriously, a foreign body should be planted in the heart of this nation to prevent the convergence of its wings in such a way that could exhaust its power in never-ending wars. It could also serve as a spring board for the West to gain its coveted objectives".

As long as there are Jews in Israel Muslims will never be at peace. They not only want to wipe out the Jewish settlement in Palestine, but also are in a fury to take revenge against the Westerrn Powers who burdened on them this troublesome race. To add fuel to the flames, the West wants to solve the Palestinian problem through the leaders like Yasser Arafat who are imbibed with the ideals of Western brand of secularism. This induced the West to consign the Nobel Peace prize to Yasser Arafat who was the prime suspect of the Hamas, a staunch Islamic organization which has vowed to liberate Palestine.

A Crusade against the Crescent with Euro-American hegemony–(Bosnian Muslims' Tragedy, an Islamic hell on earth)

Muslims conquered Spain in 8th century and made Spain their homeland. After 800 years of unobstructed rule king Ferdinand attacked the city of Granada, the capital city of Spain and killed hundreds and thousands of Muslims with the help of a union formed by the Church and the Pope. The Christian Army of King Ferdinand forcibly converted the Muslims to Christianity. The rest were expelled from Spain under heavy persecution. Muslims fled from Spain to North Africa and other nearby countries. Ferdinand plundered enormous wealth from the Muslims and became one of the richest kings of Europe. This plundered wealth of the Muslims made him to provide three ships i.e, Santa Maria, Pinta and Nina to the great explorer Columbus. This navigator was fortunate enough to discover the vast continent America with the obsession of discovering India.

Muslims of Bosnia who at present suffer from the Serbian onslaughts are the offspring of those Muslims who fled to escape the aggression of the Christian king Ferdinand of Spain in the year 1492. The same kind of incident was again repeated after an interval of 500 years.

Those Muslims who fled from Spain settled in Serbia, which was a part of the Ottoman Empire. In the first decade of 18th century Serbs in the province of Belgrade rebelled against the Ottomans and started a war for an independent state. Hence they began to kill Muslims. The killing and conversion of Muslim women and children in large numbers and in a planned way in and around Belgrade was done during March 1807. Serbia acquired the status of an autonomous principality in the year 1830. Since then the expulsion of Muslims started from Serbia under heavy pressure of persecution. The Muslims left Serbia and settled in Bosnia.

Present Muslims in Sarajevo of Bosnia are the descendants of the Muslims of Granada in Spain. The event that took place 500 years ago in Granada is once again being repeated today in Sarajevo in the Republic of Bosnia and Herzegovina. The two cities were besieged and destroyed by the Christians. It was the very embodiment of conflict between the Christian Europe and the civilization of Islam.

Meanwhile Bosnia and Herzegovina became a Muslim majority state in 500 years of conversion, population growth and infiltration. Muslims felt that the time was ripe for them to demand Bosnia and Herzgovina as their Islamic homeland. But it was not to the liking of the Christian Serbs and Croatians.

Mr. Slovodan Milosevic embarked on his project of a greater Serbia by making his intrusion into the Croatian territory. Meanwhile Cardinal Kukerjee of Zagreb rushed to the Vatican for recognition of Croatia as the Croats are Roman Catholics and the Serbs Orthodox Christians. Without any delay Germany declared its support to Croatia. Very cunningly the Euro-American combined Christian power lodged all their unified anger against the Muslims.

Since Croatia was a part of the Axis during the last World War the British almost instinctively threw their diplomatic weight behind the old allies, the Serbs. It was between the ancient Serbian–Croatian hostilities that the Bosnian Muslims got heavily squeezed. The Serbians assisted by other European countries tried to uproot every Muslim land mark on the European continent. In both the cities the Christians decided to uproot the political and socio-economic forces of Islam. Both the Serbs and Croats received full support from their European allies. The Croats and Serbs spurred on by Milosevic and Tudjmen had turned upon the Muslims in a relentless campaign of ethnic cleansing. Mass graves and death camps were as a daily fare. For nearly five years Europe watched the scene powerlessly.

The Bosnian genocide and persecution is a rare example in the history of the world. In the year 1913 the Christians in Montenegro killed about 800 Muslims, and 12000 Muslims were converted. In the year of Yugoslav's establishment in 1918, 3000 Muslims were arbitrarily killed in the region of Eastern Bosnia. In November 1924 the killing of 600 Muslims in Montenegro was no more counted as a great massacre. The Chetnics killed about 1,03,000 Muslims during the period 1941 to 1945 when Bosnia was under the communist rule. At the time of partition of Yugoslavia, more than 2,00,000 Muslims were killed in Bosnia alone in the racial clash. Most of the Bosnian children became homeless. In Bosnia there were special prisons with rape camps where the Serbs kept Muslim women only to rape them. All the men in the refugee camps were forced to dig trenches to bury the dead bodies of their own men. This reminds one of the Nazi forces who deployed the Jews to dig trenches and bury the corpses of their own men.

Rape was deliberately used as an instrument of terror and a conscious part of strategy. Ethnic cleansing and the annihilation of minorities is generally considered to be a part of nation building. But what the Christians could do to the Muslims in Spain in the fifteenth century was not feasible today in Bosnia. Muslims exchanged their blood for the autonomy of Bosnia. Now they want to take revenge against their traditional persecutor, the Euro-Americans.

Death camps, concentration camps and rape chambers mushroomed nearby areas. Muslims were taken there in thousands to be shot by the Serbs. In the detention camps 4000 to 5000 Muslims were packed inside each wooden barracks.

Having an aim only to kill the Bosnian Muslims and to distinguish the Christians from Muslims they made open the underwear of Males and then started firing the Muslims after having recognized them with their brand of Sunnat (Hithna) on the penis. This is extremely humiliating. When the genocide of the Jews continued they were given the opportunity to go to their synagogues before their execution. But the Bosnian Muslims were given no such opportunity; first, the Serbians destroyed all the mosques, then killed the Bosnian Muslims.

Muslims suffered the United Nation's embargo of weapons and mercilessly and unilaterally were butchered. The U.N peacekeepers, under the pretext of fear of the Serbians, never used force to deliver the little aid donated by some Muslim organizations. The Bosnians automatically suffered defeat as they lacked support from world organizations, the Muslim countries and the Western Governments. Hence 80% of Bosnian Muslim were defeated by a handful of Serbs and Karadzic supporters. This prodded the world Muslim union to raise up their armed hands against Americans.

The Serbian army and the paramilitary troops crossed the Drina River, the natural border between Serbia and Bosnia. Genocide in Bosnia and Herzegovina was accompanied by gang rape. According to an investigation as many as 35000 Muslim women were gang-raped. Many of them were gang-raped until they became pregnant. The intention was to produce Christian children from Muslim wombs and increase Serbian Christian population through Bosnian Muslim women. Women were dragged out of it one by one in spite of their strong resistance in supplicant tone and were raped in front of their sons, brothers and husbands.

Generally in European countries, gang rape or mass rape occurs as a by-product of war. But in the case of Bosnian women, rape by the Serbian soldiers was quite intentional. It was to produce the symbol of contempt among Muslim women, to deprive them of the noblest pleasure of having a child and to destroy the Islamic culture and seed from its very root. After the rape, some adolescent Serbs would slit their throat allowing them to die fluttered and then throw them into a dead mine.

Rape was deliberately used as an instrument of terror, as a conscious part of strategy to subjugate the Muslims of Bosnia. The Bosnian Serbs picked up the beautiful Muslim girls in the town of Foca and subjugated them to the systematic gang rape. It is a wide spread recognition that ethnic cleansing is a crime against humanity and the present judgment helps to establish that rape and sexual slavery is a heinous and beastly approach. But in war every thing goes unwittingly and judgment favours consequence.

This enraged the Muslim worldwide to fight against the Westerners and Christians. The ethnic cleansing of Muslims in Bosnia made the whole Islamic world irate to leave no stones unturned against America and its allies.

"Because the Serbs were in the victorious group, for them rape was fun. But it is an indication of indignity for the Muslims. America and other Western countries patronized those Serbs. When the Islamic Republic of Iran proposed to send a peacekeeping force of 10 thousand strong army men to Bosnia, it was repudiated by the U.N.O. Hence the Islamic countries decided to consolidate their strength to launch Jehad against the USA and its allies.

"One major impact of the Bosnian and Kosovan war for independent Muslim states has been to reshape of the Western, particularly American attitude towards Islam and the Muslim world whose military might has been magnified into a threat against Islamic existence. Muslim world as a whole has realized that the Western attitude towards the suffering of the Bosnian Muslims is an instructive example of double standards. All these principles which were always talked about by the West and the U.N. which passed 12 successive resolutions on that issue, have been nowhere in sight during the Bosnian conflict."

An angry Muslim–

"If Muslims unite and stand together, the arrogant powers can't do anything against the Muslims. Thus it is necessary for the Muslims to unite against the U.S led global arrogance". —M.Z. Abdur Razak, senior lecturer in Arabic and Islamic civilization at the University of Colombo.

Muslims are angry on the ground that they are down-trodden by other non-Islamic nations. For example in Germany there are more than 3 million Muslims but none of them got representation in German parliament. In England Islam is not constitutionally recognized as a minority race. In France the use of Hijab is a long standing debate.

Muslims always stand unilaterally united to their religion and law. Slavery is admissible in the Quran and Islam. A woman, particularly a slave girl, can be treated by her master as fertile land is treated by a ploughman, in accordance to his will and pleasure. Coition with slave girls by Muslims is recognized in the Quran. The rich Arabian Amirs keep slave girls in their service in large numbers. It is a very common practice that they rape those slave girls at the point of their pleasure. Eventually while a Seikh was happily engaged in copulation with a Philippino maid-servant Sara, she made good use of a knife by stabbing the Seikh through his stomach while raping. The old Seikh left for the other world then and there. It raised the question of implementation of the Islamic law Shariat that ordered her a sentence of death. But this led to a worldwide protest by many Human Right organizations to withdraw the death sentence.

In this case the death punishment to the victim is inevitable and justified according to the Islamic law. Now-a-days the Muslims are not able to implement the Quranic injunctions in the face of heavy pressure and criticism by the West. Presently they are not free to lead an Islamic life as they had been doing for long. So their suppressed anger is getting diverted towards retaliating the West.

The Muslims feel that they are nowhere in peace in any Western European countries. They are ill-treated and looked down upon by the European Christians and particularly by the racist groups. Turkish Muslims in Germany are the sufferers of German racist groups; Turkish opposition and pro-Kurdish groups and German Christians act as silent observers to these entire holocausts. So the suppressed anger solidified in their mind, later on takes the manifestation of Jehad against the whole of European Christians community and the U.S.A.

A few events like the success of Islamic revolution in Iran, the Salman Rushdie affairs, the Persian Gulf War, the victory of Islamic group in Afghanistan against the USSR, revolution in Algeria, etc., were regarded as the turning point of Islamic awakening in the world. This provoked Bosnian Muslims to remain stern and stiff in the face of the tough European Christians. Naturally Iraqi sufferings, Intifada, Bosnian crisis-all got jumbled up in the minds of the people. The Muslims saw west as their worst enemy.

Another point that irritates the Muslims is the imposition of Western culture by the Euro-Americans on the rest of the world. Islam as a religion is a combination of culture, politics and militancy. Each is inseparable from the other. A Muslim is always posed with his cultural appearance outwardly and a religious thought heartily and at the same time tries to enhance his number and creates a society of its own with the help of Jehad. So whenever and wherever Muslims sense a slight impediment in the way of their religion, culture, or politics they rise up with arms for Jehad shouting the slogan "Islam is in danger" - "Allah O Akbar".

The death sentence on Rushdie was backed by not only the Muslim scholars of different schools but also by all member countries of the OIC. The meeting of the British P.M. with Rushdie on the eve of the 9th anniversary of the issuance of the Fatwa by the late Khomeini and his support to Rushdie created hostility among the Islamic nations against Westerners.

Islam is very often quoted as anti-modern. Modernity now-a-days means only to Western modernity in its economic and intellectual dimensions which presents a special challenge to the integration of the Islamic world into the systems of the multinationals which is totally alien to the Islamic concepts of interest, insurance, taxation and so on. Some Muslim critics profess that modernism is a word, which may have a static definition, but it has no practical realization that modifies its definition. Every day is more modern than the previous day. A Muslim does not hesitate to fly an aeroplane, run a business, ride a horse or supply weapons or lunch missiles or promulgate guerille war-fare or create insurgency in non-Islamic nations. So there is reaction against liberalism in the modern Arab world either in the form of Islamic fundamentalism or anti-Western nationalism.

Muslims do not like the intervention of the USA and the UN in the Gulf countries. The West, as an occidental identity, is ever accompanied with its culture, civilization, democratic and secular ideology that is entirely anti-Islamic. Moreover the West challenges the imposition of Islamic law, the Shariat under the pretext of transgression of human right. The Western civilization implies a great impact on Muslim society in the Gulf countries. Hence they want to remove it for their Islamic security.

The USA is despised in every sphere of Islamic society. It is very commonly emphasized as dog, Satan, paper tiger, coward, child killer, enemy of humanity, enemy of Islam, etc. Hence the Muslims staying in the USA and England are advised to confront by all means to fight against the US and British aggression and to do their Islamic duty.

Muslim countries, if united, can exercise their monarchial power over other countries by controlling their oil supply. For instance Saudi Arabia produces 8.253 million barrels of oil per day, having its daily production capacity 11 billion. It also produces 1.65 trillion cubic feet natural gas. In the capacity of its liquid wealth reserved abundantly under its landscape it can exercise its monopoly over the European countries.

Presently the global Islamic movement has no hyper strength to challenge directly the USA and its allied forces. But it has promulgated its subversive activities as its regular practice by attacking the encampments and army structures of the USA in different countries of the world. The destruction of the USA ship in the sea, the attack on the US military base in Iraq, the blasting of Churches in different parts of South India, a kidnapping of the USA journalist in Pakistan, keeping hostage of the USA tourists in the Philippines, the demolition of a Night Club in Bali island of Indonesia and the serial bomb blasts on the peace keeping force in Iraq are nothing but the manifestation of its anti-American stand and a symbol of challenge to USA hegemony.

There is an Islamic heartland stretched over the countries from Central Asia up to Morocco. This Islamic heartland includes central Asia, Afganistan, Pakistan, Iran, Iraq, Saudi Arabia, Jordan, the West Bank and Gaza, Turkey, Syria,

Lebanan, Sudan, Egypt, Libya, Tunicia, Algeria, and Morocco. Apart from these countries there are many other Afro-Asian countries adjacent to those states forming the heartland of Islamic imperialism and culture. This part of land in the world has the highest record of baby production and migratory instinct for settlement. Almost 85% of the oil reserves of the world belong to this part of land. On the other hand the continent of Europe consists of several consolidated littoral nations which developed the art of aeronautical mechanism for space communication and exploration, navigation for the discovery of new lands over the sea, communicative vehicles and war ammunitions for industrial development and colonization. Almost 85% of world wealth has been accumulated in this Western part of the world and the U S A. The West wants the natural lore of the East and the East wants the material gains of the West. The West wants substantiation and the East wants enrichment. One is lured with the possession of the other. Civilisational barrier dissuades both to have a cordial exchange of each other's possessions. On the contrary both are infected with the virus of xenophobia that ushers the two races towards conflict and clash. Transformation of Civilization is the only way of solution, which can bring down the wall of difference.

2

Euro-America Under Global Islamic Movement

"In the United States a sleeping giant is emerging, living and growing in the hearts of millions of Americans aiding and healing the wounds of injustice, racism and immorality. It is rising from the ashes of slavery, calling those who suffer from its wounds. It comes also from the Western shores of Africa to the Horn, from the streets of India and Pakistan, Malaysia, China, Iran, Iraq, Turkey, Palestine, from the conservative countrysides of Europe to the Arabian Sea – from all points East, West, North and South – they come to join those here in the celebration of Islam. Islam has been awakened in America"

— A version of Global Islamic Movement.

The final hour will not come until Muslims conquer the White House.

— *Al Muhajirom, A British Muslims' Outfit*

7. Islam in the USA and the Super Power Under Challenge

The USA Under Jehad

It is unanimously accepted that the USA is the super power in the world. Having this stand in mind America calculates the world affairs as an infallible futurologist and acts according to its calculation. But if and when its calculation fails as enigmatic, there rises an apprehension that the perception of the super power is also erroneous and illusory.

In a report "Global Trends 2015" published by the American Intelligence community in December 2000, an assessment was made on a number of predictions about the political, financial and social landscape of the world. This report prophesied about the degeneration of the economic, social and military conditions of Russia; the political, economic and social destabilization of China, ethnic division of Iran, Nigeria and Israel, formation of geo-strategic alliance between China, India and Russia to encounter the US and Western influence, scarcity of water felt by half of the world population by 2015 A.D., the decreasing of Russian population from 146 million to 130 million by the year 2015, the growth of world population, the emergence of more mega cities, the crippling of roads, bridges and electrical system, the spreading of contagious diseases, etc.

Out of predilection, the predictions made by a group of scientists, politicians and corporate experts including the National Intelligence Council of America seems to be a conclusion of one self-descriptive version on the different aspects of different societies. But unfortunately they failed to access the future prospects of the USA in view of its present social and political analysis.

The more one rises higher, the more it becomes a subject of discussion and a centre of influence over others. America's predictions about others would have been true if it would have diffused all its central powers of influence over all the nations of the world. Most probably the USA did not use any reflector to see its own face. The self-styled most vigilant nation failed to protect its emblem of pride, the World Trade Centre from demolition made by its own plane that turned into a weapon for the destruction. It did not act sharply to remain alert after the warning was given in the year 1993 by an Egypt born American Muslim.

Now there is a programme framed to organize a final bloodbath on the soil of USA that may occur towards 2020 AD. The process has been projected since 6th century and it has been tested, animated and activated from time to time over the lands of different parts of the world during the long interval of 1400 years. This long process has been created in some 57 Islamic countries with a simultaneous expansion of one collateral civilization, with one flag symbol, one language, one script, one scripture and one culture. The name of this is Islamic Civilization and the schemed process for the expansion of this civilization is called Jehad. The ways and means by which to conquer the countries and seduce them into one Islamic civilization is (a) birth proliferation and infiltration (b) disemboweling and rape up to pregnancy (c) close contact killing with manual weapons like knife, sword, machete, and gun. This process of conquest is very easy, inexpensive and less dangerous to the invading race who consequently follows the former three principles.

The incident that took place on September11, 2001 revealed many latent points of discussion. When it was first shown on T.V. "Terrorists hit America" the statement itself revealed that Americans are not still aware of the Islamic process of attack that has been constantly promulgating itself in the USA. The cold civil war, as a first information report of Global Civil War, is on in the U.S.A. The ruling government is of course unaware of it; otherwise they would have keenly, deeply and thoroughly introspected and analyzed Jehad. Americans misunderstood Jehad as terrorism and misunderstood Jehadi fighters or Mujahids or Islamic (religious) fighters as terrorists. Europeans and Americans have conceived Jehad as a worn-out word used in the history of Islamic war.

Had they been appropriately informed on the idea on Jehad, their foreign policy, their strategy to defeat Russia, their soft corner for Pakistan and their dealing with Afganistan after the demolition of the World Trade Centre would not have been as it is now.

(a) Islam in the U.S.A.

For a long time Islam was considered as the religion of the Middle East. But in the middle of the 19th century Islam began to expand in Europe and in the USA. Right now, Islam is growing very fast in the USA. According to different census figures there are about 5 million Muslims living in the USA and almost all of them are supporters of Iran. Afro-American Muslims are quite influential among the American Muslims and they are alone expected to make Islam the most powerful religion of the USA.

Islam is the fastest growing religion in the USA. In every Islamic centre in America at least 5 to 10 Christians get converted every year into Islam. According to Farzad Darui, Manager of the Islamic Centre in Washington, almost 16,000 American Christians have embraced Islam since 1962. Latino community of New York has been converted to Islam in hundreds since 1992. They have also found an Islamic centre where on every Friday a sermon is given in four languages including Arabic.

Lahore's passport office reveals that it issues 800 passports every day. The U.S. embassy in Islamabad had announced that it issues one thousand visas a day to the Pakistanis bound for the U.S. People from Pakistan leave the land with a determination never to return again.

According to Professor H. William Martin, of Rice University in Houston, Texas, the growing number of Muslims in the US could have some impact. It could bring more pressure on Government dealings with Muslim countries. Secondly, it could impede efforts by conservative Christians to return to a Christian nation. And it would expose more Americans to Islam.

One of the most active members of the American Black Panther's Atlanta Rap, Brown who had once asked African Americans "to get a gun and get their rights by force" got converted to Islam and called himself Jamil-al-Amin. After learning Arabic he became a great promoter of Islam in the USA. As a leader of black activists Jamil called the whites "pigs", now calls them the oppressors. He is always busy with spreading Islam in Atlanta city.

Ironically the US, which heads the Christian nations of the world to preach Biblical sermons and expand the empire of Jesus has also cradled the Islamic Organisations to christen the USA to a centre of Global Islamic expansionism. Even white American ladies after embracing Islam not only preach and propagate Islam in their home land, but also they go round the world to spread the teachings of Islam through music and poetry.

(b) Why Islamization of U.S.A. ?

Muslims all over the world are very particular about the situation of the U.S.A. Their only intention is to prove that the Western civilization that reflects American society is totally vandalism, a frustration and a way that leads man towards hell. Hence Islamisation of America is the only solution to restore peace and tranquility in that country. Some Islamic newspapers have detected the following characteristics of American society:

- Nearly ten million Americans suffer from depression.
- 20% Americans suffer from severe mental disorder.
- Abortion is more than 30% among American women.
- Divorce and rape is increasing every year.
- Five million Americans are victims of child abuse.
- 7% Americans are addicted either to drugs or to alcohol
- Murder rate is increasing by 31%.
- Robbery, armed theft and rape are at 56%, 79%, and 99% respectively.
- 80% of the secondary school students use drugs.
- Nearly 26,000 Americans commit suicide every year.

Muslims perceive that the chief cause of deterioration in American society is the growing popularity of secularism in American democracy. According to them the national character of America should only be Islam which is an extraordinary elixire to extricate the USA from deterioration.

In reality the Muslim world lacks scientific and technological proficiency to encounter the West. So it is only the international Jehad through which it can face the US and the West.

It is redundant to say that when the sun rises in the East people of every corner of the world recollect the U.S.A for some reason or the other. This greatness of America has now lured the Islamic countries of the world to settle in this land. From their past experience, Islamic countries marked that a concentrated Jehadi attempt to win over a land has brought them unprecedented victory with enormous booty. A Red

Indianized America became the prey of European Christians and got converted to the present glorious USA. A concerted attempt of the same Europeans made them to lord over the extensive lands of middle and East Asia. The African countries also came under their subjugation during the course of their imperialistic invasion. So the Muslims with an aim to conquer this land have launched the Jehadi war, a matchless war that brings infallible victory both ethnically and demographically since their migration to it.

(c) Islamic Plans and Programmes for the USA

The establishment of Islamic institutions is a symbol of the presence of Islam, with a viable Muslim community in the American Christian society. Most Muslims in the USA are employees under non-Muslims and will stay as employees till they establish themselves.

"They continue to work with in the non-Islamic systems and they will not be proud because those systems are not Islamic at all. They ever want that Islamic centres and Muslim inhabitants should surround Mosques. It is the Muslims themselves who are to protect and promote such institutions. The Muslims of the USA want to set the following institutions based on Islamic ideology with an infallible hope to see the USA an Islamised USA.

- Islamic elementary, junior and high school
- Islamic college and universities
- Islamic medical schools
- Islamic hospitals and schools
- Islamic banking system
- Islamic political party
- Islamic museums to present the cultural aspects of Islam
- Islamic radio and T.V stations
- Islamic Airlines
- Islamic daily newspapers
- Islamic research, scientific, industrial and agricultural plants

- Islamic dietary laws are to be established and to supply hospitals, air lines, schools and grocery stores
- Trust funds and foundations (waqf) to take up these institutions"

In the early sixties Muslims were busy in search of identity by arranging conferences, building mosques and centres. In the eighties they started educational institutions, professional societies and business enterprises. In the nineties they were in the process of establishing Islamic hospitals, clinics and banks. In the first decade of the third millennium they are very hopeful of establishing an Islamic political party. As the next dream the American Muslims want to see America as an Islamic country.

Many American Muslim scholars, professors and Islamic activists have jointly framed those plans and programmes to implement for the conversion of the USA an Islamic country.

According to a report, if the present trend of oil consumption continues unobstructed, America's oil reserves will work out only up to 2007. But the production of oil by the rich Arab tycoons may continue up to 2014 A D. In the near future there is a possibility of the reserves becoming depleted. So the USA would find no other alternative than to surrender to the Muslim states. All the agreements regarding gulf security may come to a shocking end as soon as an oil scarcity will be visible in the Western countries. Unless and until they find any other alternative they would become slaves to the Middle East oilkings. The Middle East has two thirds of the whole of oil reserves of the world. Nevertheless they are mute about the persecution of America over Iran, Iraq and other gulf countries, for their agreement was made with the U.S.A. and its allies for security reasons.

One such instance that relates to bilateral interest is the Nixon Plan, which was first enacted on February 24, 1981. According to this plan Kuwait, Saudi Arabia, the United Arab Emirate, Qatar, Bahrain, Oman, etc., signed the pact to gratify their political, security and economic interest. Another pact signed in 1990 between the gulf countries and the USA is called the Carter Plan. According to this treaty the US could use military bases and air, sea and land logistic facilities in the gulf countries as well as rapid deployment of forces in case the U.S. or its allies are threatened or endangered. These arrangements would allow for the deployment of the U.S. forces quickly in order to protect its interest with these regional governments providing the necessary assistance.

According to the Carter Plan the NATO countries would also actively participate in the Persian Gulf defence. These countries would provide military help if needed. The plan also stipulated that the Arab countries will also be able to exercise internal control in case of any such civil law and order situation arises and pave the way for the US rapid deployment and Western forces to act.

In the 1970s the US and its allies implemented a discriminatory policy as far as military weapons were concerned which favoured Saudi Arabia. The main objectives of the US were to give protection to Israel from the persecution of Islamic countries, to take the Persian gulf security out of reach of the countries in the region and to take out the West in order to have full and sole control over the Persian gulf. In this way it could intervene in the region wherever and under any pretext that suited the interest of the USA.

The treaties on Persian Gulf security is nothing but deprivation these countries from having strong defensive capabilities. Though America has taken all possible measures through its member countries of the Persian gulf regional security council to escape from the glare of Iran, she cannot avoid or escape from the Iranian seeds in her own home.

The Muslims are anti-West in general and anti-American in particular. In a three day conference of Dar-ul-Uloom in Peshawar on April 2001 thousands of Islamic Jehadi fighters assembled there, unanimously declared the USA as their arch enemy. They disallowed America-made products. There they expressed their determination not to hand over the suspected terrorist mastermind Osama bin Laden for trial in the USA or in any third world country. A graffiti painted on the walls in Peshawar extolled the value of Jehad or holy war – "Koran and

Jehad are the ways of Islam", Koran and the sword are the Jewels of Muslims.

Although the percentage of Islamic population in the United States is far too small, the percentage of Muslim Criminals, serving out their sentences in various prisons is 17% of the total prison population.

Those Muslims who would have been slained by the rulers of Arab countries for their crime according to the Islamic laws of Shariat, are privileged to perform their Namaz 5 times in the prison. Imams are appointed with an annual remuneration of about $ 50000 to move round the prisons to teach the criminals about the Islamic tenets to become good Muslims. Besides, the Muslim criminals and Imams get a golden opportunity to convert the prisoners, particularly Afro-Americans to Islam.

There was a panel discussion on the writings by Pakistani Muslim women organized by the South Asian psychoanalytic forum in the Asia Society at the New York Medical Centre in the first week of June 2000, the conclusion of which was that Muslim immigrants in the USA were perceived as a terrorist threat. After the bombardment on W.T.C a thought wave began to spread in every nook and corner of America regarding the Islamic thinking and action. This was the first signal of a challenge to America in the year 1993.

Here one thing is obvious. Religiously imbibed soldiers are stronger than secular professional soldiers. Every Muslim is a religious soldier. He always works throughout his life with a psyche of Jehad. But those professional soldiers that are simultaneously inspired with a religious psyche of Jehadi thought is more invincible and sacrificial in war against his enemy. He cares more for his achievement than his life. This made the Talibans to capture the formidable town Khost after 15 years of war. It is a matter of surprise that a militant group of only 1600 well-armed Mujahids could defeat the Russian army and bring the whole situation under its control. At last America was boomeranged by this unbottled genie.

(d) Warmth of Islamic Brunt in the USA

More than one thousand mosques, the Muslim places of worship, have sprung up across the country from Atlanta to the plain field, Indiana to Toledo, Ohio. One of the newest and the largest mosques is rising in New York City.

Thus goes the fable – When an American Christian missionary meets a member of the mosque, both engage in conversation on the points which are common to both of their religions, such as reverence for the Mother Virgin Mary and a belief that all people are the descendants of Adam and Eve, etc. At the conclusive point the missionary, out of curiosity asks about Jehad, the word which is used as a sword that can be wielded in both sides. Jehad is the chief cause of all sorts of disturbances and transformation of a society of millions of people into another through the flow of blood. But the member of the mosque explains how the concept of Jehad literally means to struggle against evils. The missionary holds his tongue keeping in mind about the practical view of Jehad and turns back.

These Islamic centres have served as a base of operation for a statewide effort by Muslims to force California's schools to revise their social studies textbook to obliterate the offensive description given on Islam. The book depicted Islam as the religion of "Sword carrying Bedouins". They want to drive home a few basic points that "Islam proclaimed by the Prophet Mohammed in the seventh century is a worldwide faith of more than one billion followers. Only about 20% of them are residing in the Middle East. The followers of Islam consider themselves the descendents of the Prophet Abraham who is the ancestor of both the Christians and Jews. Mohammed is the last prophet. Lah Illah Illalah Mohammed Rasulilah. (There is no god but Allah and Mohammed is His Prophet).

The centre also reaches out in overtly political ways through an institution "The Muslim Public Affairs Council" directed by an Iraqi immigrant. This institution often invites politicians from city council members to U.S. representatives. Many white Americans come to this institution and take part in discussions. They often invite the Muslims to get involved in politics. This centre very often sponsors political symposium for Muslims. Now the Muslim members think to squeeze in an Islamic agenda in American politics. In the Islamic centre as many as 1000 persons get converted to Islam every year.

As the title VII of the civil rights act of 1964 prohibits employers from discriminating against individuals on the ground of of their religious beliefs or practices, Muslims in USA take every advantage of the constitution that renders equal right to all the people of the country without any discriminaion of race and sex. The act requires employers to reasonably accommodate the religious practices of an employee.

The Council on American-Islam Relations (CAIR) is a progressive Islamic institution in the USA. It is a prominent national Islamic civil rights and advocacy group. It has promulagated attempts to bring about reforfmations in American social life that would favour Islamic tenets. It sent a letter to the Philadelphia police commissioner to allow religious exemptioins in case of Muslim female police officers to wear headscarf or hijab. This institution succeeded in convincing the Philadelphia police department to allow Muslim police officers to grow facial hair. In 2001 CAIR helped a Muslim woman fire fighter in Maryland win the right to wear headscarf or the burqa.

An Egyptian clergyman of World Trade Centre bombing fame lambasted the judge for not agreeing to have Islamic experts at the court to contest the veracity of his statements. He criticized the New York city court for not giving him the chance to defend himself adding that his conviction by the court system will serve to strengthen the faith of his followers because they would see that the Seikh is standing for what he believes and that he is ready to suffer any form of indignities for the sake of his faith, Islam.

A French freelance journalist Jel Soler projected a 62 minutes long "Uncle Saddam" documentary, which ridiculously displayed Sadam Hussain, the Iraqi leader. This satirical documentary was compiled from the footage he smuggled out of Iraq. The film had been shown in the Vancouver film festival and the U.N. film festival and earned wide reputation.

One morning the journalist found the walls of his residence splattered with blood paint with an unsigned typed note attached to the mailbox of his home "In the name of Allah, the merciful, the compassionate, burn the Satanic movie or you will be dead".

All on a sudden his humorous mood over turned and he started considering either to hire a bodyguard or to flee. It is noteworthy that there are 12% of Arab Muslims remaining in America and 3.5% of the Muslims of America belong to Iran.

A website hosted on two U.S based free hosting companies displayed the cartoon of a pig with Mohammed written on it. The pig was also shown standing over a book on which the word Quran was written. Within five hours of sending a mass e-mail urging the Muslims to contact the host companies and demand the site's deletion, the Internet Muslim vigilance Council (IMVC) received a letter on September 11, 2001 stating that the site has been deleted for good.

A Muslim worker in Georgia filed a complaint in March 2001 stating that the company violated Title VII of the Civil Rights Act of 1964 by prohibiting him to clip his beard. The company Fed Ex by the decree of the court agreed to pay 70,000 dollars in back pay and compensatory damages to the Muslim worker and to hold training sessions for managers that will out-line the Equal Employment Opportunity Commission's (EEOC) obligations relating to prevention of religious discrimination and retaliation. Henceforth religiously mandatory beard is allowed in the U.S.A.

The U.S Council of Islamic Relations criticized an American news agency the "Associated Press" on an article on Muslims residing in America calling them terrorists. The U.S Muslims repeatedly contacted the News agency declaring that they would see both the News agency and the writer.

The USA Government has been pressurized by the local Muslims to print Eid Mubarak stamp, the first ever-USA'S stamp depicting an Islamic festival. The 33-cent standard postage stamp marks the two most important Islamic festivals in the Islamic calendar Eid-ul-Zuha and Eid-ul-Fiter.

(e) Islamic Terrorism, USA's Unbottled Genie (Commitintment of suicidal errors by Euro-Americans)

Global Islamic Movement deploys its terrorists to demolish the administrative and social structure of a country for the formation of an Islamic land and, after the work is over, the Islamic Movement shifts its work project to some other place. The USA is simply escalating the work of secessionism for the disintegration of European countries besides its own with the help of these Islamic terrorists.

To demolish the infrastructure of communism America supported Islamic terrorism (Jehad) in Afghanistan and provoked these Jehadi fighters all over the world to rush to Afghanistan for confrontation with the former Russia. To achieve its goal the USA had spent 3 billion dollars to allocate the terrorists in Afghanistan and embellish the Muslim militants with lethal weapons through the CIA. This encouraged General Zia-ul-Haq to come to prominence and dream of a Pakistani sphere of influence over Afghanistan, Uzbekistan, Tajikistan, Iran, Turkey and India. This perspective of the USA gave birth to Taliban with a cohabitation of Pakistan and Afghanistan. Taliban has not been limited to the territory of Afghanistan. As a combination of Turks, Algerians, Afghans, Pakistanis, etc., it has now emerged as an 'ism' employing terrorism to expand its dreadful reach. Now France is worried for the Algiers, German and Turks, England for its Pakistani inhabitants and America for its own converts.

America's foreign policy, which it has engineered to subdue its rival power has proved suicidal. In the year 1979 the U.S.A seduced Muslim militants or Jehadi fighters against Russia and provided them all sorts of assistance through Pakistan. As a result the C.I.A and the I.S.I came closer to each other. Muslim Jehadi fighters were trained in the camps of Pakistan and Afghanistan. They emerged as a fighter group in the name of Taliban. They fought against their enemy Russia. By that time Russia was on the verge of disintegration owing to its ideological debilities. As a part of Islamic ummah and global Islamism Pakistan, the breeder of international Islamic jehadi fighters, acquired all the most modern and sophisticated weapons and the strategic skill of most modern warfare from the USA. In the wake of international Islamic movement these trained Jehadi fighters of Islam will apply their war strategy against the USA and its allied forces.

America's pseudo war against Russia and the disintegration of Russia into Islamic homelands were synchronous. America took the false pride of winning over Russia. It simply unveiled the curtain wrapped over its constellation of enemies. Each of the republics formed after the downfall of Russia was an Islamic country. Each one is equal to a Pakistan or an Afghanistan.

The USSR was defeated neither by Afganistan nor by Pakistan and never by the USA. It was disintegrated by itself, by the upsurge of Islamic wave in its own territory. Its soldiers denied fighting against their coreligionist Afghans. Now it is the turn of the USA, which is going to face the same trauma that communist USSR faced.

In the year 1991 the U.S.A. helped the Kurds to weaken Iraq. In retaliation Iraq killed almost 50,000 Kurds and drove more than one million to seek refuge in Turkey. These Iraqi Kurds are the most formidable Muslim tribes who spread over in different parts of European countries. This is the process of Islamic seeds sown in the soil of Europe unwittingly by Euro-Americans.

The luxury sick Americans help Osama to become militarily stronger at least in a way. Every year the USA purchases $300 million Tanjanite stones. Bin Laden sells it to the USA and makes money to buy weapons with to fight against the same USA.

Britain is the main Christian country in the world to breed Jehadi fighters or the European Islamic militants. The British kingdom under the democratic rule of Anglican Christian Empress Elizabeth could obtain a world record to produce Islamic religious fighters. Britain, under the strict adherence of Protestant Christian denomination, could produce more than 600 British Muslim nationalists who have enlisted their names in Jehadi groups voluntarily to work in different parts of the world. Apart from this, there are almost 3000 British Muslim supporters to join in Jehad and create insurgency in different countries of the world. Modern British Muslim youths highly qualified from the technical institutions of England came out as front line soldiers of Jaysh Mohammed (Prophet's army) group that recruits Muslims in Britain to train for guerilla warfare in different countries of the world.

The bigwigs of I.S.I. of Pakistan had a safe asylum in England. England had been providing all sorts of assistance to the I.S.I. agents to continue their holy war until the collapse of the World Trade Centre. It also aided Afghanistan and Pakistan in their Jehad against Russia. The Chief of I.S.I. Hameed Gul had an easy access to London. He was in charge of supply of arms and ammunitions to Afgan Mujahiddins during the 1979-89 anti-Soviet war in Afghanistan. Only after the Osama bombardment on the U.S. embassies in Kenya and Sudan that Britain felt the burden of Hamid Gul and prohibited his entry.

Presently it is found that in every corner of the world Muslims are engaged in war against non-Muslims. The case of Lebanon and Cyprus is old enough. In Philippines the Muslim majority south has drawn sword against the Christian majority north. Muslim majority state Eritrea came out as the 57th Islamic country of the world after having a staunch battle against Ethiopia. After the collapse of Yugoslavia, Muslims from the whole world arrived in Bosnia and Kosovo to fight for their freedom against Christian Serbs. After the downfall of the USSR Muslims in Chechnya, Armenia and Georgia are fighting Jehad against their Christian compatriots. The common enemy and the archenemy of all those newly hatched but internally well formed Islamic republics is the USA.

"The USA is the enemy number one of the Muslim world"– This is the statement of no less than a man like General Mohammed Ajiz Khan, the Chairman of the joint chief of the staff committee of Pakistan. The USA fondles Pakistan like a mother her milk-fed baby.

The USA, which nurtured Jehad as a weapon to destabilize the administration of some developing countries, has now boomeranged by this sharpened religious instrument. Jehad is the proverbial genie, which was unbottled by the USA and its allies. It rose high up with a Talibanic figure and strengthened enough to demolish the WTC. America supplied millions of dollars to create insurgency in Russia, China, Saudi Arabia, Bosnia, Chechnya, the Philippines and in India. But when its own interest was threatened it exercised its fundamental right to use its missiles to destroy terrorist (Jehadi) centres violating all international laws. But the USA has not yet conceded that terrorism has become inherent in its own soil. It has to face a bipolar terrorism or Islamic Jehad. One is its internal Jehad as Civil war and the other is its external Jehad or international terrorism.

After the extermination of communism in the USSR, now it is the turn of the USA to be sacrificed on the altar of Islam. To gratify the never-ending process of Jehad global Islam has now caught the USA to be expendable for this process.

8. Disproportionate Growth of Islamic Population in Euro-America – A Death Knell For Christians

In an investigative statement it was reported that the population of Islamic countries like Oman, Iran, Kuwait, Libya, Bangladesh, Jordan, Kenya, Morocco, Pakistan and Indonesia are decreasing proportionately in comparison to the census of last decade. The main cause of this decrease in population is migration to the USA and other European countries.

There are about 5 million Muslims in the USA (Muslims claim that their population is 6 million). Now the world Islamic intelligentsia has deeply concentrated to rapidly increase the Islamic population in America by massive conversion. The best possible way to Islamise America is birth proliferation, which precedes conversion of Americans and Muslim immigration into America. The Quran favours birth fertility and polygamy. Hence a sincere and concentrated attempt has been made for a rapid increase of Muslim population in the USA. The Muslims in the USA will be 14 million by 2010 and by the year 2015 the Islamic population of the USA will be an estimated 20 million strong.

The estimated rate of conversion to Islam among Americans is 135000 per year. Every year prisoners in jail are also converted in thousands. 42% of Afro-American blacks are Muslims. Indian and Pakistani Muslims constitute 24.4% of the total Islamic population in America.

The ten states with the most concentrated Muslim population are California, New York, Illinois, New Jersey, Indiana, Michigan, Virginia, Texas, Ohio and Maryland (listed in order of population). These represent 3.5 million of the American Muslim population.

There are more than 1000 mosques, 400 Islamic schools, 3 colleges, over 400 associations, and .2 million businesses. There are more than 80 Islamic publications, journals, weekly newspapers, etc. Currently there are almost 10,000 Muslim soldiers and army men in the USA Armed services. The Muslims are in high positions in the fields of education and technology.

There are 2.5 million black Muslims in America and, if the rate of conversion of Afro-American Christians into Islam goes unhindered, Islam would be the chief religion of the blacks. Now-a-days almost all urban areas are populated by black Americans. One can find mosques, Islamic cultural and educational centres, abattoirs where animals are slaughtered according to the Islamic system in all the urban areas of America.

The Afro-Americans form 12% of the total population of America. In a country like India Muslims having 12% of the total population could raise a successful revolt to segregate India and form Pakistan in the year 1947. It is not surprising that, if all the Afro-Americans embrace Islam, they can control the American administration. The Million March in Washington has a great effect over the American society.

The population of the Christian Americans is decreasing day by day and, on the contrary, the percentage of the Afro-American Muslims is on a phenomenal rise. The city of Boston in Massachusetts has become the major city where Christian population is in the minority.

The census figures show that the Whites now make up 49.5% of Boston's population while Afro-Americans number 23.8%, Latinos 14.44% and Asians 7.5%. Other minorities and people of mixed race make up 4.8%. The Islamic star has a brilliant future in American zodiac. The world boxing champions Mohammed Ali and Mike Tyson are Muslim converts.

An increase in the number of gay and lesbian couples in a society brings unprecedented and tremendous change in the birth ratio of the concerned society of a nation. This leads to decrease the number of population in many Western countries. Surprisingly USA has 940,000 gay couples. Homosexuals lack any childbearing capacity owing to their lack of natural cohabitation. The Christians of the USA have become a target to this inhuman and unnatural distorted tradition that caused a rapid downfall in the proportionate birth rate of American Christians. On the other hand Islamised Americans in general and Afro-American Muslims in particular have been enhancing their population in multitudes to confront their adversary society. Baby breeding is a very successful scheme for those who have a future plan to win over the world through the number diplomacy. Islam encourages marriage as soon as a boy attains puberty. Early marriage and polygamy help a man for adequate breeding. Infanticide is another prime cause for the decrease of population in many Euro-American countries. There are evidences of women who are left destitute with their children after divorce. In some cases women kill their children born from their previous husbands by smothering or by some other means.

The U.S.A's immigration population is now the largest in history. Since 1970, the immigration population tripled in the U.S.A. Most of the immigrants come across the U.S border with Mexico. The USA provides a constitutional privilege of citizenship to those immigrants who marry a USA citizen. This gives a golden opportunity to those baby breeders who come from Pakistan, Nigeria, India, Bangladesh and other Gulf countries. They develop sexual relations with USA women and easily avail of the right of citizenship. Thereafter they perpetuate the expansion of their own imperialism. There are USA women who turn out to be professional wives for these citizen seekers and thereby jeopardize the country's security.

The 11.2 million immigrants who have arrived since 1990 and their 6.4 million children accounted for almost 70% of U.S population growth over the decade. Presently the U.S.A issues 70 to 90 thousand permanent residency visas each year. But more than half a million immigrants illegally enter the country The immigrant population grew to 5.7 million in the1980s and to 8.6 million in the 1990s. Mexico accounted for 28% of all immigrants, China 5% and India 3.5%. Immigrants constitute almost 26% of the population of California, 20% of New York, 18% of Florida, and 16% of Hawaii, etc. Immigration would emerge as a hot political issue in the near future. After being given some missile doses by the Global Islamic Movement the USA imposed some restrictions in its migration policies.

According to a forecast for the period between the year 1990 and 2025, Central America would require a large-scale labour force. It would increase by 50.5 millions. North America, during the same period, will be short of manpower compelling it to rely on immigrant wage earners. During this same period, in North and Western Europe as well as in Italy, active manpower will be deficient by 44.3 million. At the same time young men power in North Africa will have increased to 56.5 million. They would seek a safe asylum for them in those European countries that need them for their self-interest.

It has been forecast that in this 21st century the ocean level may rise to 30 to 100 centimeters, which is likely to submerge several parts of the seacoasts and river deltas of all the continents. According to one account 16% of Egypt's population and 10% of that in Bangladesh is likely to the rendered homeless. The density of population is very high in these two countries. So it is inevitable that they will flee from their country to seek asylum somewhere outside their country and particularly in the countries of Europe and USA.

The estimated 5 million Muslim population of the USA is nearly twice the number of the U.S Episcopalians. More Muslims live in the U.S than in Libya. An influx of immigrants and slow and steady increasing stream of home grown conversions including many black Americans constitute the total Muslim population which, according to their estimate, exceed America's 6 million Jews towards 2010.

Allah Smiles

Euro-America's exhaustive attempt to clampdown the tenacious dictator of Iraq and unravel its potential "treasure of great devastation" seems to be futile and ridiculous. It also boomeranged and falsified USA's surveillance performance and speculation capacity.

Euro-America must understand and realize that the real treasure of devastation is not preserved secretly some where in Iraq or in any other Islamic country of the world. Those most sacrificed Muslim youths dedicated to Quran, Allah and Islam are the unreserved treasure of devastation. They would be utilized in the coming Global Civil War or the apprehended Third World War. They are proliferated all over the world including all the European countries. The Global Islamic Movement is the number one enemy of the Euro-America's unchallengeable civilization. It is thrusting its human weapons echeloning everywhere in the world and particularly in the Euro-American soil. Their horrendous ballistic figure would be revealed after they become strong enough to raise a revolt from inside the western soil and fortify their strength so as to face the Global Civil War against Euro-American Civilization.

9. USA Leads to a Civil War : An Internal Jehad

The Muslim world wants to bring the USA under its subjugation and attain it as its homeland. To realise their scheme Muslims have already instituted the consecration of a civil war in the USA, which is expected to perpetuate until it reaches its goal of complete Islamisation. If their attempt at Islamisation promulgates and proceeds unobstructed their success may come to a conclusion towards the end of 2015 or before it in accordance with the intensity of their progress.

This Civil War (which is nothing but a violent and unending communal riot) will be for the confirmation of national identity of America whether it is a secular Christian country or an Islamic country, Dar-ul-Islam. Now there is open civil war for national identification in vogue in Palestine, Lebanon, Algeria, the Philippines, Indonesia and Kashmir province of India and in many other countries of the world. The pseudo civil war for national identification has already been in action in almost all the European countries and in the USA. Its warmth is much exacerbated in America, England, France, etc. The civil war for national identification in India is midway. But unlike between Christians and Muslims in European countries, it is between Hindus and Muslims in India. Christians are in tandem after Hindus are pushed to the verge of extinction.

For a country civil war is more dangerous than an external war as it completely ruins the moral courage of a country, destroys its self-confidence and national solidarity. America is facing the turmoil of a great civil war. A single Muslim in the guise of a CIA or F.B.I would be sufficient to make America surrender before Islamic aggression. It is also suspected that F.B.I's secret soft ware may have been in the hands of Osama Bin Laden. An F.B.I. spy apparently gave it to his Russian handlers who, in turn, sold it to Bin Landen for 2 million dollar.

Dr. Martin Luther King (Jr.), the Afro-American Baptist minister from Georgia, led the American blacks to achieve full civil rights as citizens of the United States. On August 28, 1963, at the height of the civil rights movement 200000 people marched into Washington D.C to demand freedom and equality for all Americans. He regretted that Afro-Americans live on a lonely Island of poverty in the midst of a vast ocean of material prosperity. He was assassinated at the age of 39, in 1968.

America faced its first civil war at the time of Abraham Lincoln and the victory of the Government strengthened the integrity of the USA. It made the people self-confident. But this time the USA is going to face a different type of civil war, which, on its success, will hack the USA into pieces.

To form a separate homeland for the Muslims in the U S A, an Islamic fundamentalist Eliza Mohammed in the Year1930 founded an institution "Nation of Islam". He named the white Americans as "blue eyed devils." Another revolutionary youth Malcom X, a converted Muslim, led the organization simultaneously with Eliza Mohammed. But he suffered a premature death. A park is named after him in Washington D.C in his memory. Presently the "Nation of Islam" is under the prompt leadership of a staunch Afro-American firebrand Muslim youth Farra Khan. This organization demands five Southern states to be allowed to continue as a separate nation.

Here it is noticeable that the demands of the Afro-Americans for a separate homeland are made under the banner of "Nation of Islam". This is indicative of the assimilation of the Afro-Americans with the American Muslims in an assumption to display that all the Afro-Americans with the American Muslims are determined for a separate Islamic homeland.

In this regard a memorable event occurred on 1995 when the Nation of Islam's Afro-American Muslim leader Farra Khan solicited all the Afro-Americans to join in a Muslim march programme to show the unity and strength of the Afro-Americans. Farra Khan asked the male members to congregate in a rally in Washington to show their solidarity, identity and socio- political power. The march was identified as the Million March.

The peculiarity of this Million March is that it consisted of only male members leaving their female wings in houses in order to show the importance and centrality of the family as the nucleus of their community. This system is analogous to the Islamic tradition where in times of mass public driving only male members come forward leaving the females in houses.

This Afro-American rally was meant to show their resentment against the racial problems of this country, which has turned into one of the most important crises that afflicts the U.S. society. The disappearance of the U.S supported Governments in different parts of the world, the revolution and political developments that took place in different continents have caused an influx of immigrants from different nationalities and races into the U.S.A. This frightened the Americans to a great extent.

In the Million March held in 1995, about 8,50,000 male members had united to show the strength of Afro-Americans. It was followed by the Day of Atonement to commemorate the anniversary of the great march. From the speech of Farra Khan on that day it was clear that he is prepared to reach the extreme end along with all his followers for the safeguard and pride of Afro-Americans.

He was very much overwhelmed on his own determination when he denounced America's unjust foreign policies and reiterated before the journalists of the U.N. – "You in the U.N should be ashamed of yourself" for the imposition of sanctions against Libya. He strongly criticized the U.N's role that is acting as a tool of America's foreign policy objectives. He criticized America by saying that America is the only remaining superpower, but she is not a moral super power.

Islamic Revolution has finally arrived in the U.S.A and merged itself in the black wave of Million March on October 16, 1995 with the terrific growling "Allah Ho Akbar". The upsurge of the Afro-Americans flowed down the Washington Hall towards Capitol Hill with the recitation of the chapters of the Quran. It was a hard slap in the face of the United States' administration and brought to light the injustice of colour discrimination in American society.

There is another Islamic organization in the U.S.A. called "Muslim of America". It has its office at New York. It is also known as "Al-Fukra" which literally means swaggered one. The Egyptian Muslim leader of America who was held responsible for the explosion in the World Trade Centre in 1993 belonged to this group. But Seikh Mubarak Shah Jeelani, the founder of Al-Fukra, exceeds the former in seditious activities. This Pakistan born Islam Leader Jeelani had his 3000 Muslim followers, most of whom are Afro-Americans. This organization was held responsible in carrying out some destructive activities in Ports Land in 1983 and ISCON temples of Philadelphia and Denver. They even stabbed to death the Imam Khalifa of Arizona for his having given the statement that the Quran was written by a human being. The Al-Fukra organization has formed a list of the enemies of high profiles who belong to America, Canada and Israel.

The presence of this terrorist Jehadi organization was found in Canada when some 5 members of this organization were nabbed while plotting to smash a cabaret and a temple in Toronto. Most of the members who stretched the net of this organization throughout America and Canada are Pakistan based Muslims. The Jehadi fighters of this organization have opened many militant training centres in Europe and the African countries with the patronage of the I.S.I. of Pakistan. This organization believes both in violence and Islamic fundamentalism.

The American Muslims are the only racial groups who openly criticize America's foreign policies. Tens of thousands of Muslims from North America held demonstrations outside the U.N. Head Quarters to protest against the Bosnians' crises. Chanting "Allah O Akbar" they protested for lifting the arms embargo against Bosnia. They condemned the performances of the U.N. Members of the Security Council and the U.S.A for their failure to handle the situation in regard to the Bosnian tragedy.

Had the Black Americans not been a mixture of American Muslims, probably the Los Angles riots would not have been so violent. In the Los Angles riot that occurred on April29, 92 an all White juries' acquittal of the white policeman who were video-taped beating black motorist Rodney King inflamed racial violence igniting three days of burning and looting. It cost 900 million dollars to America for the reconstruction. It caused 50 deaths and 2300 injuries with a damage of 1100 buildings.

Since the year 1930 Eliza Mohammed, Malcom X, Farra Khan and other Muslim leaders are leading the Afro-Americans. They lead the Afro-Americans and Afro-Europeans towards the Islamic world, which would lead them to form an Islamic nation of Christian America.

10. USA Encounters a Global Civil War

After the fall of the Soviet Union, the USA presently encounters a greater enemy, Islam. This is the statement published in the editorial of Pravda, a Mosco daily which also said that millions of Muslims throughout the world are ready to strike a heavy blow against the U.S.A., particularly for its stance to disrespect the principles of Islam.

The Iranian parliament's allocation of 16 million dollars to neutralize American conspiracies is like a command of Jehad against the plans of America. The life sentence in the U.S.A of Seikh Abdul-Al-Rehman, an Egypt-based leader of Jamat Islami, was another factor turning Muslims against America.

Very conveniently and very cunningly the USA played the British-sponsored divide and rule policy against the Gulf countries. When Iraq assaulted Iran all the Islamic countries remained dumbfounded. Iran's rib was broken for two decades. America was here in a winning position. When there was war between Iraq and America on the question of Iraq's occupation of Kuwait, all the Muslim gulf countries again helplessly looked with eyes full of distress the plight of their coreligionist countrymen. But more of them thought to disrupt the chain of their multilateral agreements with America. They have a sense of fear over their security without the USA's presence or interference in their internal affairs. They valued their national security more than their religious interest. The littoral states that are dissatisfied with the USA's foreign policy and are made silent under duress are waiting for an opportunity to strangle the USA and its allies.

When the USA is against the Talibans it is natural that Pakistan is whole-heartedly against America. The friendship of a dictatorial ruler of Pakistan cannot be counted on as a good alliance between the two nations. This relation can best be described as the relation between a tiger and a wolf in a circus. It was found that Osama Bin Laden had his hands in the bombardment of the American embassy in Kenya and Tanzania earlier in August 1998 that caused a death toll of 257 civilians. In apparent retaliation for the twin bombings the U.S.A. fired dozens of cruise missiles on Eastern Afghanistan in an attempt to kill Bin Laden.

Now Bin Laden is in apprehension of certain threatenings to his life. But he cares very little for it. A man who cares very little for his life is the most dangerous person in the world.

Moreover he is one of the richest persons and militarily his perfection is beyond question. The Ex-Security Officer of Russia Alexander Labed confessed that almost 100 small nuclear bombs have been stolen from the armoury of Russia. Obviously it reveals that these might have fallen into the hands of Islamic terrorists. It is clear that when a single person can threaten America, we must measure the great strength of support that he possesses from the Islamic countries.

America boasts as the master of global surveillance. According to a newspaper statement Washington has deployed over 100000 combatant troops in European countries and it has an Air Force training base in the Middle East. It has over 1 00000 troops in North West Asia and has participated in 70 battles beyond its borders to enforce its dominating policies. The U.S. has always depended on political and military might and assumes the role of world police. Nevertheless it is engrossed with some major shortcomings.

When the Egyptian born one-eyed old Muslim first damaged the World Trade Centre, it was expected that this matter would lead to serious steps to be taken by America to subdue the Islamic growing power with a iron hand. But it was found that nothing such happened as a later event of the explosion. Apart from this, the man accused for this conviction was put under trial and was sentenced like all other common convicts. Moreover a Christian advocate, particularly a lady Lynn Stewart could be available for trial in favour of Abdul Rehman! Democracy and secularism of America has its own shape of distinction. But extension of political ideology of every Government has its own limits. Like the people of India the people of America also remain unhurried when their national interest is getting saturated on the altar of democracy in the name of secularism. Otherwise a Christian advocate, moreover a lady, should not have come out to aid in this trial.

The USA's espionage system is also detrimental to the extent of securing its national interest. It is reported that a meeting was held somewhere in East Afghanistan where the Muslim leaders of the world had united on February 23rd 1998. All of them came to a conclusion to step down America and its allied forces. The convener of the meeting Osama Bin Laden declared America as the house of Satan. He appealed the Muslims unilaterally to launch Jehad against America and its allied nations for an indefinite period. In the same year, six months after this convention, Muslim militants bombarded on American embassy at Kenya and Tanzania on August 7th, 1998, killing 257 civilians with more than 5000 injured. This Afghanistan was once the most intimate country of America and was used as a weapon to retaliate Russia. It is an established fact that the U.N.O. is a weapon of war and court of Justice in the hand of the U.S.A. The U.N. war crime tribunal had included the destruction of historic monuments as offensive but no one could save 1500 year old Bamiyan Buddha from destruction by Afghans.

America fails to evaluate the nature and ideology of its non-Christian allied countries. During the last 50 years it has shown a distinct tilt towards Pakistan. Towards the year 1950 Pakistan joined the American sponsored CENTO and SEATO groups and became entitled to large scale American arms aid ostensibly to confront communism. But in reality the fighter jets, tanks and other related arms were used to launch attack on India in 1965, despite the USA's assurance that Pakistan will not be allowed to use these arms against India. This tilt went to absurd proportions in 1971 when Richard Nixon ordered the U.S' 7th fleet to anchor in the Bay of Bengal in order to intimidate Indian Armed forces.

The Soviet occupation of Afghanistan again saw the pumping of armaments worth billions of dollars into Pakistan. The mighty Soviet Union naturally broke up turning down Afghanistan to give access to American multi-nationals into the Central Asian regions. This brought the infamous Hank Brown Amendment gifting Pakistan roughly 400 million-dollars worth modern armaments. But the result was quite opposite to its expectation. The disintegration of the USSR did not bring about any change in the ideological animosity against the U.S.A. Afghanistan challenged to be the number one enemy of America. Gunmen inside Pakistan are repeatedly targeting American citizens.

Although USA's distinguished evil axis is spotted in the Gulf countries, it has another evil axis in East Asia, which is a combination of Pakistan, Afghanistan and Bangladesh. A man simultaneously cannot be a friend of whale and foe of shark. The USA's friendship with Pakistan and enemity with Afghanistan is only ostensible and spurious. Pakistan has the sharp intellect to extort military and financial aid from Western countries. Afgahanistn has the spirit to face the hurdles of life and fight blindly as directed. Bangladesh has the prolificity to produce the babies who can be used as vote banks, as terrorist trainees and as paid labourers and vote banks for the expansion of Islam on non- Islamic white lands.

Now it is found that the weapons supplied by the USA to the Islamic countries like Afghanistan and Pakistan are used against the Americans. The Middle East countries are the world's largest arms importers. These imported 43% of all arms traded in 1994. Saudi Arabia alone imported about $ 2 billion dollars worth weapons in 1994. It is a consensus that Arabia has no such battlable enemical country in Asia and the only enemies of the Arabians are the non-Islamic Western countries and the USA.

George W Bush is in trouble as well as in puzzle. Out of trouble he declared his determination to attack Iraq. Iraq is simply a scale of the great Islamic shark. Iraq could create an indelible impression in the minds of the Muslims that Euro-America is the deadliest enemy of Islam. So long as these Western countries have not been subdued, nowhere in the world would Islam be in peace.

Out of puzzle the President of USA is hosting the Muslim leaders of the Islamic countries including the President of Iraq. Having been the target of world Islamic arrogance he is planning to mark the Muslim holy month of Ramadan with the Islamic leaders in the White House and sharing the traditional Iftar meal. He also sent a message to the Islamic leaders of predominantly Islamic countries acknowledging best wishes and calling Islam "a peace loving faith". The idea that terrorism is a part of Jehad and Jehad is a part of Islam is hedging and evasive in everybody's mind, both in the mind of the host and the guests, in the mind of secular government and the minority Islam community. The moment the idea bursts out there will be the solution of trouble and puzzle and this solution is the Great War [or the Global Civil War] if it occurs after 2015.

When a pack of canines consisting of jackals, wolves and wild dogs concertedly attack an old tiger encircling him from all around, who suffers from the pain of hook worms sucking its blood inside the body, it is only the fool who expects the tiger's victory.

11. Europe Under Jehad

> *But the nation in every age has bowed to the religion as well as to the language of Mecca.*
>
> —Edward Gibbon, *Decline and Fall of the Roman Empire)*

European soil is gradually slipping from below the sole of original Europeans who are now identified as European Christians. They now confront the Islamic upsurge in their homeland. The banning of Islamic hijab in France and its withdrawal, the death sentence to British civilian Salman Rushdie by the Iranian leader and the British government's protective measures to him, the establishment of Islamic schools in Europe, the creation of British Islamic parliament and parties, the increasing interest of Western intellectuals in Islam, the creation of religious organizations all over Europe, the establishment of Islamic radio and television stations, the circulation of Islamic newspapers and magazines, the debate over the use of burka and hijab by Muslim women in European countries, the current conflict over the identity of the Muslims in the Balkans and East Europe are all important issues which show the Western reactions against the rise of Islam in Europe.

(a) Islamic Fervour in Europe

The arrival of Muslims to live in Europe irrevocably altered the demographic map of Europe. The warmth of Islamic fundamentalism is quite perceptible in Europe. The European powers like France, Belgium, Germany, Italy and Switzerland conduct anti-terrorist operations against these fundamentalists even for world cup soccer tournaments. The emergence of Islamic fundamentalism and militancy in England indicate the trend.

The French are particularly apprehensive of the terrorist (Jehadi) Islamic group called the GIA which belongs to Algeria and is one of the most radical and brutal Islamic Jehädi groups in the world. Apart from France, in Spain where Muslims were once the leaders and rulers of the country, increase their number in harmony with the numbers of mosques. Presently the Jehadi activities in India, the Philippines, Indonesia, and the U.S.A. and in the African countries have opened the eyes of Europeans. In all the Madrassas of Europe, students are taught to follow rigidly the tenets of Islam. In Roman Catholic countries like France, Spain, Italy and Belgium, Muslims have exceeded Protestants in number. In France alone there are 5 million Muslims and more than 3 million are in Germany.

The whole of European countries have become the eyesore of the Islamic world as its firebrand enemies. To add fuel to the fire the Western world takes extreme interest in racial apartheid that makes them a source of hatred by most non-European people particularly the Muslims. The death of a 15 years old black teenager Benjamin Hermansen towards the end of January, 2001 who was killed as a target of racial discrimination made the majority of the black people to rise in revolt against the government. More than 30 thousand people started a rally in the pitch dark night with torch lights in hands to protest against the brutal racial killing of the blacks that equals the ethnic violence in Kosovo, Bosnia or in Oslo (Norway). The three points of places were drawn in a line to manifest the centre of target by white oppressions to unite the Blacks turned Muslims to fight against racism and fascism that jointly goes against White Christianity.

Islam is averse to interest-based banking system. There are many Islamic financial institutions in Europe like Dar-al-Mal-al-Islami (Geneva) and Albarakah International Ltd. (London), al Rajhi Company for Islamic Investment Ltd. (London), etc., which are generally privately owned. These international institutions compete with conventional banks for deposits but without paying interest.

(b) Anti-Christian Stance of European Muslims in Europe

The demolition of Churches in different parts of Europe and persecution of Christians in Turkey by the Muslim majority created bitter feelings among the rest of the European countries. Presently they are realizing that Islam is a different type of religion, which cannot be separated from religious politics. Where there is a Muslim there is the quest of an Islamic state. Islam as a religion simultaneously animates religious fundamentalism. So an Islamic state and Islamic fundamentalism always follow a Muslim.

When the Muslim soldiers of the Ottoman empire began to persecute the Greek civilians in the year 1453 and vandalise the Churches the Europeans did not conceive that these sacrilegious acts are nothing but religious savagery. When the Turkish Muslims mercilessly killed unarmed Belgian Christians, the then British Prime Minister Gladstone concentrated to check the growing influence of Russia with the help of Turks. At that time it was not in their mind that every fall of a sword targeting the neck of non-Muslim Europeans is sharpened with Islamic bigotry.

In the year 1988, when the Pope was attacked by a Turkish Muslim youth and in another incident when the Pope had a sheer escape from the attack made by 11 Muslim Mujahids amongst whom was a Pakistani national it was conceived that these were the acts of Muslim fundamentalists.

Now the French feel the heat of Algerian fundamentalists. The British feel and understand the meaning of a Fatwa passed by an Islamic leader against British women on British soil. Now they understand the frowning of the Muslim youth of Hizbul Tahir who growls to throw away the derailed British young men and women into the sea.

It is interesting to know that major serious decisions to Islamise Europe in general and England in particular are being done in England and particularly in Muslim Parliament. In June 19, 1993 at a Special session of Muslim Parliament convened for the Bosnian Issue, the Muslim leaders had a grave discussion. Some of them pointed out that 500 years ago Christians uprooted the Muslim foundation from Spain only with the help of the primitive technology available. It took only 150 years to wipe out Islam from Spain. The Serbs achieved their goal within 2 years to exterminate Muslims from Bosnia and Herzegovina

Relevant to the Bosnia issue they expressed their deep anguish, grief and anger on the vulturous attack on Islamic society, culture and civilization in Bosnia by the Europeans. They unanimously confirmed the point that the attempt of the Serbs to exterminate the Bosnian Muslims has been done with the knowledge and guidance of the European countries and the U.S.A. The permanent nucleus of the U.N.O and the European community are in favour of the Serbs' aggression for the ethnic cleansing of the Muslims from Bosnia. All the economic, military, diplomatic and other humanitarian activities like peace treaties to eliminate the Bosnia issue is only an illusion and pretension to give opportunity to the Serbs to speed up their aggression. Muslim Parliament opines that the U.N and European Community actively supported the Serbs in their attempt to annihilate the Muslims from the Bosnian soil. The British government in particular actively patronized the Serbs in the continued holocaust of the Muslims.

Having a thorough investigation into the history, the Muslim Parliament concluded that the political frontiers of Europe have always been transitory. Examples are many like the reunification of Germany and the disintegration of the U.S.S.R., and the crumbling down of the W.T.C. etc. The role of the U.N.O is just like that of an old lady who can only advise but cannot realize her words in action. Similarly those who were victorious in the last world war were not successful in their plan to have a future dominance on the vanquished nations. America who was supposed to be a super power became a superfluous power state when it retreated with empty hands from Vietnam. The U.S.S.R which pocketed a large number of countries in the world was broken into pieces giving rise to numerous Islamic countries. All its plans failed in Afghanistan. The fate of Europe as an indissoluble body is also alarming.

No mundane decision, settlement is eternal or permanent. They are subject to change in course of time. The plight of the

Bosnian or Palestinian Muslims will not last long, nor are the border lines drawn by the victorious nations permanently unaltered. The fortunes of persecuted Muslim will smile again.

Thus they concluded-"When the Serbs raped Muslim women, it was not for sexual pleasure. European women have been brought up to regard men in uniform as qualifying for instant favours. Sexually satisfied men fight better than sexually deprived or frustrated ones. Offering free and frequent sex is a well-established part of European women's war efforts. Serbian men were fighting close to home, near their wives and girl friends. There was no dearth of Serbian women for sexual gratification of Serbian soldiers. But they raped Muslim women only because the women were Muslims. The Serbs developed rape as a weapon of warfare."

Islamic commentators say – "The Serbs were raping women to destroy the sanctity of Islam, to destroy Muslim family and identity. The liquidation of Islam and Muslims in Bosnia was not only essential for the survival of Serbia, it was also necessary for the survival of Europe, indeed for the self-image, purity and progress of the entire Western civilization. This is one reason the West is conniving at Serbian atrocities.

The European Union declared to break off the diplomatic relation with Iran in the year 1991. Communal hatred is the root cause for this reason. When there was plane hijacking, bombardment, firing, etc., the Europeans thought that these were the mischievous conducts of some particular persons to revolt against their government. But now they have changed their way of thinking.

If the European Muslims see no option between being European and Muslim then only there will be peace in Europe. But by that time Europe's identity would have been changed from a Christian Europe to an Islamic Europe.

(c) Ignorance of Islamic Law is no Excuse

European Christians now realize that Islam as a religion is not different from politics. The religion of Islam and Islamic politics are one and inseparable. Where there is a Muslim he tries hundred per cent to create an Islamic surrounding around it. It has become a headache for the Europeans by accepting Turkey in their Union. Now the Europeans think to walk in future in a proper way being guided by their past history. They were not clear about the Islamic Jehad in the past.

When the terrorists of Hijbul Tahir declared a Fatwa (a religious order) to throw the British young men and women into the sea then they began to think that they were not safe with their life and property in their homeland as they were since recorded history. The authority over secular England now has become debatable whether it will belong to the Western Christians or Western Muslims. England must side either of the two. But the democratic process on Islamic progress of England clearly indicates that the transformation of England into an Islamic country is not very far. The soil of England is gradually slipping from the clutch of Christians forever. No soil is meant for a particular nation or race. Both the civilizations profess and practise the theory of "Survival of the fittest."

Muslims are cautious to avail of every chance to enter into the Christian repositories to display their mark of Islamic expansionism in Christian dominated European Countries. Instances may be quoted of the Muslim women of Iran reciting the holy Quran in Vatican city, the abode of the Pope, on the occasion of Islamic Mother's Day, the birthday of lady Fatima.

The kidnapping Europeans in Kashmir and killing them in cold blood, the kidnapping of Americans in the Philippines as hostages are quite remarkable evidences for white Christians to be alert over the Islamic terrorism. Moreover the bombardment on the World Trade Centre in New York was the first that alerted the Americans about the Islamic Jehad to counteract in an open combat.

They have not yet realized the heat of Islam as a consolidated power. When they deal with a particular Islamic nation they don't conceive in their mind that they just deal with the trunk or eye or the ear of a great Islamic elephant, but an integrated body comprising these limbs.

Islam relates to a particular language, appetite, outlook, mentality and feeling, which is totally universal, and above the limitation of a particular nation or a country. But a Christian adheres to be a citizen of a particular nation; a speaker of the language of a particular country and his feelings, etc., differ from those of another. A Muslim is universal and everywhere he is one. Hence whenever a Muslim country approaches a non-Muslim country it always acts with a retaliatory mind which is preoccupied with its religious scripture that induces him to convert that country into an Islamic state by any possible means, the only means being "Jehad". So from the very day when a Muslim entered any country of Europe, it belonged to him. Instead of integrating himself in to the main stream he would try to spread his own net of culture and his own stream of Islam. This is the Islamic law.

(d) Tsunami of infiltation and disproportionate growth of Islamic population – a death knell for European Christians

According to their position there are two kinds of Muslims in Europe i.e. a) indigenous b) immigrants. The Muslims of Eastern part of Europe are mostly indigenous and have been in the region for many centuries. But the Muslims of Western Europe are immigrants from the African and Middle East countries after the Second World War.

The Muslims in East European states like the former Yugoslavia, Bulgaria and Albania have now become a part of the Central structure due to the century old reign of the Ottoman Empire. In average Muslims constitute 4% of the total European population (except the former USSR and Turkey).

In Yugoslavia, they constitute 13% of the total population. In France their population is almost 5%, Muslims constitute2.5% in Britain, 7% in Belgium, 20% in Bulgaria, 25% in Cyprus, 3% in Holland and in Albania their population is more than 75%. Muslims confirmed their minorities in the Western European countries like England, France and Germany 50 years ago. Before the outbreak of the Second World War, Muslims were insignificant settlers in the Western European Countries. But in the post Second World War period they were solicited as immigrants. But after the great Islamic Revolution, the

European Muslims are unmindful of any criticism and comments made by the European Christians against them. They are now the rightful and dignified citizens of Europe without any discrimination of East and West. They do not feel, think or even imagine that the land of Europe is alien to them. To their mind, Western Europe is not exclusively the homeland of white Christians.

In the early 1950s there were only a few tens of thousands of non-White Muslims in Britain. By the year 1991, that had risen to three million (according to an Islamic estimation), i.e. 6% of the total population. The population of the ethnic minorities has been growing at between 2 to 4% a year. Net immigration has been running at record level with 185000 new comes in 1999.

The year 1980 witnessed the growth and development of Islamic religious schools and increasing numbers of people going to the priesthood in all parts of Europe. In the year 1971 the Islamic population in Europe was 11,600,000. It increased to 15.8 million in the year 1981. But in 1991 it was marked that this population exceeded to 20 billion spreading all over the continent and has its own social historical roots.

According to some Euro-Union sources half a million illegal immigrants enter the European Union every year in addition to the 680000 legal immigrants. The European Visa Information System (VIS) has main goals contributing to the internal security of the member states and fight against the illegal immigration by supporting the common visa policy and the checks on the visa applications.

The reduction of European Christian birth rate and increase in the number of old men and women is a common sight everywhere in Europe. On the contrary Muslims condemn birth control as irreligious and anti-Islamic and hasten unhampered child production. Increased Muslim population has escalated the Islamisation of Europe. Even in a country like England the Muslim population has reached 15 per cent of the total civil population. Muslims in Islamic restaurant, abattoirs, bakeries and madrassas functioned by mosques is a very common sight almost everywhere in Europe.

Due to the healthy management of Public Welfare departments and deployment in the newly raised factories a large number of manual workers were required in European countries. Muslims in large number from North Africa, Middle East and Turkey came and settled there with their prolific birth project.

These Muslims in Europe have witnessed their third generation. The disparity in the growth of population is due to the fact that Europeans give more stress on decreasing their birth rate whereas Muslims do its opposite. It is assumed that the population of Muslim immigrants in Europe would reach 6 to 7 millions towards 2015.

An example of Belgium can be best quoted. It required a large number of manual workers for its construction work. To fulfil this demand, labourers came to Belgium from Italy, Spain, Greece and Portugal but they asked for a heavy amout in exchange of their manual labour. So the Belgian government turned their face towards Muslim countries and made an Immigrant Treaty with Islamic countries like Morocco and Turkey. According to this treaty foreign labourers were to be provided free housing facilities and modern amenities. In the lapse of time this immigration of Muslims to Europe has become a stark problem with the violently increasing number of Islamic population. Another impediment that creates problems in the European society is that Islam cannot be absorbed into the European mainstream. They create their own Islamic mainstream wherever they stay, and force others to get assimilated into this Islamic mainstream.

Friction of two civilizations has now become a practical experiment where European civilization seems to be shrinking back. Muslim spinsters hardly marry a non-Muslim and the number of such marriages in the Gulf countries is totally zero. But European ladies unobstructed and unhurriedly make matrimonial alliance with Muslims as like 21 years old Jemia Goldsmith who married 42 years old Pakistan Cricketeer Imran Khan. She even changed her European name into Islamic Sita and in course of time gave birth to a daughter. But in course of time he divorced her without caring for her European dignity. When asked, Mr. Khan said that he did it for the interst of the nation in spite of Jemima's great sacrifice for her Islamic identity. Governments of different European countries are worried about such kind of unilateral marriage. According to a speculation it was found that the number of Talaq divorcee women is gradually increasing in Euro-American countries striking a deadly lash to the socio-cultural dignity and identity.

(f) Islamic Evangelization in Europe

Traditionally it is conceived that evangelization as a word and as a process is a privilege of Christianity But now days Islam also resorted this process of evangelization for the proselytization of non-Islamic people in general and the Christians in particular. Muslim preachers have come out to spread the precepts of Islam in the societies who are far away, in the density of African forests and also in the European countries imbibed by Christian culture and civilization. Islamic scriptures now excel both in quality and quantity and compete in the world market challenging the spirit of non-Islamic literature based on religion. Besides pulverizing the evangelical monopoly of Christianity Islam has come out to proselytize in a challenging spirit to the European Christians who once distinguished the Muslims as cameleers and Islam as an Asian religion. Now Islam is at the door of Europe with holy scripture Quran in one hand and religious literature in another, which are the sources of solace to those Christians who think Bible and Christian literature distasteful, forged, a constellation of blind beliefs, full of absurdities and controversies.

Isabella, a novel is one among many such literatures of Islamic prodigy. Not only it is a symbol of Islamic aggression to proselytize exclusively to Christians but also it expresses the long cherished desire of Muslims to retain back Spain, which was their dearest homeland for over one thousand years. Spain is to Bosnians what Al Qods (Israel) is to Palestinians. Evangelization and proselytization are the best means to acquire Spain besides the growth of Islamic population. If winter comes spring is not far behind. In the novel "Isabella", Spain is conceived as a token of Christo-Islamic tug of war As a paradigm of Islamic view over a Christian land the novel 'Isabela' requires literary analysis.

Predominantly Spain was a Christian homeland. In the later period Muslims occupied Spain and ruled over it for 800 years. It was king Ferdinand of Spain who defeated the Muslims, killed and converted them and expelled the rest of them from Spain. He declared Christianity as the national religion of Spain. After the success of Islamic revolution in Iran Muslims have cast their covetous eyes over Spain, their ancient homeland It gives Muslims a glimpse of pleasure when ever they think of Spain Their long cherished desire is reflected in the most controversial novel Isabella.

Historically Isabella is the queen of the king Ferdinand of Spain. She had helped Columbus to expedite a historical voyage to find out a sea route to India. Surprisingly Columbus discovered America instead of India. Hence Isabella remained as a prominent name in Spanish tradition concerned to its glorious past.

Isabella is symbolically used in this novel as a key Character. She not only played a prominent role in changing the course of Spanish history by repudiating Christianity and embracing Islam with all her companions but also becoming a faithful and devotious defender of Islam by unleashing all the debilities of Christian theology and culture. She was born in a Christian family and was skillful in Christian theology. But after realizing that Islam is the only true religion next to none she converted herself in to Islam and withstood as a formidable Islamic revolutionary to bring a transformation in the Christian society.

Isabella is the daughter of an eminent Christian missionary and the head priest of Spain. She had unfathomable knowledge in the tenets of Christianity. Once she was sitting in the garden of Cordova chatting with her girl friends. She could hear some Muslim youths talking at a distance among themselves about some absurdities and paradoxes described in the holy Bible. The Muslim youths were adept in theological altercations of both the religions. Isabella could find some moot points from their discussions on Bible. She referred these problems at home and also asked her father about the solutions. But her father, instead of giving any solution advised her not to pay heed to the verdicts of these accursed Muslim unbelievers who are always inimical to Christianity and are the invaders of Spain and killers of Spaniards. The unsolved mysteries of Bible nestled in her mind. She couldn't console her and hence could not have a sound sleep. She asked about it to Michael, her teacher who taught her Christian theology and Peter, an expert in Arabic learning and had the honour of writing many books against Islam.

Out of curiosity Isabella arranged a meeting of Christian priests and the Islamic youths who were talking about the absurdities of Bible. One among them wa~ Umar Lahmi. He had deep erudition both in Quran and Bible. He proved the falsehood of Christianity citing the quotations from the Old Testament. It is written in the Old Testament that the religious commandmems not to steal, not to kill, and not to oppress the neighbours are opposed by the Biblical holy man like St Peter. In the second point Umer Lahmi challenged the divinity of Jesus Christ as the only Son of God. He argued that if Jesus was born from Virgin Mary and died on the cross, he is simply a human being. Jesus is never a God because God is immune from the cycle of birth and death.

Umer Lahmi also challenged the authenticity of Bible and told that it is no better than a fiction and is not the real one, which was recognized by Quran. He proved that the present Bible is a forged script and is not valid. He asserted the veracity of his religion Islam with the essence of Islamic beliefs "Ia illah illallah. Mohammad ur Rasoolallah (there is no one worthy of worship except Allah and Mohammed is his apostle). He could dare to assert his arguments in favour of Islam in the church premises.

During these discussions and commotions Isabella could gradually realize that Islam is a true religion while Christianity is a combination of misguidance disruptions and forgery.

In the third round discussion Umer Lahmi very clearly convinced the Head Priest of Spain, the father of Isabella that the 'tauhid' (Islamic unity) is far more impressive blue print of Islam than 'love', the key religious precept of 'Christianity'.

In Christianity every body from Pastor to Pope is honoured as "father", the most common word prefixed in the name of Christian dignitaries. But this Muslim fighter argued that "fosterer" is the most suitable and the highly dignified word consigned to the creator Allah whose fostering love is never withdrawn. Had the father a slight sense of love for his son Jesus he would not have killed his innocent and flaw less son for the sake of impure and sinful men. But the fosterer is one who is not injurious to anyone.

Gradually Isabella who was participating in these discussions realized that Christianity is a base less religion and it has no principle. She began to call other Muslims as brothers because there is no Papacy in Islam and here all are equal. From Ziad she came to know that Muslim's life and death, prayer and devotion, sitting and standing, sleeping and walking every thing is meant for Allah and the pleasure of Allah is the aim of. the!r life and death. Ziad also narrated that it is only Allah who can forgive sins. But Christians have made their priests and elders as rab (fosterer). They equalized man with God. Isabella also shamefully narrated how the priests forgave the sins of unmarried boys and girls in the confession days whenever they. themselves commit the ugliest sins with nuns and wash away their sins in their own capacity. Out of. grief and passion Isabella described the incidents how the Christian monks are involved in these moral depravities and even did not spare their mothers and sisters. She quoted instances from the 'History of Civilization of Europe'. Then Umer Lahmi established the idea how Islam is praiseworthy in this regard. There is no ascetism in Islam Marriage is a system Then Isabella again narrated how killing babies is a consensus in Christianity as a result of concealed adulteration between the priests and nuns and the creed of atonement has given license to Christians to commit sins. Umer Lahmi quoting from Bible said how Prophets were liars and idol worshippers. Fornication was very common amongst the Prophets of Christianity. Regarding the polygamy character of Islam he told that many Biblical Prophets indulged polygamy.

Meanwhile Isabella left her creed of Christianity and embraced Islam. Early in the morning before the 'fazr' prayer the sound of Ajan Allah ho Akbar (There is no God but Allah) thrilled her and raptured her body, mind and spirit. The sound of church bell appear-ed to be meaningless and jarring to her. Her heart filled with glory and grandeur of Allah. Tears rolled down from her eyes. She began to weep in praise of Allah. Then she fell to prostration with all humbleness and prayed Allah the almighty. "O' Allah! Grant me the love of thou and thy most loved one, O' Allah! Fill my heart with the light of Islam and tauhid (Unity) and make the obedience of thy Apostle my fate in life. O Allah! I am so grateful to thee for conferring on me the honour of following the Mercy of the Worlds. O' Allah! Grant my parents, my relatives and all Christians and the misguided ones the blessings of Islam and let us all live and die on Islam. O' my Lord! Just grant this humble prayer of the oppressed one for thou art all knowing and seeing".

After concluding this prayer Isabela felt that her soul has got solace and a great load had been lifted from her mind and she found that treasure house of endurance, firmness and elation had been installed in to her heart and she is very happy as she has secured a great wealth like Islam. She is now fearless and bold, for the tauheed (unity) has cast off from her all fears except the fear of Allah.

Isabella's parents came to know about her apostasy. They became revengeful and plotted a conspiracy to torture her and on her denying accepting Christianity, killing her. Other Christian leaders accompanied her father to trap her and put her for inquisition. According to their pre plan she was put in a secret under ground chamber and her hands and legs were chained. She was severely beaten and got fainted.

Isabella had three intimate friends. They broke down in despair knowing that Isabella has been incarcerated. Then they made a plan to extricate Isabella from the fetter. To workout their plan they sought permission from Muslim elders. They went to her father, the head priest and convinced him to let them give a chance to try to bring Isabella back to Christianity. With much difficulty they could reach her and according to their well-planned clique they not only unleashed her but also tied the legs and hands of the monk who was the chief conspirator in Isabella's imprisonment in that torture camp and left him in utter misery. The princess of Spain turned nun also was left destitute with the old monk. The releasing episode of Isabella and hoodwinking by her friends to the Christian priests, monks and the female ascetics are so humiliating and thrilling that the description of Isabella would irate any Christian reader and uncover the blind beliefs, primitive instincts and foolishness of Christians.

Isabella left her house and dear parents forever and lived with the Muslims. In course of time she became a great defender of Islam. All her girl friends had been convinced about the reality, simplicity and truthfulness of Quran and Islam. They accepted Mohammed as the only Prophet and embraced Islam. Soon after their conversion in to Islam they covered their face with Burkha as a symbol of Islamic tenet. Umer Lahmi spoke them about the fragility and falsehood of Bible and told them about how it is a forged and multifaceted script with a compound of many oddities, contradictions, absurdities, disparities and profligation.

At lasts a lady preacher of Christianity approached Isabella with great grandeur to convince and defeat her through theological argument. The Wordy altercation between them continued for days but at last Isabella made her spell bound. Gradually reputation of Islam began to spread among the Christians in Spain like the fragrance of flower and they began to embrace Islam. Islam spread throughout Spain like wild fire. Isabella spent a true Islamic life and defended Islam through out her life. Thus ends the story.

It should be marked that how Muslims as a religious entity in the European soil could dare to challenge the entire Christian world by brainwashing Christians through literature slowly, steadily and in a precised manner.

12. European Nations in Islamic Cauldron

(a) England: From Anglican Church to Dar-ul- Islam Institute

Britain deserves the honour as an illustrious propagator of nationalism. It has much contribution for the freedom movement and liberation of many lands, which were under bondage for centuries. Now Britain's own democratic secular environment has posed a great question mark on 'nationalism', which the British can't answer. The national interest of Britain is shifting and is abdicating it to a transformed national interest that favours Global Islamism. This transformationl nationalism is getting animated in the British soil that indicates the replacement of the Anglican cross by the Islamic Crescent. The process is on under the banner of Transformation of Civilization.

A magnificent mansion is designed as Dar-ul-Islam meant for the spread of Islam in England. There was a proposal to convene a conference of Islamic fundamentalists of the world in London in the year 1996. The key objective of this conference was to create an organization to fight against those who oppose the Islamisation of different countries of the world. The Jehadi fighters who were entangled in the first time bombardment on World Trade Centre at New York convened a conference in England. The Hijbullah of Beirut, the Hamas of Palestine, the Muslim Brotherhood of Algeria and the Mujahiddin groups of Afghanistan were invited to assemble to have a close deliberation on Universal Jehad. This conference had been convened on behalf of Hijbul Tahir, but the British government refused visas to the guests of Islamic symposium and banned this organization, when it was found to have connection with the Jehadi groups who planned to kill the then British Prime Minister John Major and the Jews.

There are many British Mujahhids or religious fighters who act as human bombs and participate in the Jehadi war launched in India to separate Kashmir. One such British Mujahid is Mohammed Bilal a 24-year-old Birmingham born nightclub frequenting lad who became a "born again" Muslim at the age of 15. He left his college study half way in Mid-land, left his family and came to Pakistan. After finishing his militant training, he joined with Maulana Masood Azhar, one among the three hijackers of IC 814 plane in 1999. Then he aspired to martyrdom and became a suicide bomber. He drove an explosive-laden Maruti Car right up to the entrance of the Indian army's 15 corps H.Qrs. on the Christmas day of December 2000, blew it up and died.

A British citizen Salman Rushdie, soon after he was declared an apostate and culprit for his so-called comment of the Prophet, was put under tight security. His case indicates to what extent Islam perturbed the British government even in the question of giving security to its countrymen. As a Muslim apostate, British citizen Salman Rushdie was denied life from February 1989 by the government of Iran. Muslim youths are stalking the possible moment of opportunity to shoot him. It was obvious that Britain had a sense of fear and suspicion towards the Muslim citizens; otherwise the adversity of Rushdie would not have been so pitiable. Being a British subject with the right of having full citizenship he apologized for his life to an Iranian Supremo and, after his death, to his followers. Out of compulsion and fear for his life he admitted with most humble submission that, whatever he wrote was admittedly wrong, enigmatic and unsubstantial. He wrote it when he was engrossed with an un-Islamic conscience. The British government stood a mute spectator to all these happenings.

The influence of Islam has permeated the soil of England to such an extent that multinational companies are sporadically compelled to use Islamic features and scriptural verdicts for their advertisement. Instances are numerous. McDonalds printed an Islamic quotation – "There is no God but Allah and Mohammed is his Prophet" on 2 million paper bags intended for take-away orders of Children's happy meals at the 520 McDonalds restaurants in Britain. However this declaration of faith was not a Quranic quotation, otherwise the company would have faced the plight of Salman Rushdie.

More than 1500 Muslim children from 40 schools in Yorkshire of Northern England boycott to attend the religious education classes at State Schools in protest against the mainly childish syllabus required by British legislation. Under the 1988

Education act, parents have a right to withdraw their children from religious education classes, which are required to reflect the fact that religious traditions of Britain are in the main Christian.

An Islamic Homeland in England

In the Salman Rushdie issue, England's thought wave was divided into two parts. The British lovers of democracy openly supported Salman Rushdie for his free statement on Islam. Even British P.M. John Major met Rushdie and expressed his full support. On the other hand modernized or Westernised British Muslims turned out to be the protectors of Islamic tenets in England. They insisted on strengthening their fundamental outlook and involved themselves in their Islamic spirit. That means a true Muslim always keeps himself above the nation. This temperament was palpable after the Rushdie issue. A Muslim British citizen first displayed himself as a Muslim and next only a British.

England, once the land of "Lord of sovereign" and an adorned symbol of the Church of England, has witnessed the conversion of white Britons into Islam. More amazing is the conversion rate of women, which is much more than that of men. Most of the women converted are amongst those who enjoy a high standard of education such as teachers, lawyers and physicians. Soon after the British women folk get converted they wear headscarf, cease from going to bars, night clubs and mingle with males. "The Observer" news paper in London reported that it would be the first time in history that a major indigenous population has voluntarily become a minority rather than through war, famine or disease and that the major indigenous population is the white in England who will form the minority group in Britain by 2010. According to the statistics the fertility rate of the white in England is very low, i.e. at under two children per woman. New immigrants, particularly Muslims, have higher fertility rates while the population of the British citizens is static. The global immigration of British citizens is another cause of deterioration of the white population in England.

In an interview of British Muslims 68 per cent of them opted their choice of Islamic faith above British nationalism. They asserted that they are Muslims first and British next. There is an Islamic live radio Broadcast serving the Muslim population in England. It consists of sermons and speeches of Hazrat Mirza Tahir Ahmad Khalifatul Marih iv .On every Friday the sermon is heard via the internet.

Islamic Parliament

Although Britain has a glorious history of its democratic parliament with an unwritten constitution and is highly esteemed as the mother of the Parliaments of many common wealth nations, Britain itself has a full-fledged and parallel Islamic Parliament since 1992. Hence thinking about a non-territorial Islamic state they produced a manifesto proposing the setting up of the Muslim Parliament in Great Britain.This was inaugurated on January 4, 1992 among unprecedented scenes of anger and fury expressed by the members of British Parliament and Ministers of England. The proponents of Global Islamic Movement calculated that the infrastructure of this movement in England would come to prominence towards the end of the first decade of the new millennium.

Muslims were living in England scattered, attending sectarian mosques and were adherent to westernization. But soon after the Rushdie affairs the Muslims of England awakened, united and became sensitive about their Islamic value. They became alert over global Islamisation and mindful about the formation of an Islamic parliament. They are now trying to explore the political culture and teaching of Islam in search of a solution to the problems of Muslim minority. Now they lay stress on two basic conditions (a) Acceptability to Muslims of all schools of thought (b) Political relevance to the prevailing conditions of Muslims in Britain.

Europeans have developed the belief that Islam is an Asian religion. But Muslims in general think that it is the Divine help in the form of Satanic verses and the Fatwa of Imam Khomeini that helped Muslims in Britain to define their situation and go on to set up a Muslim Parliament in Great Britain. After the

Satanic Verses issue the conversion of Christians in Europe into Muslims increased 4 times. The Muslim Parliament in Britain and its ancillary institution raised a huge fund to supply arms and ammunitions for Bosnian Mujahiddins. The Parliament at a special session held on June 1993 decided

(a) To open a European Muslim Defence Council.

(b) To convene a world conference on Bosnia Herzegovina.

(c) To work to identify, expose and punish those guilty of atrocities against innocent men, women and children of Bosnia and Herzegovina.

(d) To raise a fund in the name of Arms for Bosnia Fund from every Muslim household of Great Britain.

The Muslim parliament came to a final decision to take some steps for the promotion of Muslim interest. They are;

(a) To note the details of the massacre, rape, looting, and concentration camps, ethnic cleansing, torture, indiscriminate bombardment, etc.

(b) to enlist the names and addresses of all the criminals, political leaders, rapists, soldiers, officers and civilians who actually carried out the atrocities.

This Parliament also has a Human Rights Committee exclusively with a Muslim Chairman. It intensively concentrates to pamper Islamic interests in England as a base to propagate Islam throughout the world.

The Islamic Industrial Tribunal, a wing of Islamic Human Rights Commission, found that a woman could be legitimately dismissed form a job if she started wearing Hijab. Appropriate facilities for Muslim women are not recognized on a state level. In the health care meals, the needs of Islamic systems are not officially recognized. The system of Halal or killing of meat breed animals by ripping throats according to Islamic liturgy has not been recognized.

When the question of 'Arms for Bosnia Fund' was raised in the British Parliament, the Govt. opposed it and suppressed this Islamic proposal. The Muslim Parliament of England spread this news and this event created reactions among the Muslims worldwide.

Britain's Muslim Parliament took bold steps and came forward to aid the war-striken Bosnians. The British Muslims were the first to start relief work in Bosnia and Herzegovina. The four main groups whole-heartedly engaged in this human service were - (1) Islamic relief (2) Muslim Aid (3) Convoy of Mercy and (4) the Human Right Committee.

The "Islamic relief" institution was sponsoring 2400 orphans by running schools, printing the Quran and providing books for students, counseling service for the rape victims, instituting income generating projects, producing handicraft, agriculture projects, etc.

Another British Agency "Muslim Aid" sent some 3 million pounds of British aid to Bosnia and Herzogovina. It also provided Arabic and Quran classes at 3 different centres. It organised successful Qurbani programmes in Croatia. Besides, this camp assisted 3000 Muslim refugees for their all-round development.

A convoy of mercy had been supplying thousands of tons of food, blankets and medicine equipments, at many rehabilitation centres for the wounded Bosnians and Muslim soldiers, educational institutions having Islamic studies. It has its main centre of service in Croatia but this institution used to go to Bosnia and Herzegovina twice a week with humanitarian aid by Ex-army trucks.

The Muslim Parliament of England has also set up a Human Rights Commission in response to the genocide in Bosnia and Herzegovina. Apart from organizing demonstrations, exhibitions and lectures to raise funds for the Bosnians' cause, the Muslim Human Right Commission has shouldered the responsibility to send food and medicine to Bosnia and Herzegovina as part of the work for Bosnia Appeal. The Bosnian Children Fund (B.C.F.) has been in operation providing financial assistance primarily for the orphans of the Shahid (martyrs) and also for other Muslim children. Another branch of Muslim Parliament is "Bosnia Jehad Fund" which is set up to provide funds to the Bosnians for their most desperate needs.

In an international khilafat conference held in England, in London on August 7,1994 by the terrorist organization Hizbul

Tahir, there assembled 8,000 Muslim fundamentalist representatives of different countries of the world. Here they concluded that as long as the kingdom of Israel is not finished there is no question of peace in Islamic countries. All the international organizations whether it is the UNO or the International Monetary fund or the Arab League, they are all under the subjugation of the imperialist nations. So let the Muslims in mass declare these organizations as illegal.

"Muslim News" is an Islamic news magazine published in England with a daily circulation of more than 65,000. It reflects the society of British Muslims in England and reserves a strong opinion to protect the interests of the Muslims of Britain. For instance, when a British Metropolitan police narrated that Islam is a religion based on violence, the magazine vehemently protested against this comment. The Secretary General of the Muslim Council of Britain (M.C.B.) Iqbal Sacrami warned the British police never to pass such rebuffing comments in future. The protest raised such a wave of resentment among the Muslims that Asst. Commissioner David Venice admitted the mistake and told that they would remain careful while using the word Islam or Muslim. This is how the Islam dominates the psycho status of British Officers while canvassing on an insignificant word related to Islam. The Secretary General of M.C.B. also made it clear that Islam and terrorism are contradictory and the non-Muslims should be aware of it.

One among four Muslims in Britain is unemployed and one in 15 white Muslims is unemployed. The British Islamic Human Right Commission now demands to amend the Race Relations Act of 1976 which has affirmed Jews and Sikhs as minor racial groups ignoring the Muslims. Under the pressure of 2 million strong Muslim minorities the British government at last admitted that the law enacted in 1976 is defective and in due course it would be revised.

British Royal House and Islam

England particularly the royal family of England seems to be more compassionate towards Islam. This family poses a peculiar sense of respect to this religion. The writer John Casey in his essay 'why fear Islam' quotes about Charles' speaking sympathetically on Islamic culture and Muslims in England. Prince Charles was also pressurized to open a department for Islamic study in the Oxford University. He also hosts receptions for young people from British Muslim community to celebrate Eid-ul-Fitr at St James Palace in London. Surprisingly London, which is the epicentre for the propagation of Christianity, is getting converted as the centre of Islamic studies and strategic research.

In addition to the formation of Islamic Parliament in England, the greatest insult conferred by the Islamic world to Britain is the entertainment of Dodi Fahd with the late British Princess Diana, the mother of the heir apparent to British throne. The marriage ceremony of Diana with Prince Charles was one of the greatest pageantry the world had ever seen but it had an Islamic tragic end. The British unwittingly digested this insult, as they had no other alternative.

The British helplessly averted the world attention on the covariation of a non-Christian and non-European Arabian Muslim youth Dodi Fahd with the British princess Diana. This is a sign of great disrespect to the British Royal House. To enjoy oneself with the British princess is simply a glimpse of Jehad that can be defined in the way of exposing or dishonouring the centre of love and devotion of the British, the Kafirs. Dodi was the first human bomb, a suicidal force to launch Jehad against Europe in general and Britain in particular. But the world ignored Dodi to be considered as such.

Islamic pressure is tremendous in England. Idi Amin, the former President of Uganda, who had the notoriety of killing more than 500000 people, once went to England and persisted in visiting the British Queen. However the royal authority invited him to attend the dinner. On asking about the reason of his arrival in England he replied that he simply came to purchase a pair of 14 number shoes, which suit him.

It is redundant to note that once the British queen denied hosting the great British litterateur William Shakespeare, simply because he was the son of a cobbler.

In a recent event Prince Charles of England has been chosen for the Sultan Hassanal Bolkiah International Award for the promotion of dialogue between Islam and Western civilization. The Oxford Centre of Islamic studies declared that Prince Charles had been consistent in his public advocacy of the need of greater mutual understanding between Islam and the Western world.

The above incident emphasizes three notable points. First, if there is mutual understanding between Islam and the Western world, there will be no more a world by the name of Islam and no book by the name of the Quran. Islam advocates strong principles that strictly contradict Western culture. Secondly, for a greater mutual understanding between Islam and the West, Diana was the first lady to have sacrificed her life. It is her greatest contribution towards the world of religious understanding. Not a single Muslim institution came forward to pay its tribute to this noblest lady who became an emblem of mutual understanding between the two rival races. Not even a single Muslim poet in any corner of the world has composed a single poem in her praise. It is because Islam does not permit a Muslim to honour a non-Muslim. A non-Muslim European youth cannot entertain a Muslim girl in any Gulf country as the British Princess Diana did with a Petro guy. Thirdly Prince Charles knows that the death sentence is still hovering over the writer of Satanic Verses, a British citizen who is kept confined under heavy security. The world wants to know the riddle of the confinement in the midst of Islo-Western understanding. This is simply a jehadi stratagem of the Islamic world to strengthen their Islamic foundation in central Europe in general and Britain, the prominent abode of Western civilization in particular. Muslims are ever aware of the British interest in creating a rival state like Israel in the midst of Palestine.

England has now become a breeding ground of Islamic fundamentalists and Jehadi fighters. Extreme Muslim clerics in London have decided to celebrate September 11 by launching a militant Islamic organisatioin "The Islamic Council of Britain" "to implement the Shariat law in this country. Umar Mohammed Bakri, a staunch Islamic orator, has launched Jehad in the psychic sphere of Britain to change their mind and revolt against British democracy. It is also reported that this organizatioin will also welcome Al Qaeda sympathizers. A recently published report describes that every year about 900 British Muslims flee from the country to run their Jehadi activities in Kashmir and other foreign countries. They have the support of 30000 Muslims in Britain. Some of the British Jehadi fighters have fled abroad to create public opinion against Kashmir's integration with India. According to their policy, after the Kashmir problem is solved they will soon turn back to England with a religious Jehadi zeal to create insurgency in their motherland to convert England in to an Islamic country through conversion, immigration and high Muslim birth rate. According to the "Guardian Unlimited" — "We will replace the Bible with the Quran in Britain."

(b) France

A large number of Muslims, mostly from the North African countries, migrated to France in the interim of two world wars to meet the need of labour force for the reconstruction of Europe. Large sections of the Muslim immigrants worked in factories, mines and construction industries and Muslim inhabitations began to develop in different cities in France. Statistics show that at present there are five million Muslims living in France, the largest population in Western Europe. The Muslim society in France consists of almost 123 different nationalities, most of whom are from Algeria, Morocco and Tunisia. But the Muslim population of France is made up of three different ethnic groups; North Africans, black Africans and Turks. They arrived in three waves of immigration, the first of which began in the 1950s. North Africans (Algerians, Moroccans and Tunicians) are the biggest group with Algerians dominant in it. For decades France was inaccessible to Muslims. France as a Chrisrian country turned out to be a heaven on earth for the Muslim immigrants. A Muslim family in France is identified with a father, three or four wives, about twenty kids earning $10,000 a month without working. (This is so because in France those mothers who do not work for the reasons of looking after their young children are given a subsidiary allowance of about $500 a month per child to the mother and this is an encouragement to young mothers to stay home to rear their childen and not to look for jobs outside leaving the children unattended. Its believers occupied the lowest rungs of the economic and social ladder, lived in peripheral housing projects and practised their faith in the impoverished prayer halls. They were divided by their country of origin and continued to wear the costumes of their native villages.

That situation began to change in the 80s. By then it had become obvious that the first generation immigrants and their offsprings would never return to their countries of origin, even though they and their families were living in poverty on the margins of French society. Exposed during their schooling to France's republican ideals of "Liberte, Egalite, Fraternite," their children began to feel that they were victims of injustice. The stage was set for the defending phenomenon of the 90s, the reconversion of the second and third generation immigrants to a more radical Islam than that of their parents as a source of identity in a society from which they felt excluded. The rise of the new assertive young Islam in France is a sign of the increasing integration of France's Muslim population. Increasingly the mosques of France are attended by a cross section of blacks, North Africans and even converted white French.

In France the Islamic population is next to the Roman Catholies. The Protestant Christians keep the third position in the population chart. Out of the total populatioin of 58 million people of France, the Muslims constitute 5 million. There are about 3,00,000 white European French Muslims in France. About one third of them are French citizens. Almost 40% of them are living in Paris and in its vicinity. 90% of the Muslims in France belong to the working class. The rest 50 million French had no such religious tendency to counteract Islam in France.

The largest mosque of France is in Paris, which was built in 1925 by the Muslim immigrants from Algeria. At present this is the prime centre of Islamic political and religious activities in France. Other important mosques in France are the Grand Mosque, Stalingrad Mosque, Barbs Mosque and Galini Mosque, etc. There are about 1110 mosques and prayer halls in Paris. Outside Paris there are 600 mosques and prayer halls. The Grand Mosque of Lyon has an area of 3000 square metres and has been built with the collaboration of Saudi Arabia. This is the largest mosque in France after the Grand Mosque of Paris.

In the year 1970 there were only 23 mosques in France. But soon after the success of Islamic revolution in Iran, the number of mosques multiplied so rapidly that it went beyond expectation. Despite this increase in the number of mosques the Muslims in France feel the lack of sufficient places for their worship. Many French scholars, writers, artists, philosophers embrace Islam. Well-known French philosopher Roger Geraudi, artist Moris Bejar inc are amongst them. The wide spread immigration of Muslims in erstwhile liberal France is now robbing the French of jobs, social services and even safety of women in the streets. Presently French men are clamouring for stopping all construction of mosques in French territory. But Muslims could turn the situation of France in their favour.

Some Islamic Groups of France

(i) The Council of Islamic Thought

This is an official establishment, which was founded in 1990. The duties with which the members of this council are entrusted are attending to the religious needs of the Muslims in the hospital, issues related to the incarcerated Muslims in the armed forces, supervising the proper manner of slaughtering of cows (Halal, the Islamic process of killing animals to die in utter agony and pain) and inspecting the proper functioning of religious programmes.

(ii) Advanced Institute for Islamic studies

The Institution trains the Imams or prayer leaders and Islamologists to lead the Muslims in Europe and to preach the religion of Islam.

(iii) The voice of Islamic Association

This is aimed at protesting against anti-Islamic activities and condemning anti-Islamic publications.

This keeps an eye on the French constitution so as to amend it in terms of favouring the self interest of the Muslims in France. This association was very active in the time of the Satanic Verses wave.

(iv) National Federation of French Muslims

This federation constitutes the Muslims who are the natives of France. Its programmes of action include imparting training and familiarizing other Muslims with Islamic teachings. Different Islamic countries finance all these Islamic groups.

(v) French Association for information on Islam

This institution came to existence in the year 1993 being patronized by Persian littoral states.Its key role is to change the perception of Europeans on Islam.It has planned to raise an Islamic University in any European country, most probably either in England or in France. Roger Geraudie, a famous French Philosopher on Islam, is a staunch supporter of this organization. He himself left Christianity for its irreligious customaries and embraced Islam.

(vi) Rabitat-ul-Islami

This is the most powerful branch of Islamic group in France, particularly in Paris, It has abundant financial strength to organize many Islamologic conferences. It spends large sums of money on inviting famous speakers from different parts of the world. All the Islamic groups of France are convergent to this Rabiltat-ul-Islami of Paris branch.

Another Islamic group is "The Union of Islamic Students" in France. The union of Muslim students has its connection with the Muslim Brotherhood (Ikhwan-ul-Muslimeen) and Muslim institutions of Saudi Arabia and other Islamic gulf countries.

The numbers of Islamic groups are increasing in France rapidly. The numbers of these institutions rose from 1050 in

1991 to 2000 in 1995. Now there are near about 3000 Islamic institutions, which show the intensity of Islamic activities in France.

There are many eminent French writers, doctors, technicians and artists who have embraced Islam. One such most important French figure is Rene Guenon. After conversion into Islam he was known as Seikh Abdul Wahid Yahya. He was a great thinker of France. He converted thousands of white French men into Islam. Other such prominent figures are Dr.Dalit Abu Bakr., Roger Geraudie and professor Vincent Mansaur Montie, etc. There are some thousands of French who have been converted into Islam but have hidden themselves for fear of being ostracized.

The converted French Muslim writer Roger Geraudie in his book "Founding Myths of Israeli Policies" mentions how the Whites have killed 3 00000 children of Iraq. He also described the bombardment of the USA on Hiroshima in Japan and its use of N' bomb in Vietnam as extremely inhuman. He was found guilty for his writing and fined 120000 Franks.

Presently France, the land of Christian nationalism is slowly but steadily proceeding towards Islamic trap. The French government bowed before the Islamic pressure and out of compulsion ordered the education department to allow Muslim girl students to use Hijab, an Arabic religious headscarf, in defiance of the regular school uniform dress. Apart from this, the court passed the decree, which urged the government to give compensation to those girls who were expelled from the school for having dressed themselves according to Islamic tradition. However the French Prime Minister John Pierren Raffarin in a TV interview on September 22, 03 said that Islamic veils and other religious symbols have no place in French schools. Schools should not be the place where people display their religious affiliations. The questioin of traditional Islamic dress is at the centre of deliberations by a National commission seeking concessions on France's secular principles. Islam not only exercised its control over the socio-cultural life of France, but it also checked the advancement of French Christian crusade into the dense forest of Africa. France entered East Africa in 1637. But there was Islamic reaction against France. It resorted to the interior only in 1854 and found the largest colonial states in Africa in the name of Federation of French West Africa (AOF) comprising the present day states of Bremen, Burkina, Faso, Guinea, Ivory Coast, Mali Mauritania, Niger and Senegal. The Muslim reforms movement posed a threat to the French rule towards the beginning of the second half of the nineteenth century. Towards the beginning of the nineteenth century the colonial attitude of France was dominated by the fear of Islam. Heavy Islamic pressure forced France to relinquish its position from its colony in 1960.

French who are very generous and devoted followers of democracy watch the construction of innumerable mosques and madrassas or Islamic schools in their land. Here the bearded Mullåhs with a closed ear shout that Allah is the only God for the whole world in the coming years. "There is no God but Allah and Mohammed, his Prophet". The people of France are on the way to accept this concept.

France in Connection to Algeria

Algeria is now severely suffering from the bloody civil war between the Islamic Jehadi fighters and Military government. As a result a large number of Muslim refugees are infiltrating into France from Algeria generating many internal problems like the spread of Islamic Jehad and growth of Islamic population that strikes at the financial structure of France besides unbalancing the socio-cultural infrastructure.

The first attempt to export terrorism to France took place in the Christmas of 1994.The chosen vehicle was a plane. Four Mujahiddins from the G I A (Armed Islamic Group) armed with dynamite and AK 47 hijacked an "Air France" on the tarmac at the air port in Algiers.

France was for a long period in a dilemma to decide whether to support the military rule of Algeria or the Islamic militants who have made a bloody vow to turn Algeria into an Islamic country. The reason for this dilemma is that, though it is a

Christian country dominated by white Europeans, still the Jehadi fighters are in a dominating number with a reactionary attitude in Paris, the capital of France.

France has experienced the burning heat of Islamic communalism in Algeria, adjacent to its own soil. It apprehends the danger of a civil war in Algeria that may engulf France in transgressing the chest of Mediterranean Sea. In August 1994 some Islamic religious fighters entered the French embassy of Algeria and mercilessly killed 5 French men. After this incidence the government of France became alert about Islam.

France was the colonial power in Algeria until 1962 and now home to more than one million refugees of Algerian origin who fled from their Algerian homelands and took refuge in 1992. France is actually aware of the danger of Algerian violence spreading to its soil as it did during a bombing wave in 1995. The rapid growth of Islamic population by birth, by infiltration, by immigration and conversion has become a matter of apprehension to the Christian French as well as to Germans.

France also tried to suppress the Islamic movement by interfering in the internal affairs of Algeria. On realizing that the Algerian Muslims residing in France may react, it refrained from interference but France is in support of the military rule in Algeria and has become the eyesore of Islamic religious fighters of that country.

The French are more philanthropic than all other Europeans in relation to religion. They adapted as much Islamic orthodoxy as possible in to their social environment as a tolerant nation. Even they allowed Hizab, etc. They had a belief that during the second or third generation any other religious and national disparity would be assimilated in the French nationalism. But their notion proved to be a fool's Paradise in the case of Islam.

France quickly apprehended the danger of this Islamic enmity within. Since the last 90s, the government has gone out of its way to integrate Islam into French life, rather than treating it as a menacing foreign influence.

(c) Germany

Islam arrived in Germany at the beginning of 18th century in the time of Ottoman Sultan Mohammed II. Among the mosques built in Germany, the first dates back to 1731. The Muslims were serving as soldiers of the army of German emperor Fredrick Wilhelm as he believed in granting religious freedom to all. According to him every one has the right to live according to his own belief. This made the Muslims to flourish in Germany by residing there as army workers, having been married to German spinsters and enhancing their Muslim population and setting up their own Muslim families.

Out of 5 million foreigners in Germany three millions are Muslims. They, as usual, infiltrated into Germany to seek employment. Muslims are the largest religious group in Germany after Christianity. Their prime demand is to get recognition as a religious minority and to play an active role in German politics and in German society.

The second phase of Islamic immigration started with the Turkish workers to Germany, which took place after 1950. The Turkish labourers came to Germany to help rebuild the post-war Germany and make some money for themselves.

In course of time they began to settle in Germany with their families and increased their number through birth proliferation. Now they number about 3 million. The Turkish immigrants were quite unfamiliar with the German language and culture. Presently the German Muslims with the rest of the Muslim world are becoming stronger day by day. The strengthening of brotherly relations is being done by Islamic societies like Rabeta-Al-Alam-Al-Islami, Jamiat-e- Ikhwan–Al –Muslimeen and Islamic Countries' conference, etc.

Besides Turks, Muslims from Yugoslavia, Morocco, Iran, Tunisia, and Jordan and from other Muslim countries constitute a vast Muslim community in addition to the ethnic Muslim residents of Germany who had settled since the beginning of 18th century. The Muslim refugees from the Ex-Soviet Union amounting to some 7-8 thousand also should be taken into account. The Muslims of Germany are almost equal to the population of Hamburg.

Footprints of Jehad were found in Germany when 8 Iranians were nabbed in Germany who had been sent to kill four persons. Iran vehemently repudiated the procedure of German court to punish these Iranians claiming that this was a part of their religious war. The European Union disrupted its diplomatic relation with Tehran in 1991.

Iranians combined with Turkish Muslim community form a great Islamic Power in Germany. Iranian Muslims particularly play a great role in the economic, cultural, commercial and educational activities in the country. An Iranian German martyr Dr. Behasti who was assassinated in 1981, was an active member of the mosque of Hamburg. He remains in the memory of German Muslims as a great national leader. Turkish population forms the real Muslim power in Germany. Though the German authorities passed an act on November 23, 1973 prohibiting immigration from other countries to Germany other than those in the European Common Market, the population of Turkish Muslims rose by 50%. The immigrants' children and their fate play an important role in determining the future of Islam in Germany.

One of the remarkable characteristics of Islam is that once they step in on a new land to earn their livelihood, they never intend to return. During the last decade the main topic of national discussion in Germany was based on Turkish infiltration or immigration problems. But the authorities intentionally tried to exclude the religious aspect of the issue – Islam, from discussion about foreigners, to avoid the provocation of religious sensitivity amongst the Turks. The German Muslims' reactions are becoming stronger and more organized day by day.

Islam has stuck such an impression in the German psyche that as in Britain and France, Germans also shrink to open their mouth against Muslims. Islamic roots have been embedded so strongly in the European soil of Germany that if any question of discrepancy arises in future on national interest, Turkish Muslims of Germany are prepared to claim their share on the soil of Germany in the name of Islamic home land as it has occurred throughout the world where Islamic population is close to 20 to 30%.

Almost all the Muslim youths in Germany are associated either with a union or a society. Though the government blames the Turkish Muslims for the unemployment and pöpulation problem of the country, they can't deny the service of the Muslims because the majority of the Muslims are employed in jobs like mining, road constructions, etc., which are always dangerous occupations which the Germans refrain from. Their hopes and desires collapse under the heavy weight of racism.

Common notion of German Christians are obvious in the following verdict published in a German magazine Der Spiegel in its 8221st issue.

"These Asian nomads who have swarmed out the country like locusts and have turned Germany to an Islamic colony should be castrated and their women made barren and the looting of their shops encouraged. "They are not humans, rather descendants of monkies"- this is the time for the coming of a new Hitler."

"Get out Cameleers", "Test a Turk and not a frog in the laboratories" are some phrases which were very commonly used against the Muslims in Germany. By this time mosques in Germany were numbered in hundreds and they were also make-shift mosques. Public calls for prayer wasn't frequently observed and Islam was never an issue.

A converted mosque in Eving, which was silently active since 1978 became the eyesore of Christian Germans in January 1998. This mosque stands right next to a modestly affluent and predominantly German housing estate. This is one of the first mosques in this industrial Ruhr town to start proclaiming Ajan or Islam's public call to prayer from loud speakers on the roof. This followed a demonstration by local Eving Christian residents outside the mosque. The five times repetition of "There is no God but Allah and Mohammed is his prophet" hurt the sentiment of German Christians who are strictly termed as nonbelievers and subject to be assassinated by order of Allah and Mohammed. They started examining legal options.

The Government came to the conclusion in June 1998 that German laws must protect the call of Ajan, which is not different from Christian Church bells, on the ground of religious freedom. Now Muslims in Germany are clever enough to teach German Christians the ideals of tolerance and Muslims to tread on carefully.

A German writer Hidaytullah Hubsch was a Christian and got converted to Islam in the year 1969 after a deep study and realization of Islam as the best way. This Germany-born European Muslim wrote a book "The path of Mohammed, Islam, and the religion of the future". The book clearly depicts the important points of the Quran and life style of Mohammed. On Islamic social system the writer says- "the planet earth came into being for the establishment of the Mosque by Mohammed. That is the reason why Muslims consider this earth sacred and keep it clean." To gratify their consideration they want to cleanse the unholy people, the unbelievers or Kafirs, from this earth and create sacred lands in the name of Dar-ul-Islam. It signifies that non-Islamised lands are Dar-ul-Harab or unholy lands. According to him "God did not reveal Islamic law to put Muslims under hardship, but to guide them from the darkness of ignorance to the light of knowledge – that is Islamic life and living".

After England and France it is now the turn of Germany who came in rotation to arrive on the decision whether to accept head scarf for the Muslim women of Germany as a legal understanding. Taking the secular integrity of European Christian majority countries Islam finds its way to intrude into this non-Islamic state through the most controversial use of head scarf by a large group of women who want to be identified as a distinct religious group. Women from twenty Islamic countries gathered in Berlin on May 24, 2004 to talk about "Women in the Islamic world". Women from Saudi Arabia, Syria, Morocco, Pakistan, Indonesia, Malesia, Algeria, Sudan, Iran, Yemen, Bahrain, Afghanistan, Egypt, Iraq, etc., participated in this seminar. The background of this dialogue was the so-called head scarf debate on the question of whether a school teacher can wear a head scarf and what the scarf symbolizes. The Federal constitutional court of Germany had decided a few months ago that a legal basis was required for a head scarf ban for female teachers. The argument was made in an unimaginable way so as to compel the judiciary to hold their tongue. The question was raised- "Why were we oppressing women by forcing them to remove the head scarf? /Why don't we react when the women are used for pornography? Why don't we react when the women of Iraq are subjected to the worst atrocities?"Those women who represented Germany were well furnished with knowledge in the Islamic tenets with a reformative attitude.

Germany is also slowly and steadily leaning towards Islamic fundamentalism. A German writer Mary Shimel described that Salman Rushdie had wounded the emotions of Islamic religious people. Her comments in favour of the Fatwa have inspired Muslims. A Jehadi (misnomered as terrorist) Islamic group has also established itself in German soil since 1992. It was receiving financial assistance from the German Govt. through a charitable institution called "Association of Iranian Refugees". This association made efforts to support Iranian orphans. But after investigation the German Government detected that actually this institution was purchasing weapons for the terrorist outfit of Germany, Mujahiddin Khalq Organisation.

The murder of an outspoken German film maker by Muslim fundamentalists, discovery of suspected radical Muslim cells in Netherlands, promulgation of a parallel Islamic society in Germany, Islamic tendency of formation of Ghettos and attitude of disintegration from the German mainstream has created discontent among the German Christians against the Muslim immigrants.

Earlier, the local German Christians insinuated them as foreigners or guest workers. Now the term guest worker has been faded from use and has become politically incorrect. Sixty thousand Muslims of Turkish origin have embraced citizenship of Germany after a law enacted to favour the people born to foreign parents.

"Learn Germany and integrate" is the message of present leaders resonating across the political spectrum in Germany. On the contrary the out bursts have alarmed the Muslim groups who complain their life style is under threat of Christian national communalism. The chairman of Islamic council in Germany says, "Integration cannot be ordered from above. It is not a one-way street."

Islamic groups are now in search of a vent to percolate into the education system of Germany and European schools to introduce the study of the Quran in the syllabus.

(d) Italy

In no country in Europe has there been such a rapid growth of Muslims, mosques and Islamic cultural centres as in Italy. As to Islam, Italy is the bridge between Africa, the Middle East and Europe.

Islam as a minority religion is going to become a major player in Italy's future for the first time. Out of 57 million population of Italy, more than one million are Muslims. Muslim immigrants from North Africa, the Middle East and Albania have formed the second largest faith after the Catholic denomination of Christianity in Italy. Illegal migration is a hot political topic in this main Christian nation. Iraq, Palestine, etc., are trying to supercede the ethnic Christian population of Italy. Illegal immigration is a hot political topic in Italy. Muslims from Bangladesh, Morocco, Iraq, Palestine, etc., are trying to enter Italy and settle there as their own land. Muslim families with overloaded boats each carrying about 200-250 people stealthily reach the Italian islands like through sea route. When their population reaches a countable position, they will ask the ethnic Christian population of Italy to come to a compromise for an independent Islamic state.

As a part of an open door policy anticipating good dividends for him, Pope John Paul II had permitted a mosque to be built inside the Vatican territory although there is no Muslim population worth mentioning in that area. After the constructioin of the mosque was over, the Pope also wished a similar response from the Saudi administration. There are more than a million Catholic Philippinos living in Saudi Arabia to handle all kinds of dirty manual work. There they need a church for their congregational liturgies. Helping the Pope to have a taste of Allah king Fahd expounded that inspite of all his good will nothing much can be done in the matter of building a Catholic Church in Saudi Arabia as Allah's words clearly forbid any such constructioin of houses of worship of Kufir or faith other than Islam. The Catholic Bishop's Council is now worried about the unilateral inter marriage between the Christian spinsters with Muslim youths who are even about to grow their number to form an Islamic chunk as their home land on the sacred soil of Vatican which heads as an emancipation of suffering people from worldly misery. Soon after an Italian Catholic girl marries a Muslim youth she openly comes out with a white scarf on her head without any hesitation.

In Italy, Muslims have formed a political project named "Eurasia Islam" that symbolizes the political- cultural fight against Western civilization. The Muslims of Italy are always in favour of Iran for its leadership. A Cardinal of Vatican, Jiya Como Beefy, a Roman Catholic leader, an expected successor of Pope felt the heat of Islamic sword in Vatican. Hence he called for the Christians to carry on a Crusade against the Muslims. He told that according to a report of the U.N.O during the last 10 years the population of Muslims doubled in Europe. The first Mosque was built in Rome in the year 1995. Now there are more than 100 mosques raised in the Vatiean City.

Italy has long experience in dealing with domestic terrorist groups and is also one of the European states situated on the front-line for Islamic immigration into Europe from North Africa and the Middle East. According to the U S treasury department, the Islamic Cultural Institute in Milan is the most important base of Al Qaeda in Europe– a station from which weapons, men and money spread out to the whole world. Growth of Italy's Muslim population is under rapidity.

The fact is that those Italians who embrace Islam become more devoted to Italy having their nativity with the soil since 8th century when Italy was under the domain of Islam. Later it was dominated by Catholic denomination and became the abode of the Pope. Islam was not a question of discussion in Italy before 1980. The number of Muslims doubles in 10 years. Among the Muslims of Italy 10,000 are Italian born converts.

"Perhaps here more than elsewhere, the cross over questions of immigration and religion are vexing a nation where St. Peter's Basilica and Europe's largest mosque are just a city bus ride apart." Time will come "when the Italian brand of Islam can play a major role in the religious future of Italy." Muslims are stalking to seize the opportunity to decide the position of Italy having Rome as its capital and epicentre of preaching Islam instead of Christianity.

(e) Chechnya

Chechnya, with a population of 13 million is a Muslim majority state of the former-communist empire. It declared its secession from Russia to be the 21st republic of the Russian Federation. Chechnya has large oil reservoirs.

The soil of Chechnya has been volcanised since 16 th century when the Muslim majority region of Chechnya wanted its freedom from the suzerainty of the Czar. After a bloody battle against the Czar, the Muslims capitulated before him in the year 1864. They again started a revolt in the year 1877 but it was ruthlessly suppressed. Under the heavy oppression the Muslims could not withstand the persecution in Chechnya. They left Chechnya for Uganda and Turkey. Some of them again returned to the newly formed USSR after the dethronement of the Czar in the year 1917. During Stalin's tenure he killed 3,00,000 Chechnyans to suppress their rebellion for an independent Islamic nation. By an order passed by him on February 23, 1944 Stalin expelled the Chechnyan Muslims to the vast isolated land of Siberia. After 13 years of exile Nikita Kruschev called them back to Chechnya. Meanwhile they enhanced their population and in the year 1990 they revolted against the USSR and declared Chechnya as an independent sovereign state. The Soviet Parliament was forced to recognize it.

The USSR was disintegrated in the year 1992. Russia regained its old identity, not as a kingdom but as a democratic republic. But to its utter surprise Russia saw Chechnya revolting against its independence as an Islamic nation. Consequently Russia invaded Chechnya in the year 1994 but it had to surrender before the invincible Islamic Jehadi fighters of Chechnya. In the year 1999 Russia again inflicted a war against Chechnya to suppress the revolt for segregation from Russia. The Muslims faced more horrendous assaults from communist Russia. Most wretched were the citizens of Samski who had helped the Chechnyans against the Russian soldiers. Out of 15,000 people of the small town, 10,000 were killed so ruthlessly that the villainous carnage exceeded the historic record of Chengiz Khan. Now whenever a soldier feels a slight deflection of the body he starts firing. Soldiers drag out children from the mother's lap; throw them with hands tied up under the tank to be crushed. They pour petrol over the corpse and then force the mother to light the match. They make the best use of hand grenades on those who try to prowl into safe places. Killing people with torture everyday was a regular habit and a source of entertainment to the Russian soldiers.

However in the middest of turmoil and great holocaust Chechnya emerged as a small Muslim Republic in the year 1992. Soon after Chechnya Republic was formed, it banned Russian language. Russian army seriously attacked it by its ground forces and later by air for aerial bombardment. The artillery that included airplanes, long-range missiles and tanks inflicted a heavy attack on this part of Europe since its inception.

There are two important factors that determine Russia to remain resolute not to unleash Chechnya from its clutch. First the oil reserves of the Caspian sea and the reserves under Chechnya. Russia wants to capture the oil reserves and export it to foreign countries if it reaches the black sea with a connecting pipe through Chechnya. Hence if Chechnya is segregated then the greatest repository of oil wealth will automatically be lost from the Russian hold. It will suffer a great loss at the hands of Islam monopolists.

Secondly if Chechnya becomes independent then the regions like Dagistan, Tatarstan, Ingusetia and other small Muslim dominated provinces are there in tandem to demand their separation from Russia. A time will come when segregated Russia will remain as the last Islamic state.

Whenever the slogan "Allah O Akbar" is heard from the main square of Grozney, the Russian soldiers and tanks take position. It was the first movement among the republics inside the Russian Federation to break away and was then a severe blow to the central government in Moscow.

In Chechnya alone almost 50 thousand Muslims have been killed by the Russian soldiers. Warfare launched by Chechnyans is now directly under the strict management of Islamic militants. There is no possibility of end to this war. Chechnya is burning.

(f) Poland

Poland is another European country where Muslims have been consolidating their position gradually to stalk over the Christianity. The Tatars who immigrated to Poland from Lithuania and Caucasia in the 14th Century propagated Islam in Poland. Despite the presence of the former-communist regime, around 3 to 4 thousand Muslims were able to preserve their religious identity.

In the 16th and 17th centuries, Polish Muslims numbered 100,000. But the European tribal wars and the pressures exerted by Christians and eccelesiastical authorities caused the Polish Muslim community to wander. They celebrated the 60th anniversary of their conversion to Islam by holding special ceremonies and publishing a new translation of the Quran. Now they plan to erect a huge mosque so as to draw the attention of the whole of the European Muslims to be envious of the quick uprising of the Muslims in Poland.

(g) Bosnia

Bosnia and Herzegovina - This is a newly formed Islamic country carved out of Yugoslavia, which set a unique, exemplary achievement to get independence in the face of violent opposition. Islam reached this land in contact with Roman and Ottoman Empire. The Muslims constituted 44% of the population of the Bosnia and Herzegovina republic, which suffered from the severe aggression at the hands of European Serbs. The Serbian minority started a systematic plan to uproot Islamic existence. So they began the destruction with whatever they found in the name of Islam.

Though the Bosnian Muslims emerged in a European and Christian environment and their people have felt themselves much more a part of Europe, it is natural that they turned to the Islamic nations for large scale assistance for the formation of an Islamic country in the middle of Europe.

A Muslim based Democratic Action Party was formed in May 1990 and its success in the election in the same year was taken as sufficient proof that fundamentalists tried to establish an Islamic state in Europe and impose the Shariat law (Islamic law) and reduce the Bosnian Serbs to the status of a minority. The relationship of Bosnians with the Organization of Islamic Conference also created suspicion and fear in the minds of the Serbs. This emboldened them to achieve their Serbian national goal.

A few events like the success of the Islamic revolution in Iran, the Salman Rushdie affair, the Persian Gulf War, the victory of the Islamic group in Afghanistan, the revolution in Argentina, etc., were regarded as the turning point in the Islamic awakening in the world. This provoked the Bosnian Muslims to remain stern and stiff in the face of the tough European Christians.

Bosnia, the Muslim populated area of Yugoslavia, declared its independence on 14, September 1995 after the Dayton Peace Treaty. The Serbs of Herzegovina were compelled to fight against the Muslims of Bosnia. They declared the Serbian republic and destroyed a large number of mosques.

Muslims fought very bravely against the Islamic onslaught inflicted by non-Muslim European countries. According to UNICEF's estimation, within the two years of war from 1992 to 1994, 16614 children died in Bosnia and 35350 children were wounded. Kamal Karic was the youngest amputee in the Bosnian history, who lost his leg at the age of only 4 months. Every third child in post-war Bosnia suffers from serious psychic problems while all children suffer slight psychological danger. The most frequently observed symptoms of disorder were excessive attachment to parents, fear of loneliness, eye tics or some other kind of tics, dependence on medication, concentration problems, nightmares, speech difficulties, etc.

In the midst of all the oddities, oppressions, conflicts, unpleasant and unfavorable circumstances the Republic of Bosnia and Herzegovina was formed in the year 1991 and was recognized by the U.N.O, the U.S.A and other European countries. But the European countries wanted Bosnia and Herzegovina to remain confined only to Sarajevo and its suburbs. They wanted that an international group should govern it where the Croats would play a major role. But the Muslims wanted an Islamic nation free from Christian leadership.

Europe was in a quandary, unable to device any initiatives for fear of tripping in to a concerted Islamic invincible citadel. It was at this moment that America stepped in and resorted to a sort of balance, which led to a status quo currently being described as peace.

(h) Spain

Spain had long before been Christianized. But it came under the Islamic subjugation in the 8th century. Muslims ruled Spain from 711 to 1492. Catholics conquered Granada in the year 1492. When Philip came to power in the year 1610 he escalated the process of conversion of Muslims to Christianity and their migration from Spain. It was king Ferdinand who fought against the Islamic rule and defeated the Muslim rulers. He forced the Muslims for a conditional settlement in Spain that they would either embrace Christianity or leave the country. The Muslims were obliterated and Christianity was again restored with royal prominence.

After the success of Islamic Revolution in Iran Muslims again became thoughtful to retain their glorious and ancient homeland Spain. Islamic infiltration played a prominent role in European society, and Islamic demographic proliferation developed in harmony with the economic development of European countries. Spain was not an exception to this target. Islamic infiltration is a very common means for unbalancing the financial, cultural, political and social conditions of a country. To intercept the future destabilization Spain has taken a serious step to check the Muslim infiltration on its border with Morocco touching Melilla and Centa enclaves. But thousands of African

Muslims with a European destination sneak through the barbed wire fence with the help of professionals who teach them how to sneak through it. Spain had decided to build a concrete fence dotted with censors; Cameras and control towers have been installed and erected along its only 10 km long border in Melilla at a cost of 10 million dollars.

The Government of Spain has also planned to patrol the border by men in uniform round the clock. Trained ferocious dogs are deployed to nab the Muslim infiltrators. Nevertheless Spain is not free from Islamic troubles. In spite of all these security measures taken by the Spanish government the undercurrent infiltration on the border is still in vogue. The growth of disproportionate Islamic population within the country is again setting Spain on the epicentre of a communal volcano, which had once erupted in the 8th century.

On 11 March, 2004 there was a bomb blast in Madrid ravaging 4 trains that caused a death toll of 202 innocent civilians and seriously injured 650 persons. The Al-Qaeda, the terrorist outfit of Osama bin Laden, openly claimed responsibility for this attack which was inflicted as a warning against the crusaders. This bomb blast in Madrid brought many oblivious incidents to the lime-light. It proved the disappointment and inability of the European investigative authorities to achieve their goal in curbing the Islamic terrorists. One senior German Intelligence officer confessed in his own words-"Our security is much less integrated than our business. We have different languages while the terrorists speak only one language, Arabic. The extremists also move freely across the borders. we are far too fragmented across the borders. But the Islamic militants blend easily with the other immigrants from North Africa, the Middle East and elsewhere." This time also the Global Islamic Movement tested the nerve of Western sensibility in Spain to strengthen the foundation of Islamic renaissance in the middle of Europe.

(i) Macedonia

This ancient historic country of Europe has also been drawn into the Balkan war. About 32 per cent of the people of Macedonia are Muslims. The Albanians who now make up one third of the population largely inhabit in Western Macedonia. Now it is feared that an ethnic clash will lead to intensified fighting in and around the buffer zone separating Serbia from Kosovo and between the Albanian minority and government troops in Montenegro. Fighting has been reported between the ethnic Albanian Muslim militants and Macedonian troops near Macedonia's border with Kosovo.

Presently government, after having smelt the Islamic aggression and their dominating role in the social affairs, followed certain policies to curtail the Islamic aggression. It gives residence permit only to those Albanian Muslims that changed their Islamic names and hold a Christian name. There are many Albanian Muslim refugees in Greece to find job and good salary and now they have become the target of the Greece government's alienation policy.

(j) Kosovo

Kosovo recently has sprouted up as another Islamic sovereign nation in Europe. It is a state of South Siberia consisting of 2.5 million population. 90 per cent Kosovans are Muslims of Albanian origin. The Muslim separatists revolted for autonomy from the clutch of Serbian Christians. The Former-President of Yugoslavia, Slobodan Milosevic took some drastic steps to suppress the Islamic uprising.

Henceforth started the scene of violence and killings of civilians by the Serbian troops. Thousands were killed in the clash between the Serbian police and Muslim separatist Jehadi fighters. In this war 1.5 million people became refugees, 5000 Serbian soldiers died, 10 thousand were wounded and 12,000 civilians killed. After 9000 times of bombardment there arose the question of a peace treaty. On 10th June 1999 the military alliance of NATO stopped the bombardment on Yugoslavia.

The Serbian President Vojislav Kostunika who succeeded the former president Slobodan Milosevic admitted to the excesses of the Yugoslav security forces. Milosevic was also indicted by the U.N. Court for his security forces' crimes against the civilians of Kosovo.

Western democracy, a vulnerable ideology

Islam traps their enemies with the enemies' (non-Muslim's) net and hunts their enemies with its own weapon. To quote an example, Western jurisprudence advocates that a country would belong to those who establish their community as the majority community of that country. To define this law Prof. Holland says- "*A state is a numerous assemblage of human beings generally occupying a certain territory amongst whom the will of the majority (or the ascertainable class) of persons is by the strength of such a majority or class made to prevail against any of their members who oppose it.*"

The Supreme Court of the USA says- "*A state is a body of few persons, united together for the common benefits to enjoy peaceably what is their own and do justice to others.*"

According to these theories a society or race, whether ethnic or alien, would claim its authority over that country soon after it forms the majority of population.

This democratic theory propounded by the Western critics and followed by the non-Islamic countries all over the world makes Islam proceed to win over the non-Islamic lands with its weapon of "Grow and get."

3

The Thundering Cloud Expands

The Quran and Jehad are the ways of Islam and the Quran and the Sword are the Jewels of Muslims

– Global Islamic Movement

13. Pakistan, the Breeding Ground of Terrorists

"Pakistan is the first step of victory over India for the seven hundred year old Muslim invasion" -Arnold Toynbee

Pakistan is a vampire with Afganistan and Bangladesh as its two wings. The social infrastructure of Pakistan compounded with the religious impetus, financial bankruptcy, political imbroglio and administrative vendetta compels Pakistan to feed on terrorism.

It lacks any ancient history or any glorious past to inspire its citizens to lead the life of a civilian. This topples as a mercenary nation for its survival next to Afghanistan. Unlike the Islamic Gulf countries it has not been blessed with any natural boon for its enrichment. It is notoriously popular for its conspiracy and nefarious brain. For its survival it looks towards America for financial aid, towards Arabia for communal aid and towards India for its geo-political existence. It has an obscured past and uncertain future.

As a professional terrorist breeder Pakistan only wants sophisticated weapons from Euro-America to keep them engaged in subversive activities. It also wants to quench its thirst of terrorism by perpetuating the Jehadi war to segregate Kashmir from India as a principle of Global Islamic Movement. Afghanistan has its border with Russia. Religiously and fundamentally Afghanistan is a compatriot of Pakistan. It has the same record of non-Islamic ancient past and historic glory. Both are devoid of any historical past and national glory. Hence Afghanistan was used as a fighting force against the USSR through the mediation of Pakistan. It just acts as a commission agent of war. The weapons supplied to Afghanistan by the USA were transported through Pakistan. Thus Pakistan could acquire enormous lethal and sophisticated weapons sufficient for its military requirement.

Pakistan, the International Training Centre of Terrorists

Pakistan is the key Islmic country in the world that produces professional Jehadi fighters to be deployed in different countries for the spread of Islamic terrorism. The trainers, who are specialized in explosives in the USA, conduct these training centres. They make such instruments as are easily portable by the militants.

Pakistani militants and Talibans were operating some 28 secret guerilla camps in its occupied portion of Kashmir to train local Muslims to make Kashmir an Islamic country and separate it from India. The Talibans have stepped up their involvements since their control over Afghanistan. They are more daring, formidable and fortitude owing to their long history of fighting and war of success even against the former invincible USSR army.

On the other hand, the Pakistani soldiers are meted out to the Arabian countries for their requirement of army men to suppress their civil war and internal rebellion. Pakistan earns a lot by the supply of its army men to the Gulf countries. It has the largest Islamic army force besides the dare devil trained militants and suicide bombers in the world. Presently after the crumbling down of the USSR, America finds China as its great rival as a communist country. But Pakistan by its successful dishonest diplomacy has been able to maintain good relations with both America and China. It illegally misappropriated a large portion of land from India and consigned a piece of it to China and made her a friend in need.

Madrassas are the primary centres for the breeding of militants. There are 5000 strong madrassas in Pakistan with an enrolment of 600000 students. 300000 Mujahids have already been produced from these madrassas. By executing these camps Pakistan is doubly benefited. First, it produces trained Mujahids coming from different countries of the world and exports them to different centres of war in the world. Here war does not mean a fighting in the battlefield confined to sword and blood. Islamic war of Jehad implies multipurpose activities of attacking and curbing the enemy in different aspects of life, which is both physical and psychic. So by imparting militant training it gets enormous financial aid from the Gulf countries. America's C.I.A and F.B.I were hand in hand with the I.S.I of Pakistan for a long time. The knot of alliance has not yet been slackened. It is a profitable business for Pakistan. Apart from imparting some specific training like bomb explosion, secretly shooting of important persons, sabotage, collection of secret news and important papers, infiltration into the enemy defence force, the Jehadi fighters also get occupational training for their survival in enemy countries where they are infiltrated. Many frustrated, disappointed and unemployed Muslim youths are caught in this net to get this training and a good living. On the failure of survival in this way they are assured an enjoyable paradise after death. So this training profits Pakistan in many ways like population control, good earnings and militarisation of civil life etc.

In the year 1980 about 20,000 Islamic militant youths came from twenty different Islamic countries to get subversive training in Pakistan. Most of them were Arab Islamists. They were also the participants from Philippines, Kosovo, Bosnia and Herzegovina and Malaysia. Previously those who came to participate in the training were intended to fight for the liberation of Afganisthan committed to establish Islamic regimes in their own countries. Thus the movement that was staged to help liberate Afganisthan gave rise to a natural course of "Global Islamic Liberation Movement" with Pakistan as its centre of militant ramification with the I.S.I, its key organization. This was later popularly known as Armed Islamic movement spearheading the wave of new international terrorism. This has been sending its Mujahiddins all over Asia, Africa, the European countries and America to accelerate Islamic struggle.

As Pakistan and Afghanistan are parasitical in their national financial infrastructure, they have professionalized their training of terrorism. Pakistan is the largest producer and exporter of Islamic fundamentalists and Islamic terrorists of the World.

Terrorists fully utilize the most advanced instruments of Arab communication and information technology. They utilize the satellite telephone service and the services of powerful wireless sets. As a consequence, their activities have been more dangerous than ever before. Kidnapping, murder, hostage, exhortation, explosion, etc., are tune for them. It is also known that the terrorists produced by Pakistan are able to use atomic, chemical and biological bombs, the use of which is prohibited by International Law. But the terrorists are above the law.

Though Pakistan boasts about its Islamization of administration it also raised some institutions, which even train females in military training. Apart from imparting militant training to Islamic youths Pakistan also runs a 'finishing school', which imparts military trainings to women folk along with the Islamic tenets with reference to the holy Quran. Modern Pakistani people are now interested to camouflage themselves in this finishing school. The Gulf countries the feed majority of the Islamic madrassas used to produce fundamentalist militants.

The Islamic university in Islamabad is charged with harbouring mercenaries who had carried out terrorist acts in Egypt and Algeria. These institutions also train militants for raking up troubles in Central Asia and even in the Chinese province of Sin kiang. It is well known that the Taliban conquerors of two third portions of Afghanistan were trained Mujahids from the fundamentalist Islamic schools of N.W.F.P in Pakistan run by Maulana Hafizur Rehman, the leader of the Jamiat ul Ulema-e-Islami.

Inter Service Intelligence (I.S.I.) – A Psychic System to Produce Human Weapons for a Global Islamic Invasion

As a brain child of Mohammed Ali Jinnah, the founder of Pakistan, I.S.I was formally established in February, 1948. This body carried out its first assignment on October, 22,1947 with its mission of mercenary Pathan tribals of Kashmir valley. From its initial stage it has the notoriety of sabotage, kidnapping, plundering, etc. All these activities of the I.S.I suited well to U.S.A to use it for the debacle of communism in former U.S.S.R.

General Hamid Gul, the D.G of I.S.I had a major achievement which was the successful export of Pakistan's opium to far-flung lands all over the world in which he could accumulate huge amounts of money. Today it does not depend on the government for its resources. Apart from this, Pakistan gets the major portion of its expenditure from the business of heroine, charas, hasis, brown sugar, etc. Advertisements are published in Pakistan Magazines to meet the expenditure for the perpetuation of Jehad. There is also a huge flow of finance from the Gulf countries to provide militant training to the Islamic Jehadi fighters of different countries of the world. All these training camps of Islamic militants for subversive activities are conducted by the I.S.I.

Presently 25,000 I.S.I agents are working in different countries under 6 divisions. Those are 1) Joint Intelligence Axis, 2) Joint counter, 3) Intelligence Bureau, 4) Joint Intelligence North, 5) Joint Intelligent Miscellaneous, 6) Joint Signal Intelligence.

Out of the lethal weapons supplied by the U.S.A to fight against the U.S.S.R, I.S.I kept 60% of it for its own benefit. It also saved 35% of the total financial aid provided by the U.S.A. for the Afghan refugees.

The 2000 kms long Pak-Afghan border is used to raise militant training camps. Mercenary youths from Egypt, Algeria, Tunisia and Saudi Arab also come to get the training and create subversive activities in their own countries. It is no wonder that Muslim youths of European countries also come to be trained in Pakistan.

It generally so happens that wherever one finds a subversive incident in any part of the world, the activist must be a trained fighter under the guidance of I.S.I of Pakistan or a Jehadi fighter of Pak-Afghanistan.

At first the training procedure of the I.S.I was functioning according to the British system. But after the C.I.A of America trained more than 200 I.S.I officers according to the new system of intelligence, they are now able to spread their spider net everywhere.

These Jehadi training centres run by the I.S.I of Pakistan in Afghanistan have produced more than 300000 Islamic Mujahids popularly known as terrorists during the last 15 years. 90 thousand of them have been killed in the war fields of Afghanistan, Kashmir, Bosnia, Egypt, Algeria and Pakistan. 90 thousand of them are very active in Afghanistan under the patronage of the Talibans. 30 to 40 thousand of them have been serving in the International Islamic Brigade of Arabs. The rest of the trained Jehadi fighters are deployed in the Kashmir sector in India.

A newly formed group "Fidayeen" was first introduced by Laskar-e-Toiba. This is a post-Kargil militant group. It typically selects the mission where they cannot return alive. They have conducted some 25 sneak attacks on various army and security force installations since 2000.

The parent outfit of the Fidayeen, Laskar-e-Toiba, emerged as the most powerful pan Islamic outfit especially after the sneak in attack in the Red Fort at Delhi where three army men were killed. It is quite difficult to keep track of the Laskar militants as they use a set of code names. When a militant dies in operation; a new recruit with the same code name replaces him.

Lashkar-e-Toiba is the militant wing of the pan Islamic organisation. It has a strong troop of half a million Islamic trained terrorists in Lahore who are ever ready to fight for the cause of Islam. The well-armed militant Jehadi fighters of Lashkar are fighting in the Kashmir part of India propped up by the I.S.I. of Pakistan. Murkaz-e-dawat-ul-Irshad has its headquarters near Lahore. It runs more than 2000 madrassas with the aim to Islamise the whole of Pakistan and Kashmir. They hope that Islam will finally dominate the entire world. This organisation established the Jamia Dawat-ul-Islam (university of Dawat-ul-Islam) in 1989. Both the religious teachings of the Quran and militant training are imparted in this college. Their practical field of operation is Kashmir where many of the students either kill Indians or die for their holy cause.

Markaz-e-dawat-ul-Ershad rejects democracy as a Western form of Government, which is full of flaws. As a corollary it disapproves of all sorts of democratic means of political expressions like sloganeering, launching of strike or demonstration, peaceful protest, electoral politics, etc., as un-Islamic.

In 1987 Laskar-e-Toiba fought against the USSR in Afghanistan along with the Afghan Mujahiddins. After they won in the holy war against the largest country of the world, they turned out their attention towards India and since then the Jehad has been escalating in Kashmir. In spite of all these retaliatory, explosive and conspiratory activities of Pakistan to substantiate the Global Islamic Movement, the U.S.A doesn't realise its cunningness. Pakistan is nothing but a rootless parasitic chunk fed over mercenary business. This dollar fed, self-willed baby simply pretends as a porter of Euro-America by mediating between ex-U.S.S.R and Afganisthan in the past and by supplying on hire Jehadi fighters and Mujahids to the Gulf countries.

Pakistan is the only country in the world, which could allure U.S.A to run behind its mirage. When the USA remarked Pakistan as the terrorist producing country, the I.S.I instantly asked the Talibans ostensibly to close down the terrorist training centres. But these camps never ceased from its operation. It simply inverted its nameplate. The I.S.I of Pakistan run terrorist operation centres in Kashmir, the USA, Canada, Chechnya etc. Pakistan is utilizing the advantage of liquidation of visa restrictions made by India as a part of development of bilateral relations between the two countries. All the Pakistani students and students who came from other Islamic countries to get Jehadi training in Pakistan turned towards Indian madrassas.

On August 7, 1998 two bombs simultaneously exploded near the U.S.Embassy in Nairobi (Kenya) and Dar-es-Salam (Tanzania). More than 250 were killed and about 5,500 were injured. It was found that "Hizb Alla International" had its active hand in this bombing with Pakistan playing an important role. A man involved in this bombing, Mohammed Sadi, was arrested in Pakistan.

Pakistan conducted joint naval exercise with Iran in the Arabian Sea. The USA is the only enemy of Iran. Pakistan's ambivalent role is most surprising. It acts as a lackey of the U.S.A. and synchronomously acts as a cognate of Iran.

Pakistan has secret alliance with China. When Pakistan would raise its hood as an Islamic nation to sting America, China would automatically come forward to help Pakistan. The great Coco Island, about 20 nautical miles from the Andaman, is a strategically located isle in the Indian ocean and a part of Myanmar territory. For years it has been virtually under the Chinese control. International defence experts have detected inordinate and suspicious Chinese military activities there. The Myanmar government has allowed the Chinese to build roads within Myanmar and to mount powerful military installations near the great Coco Island and St. Mathew's island. The radar station on St. Mathew's Island is directly linked to China via its satellites.

China aims to have a strategic outpost in the Indian Occean with the aim of encircling India in its grand strategy. The Chinese-Myanmar military nexus threatens the safety and security of Singapore. New Zealand and Australia too are scared of the Chinese military presence, which is increasingly growing in the Indian ocean. These two white nations are under the protection of the U.S.A.

Pakistan, the Non-Nato Ally of the USA and the Chief Exporter of Terrorists to Create Insurgency in the USA

Pakistan is a country which produces and exports nothing but terrorists. As a nation it was created under compulsion by the colonial powers to weaken India. They were successful in their plan. But on the other hand their tilting towards and sympathy for Pakistan made them to create a never extinguishable flame in the guise of terrorism that would conflagrate like the spread of an all-consuming wild fire. Pakistan was born out of hatred and vengeance. This sense is conveyed by the Quran to the Muslims who are inspired to hate all those who are non-Muslims. This Islamic bigotry made them to continue war against all the non-Islamic nations of the world.

Engagement of Muslims in war against non-Muslim countries made them war mongers, war lords and war wallowing civilians. Political leaders diverted the attention of the Pakistani public towards India for their survival in power. Pakistan is bound to maintain an army and keep arms and ammunitions. An unproductive country shouldering such a great burden must lead towards bankruptcy. This situation favoured the colonial powers to grasp Pakistan as their mercenary sceptre. Democracy is a daydream in a country, which is synthesized by the Islamic thought. Hence the rulers of Pakistan followed the Islamic vendetta of succession "Tukth ya Takhta" (either the throne or the coffin) from Md Ali Jinnah and Liaqat Ali Khan to Pervez Musharraf. This principle of Islamic succession made the rulers opportunists, cunning and war-mongering. Pakistan has been playing a very cunning role to make both ends meet. In one way it hoodwinks Euro-American imperialist nations acting as their mercenary state against India to suppress its uprising and simultaneously shelters and nourishes Islsmic militancy as a part of its Islamic character to spread terrorism in all the Euro-American nations. Pak scientist Abdul Kadir Khan was involved in transferring atomic technology to Iran, North Korea and Lybia which are the three arc enemies of the USA. Pak first indicted the scientist to appease the USA as its ostensible ally but latter on pardoned him on grounds of Islamic racism.

Ardent youths flee from Pakistan to make their fortune in the developed Western countries. Those who are noble are not honoured. This situation favoured the developed nations to use it according to their will and pleasure. They aided Pakistan to spawn terrorists in innumerable training centres. In course of time the production of terrorists was professionalised in Pakistan. It became a factory of terrorists. Developed countries produce weapons and create markets for their disbursement. Similarly Pakistan also produces terrorists and creates markets everywhere in the world to dispose them.

Pakistan inevitably needs to produce terrorists for its survival. Moreover it became an authority of missile technology. The Gulf countries and other Islamic countries now are in need of these terrorists to take vengeance against Euro-America. Pakistan,

Afghanistan, Bangladesh, etc., are bound to stick to this profession just for their survival. Hence if the developed countries would set Pakistan free from their clutch, automatically the Gulf countries and other Islamic countries would come forward for its help. The ISI is well acquainted with the soft corners of Euro-America, particularly the USA and England. These countries maintain cordial relationship with Pakistan. Hence to use the ISI as their outrider would be more favourable for the Global Islamic Movement to penetrate in to Euro-America for a global victory. They are bound to use these terrorists for their protection, expedition, and invasion. No sooner had the pressure of Euro-American countries become lowered, the Gulf countries would come out to the open field and march ahead keeping these terrorists as their forefront army.

Pakistan's bombardment on the terrorist camps and its dissemination and propaganda that Pakistan is anti-terrorist is ostensible. There are fundamentalist Jehadi factions who oppose Musharraf's alliance with the USA for the latter's stance against Islamic terrorism and Sadam Hussain. Hence when Musharraf apprehended danger to his life after several attacks on him, he launched an attack against the Jehadi fighters. The moment Musharraf detached himself from the clutch of the USA, he would be blown off like scraps of straw. He knows it well that death is hovering over him in the stature of the same vampire who swept away the former President Zia ul Haq and his mentor Zulfikar Ali Bhutto.

14. India, the Largest Democratic Nation under the Crunch of Global Islamic Invasion

Once India, in the name of Bharat Varsh, was famous for its bravery, wisdom, naval trade, rich culture, literature and on the whole, for its ancient civilization. There were excellent heroines who braved death in the battlefield and preferred death entering into the funeral pyre, alive, rather than capitulating before the enemy force. But India failed. It failed like the great Roman Empire for one and the same reason. The reason of failure

> *of both is their lack of proper knowledge of Jehad. The war pattern of Jehad is quite different from the war pattern of all other races or civilizations of the world. Without the knowledge of Jehad and without an accurate preparation to face Jehad one cannot win in the Islamic war.*
>
> *– M.S. Golwalkar*

A secular democratic country with Muslims recognized as a national minority is the best means for the Muslims in the modern age to reach their goal i.e. to convert that country into an Islamic State. A simple example can be quoted about India, which favours the Muslims the best compared to any other country, which is in the operation theatre of conversion and Transformation of Civilizations. The political outlook, cultural enrichment, and national policies of India favour Islam. The largest democratic country of the world, with more than one billion population, India has recognized Islam as a special class minority. The present politicians with an indomitable desire to strengthen their political position have been turned down into power-loving wolves and appease the Muslims lavishly sacrificing the interest of the majority of 850 million population.

India faced the Jehadi war of Muslims since 712, which is rampant till today. One can feel the fervour of Jehadi war in every nook and corner of India. Medieval history of India is the history of Islamic aggression since Mohammed bin Kasim, Mohammed Ghazni, Mohammed Ghouri, Taimurlang, Ala-ud-din Khiliji, Mohammed Tughlak and Ibrahim Lodi who were restless invaders and true messengers of Islam. Mohammed Jahiruddin Khan nicknamed as Babur established his dynastic rule in India until India came under the subjugation of British rule.

Indians, mostly disorganized Hindus, are the key targets of Muslims. The majority of Hindus are just like puppets in the hands of corrupt politicians. Seven hundred years of Jehadi war against Hindustan presented to global Islam a land which is dividedly called as Afghanistan, Pakistan and Bangladesh. Now the above three are in unison fighting to free Kashmir from the clutch of India to declare it an independent Islamic country.

This part of India is presently under the third phase or the final stage of Transformation of Civilizations favouring Islam.

Government's Policy of Appeasement to Muslim Minority

(A nationalized policy that hastens the transformation of civilization through ethnic cleansing)

Government of India foolishly considers that it is only the ISI of Pakistan who is behind the scene to promulgate subversive activities in :ndia in general and Kashmir in particular. It has not yet realized the truth that it is the Global Islamic Movement, which is working behind all subversive activities throughout the country. Moreover Indian politicians and government authorities are quite insensitive to and ignorant of the fervour of Transformation of Civilizations, which has been difusesd over the Indian sky for about one thousand years.

Ostensibly India is a democratic secular country and it has many bilateral and multilateral relations with countries like the USA, Russia and China and it has initiated a policy of globalization to solve its economic difficulties. But practically and internally it is proceeding towards an Islamic solution to solve all its socio-cultural, linguistic, economic and all other national problems.

Indian Prime Ministers from Nehru to Manmohan Singh flatteringly favoured Islamic social development with special care and pampering attention. Mahatma Gandhi, throughout his political career, fought for Islam and died for Islam. He clamoured that the partition of India and formation of an Islamic land would be possible only over his dead body. .But soon after the partition of India he ahanged his voice and demanded compensation for Pakistan. Although Mohammed Ali Jinnah reproached Gandhi as the most inferior and nefarious person, Gandhiji flattered Jinnah. It is only Pandit Nehuru and Mahatma Gandhi who represented Hindu society but favoured the Muslims. The formation of Pakistan was a natural process of Jehad created under the strict discipline of the Transformation of Civilizations. Gandhi and Nehru only escalated the formation. Kashmir is not the end of the way. It is a station next to Pakistan. The procession of Islamic victory will reach its end at the terminus of Kanyakumari where the Indan soil touches the sea. Gandhiji died for the cause of Islam leaving behind a major political party which followed his appeasing policy very sincerely with fidelity and in a high order. Without any exception all the national political parties follow its foot prints. The first Prime Minister of India Pandit Nehru was the arch initiator to separate Kashmir and contrived another Islamic homeland in India.

In the midst of national secularism only the minority groups are privileged to impart religious education under government's full patronage. The national and traditional culture followed by the majority is completely ignored. Even if the Government enacts a law nationalizing all private educational institutions, the minority educational institutions are exempted from it because of the protection given by article 30 of the Indian Constitution.

Islamic madrasas (Madarsas) known as Islamic religious schools are the cradles of terrorists. These madrasas are the Jehadi factories. In Pakistan these create, harbour and shelter secessionists who are particularly meant to fight and kill the non-Muslims and convert a secular or non-Islamic country in to an Islamic nation. In India, some of these madrasas are found guilty of harbouring and training militants or Jehadi fighters. The Government of India spends millions to feed and maintain these madrasas in the name of privileges to the minorities. Government has least control over these institutions.

National education system of India is totally indecisive and detrimental for national enrichment. When a government changes the national policy of education changes besides bringing a change in the subject matter of history of the nation. There is also a parallel system of education in India where one is meant for the minority group and the other is for the rest of majority. People of minority community are fully guided by the government of India to teach religion in the schools where others are not authorized.

There are almost 50000 madrassas, the Islamic religious schools or breeding lands of Jehadi fighters functioning in India. A panel has been set up to monitor minority education including the modernization of madrassas on the basis of national policy of education by the Government of India since 1986. The Committee meant for the purpose will recommend the government on issues related to reservation, recognition and affiliation of minority education. Government channelises huge funds to run madrassas. Government collects tax from Hindu temples and monasteries and spends it lavishly to run madrassas and to meet the expenditure of Haj. But when the government proposes to set a National Board for Madrassas Muslim theologians term it as an imposition from above. Government of India would only finance them but cannot control it.

In Kerala alone there are 10000 madrassas, the largest number of its kind with 25000 Maulvis and 738000 students. The number of madrassas in Madhya Pradesh is more than 6000, which is next to Kerala. These madrassas impart Jehadi teaching to 400000 students through 12000 Maulvis. In Maharastra there are 2435 Islamic educational institutions comprising 4900 teachers and 20400 students. West Bengal comes next to Maharastra where there are 2116 madrassas with 10000 teachers and 90000 students. There are 1780 madrassas in Rajasthan that imparts Jehadi teaching to 25000 students through 3600 religious teachers. 4000 teachers are working in 2002 madrassas in Assam with 120000 students. There are 86 Maulvis in Delhi training up 3772 students in 1161 madrassas. Karnataka has 1884 Maulvis and 85000 students in its madrassas. The number of madrassas in Andhra Pradesh is 721. There are 2000 Maulvis and 76000 students reading in these madrassas. In the late 90's when Congress Government was in power it enhanced the salary of the Maulvis to a considerable amount to appease the minorities.

Infiltration and growth of unwanted population is considered as the greatest barrier for the development of a country. India exposes itself as a Paradise of Pakistani and Bangladeshi infiltrators. Developed countries of the world have implemented many restrictive laws to check infiltration. Some European countries don't allow the non-whites to reside in their land. Even many Asian countries like Japan, Myanmar, Singapore, etc., have resorted to stringent steps to obstruct infiltration. Myanmar evacuated all Bangladeshi Muslims from its country. Singapore implemented the policy of beating of infiltrators with canes besides minimum one-year's rigorous imprisonment.

In India, though there is constitutional provision to check the infiltration, it is quite the reverse in practice. Corrupt Indian politicians still hanker for infiltrated Muslim population who are left worthless, useless, unwanted and rejected like scraps of paper thrown into the dustbin in their motherland Bangladesh and Pakistan. They are hailed as heroes in India simply for their power to cast their votes in favour of the parties who welcome them. Muslim vote bank is nothing but a mirage that allures the infatuated and myopic foolish politicians.

About half a million terrorists are waiting on the Indo-Pak boarder to infiltrate into India to initiate subversive activities in this country.

The Indian film industry particularly Bollywood is one of the largest industries of the world. It has profound influence on the financial and socio-cultural life of Indians. The majority of the Indian film stars and producers act as lackeys of I S I agents. Daud Ibrahim spends 60 per cent of the total outlay of the Hindi film industry. Bungalows of many film stars have been converted into the safe asylums of ISI agents.

Indian Muslims with a visa in hand go to Pakistan and openly deliver their opinion in favour of liberating Kashmir from India. "Trans line of control" families make matrimonial alliances. Even the son of a Muslim leader of India can get married to the daughter of a Muslim leader staying in Pakistan although the parents of the couple are against Indian integrity and both the countries are belligerent since the day of independence.

The world famous centre of Islamic thought is in Deoband, India. Almost one and half century old this centre is the key source of expansion of Islamic thought and constitution of Islamic law on different aspects of Islamic life. This school of thought emphasizes 3 most important Islamic factors that- (1) Man is born smarter than women; (2) Music is evil. (3) Education for girls beyond 18 years is a wastage of time. The Dar-ul-Ulum (Centre of learning) Deoband's rigid interpretation of Islam is the ideological foundation on which the Taliban movement as well as many of the hardliner religious groups in Pakistan are based.

The Muslim lobby is so powerful and strong in Indian politics that militant organizations and separatist groups after the commitment of murder or bomb-blast openly claim to have committed the holocaust and they even challenge the largest democratic parliament. Whenever and whereever any event relevant to Islam takes place, Muslims in India pass their comment openly and directly, without considering its results whether it hurts the national interest or the interest of the majority.

After the destruction of the World Trade Center, the Imam of Delhi Jama Masjid openly opposed the tension hit USA and supported the call of Jehad given by the ruling Talibans in Afganistan against the USA and its allies and asked the Prime Minister of India to shut up his mouth and keep quiet on this issue. As quoted by him –"If any Islamic country or its Ulema (clergy) announce Jehad, it is obligatory for each and every Muslim in the world to support it morally and express it openly." "It would be better if Vajpayee (the then Prime Minister of India) keeps his mouth shut. We support the Taliban Jehad of cry" clearly indicates that the Imam as an Islamic leader of religious concern is above the law and constitution of a country, which is branded as a nation of the largest democracy. His statement on the Prime Minister of India denotes as if the P.M is an irresponsible authority and he would be scorned for the lapse of duty.

During the USA–Iraq war Muslims throughout India launched demonstrations and torched the USA flag and solicited the Muslim community to repudiate foreign beverege signifying that USA is against India. The Government was a mute spectator of all these scenes.

Urdu, an Islamic religious language and one of the national languages has been honoured as the largest non-provincial national language of India and the most influential language next to English. The national language Hindi is gradually abdicating its position to Urdu. India opened its first Urdu channel in New Delhi which could be heard in Gulf States, the USA and U.K.

Even there are Indian Urdu newspapers like "Da'wat" which openly gives its statement in support of Iran's nuclear power and challenges the World Islamic Community to unite and fight against the Israelis to rescue the Palestinians from their clutch.

Though India is a majority Hindu state, the homeland of ancient Aryans, Nehru did not like this to be the land of Aryan's progeny. If Gandhi and Nehru had their contribution for the formation of Pakistan, Nehru alone was responsible to convert Kashmir, a noblest chunk of India into an Islamic majority state, where Muslims enjoy first class citizenship with special privileges incorporated for them into the Indian Constitution in article 370. Successive Prime Ministers ruled India claiming themselves as his noble successors for half a century only by animating the appeasing policy to the minority communities in general and Islam in particular. Fifty years of political tendency to perpetuate the appeasing policy pulverized the original national feeling of this land and it favoured the Muslims for all round development of their social life including Islamic birth proliferation, which raised the Islamic population 4 times more than what it was 50 years ago.

Government of India is simply acting as a lackey to the minority community, which obviously proves that India is hastening to be another Pakistan with in 2020. Some instances are as follows -

The Indian Constitution advocates the right of equality to all citizens. But the minority communities in India are treated more than equal. The Muslims have formed majority community group in Jammu and Kashmir. There they enjoy special class privileges under article 370 of the Indian Constitution. As long as there is temporary article 370 in the frame of the Indian Constitution with its full swing of implementation, there is unobstructed danger on Indian national life.

While Jammu and Kashmir is burning under heavy communal conflagration Government of India is grueling for round table sessions with the terrorists to come down for an amicable settlement. In a bid to promote domestic tourism in the Kashmir Valley the Central government declared to imburse airfare for all group A and B employees who utilize their leave travel concession. Here the record of killings in the valley quite contradicts the actions of the government.

The Indian Constitution lays over emphasis on the minorities. They are given special banking facilities and many other facilities, which are not available to the common citizens of India. They are not bound to abide by the common civil code. Government of India has incorporated a National Minorities Financial Corporation (NMFC) cxclusively for the development of minority class. A huse sum of money is allocated in this corporation, which is given to them on a loan basis with a meager interest of 3-4% whereas the rest of the poor of non-minority general community draws loan from the bank with an interest, which is some 5 times more than what a minority draws. Accordingly the Government of India has allocated Rs 95686 millionin the 9th five-year plan (1997-2002) for the empowerment of the 145 million minority population.

A Muslim is encouraged to visit Mecca with full cooperation from Central and state Governments. Finance and material assistance is provided to each Muslim who qualifies for a pilgrimage to Mecca. Every year more than one 100000 Indian Muslims visit Mecca since 2000 A D and Government of India spends more than Rs. 25,000 per Muslim visitors (it is proposed to enhance to Rs. 45,000 per head) from the state exchequer. Besides, there are other facilities, which a Muslim pilgrim avails as a national religious tourist. Every non-Muslim Indian unwittingly spends from his own pocket to meet this expenditure. Very fawningly the Government of India contributes to the pilgrims, whereas the Quran strictly rejects pilgrimage with the help of other's aid. The Imam of Kaaba instils in the minds of the pilgrims that Government of India has no right to keep Kashmir as a federal state because Kashmir has become a Muslim majority province. It must be segregated from India to be declared as an Islamic country. The Imam quotes the examples of the Muslims of Afganisthan, Palestine, Bosnia, etc., who are fighting to liberate their lands from non-Islamic rulers.

Though the Government of India is fully aware of these facts, still it remains reticent simply to appease the Muslims.

The Government of India is alert about providing all sorts of assistance to a Muslim pilgrimage bound for Mecca. But it seems to be less concerned about the protection of the life and property of the non- Muslim minority community in Kashmir. When a non-Muslim flees from the land to escape from the persecution of terrorists, eventually all his assets are occupied by those marauders who had chalked out the plan to drive the non-Muslim minorities from the land of Kashmir according to their law of Islamic expansionism in the name of Jehad. In all the provinces other than Kashmir a man filching a cucumber is put under prosecution and treated as a culprit. In the prison he languishes his days even for years together. But in Kashmir those who are entangled in evacuating a community which is a part of the main stream of Indian national life are honoured as freedom fighters and not as secessionists. Government of India comes down to have discussions with them round the table in anticipation of successful agreements. They are afforded royal treatment when they are in prison and media persons disseminate them as revolutionary freedom fighters.

Indian Muslims take pride of Babur, an invader, more than Goutam Buddha, who enlightened the whole world as a revolutionary preacher and propagator of peace and non-violence. Muslims in general are irritated at espousing the reconstruction of Babri Masjid in Ayodhya as well as the demolition of Bamyan Buddha of Afghanistan.

When the Shahi Imam of Delhi stridently declared his support to justify the demolition of the Buddha statue in front of a gathering of Namajists of two lakh Muslims on the eve of Id, government of India did not react on his comment.

When Sahabano Begum, wife of Mohammed Ahamed Khan, filed a suit for her maintenance against her husband's proclamation of Talaq (Islamic system of divorce which takes no time to be worked-out) the Supreme Court made a decree on April 23rd, 1985 ordering her husband to provide maintenance to her. Except some isolated intellectuals, the Muslim Community as a whole decried against this court verdict libeling it anti-Islamic (Even some public representatives in government reiterated the honourable court as communal). The Constitution of India was again amended to preserve the religious interest of the minorities defying the national interest.

A hair of Mohammed has been preserved since 1700 A.D in India in the repository of Hazratbal mosque in Kashmir. This collection is preserved under tight security as a symbol of historical fact, archaeological monument, religious emblem and national pride. Government of India spends millions of rupees for its protection and preservation. When it was whisked in the year 1963, there was a tumultuous uproar which even sacked the government of Kashmir.The wave of fury was mitigated after the hair was put back. Nevertheless to prove its authenticity a committee was formed including many Muslim leaders of national fame and a representative from Mecca.

In the year 1993 again there was a trouble on its security by some Pakistani militants and Indian Muslim secessioinists. When attempt was made by the government of India to nab the culprits, the minority leaders raised the problem of sacrilege of the mosque by the intrusion of army men. The government failed in its attempt to nab the militants and to expropriate the mosque from their clutch. They failed in their mission when the militants threatened to blast the mosque from inside. After 30 days of seizure of the mosque the government of India bowed before the demands of the militants and announced unconditional release of all the incarcerated anti-national elements with an assurance of security provision up to their dispersion. Government of India comes with all its aids of constitutional power to safe guard the interest of the minorities even hacking the national interest.

A similar incident took place in Mecca on December 20, 1979 where 200-armed militants seized the shrine. Immediately 300 soldiers entered the mosque, killed 120 militants on the spot. The rest were nabbed and publicly beheaded for their unholy attempt on Jan 10, 1980. But appeasement has its own distinction. Government of India, representative of more than 1 billion civilians, is ever ready to sacrifice the interest of the nation for the interest of its vote bank.

Presently the militants are the most power controlling authorities in India. Their release from imprisonment is made easy. As formalities they kidnap the daughter of a central minister or hijack the boeing plane or some often officers of high profile for a conditinal release of imprisoned terrorists. The terrorists and the seccessioonists of Kashmir are given the statues of freedomfightes.

Every nation has its national song that reflects the national significance and so is the case of India regarding its national song Vande Mataram. During its freedom movement the revolutionary freedom fighters proceeded towards the gallows to be hanged chanting the song Vande Mataram. This song inspired millions of people to emancipate the country from the clutches of British colonialism. But because Md Ali Jinna the founder of Pakistan opposed it during the Kakinada session of Congress emphasizing the song to be non-Islamic. This most highlighted song was later stepped down simply to appease the Muslim minorities. In the post independent era Congress posed itself to be the party responsible to abolish slavery. It entertained the chanting of Vande Mataram at the beginning of its party sessions. But this tradition of Congress also came to an end when it was strongly opposed by its Muslim members in its Calcutta session.

The beginning of this century saw the BJP emerging as a standard bearer of all that was akin to nationalism. On March 11, 2004 some 54 Muslims belonging to the BJP were ostracized from their society and were forbidden to have relation with their family members. Their only sin was that they favoured Vande Mataram as a national song. Their marriage was also proscribed by the Mufti, the religious head of the mosque of Agra, who also corroborated that the song would lead Muslims to hell. If the expelled Muslims wished to revert to Islam they were required to cleanse their soul of the unclean thoughts and remarry according to Islam. None of the political leaders dared to openly come out to protest against this prohibitory order, which is not conducive for a healthy social and national tradition and particularly that which declares the chanting of the national song a sin. All the people sipped the shame in a draught. Such incidents take place in a country that comes under the orbit of the second phase of the Transformation of Civilizations. At this stage people lose their conscience to differentiate between the code of conduct that suits the nation and that which injures the nation. Countries coming under this stage also declare that chanting of national song by the civilians is not compulsory.

Being pressurized by the minority community the government of India recognized the optional choice of chanting the national song. Owing to an objection made by a student of a minority community in Kerala the Supreme Court passed an order that nobody can be compelled to chant the national song. The people of the Philippines where the court asked the government not to compel its citizens to chant the national song experience the same fate.

The cow is the most respected species of 850 million Hindus in India and the national animal of the land since the beginning of Indian cultural tradition. It is butchered every day in thousands in almost 7000 abattoirs of India in spite of violent protests made on behalf Hindus to ban cow slaughter. To have an Islamic link all the animals including cows, calves, buffaloes, etc., are butchered by Halal, the Islamic process of killing an animal by cutting its throat leaving it to die fluttered in utter pain. Abul Ala Maududi, the founder of Jamat-e-Islami in his book 'Rasila and Missile' writes- 'In countries where cow has not been considered as a sacred animal, slaughter of cow may not be essential but in a country like India where it is considered as a sacred animal by Hindus it is necessary to slaughter cows and it is necessary that those Hindus who are converted to Islam must consume beef to become a reliable convert.'

This principle has been followed as a rudimental religious principle of Islam by majority of Muslims in India. Different political parties who compete to appease the Muslims to get their community vote have also raised this to the rank of a key point in their national political agenda; that they will not ban cow slaughter in India if the Muslims would help them to come to power with their organized community vote.

Regarding the appeasement policy of the Government of India to the Muslim minorities the case of Sri Ram temple versus

Babri Masjid may be quoted. There was a temple in the U.P province of India, which was constructed in memory of an Indian hero Sri Ramchandra, on his birthplace. This hero has been worshipped as an incarnation of God since the inception of Hindu Culture and religion. This is a matter of prehistoric antiquity, which dates back some thousands of years. Temple after temple has been constructed on this site after the existing one gets dilapidated. Millions of people of India and abroad visit this temple every year.

It was only after the invasion of an Afghan invader Mohamed Jahiruddin Khan nicknamed as Babur (tiger) for his ferocity who demolished the cliff of the temple and gave it the shape of an Islamic expansionism. Since then it is termed as the Babri Mosque. The Government of India knows it well but dares not to return it to Hindus for fear of Muslim minorities.

On the other hand a large number of mosques and monuments are demolished by the Saudi regime for the extension of hospital, kings palace and for the beautification of the city.

Minorities are represented in every sphere of life. Infiltration from Bangladesh and Pakistan into India continues unabated in millions. Still it is unobstructed and on the contrary many politicians for narrow gains welcome the infiltrators. Arabic, as the religious language of Muslims, is propagated through Sahitya Academies, literary institutions incorporated in all the provinces of India although each province has its own 2000 years old flourishing language, literature and script. Madrassas or Islamic religious schools are encouraged in thousands throughout India to impart Islamic religious education, which is completely denied to the Hindus. The preservation and propagation of Hindu culture, the national culture as defined by Westerners according to law, is completely denied priority on Government level on the ground of the Government being described as secular. The conversion of Hindus in to Islam and marriage of Hindu girls either by force or by coaxing is a common phenomenon.

Although the people of the majority class of India, the Hindus, want the government to take drastic steps to control the birth rate and amend the Constitution of India honouring the common civil code to this effect, the government is quite reluctant and indifferent to take any steps to minimize the spate of growth of population. The only reason is that the Muslims as a minority community are not in favour of birth control. They have the capacity to tug down a party in power if it takes any step in this regard and hurts their Islamic sentiment. The norm of minimum age limit for marriage is strictly obsertved for the Hindus. No sttention is given to stall the minimum age limit of marriage for the minority communities. Muslim boys in rural areas marry within the age limit of 13 to 14 and breed children to help increase the Islamic population in the national and international level. When Salim, a boy of 18 of the village Mewat (Gurgaon) spurned to marry a girl of 14 for the sake of higher study, it became national news.

Though the population of India exceeded one billion and life existence has become a serious question for millions of young men and women, suicide and death out of hunger has become a day-to-day affair, unemployment problem has exceeded its limits, the Government is completely unconcerned about population control as it seriously hampers the minority interest. The Non-Muslim population of India including the business class, bureaucrats, farmers and the Christians strictly adheres to birth control. A tendency has developed in the couples of 1980s to be satisfied with one or two children. Those who married towards 1990 restricted their number of children to one. Except some countable Muslim bureaucrats the rest of the community observe their religious policy very strictly, adding fuel in the fire of birth proliferation. Many Muslims in India have in their mind that the only way to bring back the Islamic dominance over India is to increase Muslim population.

Some preventive measures like TADA, POTA, etc., are disgraced and violently condemned by the political parties on the pretext that these are anti-minority acts. Condemnation of any law, any amendment, any argument or any debate that goes against the interest of the minority community is a common practice of present politicians, particularly Communist, Congress and congress-oriented political parties.

The post of Chief Minister of Jammu and Kashmir for half a century was streamed on family tradition. Invariably all the Chief Ministers of Jammu and Kashmir plead for the special status of Jammu and Kashmir owing to its Muslim majority. The Chief Ministers of this state are projected with high profiles and the state provided with special financial packages, which in comparison are far above all other states of India. The Prime Minister's announcement to make the airport of Jammu and Kashmir international is another step of appeasing this state.

Adding fuel to the fire the Government of Jammu and Kashmir took a decision to implement the controversial "Grant of Permit for Resettlement Act 1982" which enables the settlement of the Muslims who had migrated to Pakistan after partition.

The State Government formed with the majority of Muslims always sticks to the policy that suits the interest of the Muslims only. In spite of the request, warnings and comments of the Union Government and the people of the rest of India to the state of Jammu and Kashmir to be alert and take legal action against the terrorists, the Jammu and Kashmir Government released the dreaded terrorists defying world opinion. As a result of such steps that favour the militants, more than 150000 people have fallen victims to the Jehadi fighters.

Spate of Infiltration and Disproportionate Growth of Islamic Population – A Death Knell for Hindus

"Disproportionate growth of Islamic population" that disintegrated India in the year 1947 is again on the rise in many parts of this country threatening its national integrity. After Kashmir fell into the Islamic cauldron of Jehad the Global Islamic Movement has targeted other parts of India for the formation of another Islamic homeland.

Pakistan was divided into two parts at the time of its formation – East Pakistan and West Pakistan. West Pakistan had a thin population but vast land. East Pakistan was overpopulated but land was not comparatively extensive. Soon after the formation of Pakistan in August 14, 1947 West Pakistan started financial exploitation of East Pakistan. Earlier non-Muslim (Hindu) refugees came to India in millions as permanent settlers. But after the partition of India and formation of Pakistan, Muslims of Bangladesh came to India as infiltrators to escape from their financial adversity. During the sixties the Government of Pakistan was informed by a secret survey that the explosive population of East Pakistan would reach 200 million towards the end of the last century. So to escape from this dreadful situation the Government of Pakistan directly and indirectly encouraged infiltration into India.

After East Pakistan was converted into independent Bangladesh, the process of infiltration accelerated more than ever before. The Government of Bangladesh also realized that the expulsion of its own people into India is the only way to solve the population problem of its nation.

Apart from Bangladesh government's attempt there were numerous agents and organizations in Bangladesh whose profession was to assist the people of Bangladesh to have an easy access to India. Bangldeshi Rifles also swell their pockets by helping infiltration.

Like any other Islamic countries of the world, there is no provision for the protection of minorities in the constitution of Bangladesh. Between 1979 and 1984 the Government of Bangladesh settled 400000 Muslims in the beautiful tract of Chittagong. When the situation became explosive the Government sought a military solution and thousands of refugees crossed over the border to India.

Between 1971 and 1981 Bangladesh census records show a reduction of 3900000 in the minority population. Between 1981 and 1989 people with a population of 3600000 from the religious minorities were missing from that country. Tripura has a 867 km border without any natural barrier with Bangladesh and Assam has about 300 km border with Bangladesh.

A group of intellectuals in Dacca is seeking to legitimize the migration of Muslims to the adjoining areas of Northeastern regions of India by incorporating the theory "lebensraum" or living space in support of infiltration.

Infiltration into Manipur has been in full swing. The Muslim infiltrators have settled in different corners of the state. Neither the government of India, nor the government existing in Manipur is alert or vigilant of this dreadful situation.

Owing to his Islamic bigotry Saadullah, former Chief Minister of Assam, allowed infiltration from Dacca and Rajsahi districts of pre-partition Pakistan. Silcher and Nowgang districts lost their Assamese character. Muslim strength in the state Assembly grew from 6 in 1957 to 28 in 1978. In 1983 the number of Muslim infiltrators was 5 million in Assam.

Muslim population unprecedently grew up in the lower and middle parts of Assam besides its two hilly districts since 1971. According to the 1991 census the minority Muslims constitute 28% of the state's total population of 22 million people. In the census report of 2001 their population increased by more than 30%. It became 63,73,204 in the year 1991. In the districts of Golpara and Barpeta, the Hindu population is left far behind the Muslim population. Muslims are trying to topple their population in the districts of Dhubri, Karimganj and Helakand. Census report of 2005 reveals 74% growth of Islamic population compared to 30% of Hindus. Similarly Muslims grew up to 66.57% compared to the 33.03% of Hindus of Kachhar district. In the district of Karimganj growth of Muslims was 57.63% in proportion to the Hindu growth of 21.20%. Muslim infiltrators out numbered the indigenous Assamese particularly the Bodos in the Bodo Autonomous Council areas.

Out of 23 districts of Assam, the Muslims have over populated the Hindus in 6 districts. Out of 126 legislative assembly seats, the Muslims are the deciding factor for 55 seats. The minority vote bank is obviously vital to all parties.

Infiltration from Bangladesh is beyond the capacity of the Government of India to control. It is not tenable to check on the Indo Bangladesh border, which is 1060 km. long along north Bengal. There are many entry points of illegal immigrants (like Hili in south Dinajpur) where everyday nearly one hundred people cross over into India. The B.S.F. authorities catch only one out of 200 infiltrators. Others escape after bribing some middlemen who facilitate their smooth infiltration.

In a conference held at Chandigarh, the Defence Minister George Fernandes informed on September 24, 2003 that every month 100000 citizens from Bangladesh infiltrate into India which fact in a threat to its internal security.

As Islam is directly linked with politics, the growth of Islamic population has a direct effect in the state administration. One such instance can be quoted from the State politics of West Bengal in connection with its Islamic population. In the year 1952 a number of Muslim M.L.A.s in West Bengal were 22. In the year 1982 this number increased to 43. Just in 30 years and in 8 consecutive elections the number of Muslim M.L.A.s doubled. This was in proportion to the growth of Muslim immigrants from Bangladesh to India by infiltration. The number of infiltration every year remains almost 2 million. Similarly in the Dhubri district of Assam, 5 M.L.A.s out of 7 are Muslims. Now it has become a Muslim-dominated area of infiltrators.

Nine border districts of West Bengal viz. South 24 Parganas, North 24 parganas, Nadia, Murshidabad, Malda and West Dinajpur, 4 districts of Bihar viz-Purnea, Katihar, Kishanganj and Araria and 10 districts of Assam viz. Dhubri, Baspeta, Bongaigaon, Nalhari, Kokrajhar, Lakhimpur, , Darrang, Nasgaon and Kamrup have become highly explosive of infiltrated population. It seems as if these districts are extensions of Bangladesh.

According to an intelligence report these are one million infiltrators in West Bengal. There are almost one hundred villages in West Bengal, which is entirely devoid of Hindus. Hindus of these villages are either killed or expelled or converted into Islam. Out of 224 Assembly constituencies in West Bengal Muslim infiltrators in 80 constituencies decide who would come to power.

There are unrecognized madrasas in West Bengal whose number far exeeds those of the recognized ones. The numbers of such madrassas and Khaliji madrassas (schools run by mosques) are over 4000 in West Bengal while the government aided and recognized ones are almost 500.

Infiltration has reached an alarming stage in West Bengal and the North Eastern States. The entire area of North East would very soon plunge into a Kashmir-like situation. Around the suburbs of Kolkata, Bangladesi infiltrators are crossing over and settling down in Jhuggi clusters. Mostly these infiltrators are involved in large-scale illegal trading. They have set up their colonies and now dominate the local community.

As per the 1971 Census report, the population of Murshidabad was 2,94,024. But in the 1991 census report it reached 6 million. Within a span of 20 years the population increase in Murshidabad had been to the tune of about 2 million, which means an increase of 66 per cent.

An example can be quoted about the demographic change between Muslims and non-Muslims residing in two different places of a Muslim dominated and non-Muslim dominated country.

In August 15, 1947 Murshidabad district, which then had 52 per cent Muslim population, was initially slated to be included in Pakistan. Khulna district, which had 52 per cent Hindu population, was to come to India. Later, as per the terms of Radcliff award, the Murshidabad remained in India and Khulna went to Pakistan. Today there is about 14 per cent of Hindu population in the whole district of Khulna as against 52% in the year 1947 whereas in Murshidabad district today's Islamic population is 70 per cent. The demographic change of these two districts shows that the Hindus in Bangladesh and Pakistan are reduced from the a minority to a microscopic minority whereas the Muslims in India are increasing their number by leaps and bounds. Bhatia Muslims' infiltration from Bangladesh into India would again one day stand it on the verge of partition. It is expected that the number of infiltrators in Bihar would exceed 1.5 million towards 2000.

The river Padma, in the district of Murshidabad, was divided in to 8 parts. Each part was used as an infiltrating track for the migrants. Indian Bhatia Muslims helped Bangladeshi Bhatia Muslims in infiltration. After crossing the river it was not tenable to identify who is an alien and who is a national. Also there are some places where there is no trace of any line or mark of partition between the two countries. This helps the infiltrators a lot.

After the formation of Bangladesh many Urdu-speaking Muslims who could not return to Pakistan, stayed back in Bangladesh. There they were persecuted and ill-treated by the Bengladeshi civilians. They gradually infiltrated and settled down in Kishanganj in Bihar and Khidirpur, Matiaburuj and Raja Bazar areas at Kolkata.

The most infiltration-affected district of Bihar is Kishanganj and of West Bengal, Maldah. These two districts are the gateway of infiltrators from Bangladesh. There are many Indian agents or mediators who help the infiltrators reach a safe place or the place of destination. In Bihar the districts like Kishanganj, Madhubani and Ardia are declared Muslim majority districts. Police report confirms that thousands of Madrassas are opened in the border areas of Indo-Myanmar as a symbol of Islamic demographic invasion of India.

In Kishanganj district of Bihar Bhatia Muslims double the population of Hindu natives of that district. "Necky passport" is a word, which is rampart in these areas. It implies that the soldiers of Border Security Force after receiving their due share of bribe push a kick holding the neck of the infiltrators. The infiltrators create a situation of terror in the border areas to such an extent that even the Indian Muslims fear to open their mouth against the infiltrators. The local non-Muslims, out of fear, sell their immovable properties and flee to a safe place.

Those who are nabbed are put into prison. After their term of imprisonment is over they are taken back to the border to be handed over to the Bangladeshi rifles. But the Bangladeshi authorities don't take any interest to receive them citing their non-availability of Bangladeshi identity. Again they are brought back.

Bangladeshi infiltrators have settled down in millions in the slum areas of Bombay particularly in Prabhadebi, Andheri-Sakinaka, Dongri, etc. Due to the change of policy in the exports and imports of gold, no profit remained in this smuggling.

Hence the foreign dwellers launch the smuggling trade of AK-47, Sten gun and sub-machine gun that are available for half the rate of the original price. The selling of these weapons has an unexpected rise in these areas.

Population of Muslims in the border areas of Gujrat has unexpectedly increased and the Hindu majority towns have almost been converted into Muslim majority cities. In many areas of Kutch like Koteswar, Lakhtar, Luna, Hajiipeer, Khabdi, Bela, Lonadara, etc., are under the rapidly growing population of Pakistani infiltrators. At every 5 kms. one can find a mosque. Presently there are 400 mosques on the frontier tract where the Maulvis from U.P., Bihar, Maharashtra, West Bengal and Haryana come and teach Islam. Being directly under the care of the I.S.I. agents of Pakistan, these institutions have close contacts with Muslim education and welfare society like Jamia Sofia and Dar-ul-Ulum.

The border of Rajsthan is also not an exception. A large number of Muslim infiltrators have begun to settle down in the border districts of Rajasthan as daily wage earners. Now they have become a unit of terror for the natives of these areas. A large number of mosques are being constructed in the border areas, which are the breeding ground of communalism. Many districts like Jaisalmer are becoming over-crowded with the Muslim infiltrators.

Pakistani infiltrators coax Hindu girls and later marry them. Then they send the women folk to Pakistan. Among these infiltrators are many Pakistani spies who are deployed by the I.S.I in subversive activities in India. If they are nabbed with much pain and strain, the court easily releases them on bail giving them an opportunity to join their infiltrator relatives in the districts of Jaisalmer in Rajasthan.

Earlier Bangladesh infiltrators were in countable numbers in Punjab. But after they detected their bright future in Punjab owing to the growing demand of cheap labourers in the state they moved towards Punjab. The small-scale industry-adding farmers are naturally inclined to exploit this factor to their advantage without considering the ill effects of their concentration in the state.

In Punjab and Haryana they are indispensable as farm labourers during their harvest season. The terrorists of Punjab and rangers of Pakistan use them as expendable couriers. There is a Bangladeshi colony in trans-Jamuna area in Delhi.

The whole of Kerala has been coming under the glare of Muslim fundamentalists. Mosques are mushrooming in Kerala over-night. Increasingly the mosques have become the focal point in people's lives and it is from here that extremists are seeking to effect fundamental changes in the psyche of the north Kerala Muslims. Babri Masjid was never an issue to Kerala's Muslims. But today people have been urged to rise and protect their religion against the Hindus who are tainted as a whole to be responsible for their hurt of religious sentiment.

Hundreds of people back from grueling years in the Gulf find that they have neither employment nor income. What they had earned in the Gulf does not suffice them even to complete their houses. The local mosques provide a welcome refuge to vent their frustrations against an ingrate state. Pushed by the grinding poverty and severe psychological trauma of years in the deserts of the Gulf, they become easy prey to this Islamic communalism.

The heart of national administrative operation, New Delhi, is also not free from this contagious disease. There is a swarm of Muslim infiltrators from Bangladesh stretched in all parts of this metropolis. In New Seemapuri there are more than 2000 slum houses of Muslim infiltrators. Such slum areas are stretched in Jahangirpuri, Karawal Nagar, Sarai Rohilla, Sanjay Colony, in New Delhi, Narudra Niketan, New Kamchanpuri, Motia Khan, Matiamahal, Shaheed Basti and Adarsh Nagar. As they are the immigrants and have come with an aim for their livelihood, they offer their service in a comparatively cheaper wage and humble behaviour This affected the local wage earners and decimated the balance of service. But they are well treated by the foot-licker politicians with a provision of ration cards. In Delhi alone there are more than 1 million Muslim infiltrators.

121 madrassas and 146 mosques have been raised in the border of U.P and Bihar. On the border of Nepal and Bihar

hundreds of mosques are under construction. They are used as asylums. The I.S.I. use Bihar as its entrance gate into India. Bihar is the most suitable place for militants, the I.S.I agents or any other subversive activists to spread their network. The I.S.I. agents easily enter into India through the 1700 km long stretch of Bihar-Nepal border.

The states like Karnataka, Madhya Pradesh, Odisha, etc., are not far from the clutch of the I.S.I. Fact is that the I.S.I. activities in these states don't come to light. Hence it does not come to a national level discussion. The case of Odisha may be taken as an instance. One can find in all the districts of Odisha hard-core I.S.I agents and infiltrators. The I.S.I. agents play monopoly in business in the Malkangiri district. They infiltrated into Odisha through Andhra Pradesh in the guise of Naxalites. But they are all wolves under sheep's skin.

In Odisha the illegal Bangladeshi migrants pose security threat. They air programmes from unauthorized underground radios in the coastal districts of Kendrapara, which also harbours the missiles test centre, a very sensitive defence establishment. After the king of Kanika allotted 5 acres each to 200 migrated families of Bangladesh, they surreptitiously allowed their near and dear ones to live with them. Vote bank politics of many leaders helped these migrants acquire government and forestlands. After these got converted into prawn farms, they became millionaires.

In the port city of Paradeep, the increase in the population of these infiltrators is extremely alarming. After the port was established in the year 1962, infiltrators from Bangladesh came and settled here in large number. Due to the non-cooperation of the State Government the port authority failed in its attempt to evacuate them from this area. Gradually their number is increasing in addition to the number of new infiltrators. As such the majority of them went to Bangladesh to participate in the last general election and again returned to their new place of settlement in Bijay Chandrapur, adjacent to Paradeep.

Moreover Odisha is a combination of refugees and infiltrators. Hindus from Bangladesh came to this state in millions since 1947, the partition year of India. In the process of infiltration Muslims have been coming to this state un-objected and un-obstructed since 1947. Now there are presumably 3 million infiltrators residing in different Muslim-dominated districts of Bhadrak and Kendrapara and in the wildly uninhabited districts of Koraput, Malkangiri and Nabarangapur. Incidently a progeny of the refugee family out of his good luck got elected to the state assembly and became a cabinet minister. Presently a Muslim infiltrator, supposedly an I.S.I agent has emerged in the same locality as a crownless leader creating reign of terror and challenging the laws of the land. The refugee-turned minister's newly constructed mansion in the district of Malkangiri was blasted and pulverized by the infiltrator turned militant towards the end of 2001. This is how the Bangladeshis play their roles in India. The Government acts as a dumb-founded winking spectator.

Officially there are 18 million Bangladeshis residing in India. But/in reality there are more than 25 million infiltrators scattered about in all parts of this country. Up to the year 1993 there were 17million Bangladeshi infiltrators in India. In the year 1992 a conference was held in Bangladesh on the country's demographic situation. It was admitted that the whereabouts of about 12 million of its population were not known.

Government of India's extreme compassion, too much leniency, and frequent order to ceasefire helps the terrorists cross the boarder. The infiltration routes of Chor ghali, Tarkundi Ghali, Peer Badesar, Sokar and Sona Ghali in Rajouri and Punch sectors have witnessed this fact.

The most affected states are West Bengal, Assam, Bihar, Tripura and other northeastern states. But these infiltrators are found in almost all the states of India.

These Muslim infiltrators from Bangladesh tremendously add to the existing population of Muslims in India. The Census Commissioner of India has done absolutely nothing to locate these Muslim infiltrators from Bangladesh. Millions of Bihari Muslims of Bangladesh who are acceptable neither to Bangladesh nor to Pakistan infiltrated into India and disappeared among their co-religionists.

The Chittagong hill tract of Bangladesh, which was the traditional abode of non- Muslim Buddhist Chakma tribals, has undergone a total metamorphosis due to the forcible occupation of millions of Muslims by dislodging the native tribals from their homes. The Bangladeshi army on the gunpoint handles this evacuation task.

Apart from infiltration, the expulsion of non-Muslim Hindus (Buddhists included) from Bangladesh also adds the number in the population list of India. To pacify the spate of Islamic population and to rehabilitate the Muslims who came from Myanmar, Bangladeshi Government launched a programme of expulsion of non-Muslim Buddhist tribals of border areas of Bangladesh. More than 100000 people again entered into India as refugees from Bangladesh and took shelter in the camps of Tripura.

As this expulsion was made under the direction of Government of Bangladesh and at the point of gun, no refugee wished to retreat. An incidence of April 13, 1991 may be quoted that took place in the Logang village of Chattagram of Bangladesh. A Muslim youth raped a Chakma tribal woman while she was tending cattle in the field. Her glared relatives attacked the Muslim youth who was accompanied by his friends. This was simply an opportunity. In retaliation the Muslims of that locality wielded their machete and the Bangladeshi army who were deployed to expel the people directed their gun toward these villages. More than two hundred innocent people including many women and children faced instant death by stabbing and firing. The rest 5000 Buddhists of that locality left their sweet homes and came to India crossing the border. The Prime Minister of Bangladesh Begum Khalida Zia was a mute observer of this massacre. She was perhaps counting the decreasing number of non-Muslim population of Bangladesh to her utter satisfaction of conducting her religious duty.

The Indian parliament and the people are continuously fed on wrong information and to the ever-lasting misfortune of the nation. No Muslim leader in India has ever raised his voice against the Muslim infiltrators of Bangladesh. Some power-loving politicians are ever ready to appease these infiltrators only to get their organized votes. The Government of India of last decades criminally neglected the very serious problem of Muslim infiltration from Bangladesh.

It can be said that the state legislatures of West Bengal, Assam, Tripura, Bihar and even Parliament of India are illegally constituted because many members of these bodies have won their elections with the vote of the foreigners who are not the citizens of this country.

The national media in general has failed to highlight the gravity of the problem.

After 1971 it was found that in the border villages there is a regular influx of people from Bangladesh. The smugglers engaged in their trade across the border had helped these people to settle down as they helped them in the smuggling. These people engaged in smuggling are the Muslims of Bangladesh.

However it is in the neighboring states of Assam, Tripura, West Bengal and Bihar that the impacts of Bangladeshi infiltration is overwhelming. In Tripura the demographic picture has undergone a total change after the partition.

At present there are more than 3500000 Muslim infiltrators in Assam. They have been given citizenship rights. Even in Jammu and Kashmir, the number of these infiltrators is more than 100000. More than 12,00,000 infiltrators reside in Bihar. In Sikkim their population is more than 100000. In Gujrat they are more than 200000 and in Rajastan these infiltrators exceed 300000. In the Andaman and Nicobar Island there are some 16 thousand Muslim infiltrators. More than 6 million infiltrators reside in West Bengal.

The Muslim population due to its polygamous nature has a much higher growth rate. In a non-Muslim country like India, the Indian Muslims take to this kind of population enhancement with a vengeance and the growth rate of the Indian Muslims is today much higher than that of the Muslims of Bangladesh and Pakistan. While the Hindu growth rate partly influenced by the government of India's birth control propaganda among them is only 2.2%, the growth rate of Indian Muslims, who do not go by any birth control publicity of a Kafir government, is nearly 3.5% per year.

The infiltrators have found their own organizations like United Minorities Front, Bangladesh Muhajir Sangh, etc. These infiltrators are so confident about their tenacious unity and unhurried settlement in India that on February 12, 1991 they held a press conference at the press club in Central Kolkata under the banner of Bangladesh Muhajir Sangh (An association of Bangladeshi infiltrators). There they asserted that more than 1000000 infiltrators have already settled in and around Kolkata and that others have scattered themselves in Bombay, Delhi, Ahmedabad and other parts of the Country. Hence it is their demand that they must be given Indian citizenship. The police also failed to arrest the infiltrator processionists marching through various parts of the city with the mysterious comment that they (the police) are not instructed to take them into custody.

There are fifty million more citizens of Bangladesh ready to cross over and infiltrate into India. The rate of population growth in Islamic Bangladesh is so fast (2.7 per cent per year) that it is unable to hold the increasing numbers within its boundaries. There is open or tacit connivance to let them loose across the Indian border. The Government of Bangladesh want to take a sigh of relief after unleashing these unwanted 5o million Muslim citizens into India.

During the last decade of the last millenium the Chief Election commission passed an order denying the 370000 Muslims from their right to vote owing to their ambiguous nationality. Indian Muslims could not digest it. They appealed against the decission of the Chief Election Commission to the Supreme Court.

Unilateral marriage by Muslim males to non-Muslim females under the strong protection of their religious previlege helps them to increase their population. Most visibly the majority of Muslim film actors, cricketers and high-ranking politicians have Hindu wives and daughters-in-laws. On the contrary never once have they opined in favour of hypergamy with Hindu society to maintain national harmony.

Children in India form 15000 of total population. Statistics reveals that when 15 children are born in Hindu families, Muslim families give birth to 19 children in the same period.

It is a fact that Islam stresses the religious uniqueness and cohesiveness of the Muslim community. This theme is constantly preached in sermons that are delivered in mosques every Friday. It is a common phenomenon for Muslims to demand a separate nation within a nation because it confirms the basic theme of Quran and the sermon they listen to in the mosques.

The two-nation theory or demand of a state within a state is a natural corollary of how Islam is taught and preached in the mosques. The political leaders who pretend themselves to be very wise both educationally and philosophically don't have any knowledge of the Quranic concept of Islamic ummah and the transformational conept of ethnic cleansing.

Government of India's Erroneous Policy of Population Stabilization

Government's timely warning to control the population touched the Hindus and other communities They resorted to family planning and other measures to control the population on the face of heavy infiltration. Consequently the census report indicated a violent mark of danger for the majority community favoring Islam to turn India In to a land of Muslims like Pakistan and Bangladesh. For the transformation of a chunk of India as Pak!stan it took 700 years to complete the process. But the rest of India would hardly take 70 years since its attainment of Independence to witness the bloody process of Transformation of Civilizations. Such bloody process took twice In the recent past on the chest of ancient India i.e., in the year 1947 and 1971.

According to the census report of 1981 growth of population rate of Hindus was 28.3%. After the heavy toll of Infiltration the balance of population dwindled and ratio of Islamic population rose up higher than the majority community to a considerable extent. Hindus strictly adhered to family planning and down graded its birth rate that again indicated a decrease in its population and it came down to 25% according to the census report of 1991. In the year 2001 the census report marked a decrease in the Hindu population to a vulnerable position of 20% An increase of 20% in the national population of Hindus is a stand still position of population statistics. On the contrary Muslim population which was28% in the census of 1981 increased to 32%in the year 1991 defying the controlling measures of the government. It went up to 34 % in the year 2001. This report startled the whole nation. To mitigate the irate reaction of this imbalanced disparity government of India withdrew the report and declared that the statement was wrongly produced. Growth rate of Muslim population in India was downed to 29% instead of 34% apart from 20% of Hindu growth rate. In spite of government's reannouncement of a gravest information based on its national population, 10% growth of Muslim population over the majority community of the nation is enough to dominate and turn up the wheel of civilization of India with in a very short period according to the process of Transformation of civilizations After the congress government came to power under the wrapper of United Progressive Alliance it implemented a programme to control the explosive population growth under the banner of NCMP (National Common Minimum Programme) Government's attempt to control the growth of population was quite ostensible. It gave vents to the infiltrators to percolate through its schemes and violently increase its birth rate unobstructed to fight against the majority through demographic attack and win in the war of survival as the fittest race.

According to the population control plan of the government trained birth attendants (TBA) will be deployed as the points person in spreading awareness on family welfare issues including advice on antenatal care and postnatal care. As usual the attendants would go for approach to each door including the infiltrators to create awareness in them to have smooth birth of their issues. The attendant will also ensure timely medical attention and will be paid a transaction cost of Rs 400 per case of a baby in each infiltrators house. This is our strategy for population control!

Government's plans for safe motherhood clearly indicates that the government aides will attend each pregnant woman of these infiltrated families and attend its glossy delivery and will be paid accordingly. Indirectly this would encourage the infiltrators' confirmation of settlement in this country with confidence of being benefited by a national scheme for enhancing their population.

These illegal migrants will never like to lessen their population ratio. They are very cunning and aware of their personal values as the most wanted vote bankers. Out of growing poverty and sufferings, our people will only be an easy prey of this plan and thereby help the nation to have a decrease in the national population. On the contrary these infiltrators will get government assistance to increase their number.

Besides, if a man has four wives and each wife blessed with at best two children, shall the government have any legal or constitutional instrument to cut sort of number of children of such persons who fathers eight children from four wives?

India is the only land in the world, which is the worst sufferer with heavy burden of infiltrators. Nowhere in the world a country shelters such infiltrators and looks it at par with its bonafide citizens. Pakistan never consigns citizenship to any foreigner. Take the case of Jemima Gold Smith, the descendant of one of the richest family of England. She married to Pakistan cricketer Imran Khan and eventually she embraced Islam to modify her personality to suit the nativity. She also became a good housewife and mother of Imran's children. Even then Imran was pressurized to leave her on grounds of her foreign origin. England is also friendly to Pakistan. But British nationalism is not to the core choice of Pakistan Issue of citizenship by Pakistan to Indians is a daydream. Not only Pakistan, Bangladesh also never allows citizenship to any Indian. Indians not only allow the infiltrators to flourish in their country but also take care of their population growth through national scheme. 'Janani Suraksha Yojana.'

Government's plan for population control is both ambiguous and ridiculous. Presently government plans more aid for safe motherhood and particularly in case of BPL mothers under the banner of Janani Suraksha Yojana up to two live deliverres According to this scheme each mother would get Rs 1000 and Rs 400 In the case of delivery of a female baby or male baby 'respectively In addition a traveling allowance of Rs 150 will be sanctioned to each expectant woman who attended the clinic. For adoption of permanent methods of contraceptives each mother would be given Rs 200 as compensation. There is also provision to sanction Rs 1500 to each woman in case of acute delivery. Midwife attending the delivery would get up to Rs 200.

This is the programme of government to decrease the mortality rate from present 407 to 100 out of 1000 birth rate by the year 2010. When government adopts such safety measures for smooth and live delivery that challenges high rate morality, than how does the government promise for a plan to decrease the population? In one hand the government assures safe delivery and simultaneously on the other hand it takes strident steps to curb growing population!

No doubt, this scheme is exclusively meant for the women who are below the poverty level to check high mortality among the poor class and it is meant to evade disparity of birth proportion among the rich and the poor.

Here one thing is clear that the scheme is not meant for population control. Had the government any real intention to stabilize the explosive growth of population it would have followed the policy of China by strictly adhering "We two, our one" or at best "We two our two". Rather the policy of government helps increase the national population. It is a blessing in disguise to those who think that delivery is a God gift and birth control is anti religious. There are women who would be encouraged by the scheme of the government realizing that their each delivery entails an amount up to Rs 1000. They would continue and compete to be pregnant till they remain productive. Besides, this scheme will be a boon to the immigrants' family who all belong to the 'below poverty level' class and are in a need of national hand of co-operation for their birth proliferation They would receive the entire benefit of the government scheme meant for the smooth delivery of women under BPL.

Generally one miracle takes place in border hospitals. To destroy the foreign identity the Bangladeshi pregnant women after they cross the Indo-Bangladesh border and enter into India they get admitted into the hospital for delivery. The babies born in Indian hospitals become natural Indian citizens!

Moreover gender discrimination is man-made debility. Feticide is a contribution of materialistic ideology. It is not natural. A male baby is not different from a baby girl at birth. Our scrupulous government is going to implant a gender-based discrimination from the very delivery of a baby; when a mother is prized with Rs 1000 at the behest of the birth of a baby girl We must all remember that a mother would never strangle a baby when she finds that it is a boy and not a girl. On the whole in each time she only helps increase one number in the gross population.

Activities of Global Islamic Movement in India through the ISI of Pakistan

> *"Peace could be achieved only with the break up of India into smaller units."*
>
> —Gouhar Ayub, former speaker of Pakistan

At the time of the partition there were approximately 30 million Muslims in India. After 50 years now their population is 160 million. Simililarly there were 25 million Hindus in Pakistan in the year 1947. Now they form only one per cent of the total population.

Pakistan has launched its Islamic expeditions through different Islamic Terrorist organizations in India. The extremists of Manipur are preparing to launch a war against the Government of India with the assistance of I.S.I of Pakistan. All the subversive activities taking place in different parts of India are directed by the I.S.I.

The most dreaded militant outfit of the North East, the National Socialist Council of Nagaland (NSCN), has spread its dragnet far and wide, establishing links with almost every small and big insurgent group of the seven sisters. Its writ runs throughout Nagaland and parts of Manipur. In fact NSCN has virtually set up a parallel government in Nagaland and remains as an unchallenged force. The Central and State establishments and banking institutions have to pay hefty amounts to its coffers. Buses and trucks must pay fixed taxes. Businessmen under pressure have started fleeing the State. Through ambushes, skirmishes and killings NSCN's objective is to assert its supremacy in Manipur too, and to some extent it has succeeded.

Besides, the extremist outfit has gone the whole hog to rope in new recruits who are being sent to Bangladesh for detailed training in jungle warfare through newly found routes with the active support of the I.S.I. of Pakistan. There are almost 30 training camps of militant outfits scattered in various areas of Bangladesh. Apart from clandestine training of the militants the extremists are detailed in software subversion in the pattern of militancy. Extremists trained by officials of Bangladesh rifles are put under the direct supervision of the I.S.I. After their subversive training is over, the militants are given professional training for their earning and livelihood. Then they are carried to the points of easy access on the Indo Bangladesh border for infiltration into India.

The I.S.I's link with NSCN and United Liberation Front of Assam is now no more a secret. Both the insurgent groups are receiving generous material and monetary help to create large scale violence and blood-shed as a part of its grand design to destabilize the region.

The sinister machination of the I.S.I in creating lawlessness in the region is meant to divert the government's attention from Kashmir. In order to co-ordinate with NSCN, in respect of its alliance with other militant outfits and supply of sophisticated weapons the I.S.I. has set up a field station in the town of Sylhat in Bangladesh. The field station under the command of the I.S.I. is to help the NSCN rebels target military and police outposts, airports and drilling projects for attack and sabotage.

The Islamic groups in Bangladesh and Japan have formed a network to protect the minorities in India who they believe are under threat. There was a three-day meeting organized by the (I.M.J.) Islamic Mission of Japan on 1.1.2001 held at the Prefecture Yogasima (Mikakiyuchi) youth hostel, Kanagewa.

Islamic scholars from Japan and other Asian countries participated in the meeting to discuss the Islamic movements and activities of the Islamic world. A 10 member central advisory committee had been set up for the year 2001-2002. Tanseem Alam, a member of the senate and syndicate of Rajashahi University of Bangladesh who was the chief guest of the conference, administered an oath to the delegates.

The I.M.J. meeting decided to set-up an Islamic Development Fund (I.D.F.), which would be used for helping the Islamic devotees of Bangladesh, India and Sri Lanka and organize Islamic movements. The Chairman of Japan's Islamic cultural foundation Imam Hafiz Md Alauddin will be touring Bangladesh, India and Nepal to meet the Islamic leaders of these countries. The President of I.M.J, Kari Farooq Ahmed, reportedly disclosed that he was already in touch with Maulana Ahmmed Bukhari (of Delhi's Jama Masjid) to work out the modalities of the Islamic movement project.

There are 12 terrorist groups workout in the North East area of India under the direct supervision of the I.S.I. They are Muslim Liberation Front of Assam, Muslim Volunteer force, Muslim Liberation Tigers of Assam, Islamic Movements of India, Islamic Revolutionary Force, Islamic United Liberation Army, Assam Minority Liberation Army, Muslim Liberation front, United Special Reform of Assam Tiger, Liberation front of Assam, Islam Revolutionary Army, and Sadam Bahini.

Apart from these Jehadi organizations, the I.S.I has united 10 non-Islamic organisations and spurred them on to continue the subversive activities in the North Eastern part of India. These non-Islamic organizations working under the guidance of the I.S.I are Nationalist Socialist Council of Nagaland, Karbi National Volunteers, Hamar People's Convention, National Liberation Front of Tripura, Kangbi Mabol, National Democratic Front of Bodoland, Bodo Liberation Front, Hilltop Liberation Council (Meghalaya) Cooki Battle Front, United Liberation Front of Assam (ULFA), etc.

The major thrust of the I.S.I activities in U.P is now in the Terai and the districts of Kanpur, Aligarh, Varanasi, Lakimpur, Khiri (all bordering Nepal), Gorakhpur, Basti, Haridwar, Dehradun, Saharanpur and Nainital areas are the most affected ever. Of the 14-border transit checkpoints two falling in Pithorgarh-Lohaghat and Dharchula, adjoining Dilihat are at present most vulnerable.

In South India Hyderabad, Banglore, Kochin, Kozhikod, Bhatkal, Gulbarg, etc., have become the centres of the I.S.I. Hizbul Mujahiddin and Ittehadul Muslimee have engaged themselves in subversive activities in Andhra Pradesh. There are almost 20,000 Muslim infiltrators who have settled down unauthorized in Hyderabad.

The I.S.I. has infiltrated in India through Indian journalists. In India to become a journalist or a columnist is the easiest of processes. Except a few, no papers in India make healthy payments to their journalists. The majority of journalists don't get any remuneration. Many of them become the target of the I.S.I to supply them the secrets for a penny. To avoid the suspicion of India espionage the I.S.I has appointed Hindu journalists in place of Muslims.

The blasting of the magnificent Rashtriya Swayam Sevak Sangh's head office made the consecration of Islamic explosion in Tamil Nadu.

Later this sound of detonation was spread like the wild fire throughout the state. All India Jehad committee is a militant outfit operation in Tamilnadu. Its president is Ahmed Ali, alias Palani Baba, the undaunted Islamic spirit who has master-minded the Jehadi projects throughout the state.

Muslim young-men have been being recruited for training in arms and explosives through organizations like SIMI and Islamic Sebak Sangh, Christened as "People's Democratic Party" in Kerala. SIMI (Students' Islamic Movement of India) has its relation with many terrorist (Jehadi) organizations and the Jehadis of Kashmir. The Jehadi miscreants who were arrested from the Aligarh Muslim University campus and belonged to SIMI did the explosion that shook U.P in August 2000.

The appeasing policy of the Government of India has enabled the I.S.I to extend its area of operation unobstructed in India. In March 13, 1993 there were 13 explosions in Bombay at a time that caused a death toll of 300 persons. There are many riot prone areas in Maharastra in general and Bombay in particular which may even threaten the safety and security of the whole nation. There are certain places in India which may cause havoc in international level. Take for instance the mosque that stands at the airport of Calcutta. After it attained the international statues, the modernization and expansion of the plain ground became inevitable. But nobody dared to shift this mosque for the expansion of the field. Neither the Chief Minister of West Bengal nor the Chairman of the Minority Commission has guts to open their mouth to clean the area. When the matter was brought to the notice of the Imam of the mosque he told that Allah was the only authority to finalize the matter.

After the incident of September 11, 2001 plane bomb blast some I.S.I agents were nabbed in Kolkata. The police rushed to this mosque for enquiry. But nobody is conscious about the planes of Kolkata International Airport, which may harbour hardcore militants for their international transportation.

The militants are equipped with high velocity telescopic sniper rifles, light and medium machine guns. The explosives include RDX and PETN-based triggering devices including trip switches, remote control mechanisms, light differential relay switches, high frequency based triggering devices, time pencil and electronic timers.

The I.S.I also trains Islamic militants to infiltrate into India by cutting the barbed wire connections at the border. The I.S.I of Pakistan also circulates fake currency notes in abundance in India. All activities of insurgency in Kashmir have been directed by the I.S.I with the deployment of its mercenary Mujahids. At present there are half a million Jehadi fighters ready to infiltrate into, and fight against, India. After the advent of Osama bin Laden in the scene of International Islamic expansionism, now the process of Islamisation has been excalated by the Taliban forces since 1998. The Taliban-I-Kashmir has been organized by an assembly of Afghan and Pakistani terrorists in the ranks of Kashmir National Liberation forces. Osama bin Laden is highly esteemed as a great saviour of Islam.

In the year 1998 Laden had planned to blast the U.S Embassy in New Delhi and the U.S Consulates in Chennai and Kolkata. But the Indian army thwarted the attempts.

Apart from the militant organizations stationed in Jammu and Kashmir, there are other subversive militant Islamic Organizations which are monitored by the I.S.I. to convert India into an Islamic home-land.

The following are the fundamental Islamic organizations supported by I.S.I.

1. SIMI (Students Islamic Movement of India)
2. MULFA (Muslim United Liberation Front of Assam)
3. USRA (United Social Reform Army of Assam)
4. M.V.F. (Muslim Volunteer Force)
5. MALTA (Malta Liberation Tiger Force of Assam)
6. AMLA (Assam Minority Liberation Army)
7. UILA (United Islamic Liberation Army)
8. I.R.F. (Islamic Liberation Front)
9. Muslim Liberation Front
10. I.S.S. (Islami Sebak Sangh)
11. Paswar,
12. Jama-ul-Fukra
13. Saddam Bahini
14. Chhatra Sibir
15. Islamic Revolution Army.

Islamistan – Plan of ISI to Create Another Islamic Homeland in India

Memories of Muslim rule in India not only remained alive particularly among the upper class Muslims, but were constantly used by them to impress upon the Muslim

> *masses that having ruled India. Muslims should not allow themselves to be ruled by Hindu majority. It was because of such separatist tendencies and memories of former Muslim rule in that there was little deep-seated love for India as their motherland on the part of the Muslim elite.*
>
> – *"Pakistan, the Formative Phase" by K.B. Sayed*

A news was published in the weekly "Family" of Pakistan in July 31,1999 with the heading "Kargil-victory or defeat". There it was described, "India is not only facing the Islamic challenge in the Kargil or in Kashmir, it would also face the attack of Mujahids in different parts of India. India has entarnished them as terrorists. But they are the Muslim youths fighting Jehad, the religious war against the non-Muslims."

This statement clearly defines what a terrorist is, what a Mujahid is, what Jehad is and what the ultimate aim of Pakistan is and after all, what Islam is.

After the creation of Pakistan another big plot has been hatched out by the I.S.I to create a separate state in the name of Islamistan consisting of Meghalaya, Assam, Tripura, Nagaland, some parts of Arunachal Pradesh, Malda, Murshidabad, Jalpaiguri, West Dinapur of West Bengal, Purnia, Arakia, Bhagalpur, Kishnganj and Munger, etc., of Bihar.

Impenetrable mountain tract, linguistic variations, open international boundary lines, infiltration of innumerable Bangladeshi citizens and many other events help the I.S.I to go on stretching its unobstructed net around this area to turn it into an Islamic land.

The I.S.I has established its headquarters in Bangladesh to create Islamistan in India, as it would be very easy to operate in the North Eastern Frontier Province of India through Bangladesh. The I.S.I has ordained the local Muslim youths to some different Islamic organizations for subversive activities in these areas and plebiscite. With the organizations of this taskforce the I.S.I. would proceed towards the formation of Islamistan step by step. The first step of this progress is called operation Tehelka.

Assam is going to be incorporated in Bang-e-Islam as proposed by Fakiruddin Ali Ahmad or in the map of Mughliatan, a recent proposition advanced in Bangladesh, a state emerging as eastern Taliban. The late President Zia ul Haq had launched operation Topac pointing India to be million bits and gobbling up one peace at a time. After that non-Muslims according to the theory of Islamic Movement will either have to accept Islam or fasce massacre or leave the place as happened in Bangladesh and elsewhere.

After the formation of operation Tehelka the I.S.I. has collected sacrificial. Muslim youths to give them training to use the weapons, to explode bombs, to stretch mines, to hoodwink the police, etc., in different training camps of Bangladesh. The modern techniques of guerilla war are also taught with key importance in those training centres. The flow of financial aid continues from the Islamic countries of Asia, Africa, and Mid Europe.

These organizations have their own language and media channels. The agents and trainees use Assamese and Bangali languages with misnomered words.

This plan of the I.S.I was confirmed with the flash of the press statement made on 1.2.94 from a military regiment of Tejpur (Assam). This statement was announced on behalf of the information centre of Defence Dept. Information on the increasing Islamic fundamental activities and infiltration from Bangladesh was also given. The narrow-minded, myopic politicians like the defunct Chief Minister of Assam Hiteswar Saikia and others were patronizing infiltrates for their number politics to win Muslim hearts and hence opposed the statement of the Defence Department as baseless. Hence they did not take any steps to drive out the illegal infiltration.

Numbers of these subversive organizations have been increased in the states of Assam, Manipur, Meghalaya, Arunchal Pradesh, Nagaland, Tripura, Mizoram and in the frontier provinces of West Bengal and Bihar. These organizations came to light and in a quick process of consolidating their plans for the formation of Islamistan soon after the demolition of Babri Masjid at Ayodhya in 1992.

They are taught that if they performed their duty most sincerely and get success, they did the best for Allah and Islam and if they die during the tenure of fighting, Islamic Paradise is reserved for them for ages to come.

15. Expansion of Islamic Fundamentalism in Afro-Asian Countries

(a) Palestine, The Apple of All Discords

Palestine was under the Ottoman empire of Turkey since 16th century. After the extermination of the Jews, the Arabs became its main settlers. The Turks had alliance with Germany. Hence during the Second World War the British forces occupied Palestine and supported the revival of a Jewish state in the middle of Palestine. Hence the state of Israel came into being in the year 1948 in Palestine, with Tel Aviv as its Capital.

The Jewish settlement in Palestine is a long story of imperial conquest. The bulk of the Jewish population dispersed from the region beginning from the 6th century B.C. In the 20 th century there was a need for a Jewish homeland. A Jewsh leader Chaim Weizmann wanted Palestine to be the homeland instead of it being somewhere in Australia or Uganda, which were thinly populated areas. He succeeded due to his relation with the British foreign secretary Balfour. Thus came the Balfour Declaration of 1917 recognising Zionist homeland in Palestine.

After the formation of Israel in the state of Palestine, it was declared as the Jewish homeland. Jews all over the world started migrating to Israel and their number increased hundred times from 1948 after the Jewish government declared double citizenship to all the Jews settled in different countries of the world. Jews who had settled in Europe and Asia, particularly in India rushed to their homeland with a new hope of enriched independent life. The more the people rushed to Israel, the more was the demand for extensive areas. Jews occupied the villages and towns of Palestinian Muslims in 1948 and instantaneously the Palestinians became homeless refugees. Hereafter continued the war of expansion and extermination between the Jews backed by the U.S.A and European countries on the one hand and the Palestinians under the leadership of

Yasser Arafat backed by Iran and the Organization of Islamic Conference on the other.

There was a six days' war between the Arabs and Jews in the year 1967. The whole of Jerusalem, the West Bank area of Jordan, the Sinai Peninsula, the Gaza strip, the Golan Height, East Jerusalem were almost integrated into Israel.

Jerusalem has its own distinction. It is a centre of confluence of three Semitic religions i.e. Judaism, Christianity and Islam. Israel is the testing ground and balancing point of power politics between the Christian world adventured by Israeli Jews and the Islamic world represented by Palestinian Arabs.

Jerusalem has its Islamic name "Qods". Muslims never say it "Jerusalem" which is presently under the dominnation of the Jews. For Muslims this is one of the holiest places next to Mecca and Medina. This is the place from where Mohammed supposedly ascended to heaven on the blessed night of his ascension. In this place there is the famous Al-Aqsa mosque, the centre point of worldwide Islamic devotion. According to Muslims Qods is misnomered as Jerusalem, though Jerusalem is the oldest name of this land and popularly known by all non-Muslims.

The importance of Jerusalem to Islam is tangible from another point. At the advent of Islam Muslims prayed facing towards Jerusalem for 16 months. The Islamic Qibla was first set at Jerusalem. In the later period the Qibla was shifted to Mecca that now became the centre place of the largest human confluence every year.

Jerusalem is the holiest place for Christians as the birthplace of Jesus, the only son of God. The evolution of Christianity and Biblical history is entangled with the ancestry of Jerusalem. Every Christian aspires to visit it at least once in his lifetime.

To the Jews this is the Promised Land. God has confirmed this land exclusively for the Jews. Jesus by birth was a Jew and a baptized Christian. Present Christianity and Judaism have more internal reciprocal relations than Islam. Both the religions-Christianity and Judaism – have the view that the creation of Israel in Palestine is a fulfilment of the Biblical prophesies and precedence to the re-manifestation of Jesus. Because Jesus Christ was a Jewish descendant, the Christian world doesn't have any racial enmity with the Jews. Moreover the founding fathers of Israel are Euro–Americans. Ben Gurion was from Poland. Golda Meir was from the USA. Menachem Begin was a Pole.

The Jews claim Israel as their homeland. The Muslims say that it is their holiest place of religious importance. In June 7, 1967 the Jews confiscated the keys to the mosque immediately after they had seized the town from fleeing Jordanians.

The Jews want to convert Palestine into a great Israel. They want to retain the great Biblical Israel. The Muslims say that it is inconceivable. It is like the inhabitants of Rome waiting to return to the great Roman Empire or the Mayas and Aztecs returning to their vanished empires.

In the case of Palestine there is a religious argument for the control of Jerusalem. The rest is negotiable. According to the Muslims, Jerusalem is a holy city of the three monotheistic religions of the world. It can't belong exclusively to one ethnic group or political power.

This disputed Al Aqsa (Al Masjidul Aqsa) Mosque, which was liberated from the dominion of Christians in the year 1187, now came under the subjugation of the Jews. In June 21, 1969 the Jews set fire to the mosque and demolished it. On August 14, 1970 a group of Jews dedicated to the rebuilding of the temple of king Solomon on the site of Al Aqsa after it was demolished, forcibly entered the premises of the Harem by gunning down the Muslims.

On August 1980 the Jews decided to liberate the Temple mount from Muslim occupation. Accordingly they warned the Muslim waqf authorities to abandon the temple by sending them death threats. Later they gunned down over 60 Palestinian Muslims on April 11, 1982. The Jews secretly dug a tunnel right underneath the Waqf department in August 1982, which collapsed in March 1983. In August 1985 Jews started prayers in the Haram Al Saraf.

On July 25, 1995 the Israeli High Court issued a ruling allowing the Jews to pray at the Temple Mount.

The world Islamic community got irritated over the treacherous deed of Christian kingdom that divided the sacred city of Qods and snapped it from the hands of its most devoted persons, the Muslims, and handed it over to the Jews, their bloody enemy. Streams of Islamic blood has been oozing from that day on the sacred soil of Jerusalem.

However, shortly after the Islamic revolution in 1979, the Imam declared the last Friday of the holy month of Ramadan as the global day of Qods. This announcement, a turning point in the history of Islamic revolution, had a tremendous impact on the world of Islam, inviting a massive number of Muslims to participate in an all-out struggle against the Jews. The goal behind Imam Khomeini's call was to mobilize the western Islamic community in all political, social and economic strata and to wage a full-fledged war against world arrogance, particularly the U.S.A and Israel. The Imam firmly believed that while the Muslims constitute one fourth of the world population and enjoy the natural resources along with huge petrodollar wealth, the Islamic governments ought to play a decisive role in liberating the occupied territory, still under the control of Israel?

On "Qods Day" Islamic nations display their solid determination to struggle against Israel. On that day they shout slogans against the US and European Countries for their creation of a never-ending racial imbroglio on the sacred soil of Palestine.

Jerusalem, which was one of the centres of all spiritual bigotry destined to preach the message of peace and non-violence, has now been converted into a volcano that erupts the lava of violence and terror of religious discordance. As long as the problem of Jerusalem remains unsolved, there is no question of peace, mutual understanding and coexistence in the world.

Israeli Arabs who constitute 1.2 million population living in Israel commemorate "Land Day" since 1976 as a symbol of protest against the land expropriation by the Israelis. In Gaza strip the Fatah group of Yassar Arafat march chanting "Sharon! Wait, Fatah is going to open your grave in Gaza". They burnt the effigy of Israeli Prime Minister and the flags of Israel and the U.S.A.

At least 118 people, all but 8 of them Arabs, died in clashes that erupted on Sept 28, 2000, after the hawkish Israeli leader Ariel Sharon visited an ultra sensitive holy site in Jerusalem venerated by both Muslims and Jews. Jerusalem's hilltop is known to the Jews as the Temple Mount and to Muslims as Haram al Sarif, a noble sanctuary. Al Aqsa is one of the two major mosques in the walled compound.

Saudi Arabia's crown prince Abdullah proposed that Arabs raise 200 million U.S dollars for the Palestinians and 800 million dollars to retain the Arabic and Islamic character of Jerusalem.

On the other hand Israel is not prepared to part even a fraction of an inch of land to Palestine. When the then U.S President Bill Clinton launched an effort to clinch a peace deal with an intention to divide Jerusalem, the Israelis thronged to the streets of old city of Jerusalem to protest against his decision. There were reportedly 4 hundred thousand people present in the rally which they called the largest of its kind. The Palestinian negotiators also rejected the peace proposal of American President to have their occupation over a part of the city.

In the year 1993 Israel banished 415 Palestinians from Israel alleging them to have been Islamic Jehadi fighters. They had to stay for weeks under icy cold and open sky. Even Lebanon also did not dare to come to rescue this wretched group for fear of the Israelis.

There are many Islamic fundamental organizations working to continue Jehad against the Jews. One such organization 'Hamas' declared that it would fight against any party, nation or person who ever would have a helping hand with Israel. The Jehad seems to have no end.

The sanguinary history of the ancient abode of the Jews impels the Jews to exterminate the Muslims from the soil of Palestine, which was once an enriched nation of Jewish civilization. The same history provokes the Muslims of Palestine to wipe out the Jews. The present Muslim community doesn't want to suffer at the hands of the Jews for the misdeeds of their ancestors. But the critical situation indicates that the dissolution of either race would automatically lead the other to have a peaceful life, as there is no feasibility of co-existence with mutual understanding and co-operation.

Twenty years after the occupation of South Lebanon Israel was forced to withdraw its army after having a staunch battle with Hizbullah in the year 2000.

A militant team has been formed in the name of Al Aksa Brigade who are very active in the West Bank. They have increased their number and deadliness after January 14, 2002. Their only destination is to liberate the Al-Aksa Mosque from the dominion of the Jews of Israel.

The Jews are a nation of 4 million population in Israel, in the middle of Palestine. The Arab nations from the Atalantic to the Gulf number 170 million. The Jews control only 18000 kms of land for their survival as a nation from the grave. The Arabs possess a landmass of 14 million square kilometres of land. For the Israelis or the Jews the issue is not one of territory but their very existence. For the Arab Muslims the issue is not one of territory but their self-respect. As long as there are Jews as a nation in Palestine, the Muslims as a community are never at peace. There is no solution to end the war because this is the war of two tails of two large serpents. Perhaps the flame of war would be carried to Armageddon from this field of Olympic war.

(b) Lebanon

Like all other countries of the world, which demographically turned out into an Islamic country after the manifestation of Islam in the 6th Century A.D., Lebanon has also its history of Islamic process. In ancient times the land of Lebanon was inhabited by the Cananites who established the Phoenician cities and later established a commercial maritime empire. In 64 B.C. the Romans occupied this region and the land was later christianized.

Islamic virus infected Lebanon at the very outset of 8th century and gradually the natives were Islamised through Islamic processes and religious expansion. Thence started rapid changes in the social structure unobstructed for 400 years. The Druze emerged in South Lebanon in 11th century and there was continuous friction between the Maronite Christians and Druses. At the same time invading crusaders from European countries entered the region and supported the local Christians against the Muslims.

Lebanon was invaded by the Mongols in the 13th Century and later by the Ottoman Turks in the early 16th century. Since then it flourished as a powerful Islamic state. As usual, friction started between Maronite Christians and Muslims, which forced France to intervene in 1861 and Ottoman Sultan was forced to appoint a Christian Governor for Lebanon. After the Second World War was over and after the disintegration of the Ottoman empire, France, with its power of mandate, alienated Syria from Lebanon in order to create a homeland in Syria for the Maronite Christians. Lebanon became independent on the 1st day of 1945.

In 1968 Israel raided Beirut airport and destroyed 13 Aeroplanes to take revenge against Lebanon's support for Palestinian Muslims. In 1982 Israel's attack on Lebanon was so severe that nearly 370,000 Palestinian Muslims had to flee from Lebanon. America and other Christian Western countries always backed Israel.

Hizbullah led Guerilla war in the occupied territories of South Lebanon with its 22,000 Shiah combatants. This organization was founded on 1972. It has its representatives in Beirut's parliament. It imparts 36 months rigorous militant training. The Hizbullah party fought to liberate the occupied areas of South Lebanon. Under duress Israel withdrew its forces deployed in South Lebanon. Hizbullah party has vowed to liberate all the occupied areas of the Zionist forces including Qods or Bait-ul-Muqaddas. Hence it will continue its war until the name Israel obliterated from the world map.

However the acquisition of South Lebanon by the Muslims towards the end of the last millennium, i.e, on May, 2000 was celebrated as an era of victory by the Muslims over Israel and its components.

(c) Turkey

Geographically Turkey is more Asia than Europe. The bi-continental spread of the Turkish Ottoman Empire (13 to 19th century) and its continual interaction with the West enabled Turkey as a wonderful land of Euro-Arabic culture. Turkey is the only Westernized Isamic nation in the world. Out of its 70-millioin population 99% people are Muslims. The constitution of Turkey separates politics from religion. Mustafa Kemalpasa modernized it from the grass root level in the year 1922. He seized the executive during the First World War. The 641 years of Ottoman dynastic rule came to an end on November 1, 1922. During his 15 years of dictatorial rule the Ataturk or 'father of the Turks' rapidly Westernized Turkish society and completely changed the public and private laws. On March 3, 1924, Mustafa abolished the Caliphate and declared the laws of Shariat unlawful.

On the same day he ordered the closure of the sections of Topkapi palace where a mantle attributed to Prophet Mohammed was kept and where the holy Quran was recited day and night incessantly since July 25, 1518. In the year 1925 he banned the wearing of the cap and the fez as a criminal offence. In the last month of the same year he replaced the Islamic Hegira calendar for Christian Gregorian calendar and declared Sunday as the weekly holiday instead of Friday.

In 1928 Mustafa imposed the Latin alphabet in place of the Perso-Arabic script of Turkish language. Ataturk made practical decisions on governance, adopted new technologies and reformed age-old Sharia laws. He allowed the charging of interest, which is denounced as usury in Quran and abolished slavery despite strong resistance from Muslim religious groups.

He ordered Ajan (Public call to prayer given from the mosque), which is delivered worldwide only in Arabic, to be replaced by Turkish language in the year 1932. He made compulsory the unveiling of Muslim women and the use of European dress was imposed on them. The Turkish constitution was made secular in the year 1937.

Ataturk raised an army which itself would act as a guardian for the protection of European interests in Turkey by making sure that the schism between religion and state would be the final one. That is why a public representative backed by the electorate, cannot sport a beard if he is a male and a headscarf if she is a female, just because the U.S. supported generals may consider the observance of the basic tenets of Islam by public officials as a dangerous threat to Kemalism.

Turkey has been an associate member of EU since 1963 and a member of NATO since 1950. But it has not obtained full membership like other European nations. It has as strong a claim to full membership as any of the new East European EU members. But some member countries like France, Germany and Austria etc. strongly oppose to sanction full membership to Turkey.

Now this country is proceeding towards Islamic fundamentalism through practising the Islamic tenets. After the victory of the Democratic Party in 1950, the Ajan was restored to its original Arabic form. One female M.P, Ms. Marve Kavakci became the key point of discussion amongst the people of the Western world when she entered the Turkish parliament by wearing a headscarf and spurning Kemalism. This gave rise to a billow of protest and anger throughout the Western world.

The Turkish Prime Minister Necmettin Erbakan was a practising Muslim. His installation as a Prime Minister itself is an indication of the Islamic interest of the people of democratic Turkey. Present politicians try to show the people that they pray in mosques. The circulation of Islamic newspapers is on the increase. In parts of Istanbul with a population of 11 million, the women are seen in complete Islamic Hijab and Burqa.

The founder of Rifah party Necmettin Erbakan created turmoil in the party politics of Turkey by capturing more than 20% public opinion in his favour. His agenda put forth before the Turkish public was to cut off Turkish relation from NATO membership, to close down the aero privilege of the USA in Turkey, to close interest payment system in banking which is unIslamic, to abolish article 24 of the Turkish constitution framed by Mustafa Kemalpasha which emphasizes Turkey as a democratic country and to bring necessary changes in the constitution that suits Islamic rule in Turkey. Erbakran has more than 6 million members in his party.

This Turkish Islamic fundamentalist leader openly declared "We (the Rifah party members) are like a volcano and our explosion and detonation is also like that. We are not only going to open a 'Muslim Open Market' system but also going to lay the foundation of "Federation of Islamic Nations and World Islamic Union".

There is also an apprehension that Turkey may come into the hands of Islamic fundamentalism. Its devaluation of currency has gone up to a dangerous level of 100 billion dollars. Usually it spends 7 billion dollars per year to suppress the Kurdish rebellion for long 15 years. Thousands of people have lost their valuable lives in this civil war.

Growth of population and poverty escalates the Islamiation in a secular country where Islam plays a prime role in politics. Iran is directly and indirectly inciting the Turks to transform democratic Turkistan into a Muslim Republic. It is a much more expected country to be Islamised only because 98% of its population are Muslims. When a small Balkan region Bosnia having 48% of Islamic population and 120 years of separation from Muslim world came out to fight for a holy war then why not Turkey. And if Turky will be Islamised, then Iran will be doubly strengthened to fight against its arch enemy, the USA.

The downfall of secular democracy in Turkey would completely bring about a change in the economic and socio-political feature of the whole of Europe. It would also impose a shock wave in America's foreign policy, because Turkey is presently the most faithful flawless non-Christian Westernized country of the U S A. America used the airport of Turkey in the Iran America war and at the time of Iraq's assault on Kuwait. In the flight-prohibited areas of Northern Iraq, America has put its sharp eye on it only through Turkey. So an Islamic Turkey will bring as much trouble to the European countries as to America. At the time of the cold war against the USSR, the USA had taken the assistance of Turkey to a great extent.

It is not redundant to say that the defeat of Russia against Afghanistan is the defeat of Europe against Islam because Russia was no less than the USA in manpower, weaponry and preparation of war. The country, which had dominated a large part of Europe, was not only defeated by Afganistan but also was burst out into many Islamic countries.

The Kurds who made themselves a history of 3000 years, now prowl in different countries of Syria, Turkey, Iran, Iraq and as far as Armenia. Their place of birth is in the hilly tract of Turkey. They are so formidable that it compelled the Turkey government to deploy 10000 soldiers to exterminate the Kurds. On the other hand the Kurds want to eliminate the democratic Government from the South East province of Turkey and declare it their homeland "Kurdisthan". They are even prepared to transform the whole of Turkey's present administration. They are staunch Islamic fundamentalists with a communist bent of mind.

The present Kurds are the most dangerous terrorist groups of the world under the banner of P.K.K., which was first started by Abdul Okelan. To show the strength of Kurds once in June 1993 he passed an order to his followers staying in 28 towns of European countries to kill the local Turks of those respective towns. As a result the Turk born officers and bureaucrats were mercilessly and surprisingly killed around the whole of Europe.

Assuming that the Turkey schools are symbolic of Ottoman imperialism they set fire to more than 100 Turkey schools and killed hundreds of school teachers. They killed more than 500 Kurdish women and children on the ground that their women folk by no means associate with the Turks. All the people of Turkey and all the member countries of NATO are terrified of these Kurdish incidents observing how the civil war stricken Turkey, the only Islam dominating Westernized secular country of Asia, is gradually slipping down towards a division in the name of Turkeystan and Kurdistan. Turkey, if converted into Turkeystan and Kurdistan, the Islamisation of the whole of Europe is not far behind. Europe today is uneasy about its Muslim minorities. The alarmists feel that Turkish membership could turn out to be an Islamic Trojan horse. Europeans now begin to think that Turkey compared to its lower per capita income will be a drag on the EU.

(d) Malaysia

> *"The Islamic nations should modernize weapons expertise for the restoration of Islamic civilization and defend against non-Muslim aggression. Muslims will never be able to bring back the honour and the respect for Islam unless they become capable again of defending themselves."*
>
> – Mahathir Mohammed, Former Prime Minister of Malaysia

Evidences are obvious that Malaysia was a very peaceful nation under its peace-loving, eminent economist and reformist leader Mahathir Mohammed. After his departure the nation is going to be put on the cauldron of Islamic extremism. The present Prime Minister Abdulla Ahmed Badawi is being pressurized to convert this nice chunk of the world into an Islamic country. But the government postpones this proposal for the time being for fear of decimation of economic balance and impeachment of bilateral agreements made with the Western countries. Jehadis of Malay go to Afghanistan to get subversive training of using of explosves and automatic guns. They are well acquainted as K.M.M. (Kumpular Mujahiddin Malaysia) having political potentiality to bring about a change in the secular character of the constitution. Many Malaysian youths joined in the Russo Afghan war. Even there are evidences of Malaysian Muslims participating in Indonesian Jehad against Christians.

The steady rise of religious zeal in Malaysia is clear for a speculation. The Orthodox Islamic party is recognized as the most serious challenge to the present government of Malaysia. Many Malaysian students go to Saudi Arabia, Egypt. and Jordan for higher studies and on their return they get inspired by these ideas of insurgency.

The number of foreign Jehadi fighters trained in Afghanistan is almost 14,000; mostly Saudis, Yemenis, Egyptians and

Algerians are active in Malaysia. They number about 14,000 in this country. The USA is held up as their principal enemy. The growing religious sentiments have become a challenge to the non-theocratic character of the nation.

In a recent development in Malaysia the Islamic party proposed to turn Malaysia into an Islamic country which includes strict Ialamic laws that would punish criminals according to the Ialamic system like the amputation of limbs and killing by stoning. It also proposed to frame laws that would ban a non-Muslim to become the Prime Minister. However this proposal was rejeced for the time being. But when winter comes can spring be far behind?

(e) Philippines

The Philippines has also become a hatching centre of Islamic Jehadi fighters. Out of 70 million of total population the Muslims constitute almost 5 million. Nevertheless the Islamic organization "Moro Liberation Front" (M.L.F.) has been promulgating to form a sovereign independent homeland for the Muslims since 1970. It is a Christian majority country where Islam plays a momentous role to dominate in the national administration by spreading the terrorist network throughout the country and defying the Christian majority government. Even an attempt was made to assassinate the U.S.A President in 1994 and the Pope in 1995 during their visits to the Philippines. The Sunni Hamas and Hizab Allah are the two dreaded militant organizations of the Philippines who play the most important role in subverting this country and leading it towards Islam. They have even gone to the extent of challenging to combat America and its allies. Apart from their distinct characteristics of making attempts to convert the whole of the Philippines into an Islamic country, the Jehadi fighters have advanced their activities by killing the unarmed Christian natives of the Philippines mercilessly. They drag them into the Masjids and shoot them out in the holy shrine of Allah. They even don't hesitate to kidnap and kill the American dwellers in the Philippines on the condition of freeing the Muslim terrorists imprisoned in the U.S. jail related to the bombing of the world Trade Centre in 1993.

But in the same decade in an agreement the government of the Philippines and M.L.F consented to continue their talk for a peace treaty in Tripoli, the capital of Libya, instead of in the Philippines. Due to the ignorance of the Moroist Islamic view of secession from the Philippines, the government of the Philippines showed much generosity towards the M.L.F. and came to a conclusion to meet at Libya under the banner of an Islamic congress. It was decided to hold a plebiscite in April, 17, 1977 and collect the public opinion of 13 South frontiers province of Mindanao, Tabi Tabi, etc.

But before the commencement of this plebiscite the M.L.F withdrew itself from this agreement and again started the movement for an independent Moro Islamic homeland. On the failure in its attempt it again consented to come to attend a round table conference. On the appointed date 32 government representatives, all military officers including 5 Colonels attended the meeting. Just before they shook their hand with the self styled leader of M.L.F all the government representatives fell down on the ground in a pool of blood. The whole world was startled by this nefarious treachery.

In course of perpetual Jehadi fighting in the guise of civil war the government was stupefied to give the right of self-rule to the inhabitants of Mindanao in the year 1996. Again there started another Islamic secessionist movement in the name of M.N.L.F (Moro National Liberation Front) with the partition of the root organization M.L.F. There is another Islamic terrorist organization Abu Sayaf (meaning the Sword of Islam) enlivening its subversive activities under the leadership of Abdur Rajak Abubakar Janjalani who succeeded in pulverizing many Churches and film auditoriums in the Philippines.

After the assassination of its founder Abdur Rajak, this organization is active under the leadership of his brother Gaddafi Janjalani who kept as hostage many foreigners of France, Germany, Finland, etc., to pressurise the government to bow before their demand.

After the formation of this new Islamic state the demand of a broader Muslim autonomous region is the next issue of struggle. Mindanao is at the centre of a potential lucrative growth encircled by Brunei, the Eastern provinces of Malaysia and Indonesia. Fidel Ramos, the then President of the Philippines, a former general who fought for years against the Muslim insurgency at last bowed before the Islamic armed struggle. He invited his nemesis to join in the constitutional fold under the aegis of an honourable and enduring peace and participate in the supreme task of nation-building.

The Jehadi fighters are gathering their strength and power to convert the Philippines into an Islamic country. An Islamised Philippines will enhance the strength of the World Islamic Movement to proceed further in its own mission.

(f) Indonesia

This East Asian country is a constellation of islands and was a centre of attraction for its ancient cultural heritage. After a strong Islamic storm blew over the whole of the Middle East, Central and Eastern part of Asia, Indonesia was crunched vigorously by the Islamic force and got converted into an Islamic country with a 90% Muslim population. But its cultural identity remained unchanged. By religion the people were Muslims but culturally they were Indonesians. The government was purely secular.

It got independence in the year 1945. Having a population of 210 million this is the 5th largest Islamic state in the world. Sukarno, the first prime Minister of Indonesia, had implemented 5 point programmes for its all-round development. America supported insurgency in Indonesia by favouring the uprising of Muslim militancy and disfavoured Sukarno for his support to communism. However Indonesia was able to suppress the Islamic militancy up to 1958. Many revolutionary groups hatched out to form Akeha Mardeka or independent Akeha movement, independent Papua movement, etc.

As long as Suharto was the President of Indonesia, he kept the Muslim fundamentalists out of power. After he was dislodged in the year 1998, there came a great change in its internal politics. His dethronement was synchronous with the revival of Islam in Indonesia. The Islamic supporter Abdur Rehman

Wahid succeeded him. The Islamic thought based political groups made widely popular moves to grab their place. Wahid was the leader of one of the largest Islamic parties, Nihjat ul Ulema that consists of 30 million strong members. This Muslim cleric A.R.Wahid came to power in the election held on June 1999 with an alliance of Islamic parties called the "Central Axis". As a result thousands of moderates were killed by this changing move and Suharto was locked with his followers in a tense battle against Islamic social reformers. In course of time, Wahid was dethroned and Meghawati Sukarnoputri came to power through popular election.

In course of time Jakarta based Islamic leaders called for a Jehad against non-Muslims, particularly Christians who had been staying there for centuries peacefully with the moderate Muslims. The Jehadi fighters killed thousands of Christians in the Christian populated Moluca Island. A Java based Islamic group 'Laskar Jehad' trained and sent thousands of these religious Jehadi fighters by boat to slaughter Christians. Death toll had already reached 6000 in this Island and this communal fire spread to the neighbouring Island Sulawasi and as far as Northern Sumatra. Islamic Jehadi fighters carried on their violence for its own political and financial gain.

Laskar-e-Jehad and other Islamic organizations are active in accelerating ethnic cleansing of Christians and inciting communal hatred in different parts of the country. They organize Muslims to butcher Christians, their only religious enemy in Indonesia. Imposition of Islamic law among the moderate Muslims by the Islamic soldiers known as 'the Talibans of Indonesia' is a very common sight in the present day society.

These Jehadi fighters begin imposing the rudiments of Islamic laws among moderate Muslims like closing the bars, nightclubs, etc. Christians were compelled to raise a new resistance force for their existence in the name of "Laskar-e-Jesus". They have also requested the U.N.O to deploy its peacekeeping force.

Indonesia became a peaceless region. East Timor's independence was announced. The situation got out of control in Ache, Boyan, Molucca and other Indonesian Islands. Dr. Hennery Kissinger, a former adviser of American President, got appointed as the advisor to the President of Indonesia to tackle the chaotic situation.

Besides 210 million peoples' consumption market, Indonesia has rich mines, minerals and cheap labour force, which allures America to consume this Muslim nation's natural wealth. But the worldwide uprising of Islam and its hydra-headed Jehad prevents it to advance any further to gratify its aims and objectives. The recent Bali bomb blast, the worst holocaust since the 9/11-suicide attack, flashed the intensity of Jehadi activities in the excepitionally secular Islamic Indonesia. In the nightclub attack that cost a death toll of 200 persons including 89 Australian tourists was suspected to be a Jehadi plan to provoke the USA.

Though Indonesia is a democratic secular country, it is deeply concerned with the catastrophies of other Islamic states of the world owing to its Islamic fraternity. Hence the Indonesian ruler on the 50th anniversary of the U.N's. establishment declared it as a day of mourning instead of a day of celebration for the U.N's failure to maintain peace in Bosnia.

Islam is growing stronger in Thailand and Islamic terrorism has nestled in this land, which was once famous for its religious co-existence. Party Islamic Se-Malaysia (PAS) is the fundamentalist opposition Malaysia party which harbours separatist guerrillas. Devout Thailand Muslims say that they want primary as well as secondary school girls to wear the modest attire known as Hijab. They try to end the compulsory Thailand dancing lesson in schools and factory workers to be allowed time off to pray. Even when the storm of Western culture rushes into Indonesia it is forced to mould into Islamic culture. So the girl who becomes the first finalist in the annual Miss Indonesia pageant, she wears Muslim headscarf.

(g) Nepal

The Muslims play a dominant role in Nepal, the smallest kingdom and the only Hindu kingdom of the world. In the year 1954, the Muslim population in Nepal was 2.6%.Presently they constitute almost 20% out of the total 19 million population of Nepal. Muslims are financially very sound in Nepal and are reputed in every sphere of life. There are six Muslim M.Ps and 2 Governors in the different states of Nepal. The I.S.I. of Pakistan is very active in Nepal to play its game of insurgency in India. The involvement of the ISI of Pakistan is suspected in the assassination of the Nepalese king Birendra with all his family members.

The Islamic institutions like the World Muslim League of Jeddah, World Islamic Youth League of Kuwait and the Islamic Conference with its headquarters in one of the Gulf countries are engaged in the propagation of Islamic values and conversion in this strategically located Himalayan Hindu Kingdom. The avowed purposes of these organizations is to fuel communal politics and convert poor people to Islam, for which vast resources of petrodollars at their disposal are liberally used. Nepali Muslims are encouraged and financed to attend Islamic institutions outside the kingdom for higher studies and on their return they are motivated to engage in the propagation and conversion of Hindus into Islam.

Some of the agents of these organizations occupy positions of power in the government and are actively working behind it. There has been considerable flow of funds in the name of building of mosques, madrassas, hospitals, colleges, etc. Indian Muslim leaders of national fame also patronize these institutions with an ultimate aim of converting this only Hindu kingdom of the world into a Muslim country.

At the heart of Kathmandu, the capital of Nepal, there stands a multistoried mosque, which is popularly known as the Jama Masjid of Nepal. This is the tallest structure of Nepal and is strategically located barely some 500 metres from the Royal Palace of Nepal. Not farther from this Sunni mosque is another mosque of Shia sect called Kashmiri Takhiya.The Nepali Jama mosque has grown in to a powerful Islamic centre. In this multimillion worth proselytization centre, Friday Namaj is offered under the strict security of police and Gorkha platoons.

There are some terrorist training centres established in the villages of Nepal. A large number of Muslim youths from the border areas of India are conscripted to get the training to create insurgency and the use of sophisticated weapons. In the Narayan ghat of Nepal there is a factory run by a citizen of Pakistan. A retired military officer of Pakistan was appointed there as the chief Managing Director. Ther is an Islamic training centre Jamiya In Way Tamiya situated in the Chandan bara village of Nepal which is a centre of subversive activities. Many alien Muslims get Nepali citizenship in the pseudo name of Hindus. A temple of Lord Srikrishna was demolished in Nepal in retaliation of the Babri demolition in India. Nepal's identification as the only Hindu kingdom in the world is in jeopardy.

(h) Russia

Though communism ideoligically differs from Islam, communist countries are the most suitable lands to hatch out Islamic nations. After the communist revolution in the year 1917, the ever-victorious Islamic revolution has vulcanized the Russian soil for the eruption of Ialamic nations. As a result of this metamorphosis, the former USSR delivered many Islamic nations like Kazakhstan, Uzbekistan Tazikistan, Turkmania, Kirgizia, etc., after the labour experimentation of Glassnost and Perestroika. The Islamic under-current in Russia is expected to create too many Jehadi nations like Dagistan on its soil, which is highly fertilized for Islamic growth.

Russian Muslim students are privileged to study in Muslim Universities outside Russia and now gradually they are gathering strength. The changes occurring in recent years have allowed the Muslims of the former Soviet Union to establish mosques and religious schools and to fulfil their religious obligations such as the pilgrimage to Mecca and Medina. The recitation of the holy Quran can be heard all over Russia.

Some of the old schools are being opened and new schools have been started. There are more than twenty million Muslims in the Russian federation. They are trying to stand an Islamic religious federation in Russia and Islamic revival is taking its initial steps.

After the disintegration of the USSR the Tatar Muslims who constitute a population of 27,000 are trying to revive their ancient Islamic tradition and culture. The Tatars are the most invincible and tough race who were famous for their ruthless attack and infallible victory recorded in the indelible pages of history of many Asian countries.

Iran, which is inimical to the U.S.A, is ideologically a friend of Russia. It asked Iran for military co-operation much to the chagrin of the U.S.A. Accordingly the Russian defence minister Igor Sergeyev visited Iran in his first ever visit to Tehran on December 2000 since the 1979 Islamic revolution. Presently Islam in Russia is under the nursing care of Iran which has confirmed that this old prolific mother is expectant enough to beget the rest of the Islamic republics.

To substantiate this view an international symposium was held at the National cultural centre in Kazan in June 2001 under the theme Islamic culture in Volga Ural Region. The activities in Russia again symbolize the creation of new Islamic states in Russia.

Vladimir Putin proclaimed in the Organisation of Islamic Conference held on 16.10.03 at Putrajaya, the new capital of Malaysia, that Islam has no connection with terrorism. But when the Russian leader Mufti Talgat Tadzhuddin called for a Jehad against the USA before the Muslim multitude gathered in the heavily Muslim populated city Ufa on April3, 03, he did not define what Jehad meant according to his view.

The hostage of 1184 people in Baslan and killing of about 400 innocent children with their parents during the first week of September 2004 might have taught the secular political leaders of Russia about the Islamic Jehad and its expectations.

(i) China

For long Islam has set up its deep footprints in China. As the census account is averse to religion, the accurate number of Muslims in China is not known. But they are a developing society in the society-less communist country. Presently they are in search of an opportunity to shatter communism as they did in the USSR. Islam and Christianity are extremely inimical to communism. Though Christianity and Islam are inimical to each other both fought in their own ways against communism in Russia and their combined effort blasted communism. Both the groups in China are making a similar attempt. Mao applauded pork as the greatest national substantial food treasure of China. In 1993 the Muslims protested against a Chinese book with insulting illustrations of Islamic faith on pork eating. Earlier to this, in the year 1989, the Chinese Muslims protested against the publication of a book written on sexual practices. In both the cases the government complied immediately on the reaction of the Muslims and closed down its printing.

Having established diplomatic relations with Saudi Arabia and other Islamic countries, the Chinese government came under their pressure and began to act sympathetically towards the Muslims of China. The ever-struggling nationalism of the Chinese Muslims will be an important factor in showing their ethnic identity, especially their behaviour, culture and ruling system of China. The present Chinese Government is worried about the growing strength of the Muslims in China. The I.S.I is also trying to intrude into the Sinkiang area of China and in the Muslim region of Tibet.

China in alliance with Pakistan is a combination of Islamic fundamentalism, which does not permit co-existence in peace on equal terms between Muslims and non-Muslims and of Chinese expansionism and hegemonism. The communism in China is functioning with the point of the gun. The pellet of a bullet can penetrate every animated being but Islam is such a tenacious ingredient that a pellet is fruitless to terrify or stupefy it. So China would face its doom before the magnificence of Islam like the former USSR.

Some 9 atomic scientists of Pakistan who were absconded in the year 1997 are known to have been working as engineers in an atomic reactor centre in China. A Pakistani magazine "South Asia Team" has revealed this fact. This incidence enhanced the suspense of the USA. If the technology of atomic weapons comes to the hand of Osama bin Laden, it would cost the security of the USA a lot.

(j) Algeria

Algeria was a French colony. It got its independence in the sixties after a long and hard struggle against France. There was a time when Algeria was world famous for its music orchestra. Now the music director himself comes out to advise his escorts not to participate in any music entertainment programme because it is anti-Islamic. Women are directed to see that no part of their body should look out of Burka. Servicing women who attempt to beautify their appearance lose the security of their lives. Even there is no security of girls who go to school. The Jehadi fighters cut their throats and kill them on their way to school if they are found with their heads uncovered with Hijab. The runners of beauty parlours are no more an excuse. They fall an easy prey to the Islamic sword.

The turning wave in the political and social life of Algeria, a Muslim dominating country, shows how a Muslim majority country resorts through a process of change to convert it into a fundamentally Islamic country. The great revolution of October 1988 in Algeria expressed the people's dissatisfaction towards the government policies. The government made some political reforms and implemented a multi-party system. Then the Muslim leaders formed the Islamic Salvation Front (FIS) with Islamic slogans in the agenda. The FIS won the municipal election and first and second round parliamentary election. The Algerian army backed by the Western countries in a planned scheme forced Chaddi ban Jadid out of office and declared Algeria under army rule on 11 Jan, 1992. Hundreds of Muslims were sent to the firing squad and more than 70,000 were imprisoned.

The Islamic Salvation Front is the strongest Islamic organization, which attempts to snatch the administrative power of the country. After the Government came to power in 1992, it amended the constitution, enhanced the power of the President and suppressed the Islamic rebellion to convert Algeria into an Islamic country. All the ways and means of capturing the power by the Jehadi fighters were closed forever. Laws were enacted not to allow any religious organization to form any political group. As a result a chief Jehadi (Militant) organization Armed

Islamic Jamat has become very active and a war monger. It has taken some severe steps to invalidate the government by killing the election Officers. Consequently military rule has been promulgated in Algeria since 1994. Every year the death toll exceeds 15,000 in civil war in Algeria. If the military force of Algeria is withdrawn or it remains silent, then millions of non-Islamic civilians will be massacred mercilessly until their obliteration.

The Islamic fighters have set fire to 600 schools and universities of Algeria on the ground that the education imparted in schools and institutions are all signs of Western colonialism. So when the ruling army kills the common man on suspicion of being extremists, the extremists kill the common man in the name of Islamisation. But the reason for their association with the terrorists is first to escape from premature Islamic death and second to gratify their brutality by sacking women, which is quite easy and unobtrusive in the role of Mujahids.

A large number of Algerian religious fighters had participated in the USSR- Afghan war. After the disintegration of the USSR they returned to their homeland as victorious Mujahids. Presently they entertain with their bloody game of Jehad in Algeria, which forced 50,000 bureaucrats and intellectuals to leave the country and take shelter in France in the year 1995. Presently there are more than two hundred thousand Muslim infiltrators or refugees excluding 3 million original Islamic population.

At present the USA and other European countries are not in a position to mitigate the heat of Islamic fundamentalism and establish democracy in Algeria by making a fresh and free election. Because if any attempt is made in this field it is quite obvious that the Islamic front which is supported by the Islamic terrorist group will come to power easily as it happened in the year 1991. On the other hand to support the military rule in Algeria is also very troublesome. Because the more the army rule takes stern and stiff steps to suppress and control the Jehadi fighters, the more grows the number of killing of innocent people both by the army taking them mistakably for Mujahids and by the Islamic fighters misunderstanding the public as supporters of the army.

Office personnel, journalists, intellectuals, artists and women having embraced modernity or Western culture have become the target of these Jehadi fighters. It is a very common incident to find 600–700 people assassinated every week in Algeria. Dead bodies, the majority with their throat slit, are found thrown either at the road side or at the entrance gate of a house.

The act of assassination is so extensive that even the most humble village farmer in the field does not escape from the Jehadi hands of these religious reformers. To convert a country into an Islamic state inevitably leads to a civil war where kindness, sympathy, humanity, etc., remain confined only to the pages of a dictionary. These Algerian Jehadi fighters went up to hijacking a French plane to draw the world attention towards their bloody activities. France, the one time imperialist country, is always in apprehension of danger from these Jehadi Mujahids. East European countries also feel suffocated realizing the Islamic danger at their doorstep. Islamic Jehad or religious terrorism has also been successfully exported to Spain, Italy, Tunisia, Morocco, etc.

Armed Muslim activists and security forces have been struggling down to death since 1992 and it shows no sign of ending. According to estimation almost 100000 civilians of Algeria have lost their lives since the army intervened in 1992 to cancel the general elections in which the Islamic Salvation Front (FIS) had taken a landslide lead.

The violence that erupted after the invalidation of the election started with the killing of mostly security forces and male civilians. Women, children and babies later joined the bloody toll.

The killers who started with gun fire and bombs increasingly turned to throat cutting, beheading and even disemboweling of pregnant women. Some victims were even burnt alive. The majority of the people still support the Muslim activists but the officials blame the Islamists for the killings. Besides the desire of most of the country's 29 million people to live in peace, the authorities have a military network. Many villagers have their voluntary groups, armed by the military government. On the other side of the conflict, the security forces kill numerous Islamists. Most of these killings go unreported officially and the press is heavily censored. Any mediation draws fierce rejection from the Algerian Military rulers, who would have to be party to any negotiation. The military thinks that they have apparently won the civil war against the Islamists. In Algeria there is constant war between the military and militants.

Mr.Kofi Annan, the Secretary General of the UNO, wanted to step in the Algerian crisis but the Algerian President Liamin Zeroul bluntly refused him to interfere in Algeria's internal affairs.

The military administration of Algeria does not give journalist visa to foreign journalists. Moreover it does not want that the incidents happening in Algeria should leak out. On the other hand the Jehadi fighters like the Islamic Salvation Front frowns over any news that carries out the reformatory deeds carried out by them. Hence it is very difficult to know the incidents happening in this country. In the year 1994 the Jehadi fighters of Algeria killed 27 journalists of different news agencies indiscriminately. According to them to be a journalist is unIslamic and its only punishment is death. If any body attempts to fight against the Mujahids or Islamic militants with the pen he should be punished by the sword. Even all sorts of entertainment programmes in public is declared kufr (sin) or anti-Islamic.

The Islamic Salvation Front is the Prime Jehadi (Islamic terrorist) group of Algeria, which has aimed at making Algeria an Islamic country or Dar-ul-Islam. The intention of this front is only to confront its key target, the military rule. There are other Islamic terrorist groups in Algeria like the "Armed Islamic Groups" which have undertaken the responsibility to assassinate the foreigners, particularly the Europeans. It also opposes all sorts of negotiations. It seems that the opposite party, which represents 85% of the Algerian people with full Islamic value in agenda, is the only alternative to solve the problem in Algeria.

(k) South Africa

The first Immigration of Muslims to South Africa took place 300 years ago from Indonesia. The first group of exiled Muslims from Indonesia was sent by its Dutch rulers towards the end of 17th century as slaves to plantations in South Africa. A 14 member Islamic group consisted of Seikh Yussuf with his two wives and children who was considered to be a rebellious Muslim leader in Indonesia against their colonial rulers was deported to South Africa. Thereafter began perpetual deportation of Muslim slaves from Indonesia to South Africa. These Muslims converted the local Africans and formed the first minority group of Muslims in South Africa. They celebrated their tercentennial festival of their arrival in the Cape of Good Hope in the year 1994. Presently the population of the Muslims of Indonesian origins in South Africa is more than 300000.

The second group of Muslims belongs to Indian origin that were migrated to South Africa by the British. However the Muslims as a community have its forceful pressure over the whole of South African state. Their number is also estimated to be about 250000.

Although Muslims constitute 2% of the total South African population, they hold most important positions in government affairs including higher posts of administration. The South African government has provided one of the halls of the Parliament for worship of its Muslim members. The Muslims in South Africa are given all sorts of religious freedom like prayer calls for Azan, 5 times prayers in the mosque, shearing of animals by Islamic process (Halal), nomenclature in full Islamic style, following all traditions and costumes.

Nevertheless the "Bill of Right" contradicts to some extent the Islamic status of the Muslims. Hence the Muslim community in South Africa is engaged in debating to submit to the government a draft of a law on the status of the Muslims. They want to gain their share of right as they had paid a heavy price in the South African freedom movement to throw away the colonial yoke.

The Muslims of South Africa have developed a sense of hatred towards the Europeans. The key reason is that whenever they arrived in any part of the world whether it be in Hindu India, or Buddhist Sri Lanka or Black Africa, they were encountered and obstructed only by the European Christians. From Indonesia to South Africa they had to encounter the Christians first.

The South African president Thabo Mbeki expressed his full support fo. Yasser Arafat's P.L.O. and the struggle of the Palestinians. Muslims of South Africa asked the government to break off diplomatic ties with Israel. Mbeki said on behalf of the ruling African National Congress, "we extend our solidarity to Palestine Liberation Organization. PLO, who has always stood with African National Congress and now when A.N.C is in power it has to return the favour".

(l) Somalia

Another African country Somalia has undergone a horrendous civil war to finalize its national identity in the line of Islam. Besieged by the adversities of the starving Somalians, the USA decided towards the end of 1992 to send a large military force on a humanitarian mission to deliver food to the starving people. But the Somalian Muslims without any consideration repudiated this noble intention of the USA. The peace-keeping force which constituted an army of about 21 thousand soldiers from 29 countries of the world are also in a quandary whether to stay there or return to their homeland.

To encounter the charitable organization of U.S Muslims came forward with "Islamic world Association" and "World Muslim Relief" claiming that they are the only organizations which do real charitable work in Somalia unlike the West which comes only to gratify their own interest.

Mohammed Farrah Eidid, the formidable Islamic leader, has been receiving all sorts of military aid from Iran, Sudan, Egypt, Pakistan and Afghanistan to combat against the USA and the U.N led forces with an intention to stop their intervention into the land of Somalia. Hence in the face of death of thousands every day the militant terrorist training camps in Somalia are on. They proclaim that the intervention of the U.S military force in Somalia would consolidate the occupation of the United State's power in the Arabian Peninsula and the Gulf countries. All the Muslim factions stood against the U.S. Iran used the Sunni Islamic Terrorists and Afghan refugees as its terrorist assets in Somalia against the U.S. force. Even Iraq also participated with the Iran- Sudanese alliance to oust the U.S force from the Islamic land of Somalia. Iran has deployed the Hizb Allah suicide force to launch an all-round attack on the U.N force that would compel it to withdraw from the Somalian land as it had happened in Beirut. It has become a question of prestige for the U.N and the USA to withdraw their troops from the land of Somalia and pave the way for Islam to have a global victory.

The Islamic Jehadi leader is very cunning and is a dare devil. His rebellious Islamic militants killed 35 UNO army men. It became a day-to-day affair of fighting between the peace-keeping force and the revolutionary army of Somalia headed by Md. Edid. With a motive to nab Edid and bring the matter to an end, the USA bombarded a hall where General Eidid was in close deliberation with his top leaders. The house was completely destroyed, but Edid escaped sharply.

The whole of UNO army has been put under a shameful failure to nab red-handed the Islamic revolutionary Md. Farah Eidid. This single Jehadi fighter has shattered all the plans of the peacekeeping force of the UNO to capture him. After he killed 4 American soldiers of PKF, America deployed 400 more soldiers besides 1200 American soldiers who were sent earlier. There is also a special commando force deployed with [illegible] helicopters. An award of 25,000 dollars has been announced for the head of Edid either dead or alive.

Such a precarious condition of Somalia forced the people to die out of starvation and hunger. Millions of Muslims take refuge in neighbouring countries like Kenya. Every day an average of 1000 people die of hunger. The incessant civil war turned more than 1 million people homeless.

Somalian Muslim students have established an organization called Hizbollah (Hizb Allah) to struggle against the opponents of Islam. However Somalia is the testing ground of strength and power of the Western block. The tug of war between the Islamic force and the UNO would decide whether the UNO would be able to curb the growing Islamic strength in world scenario or it has to retreat with bag and baggage from the international altitude of power exhibition for ever.

(m) Nigeria

Out of the total population of 110 million, 60% Nigerians are Muslims. It got independence from the British in the year 1960. Eight Northern states of Nigeria are Islamic states, which has implemented the Shariat law. Gradually the whole of Nigeria is going to be declared a Muslim country. Hence America and other Christian countries are trying to create communal tension in Nigeria. At the time of U.S President Mr. Bill Clinton's visit to Nigeria in August 2000 there was a strong voice of protest against him besides the burning of the European flag and giving anti-USA slogans.

(n) Sudan

Sudan is an African country with a population of Islamic majority. Here Islam and slavery go together. After it got independence in the year 1957 it fell a prey to violent civil war. Its capital Khartum is under Muslim majority. Out of the 30 million people of Sudan six millions are animists and Christians. The fundamentalist Arab Government in Khartum has been imposing the Islamic Shariat law on the religions and ethnic minorities of Sudan. About 2 million people have been killed during the civil war between the Cross and the Crescent. Christian majority dominates its southern part. In this country more than one lakh people have been languishing under slavery. The Muslim majority who reside in the northern part of the river Keer says that the Quran has sanctioned them the privilege to convert the blacks into slavery. So the Muslims keep use of the Dinka tribals as their slaves. They use the selected women folk of this tribal race as their concubines, convert them in to Islam and proliferate children.

These Sudanese people are collectively tied with ropes in chain and asked to go to distant places to be deployed by their

Islamic masters as slave labourers. Islamic groups like the People's Defense Force (PDF) drive them and guide them to the place of destination. These Islam masters regularly rape the "Dinka" women as many times as they can until women go senseless. After they regain their sense they are sporadically asked to drink their master's urine. At times as an aftermath action of rape the Muslims shear the breasts of the women and throw them to be eaten by stray dogs.

There was a time when Sudan was noted for its religious tolerance. In the year 1989 the government of Sadiq al Mehdi was dissolved. Soon after it, Sudan became a target of extremists. After Al-Basir took over the charge of Sudan he patronized Islamic fundamentalism. He forced the bureaucrats of Sudan to take 45 days military training to keep their service intact. The key slogan that echoes around the training camps is "Allah Ho Akbar. Lah Illah Illalah"(There is no God but Allah and Mohammed His Prophet) During the training period the trainees are required to get Islamic education and Anti-American stance. The USA is the key target of the whole of the Muslim population of Sudan.

Islamic fundamentalism and anti-American stance go hand in hand in Sudan. Al-Basir's government banned almost all the political parties and expelled more than 5000 military officers from their post who seemed secular and non-fundamentalist. Those who are suspected of being anti-Islamists are instantaneously put in prison and highly persecuted. An organization called "Islamic Popular Police" exercises its highhandedness and is assigned to Islamise the society. Preaching Christianity and imparting Christian education is a day dream.

Although Sudan does not seem to have sufficient means for confrontation, it holds the aim to create Islamic holy war or Jehad worldwide and convert the earth into a holy land of Allah. The door of Sudan is always open for the Islamic extremists or Jehadi fighters of all the Islamic and non-Islamic countries like the Jehadi group Hamas of Palestine and the Hijbullah group of Iran. Sudan also used to send war ammunitions to the extremist leaders of Somalia.

The Muslim inhabitants of Northern Sudan are in violent war against the Christians of Southern Sudan since 1976. The population of African Christians residing in South Sudan is almost 750000. They are on the verge of extinction by the fierce attack of Sudanese army which is an assimilation of young Muslim Mujahiddins. Christians have their own organization"People's Liberation Army" which is nothing before the army formed by Muslim Jehadi fighters. The civil war in Sudan has caused a death toll of more than 1million people and more than 3 millions have taken refuge in the camps pitched by the UNO.

Majority of Blacks have embrassed Islam. Egypt, Libya, Saudi Arabia, Ethiopia and Kenya etc., surround it. Although the European rulers converted the Blacks of Sudan into Christianity, Muslims exceed Christians in Sudan. Islamic extremist groups have been formed to expel or end the Europeans and Jews from this soil. They are very active in Sudan for ethnic cleansing. Islamic government in Sudan patronizes Arab militia for the exodus of ethnic Christians who have taken shelter in refugee camps for fear of pogrom by Muslim militants. The security situation of Darfur is compelling the United Nations to come out of its burrow to talk with the government for the security of the Christians of Sudan. The Jehadi fighters with an Arabic patronization called Janjaweed (devils on horse back in Arabic) now have started to loot and burn farming villages as a plan to cleanse the ethnic citizens from the locality. United Nations called Darfur the worst humanitarian crisis in the world. The UN workers are also denied access to the camps filled with refugees and malnourished children.

Muslims come successful in their attempt to exterminate the foreigners as the government is backing them. They are so influential in Sudan that when the oil reservoirs were detected, they invited many foreign companies but ostracized American farms. America and its allies have kept an eye on Sudan. Hence Ethiopia, Uganda and Eritrea are on the ready position to attack Sudan. Although foreign aid to Sudan is stopped from 1990 and numerous domestic chaos have been hatched out, the Muslim youths of Sudan are prepared to answer with their best of strength and unity. American firms tried to poke in their petroleum reservoirs but the Muslims could stand as a great barrier against foreign aggressions. The bombardment on the American embassy was a symbol of expression of Islamic anger over the USA.

At last a peace deal was signed to bring the Sudanese civil war to an end. Sudan's vice president and the country's main rebel leader signed a comprehensive peace agreement to end Africa's longest running conflict on January 9, 2004 concluding an 8 year process to stop a civil war that cost more than two million lives since 1983. But peace treaty does not seem to be a solution to bring a civil war toan end. It is only an ointment applied for a temporary relief.

(o) Egypt

Islam, though not so old compared to Christianity, flourished in many countries of ancient civilizations. Wherever it flourished, it expanded not like a cloud in the sky but embedded like a root in the soil. Egypt is a typical example of such characteristics. It had an ancient civilization on its soil, which dates back 5000 years. But today Egypt is no more proud of its Sphinx and Pyramids. It is proud of its one thousand year old seat of Islamic learning. The best of its example can be quoted from Al Azhar who plans to make its entire collection of 44000 Muslim manuscripts for the first time on the Internet.

As an inheritant of one of the most ancient civilizations of the world, Egypt feels the pride of an Islamic country. The Romans took over Egypt from Cleopatra and her Greeks and made it her repository. When Constantinople imposed Paul's version of Christianity in the Roman Empire, Egypt's Monophysite Christians resisted the innovations. The Roman Catholic Church declared the Coptic Church of Egypt heretical in 456 and the rift between the two Churches continued ever since.

Almost 20 years after the emergence of Islam in the Arabian Peninsula, Egypt became an integral part of the Muslim world. Islam completely transformed the texture of the country and thoroughly Arabicised its society. Consequently Egypt became an important centre of Islamic art, architecture and learning.

This noble and peace-loving country is gradually leaning over Islamic fundamentalism to be administered according to the law of Shariat. To reach its destination Islamic fundamental institutions like Muslim Brotherhood, Al Gama'at-ul Islamiya etc. are functioning very sincerely. Hasan Al Banna founded Muslim Brotherhood in Egypt in 1928. From the very beginning the Ikhwan movement aimed at finding Islamic solutions of the problems of education, economic organization and social justice in the Society. It advocated an Islamic nation without any separation of religion and state. Next, it proposed an Islamic educational system whose goal was to create Muslim individuals, Muslim houses and a Muslim Government. It also created an economic infrastructure based on Islamic principles to solve social injustice.

In the midst of this heritage, weighty of the consequence, the mission of the Ikhwan was (a) to free the Islamic fatherland from all foreign domination and (b) to help a free Islamic state arise in this Islamic majority land.

The profound feeling of Islamic fundamentalism gradually forbade the sense of secularism and religious neutrality from the Egyptian administration. This led to the assassination of the former president Anwar Al Sadat in October 1981 in a military parade in Cairo by Jehadi fighters. His only crime was that he signed the Camp David Treaty with Israel and he was friendly with the U.S.A. His human right record and philanthropic attitude did not matter to Islam.

Emergency was declared in Egypt since 1980, possibly to suppress the growing Islamic fundamentalism. The emergency was again extended up to 2003 to normalize the situation. The killing of Anwar Sadat warned the rulers of Egypt to be conscious of their position and security for life owing to the growing fundamentalism in Egypt and the anti-American stance of Egyptians. However the anti-Islamic attitude of Hosni Mubarak subsided following improvements of Egypt's relation with the Arab and other Muslim countries and the relation of the Arab league membership in 1989. Inspite of his attempt to maintain a balance of neutrality among the European countries, he favoured Islamisation of Egypt. He emerged as the first Egyptian President to visit Lebanon. He is an active member of the Organisation of Islamic Conference. His neutral policy makes him keep good relation with Israel. But some fundamentalist Islamic countries are pressurizing Egypt to change its policy and realize that Israel is an illegal entity and ought not to exist on the map of the Middle East. An attempt has been made to implement Islamic law Shariat in Egypt. The Muslim lady pilot Nerin Salem's instance may be taken into consideration. She was a co-pilot of Egypt's Shrouk Air who used head scarf (Islamic Hijab) in addition to her pilot uniform.

Al Banna considered it the duty of each Muslim to help build such a state "for as long as the state does not emerge, the Muslims in their totality are committing sins". It is now apprehended that Ikhwan-ul-Muslimaeen party, the largest anti-Mubark faction, will establish the foundation of Islamic government in Egypt.

(p) Canada

Canada, the neighbour of the USA, is also of no exception in this regard. The government is now under heavy pressure of Islamic expansionism on its soil. Muslim migrants from the Afro-Asian countries have strengthened their foundation in this nice soil of eternal tranquility. The Canadian Broadcasting Corporation (CBC) has apologized to the Canadian Muslims for a news report (broadcast on July 13, 2001) that seemed to link Muslim prayers to the issue of terrorism.

(q) Argentina

Countries like Argentina are gradually coming under the power of Islam to encircle the USA and help the process of transformation of Civilizations. After the Spaniards conquered Argentina towards the end of 16th century, the Spanish Moriscoses were among the early Muslim immigrants who landed in Argentina and settled there forever. These Muslim immigrants were actually forced to leave Andalucia and after arriving in America they followed their Islamic tenets very strictly and simultaneously became the eyesores of the local Christians. Enemity continued. The Spanish Catholic Church burned many of them alive; nevertheless they kept the Islamic tradition still alive.

History reveals that Islamic immigration from Palestine, Jordan and Syria in large numbers continued to Argentina from 1880 to1955. Soon they speedily increased their population by migration and birth proliferation. They constituted the third largest society after the Spanish and Italians. But religiously they have formed the second largest society after Christianity. Now the Muslim population is more than 500000 and the majority of them remain in Buenos Aires, the capital city. The rest are scattered all over Argentina and mostly live in the Northern provinces.

Muslims in Argentina established their first Islamic institution in the year 1918 in Buenos Aires where a large mosque has been built by the Al-Azhar. In addition to the centre a number of Islamic union have also been established, the most important being "The Islamic Union of Arab Argentines". This union set up the first Islamic school in the capital, which teaches Arabic and Islamology in Argentina.

Observing the overspreading population of Muslims, the government of Argentina imposed certain rules to check their progress and this put them into inconveniences. This caused the Muslims to admit their "enemies" in to their circles on the grounds of being compatriots and instead of convening in mosques they get together with their compulsory friends of different religions in clubs constructed in different parts of the country.

Such an attempt to check the Islamic aggression by the government in Argentina has made the community tremendously irate and reactionary. Because never does a Muslim in general want to remain outside of its ghetto or community and he never allows others to find out its secluded Islamic social structures. The Muslims have now undone to gratify their anger against Christian Argentineans whom they ascertained as their enemy.

Besides, the Muslim youths don't receive any financial assistance to learn Arabic, the language of the holy Quran. They cannot nomenclature themselves by Arabic names, for the national laws force people to use Christian names and not converse in any other language other than Spanish or Italian. The enemies also try to convert Muslims to Christianity. The situation is made so desperate that some Muslims hold their wedding ceremonies in Catholic Churches. Islam as a religion is completely ignored in Argentina. Presently the Muslims of Argentina are in search of an opportunity to vent their anger.

(r) Sweden

Gradually Sweden is melting itself to be reshaped and squeezed into the Islamic mould. Immigration of Muslims to Sweden is just in a primary stage and Islam is not in tune with the utter bewildering birthrate. Hence very cunningly they use the Church for their prayer. After the prayer is over on every Sunday the church is crowded by Muslims. Presently children in Sweden are found having nomenclature prefixing Mohammed and they outnumber the children with Swedish names.

(s) Thailand

Thailand is another Islamic majority country. Though the people are religiously Muslims, their cultural heritage quite differs from the Islamic tenets of the Arabs. Generally it is supposed that what is Islam must be Arabic. But the Thailanders are exceptionally different people viewed from this conception. In the present Islamic spate propped with militancy to submerge the world civilization could not keep the dance-loving Thai youths aloof from the influence of Global Islamic Movement. To imbibe the country with pure Islamic Ummah the Muslim youths raided some village defence units with machetes in hand. The security force was tipped of it earlier about their maiden attempt and it instantaneously opened firing and gunned them down killing more than 100 youths most of whom were teenager sorcerers. The rest took shelter in a 16th century mosque but did not surrender even after six hours standoff. At last the security force seized them and killed them all.

Killing of these machete armed Muslim zealots without any provocation touched the heart of Muslim thinkers of the state and infuriated the Jehadi terrorists abroad. The Laskar–e–Toiba of Pakistan and Harkat ul Jehad al Islami of Bangladesh have approached this land to give the land a Jehadi touch.

Ethnic cleansing of Buddhists in Thailand has been promulgated to end religious unrest and boost Islam as the religion of peace. The Thai Buddhists constitute 20% of the total national population. They are presently on the verge of extinction by regular explosions and shootings by the fighters of Muslim separatist movement.

Apart from the prominent European countries like England, France, Germany, etc., small nations like Sweden and Norway have also became the target of Islamic terrorist network. These Islamic militants have been trained in Pakistan and Afghanistan, operate in Sweden and Norway to collect money and spread terrorist propaganda.

(t) Bulgaria

Muslims are now tightly closed with the politics of almost all the European countries. Take the case of Bulgaria. The Ex-king of Bulgaria Simon–II fought in the general election held on June 17, 2001 through his National Movement Party and won 120 seats but was short of absolute majority in the Parliament of 240 seats. The Turkish Muslims having a population of about a million had won 21 seats in the Parliament and on the request of the Ex-king and leader of N.M. Party they consented to share in the formation of a new government in Bulgaria.

(u) Denmark

In the Scandinavian country of Denmark Muslims too are searching for new methods to achieve spiritual liberty. Islam moves slowly but with confidence amidst the battle of Danish life. This movement mainly started from the 1960s when thousands of workers and Muslim professionals immigrated to those regions of Scandinavia with a good climate in search jobs.

The immigrant Muslim population in Denmark is mostly comprised of Pakistanis and Turks. Other nationalities such as

Yugoslaves, Albanians,North Africans(particularly from Maghreb) also form the Islamic population of Denmark.

Apart from the immigrants there are also a large number of political refugees such as Palestinians, Qurds, Iraqis, etc. The population of the Turks is about 3000 thousand. Arab Muslims number about 15000, almost half of the Turkish population. Out of 5 million total population the number of native Danish Muslim is about 3000. Muslims had to undergo a hard struggle for their survival. Many rented buildings have been used as mosques for prayer. Local Christians are well aware of the tenets of Muslims like Islamic fastings, hijab burka,halal etc.

(v) Saudi Arabia

Saudi Arabia, the supreme centre of Islamic religious confluence, is also not free from the sting of hydra-headed Islamic Jehad. It is an Islamic country with secular attitude having security ties with the USA and other NATO countries. The bomb explosion that shattered the town in November 1995 in Saudi Arabia proved that the attack would continue until the last man of Euro America departs from the Arabian soil. The successive bomb blasts in the USA military establishment in Saudi Arabia since 1995 signifies the profoundness of Islamic militancy.

A migratory bird belongs to that land so long as the bird hovers over it. It is destined to cross over hundreds of demarcated lands during its long journey.

A Muslim belongs to that land on earth where he is currently present. He is a citizen of a world community and above of all nationalism. Daud, Osama, Omar, Anees, Edid are like each one among the millions of migratory birds. You cannot determine their citizenship. If you have targeted one amongst them considering him to be the citizen of a particular country, it is obvious that you are groping foolishly.

4

Transformation of Civilizations

"Nations and tribes flourished and vanished and history gives reasons for it.

One single, simple, naked reason in all cases that the people were not fit." – Anonymous

"The day will surely come when unbelivers will wish that they were muslims."

– Prophet Mohammed in Quran, 15/11

16. Transformation of Civilizations, the Greatest Apprehension of this Millennium

Theory of Transformation of Civilizations

According to this theory, in a society where people are disorganized, comfort-seeking, extremely kind-hearted, even tolerant towards their enemies, cowardice, peace-loving, believe in secularism, extremely generous and philanthropic in nature, the society loses its national civic immunity or the ability of its 'civic defence'. When such a society comes into contact with a barbarous invading race, then starts a stream of collision, and the lustre of its social life gradually deteriorates and comes under the threat of extinction.

The struggle for existence always follows the survival of the fittest. People of a stronger civilization always try to dominate the people of a weaker civilization and this dominance of one over another has been going on since the beginning of civilizations in the world. A time comes when the population of the society (of the weaker civilization) deteriorates either by migration or by conversion into the stronger society (civilization) or by death. Naturally the society of the stronger civilization dominates over the land of the weaker civilization and lords over the land either by wiping out the weaker society or keeping it as a minority community. In this way a civic defenceless society, although majority in population, gets transformed by the stronger minority society abdicating the land and its "majority" statues to the former minority community and itself turns down into "minority" or extincts. This process is called the process of Transformation of Civilizations.

Every society is subject to a perennial stream of change in its social life or transformation of its peripheral structure with the sporadically varnishing of superstition and wave of reformation in a cyclical movement. But Transformation of Civilizations is such a billow of tide that completely changes the infrastructure of a society by pulverizing its shape from its very root as is marked in the dissolution of ancient Persia in the Iranian soil, the ancient Vedic civilization in Afghanistan, Pakistan and Bangladeshi soil and the ancient Egyptian civilization on the soil of Egypt. There are people civilized and flourishing on all the above countries but nobody is there to claim their ancestry linking with the extinct civilizations which had once flourished in those lands. The former perished civilizations were absorbed or usurped by the latter civilizations due to their debility to withstand before the pressure of the latter. This is the spirit of Transformation of Civilizations.

The initial decades of the third millennium of the Christian era will mark the confrontation of two biggest civilizations that would give rise to the great Transformation of Civilizations. The collision of the two civilizations that would lead the great Transformation would cover the entire human race on the surface of the earth. The great process would lead to a large-scale massacre and absolute change of societies. All these transactions would occur through the moving cog of the Great War that would activate the great Transformation of Civilizations. This change shall be the biggest of all past changes and the war shall be the greatest of all past wars. But the chief category of the war would be the Civil War.

When a country inimically confronts another country to wage a war, there stem the transfer of wealth, pride and territorial ownership of a kingdom or a country to another. But when a civilization stands inimically against another civilization the confrontation causes the dissolution of culture, religion, language, etc., of the counter civilization.

Some 17 hundred years ago there flourished Christianity in the European countries. In the later period it was introduced and developed as the Western pattern of Modern Civilization. Some 14 hundred years ago there started Islamic thought sponsored by Mohammed. Both thoughts stormed over different parts of the world absorbing and imbibing different nations into their respective folds. Christianity advanced with Cross, the Church, the Bible, the Missionaries and the Crusade. Islam also advanced with the Crescent, the Mosque, the Quran, the Mullahs, the Mujahids and the Jehad. Both are unique in their respective fields. Many nations each with a specific brand of civilization dissolved their identity into oblivion when they came into the contact of either of the two civilizations. The ancient civilizations of Afghanistan, Pakistan, Iran, Iraq, Greece, the USA, Egypt, etc., all perished, as they could not withstand before the storm. As a large fish swallows the small ones for its survival, a bigger Civilization also absorbs or digests other feebler civilizations according to the law of the "Survival of the fittest". With few exceptions Islam and Christianity, after digesting all other civilizations, now stand in an atitude of confrontation to absorb each other. This attempt to trap or digest one another would lead to a war, a global civil war, and the greatest of all the wars, signifying the Transformation of civilizations.

The Transformation of Civilizations has its implications over all the countries of the world without any distinction of West and East, South and North. The distinction is with its fervour in respect of its different phases that the country has undergone. Many Islamic countries like Turkey, Malaysia and Thailand, which observe non-Islamic cultural tenets, also come under this purview. The non-Islamic African countries and other Christian countries having a strong Islamic lobby as the minority race, also come under the perimeter of this Transformational upheavals.

Bipolar Power Horn

No sooner had the Twenty-first century opened its eyes, it first saw Islam as the most luxuriant and dreadful power structure with its strong infrastructure challenging the supremacy of Western Civilization.

After the demolition of the World Trade Centre there rose a great question mark along with the pervading dusts of the debris –"What is that vital force behind this attack that could dare to take such a bold step the world had ever seen?" Amazingly the U.S.A. also misquoted it as an attack made by some terrorists and the process started accordingly to nab them.

Regretfully, the U.S.A misunderstood Jehad, the Islamic Invasion or Islamic religious war, as attack by some terrorists. As long as one has not understood the nature and origin of terrorism, one can affoıd least security to one's nation, however sincere one's attempt would have been.

One can find in the Quran the spirit of the present religious fighters or Mujahids whose horrendous acts are described as the holiest of duties. Many nations have lost their ancient glorious civilizations under the onslaught of Christian and Islamic invasions. The current position of different nations, whether developed or underdeveloped, is on the same track and in the same trend, heading to be obliterated into the Islamic oblivion.

The root cause of extinction of civilizations is their lack of capacity to assimilate what they accepted or introduced in their social life to pull on together with. The example of India may be taken into consideration. The Aryans were great thinkers and their social infrastructure was strong and perfect from every point. In course of time the Aryans became more philanthropic and universalized. Their social structure with a great defensive force crumbled down by the nonviolent movements and movements of universal humanism propounded by Gautam Buddha, Mahavir Jain and later by Mahatma Gandhi. Consequently India became disintegrated. The modern Aryan descendants did not think about the reconciliation of their disrupted roots. Now if the present situation gets promulgated unhampered, apprehension of segregation of India is inevitable with in 2025.

A similar plight is marked in the lives of modern Americans and Europeans. They are extremely nationalistic. They love their respective nations, which are the combinations of their language, culture, social customs traditions, etc. confined to a particular chunk of land or political territory. But having inclined extremely towards luxury, materialistic enjoyment, determination for birth control, interest to lead nuclear family, homosexual life, philanthropic attitude, etc., paved their social infrastructure to a hectic state day by day. Their universal inquisition, irresistible temptation to liberate the heathens of different countries of the world and extreme interest in universal tourism deteriorated their population. On the other hand the large number of Muslim immigrants and infiltrators and their proliferated descendants filled up their population vacuum created in their absence, in their attempt at decreasing their population by birth control and their plan of accommodation to innumerable immigrants in their respective countries for building constructions and other menial jobs. Confrontation betwen two civilizations on the chest of Europe and the USA is rampant and clearly visible.

There is a second great question which stands on the tomb of the World Trade Centre.- "What would be the national identification of Europe and the USA towards the year 2020 ? Will the civilization be identified with the Muslim civilization or the Western (Christian) civilization?"

The ancient civilizations of Iran, Iraq, Afghanistan, Pakistan, Egypt, etc., faced its doom. These were completely rooted out and were usurped by Islam. India has been in the experimental stage of the great Transformation for 1000 years. Present India has lost its true national ethos. Civil war has been promulgated among the majority and minority communities in the shape of invasion of minority civilizations over the majority civilization as a part of strategy of Transformation of Civilizations.

One Hitler was noted for his notoriety in killing off the Jews with the avowed intention of ethnic cleansing. But Hitler was an embodiment of destruction that suited a world, which is now

60 years old. The death of Hitler dug the grave of Hitlerism or Nazism. But Osama bin Mohammed bin Laden is a thousand times more powerful and dreadful than Hitler. He is not imbibed with any regionalism or territorial nationalism like Hitler. He is a part of the great Global Islamic Movement that can produce thousands of Ladens in every comer of the world. Ridiculously the U.S.A is chasing after one Laden. Within the year 2015 Ladens will be found in thousands in every corner of the USA, in its assembly halls and also in the White House.

When the words flashed on the television on September 11, 2001 "Terrorists hit U.S.A" it angered Muslims as never before. Because according to Islam they are not the terrorists. They were never terrorists. They are the most religious persons, devoted to Islam and what they performed is the most sacred and holiest duty with much devotion and fidelity in the name of Allah.

The U.S.A misunderstood the acts done by some Muslim Jehadi fighters as the acts of terrorists. It is a great blunder. It perhaps misunderstands the idea that a Muslim, as a part of his religion, must try to wipe out non-Muslims. To create terrorism is a challenge to wage the war and to test the strength of the opposition. Hence one should read a 'terrorist' as a Mujahid or Islamic religious fighter or Jehadi fighter. "Terrorism" is itself the war against non-Muslims. In Islamic terms it is called Jehad or the religious war.

Presently almost all the countries of the world are put into a cauldron of cold war. This is closely interlinked with the Transformation of Civilizations. The attack on the World Trade Centre and its counter attack on Afghanistan and Iraq is simply its sparkling revelation that would sporadically take place when the colliding force of cold war bursts out.

When the U.S.A expanded its imperialism by threatening with nuclear power, it found the U.S.S.R as its rival to face the challenge of the USA's expansion of colonialism. After a long confrontation the U.S.S.R collapsed. When the wrapper of communism was removed from the carcass of the USSR, most amazingly people found in it a hydra headed Islamic cobra hibernating to wake up simply to participate in the acceleration of the Transformation of Civilizations.

The war meant for the Transformation of Civilizations always accompanies by a stream of bloodshed where the nation under the process of transformation takes a sanguine bath. This is inevitable and infallible like the principles of mathematics. More than 10 million people lost their lives in India for this Transformation of Civilizations for 1000 years. In Uganda it took a death toll of more than half a million people. In the U.S.A it was about half a million that exterminated the Red Indians. For the formation of Pakistan the ethnic cleansing witnessed a death toll of 1 million Hindus in the year 1947 and the flight of more than six million people as refugees. In the year 1950, Islamic Mujahids in Bangladesh (Then East Pakistan) killed half a million non-Muslims with an exodus of four and half million refugees. At the time of formation of Bangladesh 3 million Hindus were sacrificed on the altar of the Transformation of Civilizations in the year 1971. Communism vainly participated in the Transformation of Civilizations in the former Russia in the year 1917 to form a temporary cabin in the name of the USSR. Owing to the lack of a strong foundation of stipulated principles the U.S.S.R was dissolved in to Russia in the year 1989 and silenced with a death toll of 12 million, mostly at the hands of Stalin. Carnage in the former Yugoslavian states also comes into account. Squeezing the people to drip blood for this Transformation of Civilizations in the countries like the U.S.A, Chechnya, Indonesia, the Philippines, Algeria and India are under process. The European countries like England, France, Germany, Italy, etc., are put in the cauldron of Transformation of Civilizations.

As a self-styled reformist Euro-America has been endeavouring to educate, reform and enlighten the so-called heathens, and blind believers of different nations of the world have been at last trapped by the Islamic fowlers and it is difficult to escape from its claw. A great danger writ on the fortune of the Euro-Americans relevant to its cultural transformation will be unavoidable as schemed by the Global Islamic Movement towards 2015 A.D. The process of action revealed during these days also indicates the veracity of the prophecy.

Islam is on the rise. Islamic Jehadi fighters are consoled with a promise of attaining Paradise filled with indescribable pleasure of wine, women and nectar. Fighting against its enemy or non-Muslims simply means the fighting for Allah and the attainment of a pleasurable Paradise after their Islamic death.

It is not a matter of surprise to note that America helped a lot to Afghanistan to fight against the USSR who had extended its octopus like tentacles towards Afghanistan. The USSR had a colonial administration in Afghanistan under the leadership of Dr. Nazibullah. But at the end Dr.Nazibullah was electrocuted and hanged. In due course Afghanistan rebuffed America's unquestioning supremacy.

Islam now stands as a global mentor to crane the process of world civilization. The world of Islam extends from the West Cost of Africa and Atlantic Ocean to the borders of Sin kiang (China) and Bangladesh in the East. Its northern boundaries are in Central Asia and extend to south up to Somalia on the equatorial line in Africa. In Asia its boundaries extended eastwards to include Indonesia while in Africa its importance is such that some Western writers often mention Africa as an Islamic continent.

Islam is coming out of the hold of Christian imperialism. The situation of Islam in North Africa, Asia and the Middle East bears evidence to this fact. The Muslim minorities in Europe and the U.S.A now show more commitment to Islam than they did in the past. The tendency shown towards Islam by the Bosnian people and the establishment of an independent Bosnian state in the heart of Europe substantiates this fact. Muslim nations cannot accept the sovereignty of the West in their own countries. If the European countries respect the rights of the Muslim nations there will be no friction. On the contrary if the Euro-Americans will not react to Islam, European culture and Western civilization besides Christian religion will no more exist except in the pages of history. There was a time when Christianity stormed the world with the enlightenment of modern civilization but now it seems to have cooled down. The undercurrent of Islam is felt everywhere, from the pulverized World Trade Centre which has preserved a historical memory of about 20,000 (the number may be something more or less) tormenting spirits under its relics to the Kaaba Mosque which is encircled with an annual confluence of 2 million Muslims jubilant, raptured and blossomed in inexplicable joy.

The Transformation of Civilizations does not occur with showering of milk or raining of beverage. History hands down the witness that transformation of one culture in to another entails a large-scale bloodbath during the interim period or the period of transformation.

A nation formed on a particular land becomes accustomed to a particular culture and this gives way to the formation of a particular civilization on the foundation of that culture and cultural aspects. But when the strength of its social life dwindles, becomes imbalanced and shaken, accidentally or unwittingly the culture fades, civilization deteriorates and nation breaks down. By that time if there exists another stronger, integrated and aggressive society, it tries to confront the dwindling and disorganized society to win over it as a part of its invasive social instinct. Then there appears a situation of separation in that country, which automatically leads to the line of division in the midst of that integrated land. Then there appears the expansive stature of the stronger society with the imposition of its civilization.

The culture and civilization of a stronger nation is forcibly imposed upon a comparatively weaker nation or a nation which loves co-existence, opening its windows to all sides with the solicitation of a cool breeze through the windows. Nobody expects the inflow of a venomous air that is inhaled into his body and kills him. *Euro America gripped this phenomenon for its imperial expansionism monitoring the Bible with a sacrificed Jesus, whose existence with such greatness experimentally seems enigmatic. Amazingly Mohammedanism appeared with the dictation of a single man Mohammed pioneering the Quran and glorifying Allah whose existence is exclusively known to nobody but Mohammed.*

Christianity stormed over many parts of the world, imbibed almost the entire Europe, the USA, Australia and a large part of Asia. Simultaneously Mohammedanism drenched the Asian countries, drowned many ancient nations, diffused over Africa and, when collided with Christianity, thundered over the World Trade Centre. It first damaged the W.T.C in 1993 and pulverized it in the year 2001.

Some Pre-Indications of Transformation of Civilizations

Some symptoms appear in the internal and external affairs of a feebler nation by the pressure of a stronger civilization other than the civilization of the feebler nation at the time of Transformation of Civilizations. These pre-indications are as follows.

(a) Development of the tendency of disputed nationalism

Under this circumstance a citizen abandons its national identity and embraces an alien national conscience. He hates the cultural heritage of his motherland and loves and respects the national life of the alien nation, which may even be inimical to his motherland. Under this process a man becomes antinational in his own nation and acts against the national interest. The formation of the Islamic Parliament in England is such an example. As a mark of directly condemning the government policy of Britain, the Muslims of Britain issued a fatwa for the elimination of General Musharraf for backing the American plan to strike at Afghanistan.

In a similar statement the Indian Muslim League President G.M. Banatwalla stridently warned the government that any move by India to facilitate an American attack against Afghanistan would be seen by them as a move against the Muslims.

The citizen of a country represents its nation and its national flavour in a foreign land. He always possesses to be a patriot of the very nation, which is his motherland. But in this changing situation a man staying abroad acts against its nation for the interest of its own religion, which, in his eyes, is above the nation.

(b) Incessant civil war in affected countries

In the process of Transformation of Civilization the social life of a nation loses its unity and strength. A nation gets divided into many societies degenerating its national strength and security. In a multi-social nation a weaker society always becomes the victim of the stronger in course of unending communal riots. A stronger society, which is founded on violence and cruelty, always makes attempts to crush its opponent society, which is defenseless and believes in non-violence or is averse to violence or less violent in nature. This is the indication of deficiency of resistance capacity or immunity of the society.

(c) Adversary scenario in the International relations

Cordial relations between nations get seriously jeopardized when this dreadful Transformation is under process. It seriously affects international relations and puts the nations in an ambiguous and precarious condition. Instance may be quoted of Sheikh Omar, a British born Muslim who slit the throat of Daniel Pearl, the reporter of Wall Street Journal, a citizen of the U.S.A though both the countries are having good reciprocal relations. India, Pakistan and Britain are nations with cordial relations. But presently 900 British Muslims leave the country every year to get subversive training in Pakistan to fight Jehad in Kashmir for its segregation from India. It creates misunderstanding among them in the international level. Presently the feasibility of such instances seems very rare, but the next decade would see these occurrences very commonly as these are the pre-indications of transformation of civilization.

(d) Spread of distorted culture and emergence of a distorted society in a nation

In the conflict between the civilizations, a distorted society cannot withstand to encounter a powerful invading race or civilization, which is both internally and outwardly strong and formidable.

Increase in the number of child abuse, individual insecurity, social insecurity, homosexual tendency, occurrences of rape, divorce, suffering of people infected with incurable diseases, poverty, unemployment and after all, lack of precise and well defined national character are the symptoms of deterioration of a national life. Development of a bastard culture or a mixed culture in a society, which is a symbol of extinction of civilization, leads the nation towards its doom.

Euro-American countries are infected by the above symptoms like the development of unnatural carnal tendencies among the people in the society. India, which even would topple China in population in the coming years, is still groping to find out its national identity. Its definition of secularism is a ridiculous and grotesque idea that restrains its citizens to ascertain a definite form of national characteristics. Hence the nation is hastening towards segregation like the former USSR.

Although there is the apprehension of Transformation of Civilizations in the near future there is no possibility of a great war like the last World Wars. The spirit of a universal war converted into a Global Civil War will be limited to machetes, knives, guns and at best to some explosives. But such a civil war will be bloodiest and beyond comparison to those that happened in the past including the last two world wars.

Some Significances of Transformation of Civilizations

(a) Loss of Ethnicity

This leads to conversion of the indigenous population into an alien culture and religion. When a country comes into the orbit of Transformation of Civilizations there develops a wonderful significance. People who belong to the soil for many generations and are fixated with the ethnic culture soon get declared as aliens in that land either on their turning down into a minority community or owing to their slim strength for protection. They are declared as the rightless and disgraced second-class citizens and permissive occupiers of that land and are deprived of all the rights of independent citizens.

(b) Promulgation of three major factors in the affected society

The Transformation of Civilization is substantiated by three major factors (a) conversion (b) expulsion and (c) extermination. Unfortunately the whole world has become the field of operation to saturate the transformation, and all the people of the world have become the target of these three factors to make the Transformation of Civilizations a great success.

These three factors i.e. conversion, expulsion and extermination proceed simultaneously and collaterally concentrating on the social lives of different nations. If one out of these three factors is under operation, then one must be sure of the presence of the other two factors stalking behind it to surface. They only wait for an opportunity for their manifestation. The process of Transformation of Civilizations has been accelerated after the manifestation of Islam.

(c) Disparity in balance of power

The Transformation of Civilization takes place in a country where the opposing societies are not equally strong. To resist the process of Transformation of Civilizations, the confronting powers must be equally strong in one-way or the other. When a society is engulfed in fear and disunity and the other one is with chivalry and solidarity in a country then starts the action of Transformation of Civilizations in that country until one society obliterates the other.

Strength does not mean here the military superiority of a nation. Military power is utilized in the field of external defence and suppression of administrative destabilization. When the action of *Transformation* galvanizes through civil insurgency there is no necessity for a vast and well-equipped army to resist it.

(d) Obliteration of Secularism

A country enlightened with the idea of secularism becomes an easy prey and is used as the Armageddon of Transformation of Civilizations. The more secular a country is, the more it is vulnerable by the fervour of Transformation of Civilizations. Secularism, whatever its form and definition may be, cannot withstand itself before the storm of Transform of Civilizations which is carried by strong invasive religious fanaticism. Secularism, particularly interpreted by the Indian constitution can be compared with a graminivorous pachyderm that feels everybody's presence equally around him in a forest destitute of any carnivorous animal. But when it encounters a ferocious canine in the area of its dwelling it lacks the capacity to defend or escape from its crunching activity. Ever since secularism has failed to withstand the wave of religious fanaticism.

(e) Transformation of social values

Although both society and nation are interlinked and both are constituents of a civilization, society is the prime target of the Transformation of Civilization. The basic difference between the two is that society is a life stream that is fuelled by the feeling of religion, and nation is a life stream, which is fuelled by the feeling of a particular land or birthplace. Culture is more collateral to a society than a nation. The Transformation of Civilizations is related to the social life style of a nation. It lays its octopus-like hands on the society, which lacks a strongly protective or defensive structure of its own.

(f) Launch of a civil war

The Transformation of Civilizations or the amalgamation of one civilization with another leads to a large-scale civil war, which is popularly known as communal war. So when there occurs a civil war around the world to gratify the global trend of the Transformation of Civilizations, it is called a global civil war. The following are the characteristics of a Global Civil War waged for the Transformation of Civilizations.

(1) This is a game of war where human weapons are more in demand than lethal weapons.

(2) Manual weapons like knife, chop, machete, sword, trident would be more prominent than machine-made sophisticated weapons. But the weapons like gun, pistol, revolver and other limited explosive materials would be used.

(3) Womenfolk would be made prolific and wombs would be widely used for the production of children for utilization as human weapons.

(4) As the Global Civil War would be basically a global communal riot, all the people willing or not willing to participate would be inevitably treated as participants in the war.

(5) All human beings invariably from the embryo in the mother's womb to those who are on imminent death would be treated as inevitable participants of the War.

(6) Civilians who rely on the government action in this regard and remain slumbered would get defeated and slaughtered.

(7) A government that favours racial bigotry would finish its rival group or the minority group through ethnic cleansing and declares the Transformation a great success.

(8) Besides planes, trains and other conveyances to be used for the transportation of weapons in the ensuing Global Civil War; infiltration and immigration of aliens would also be treated as the best means of transportation of modern weapons. The more is the number of foreign infiltrators and immigrants in a country, the more would be the insecurity of defence of that land.

(9) During the intensive period of transformation there would be sporadic visions of field wars like the past world wars. This will be fought between two belligerent nations out of which one would be either a supporter of the fighting race of the Transformation or it self is an atheistic nation which is forced to face the situation created by the fighting race. In this case only air and sea would be used as a field of war apart from the land.

(10) Apart from death camps, make-shift sheds for incarcerated men and women would be rampant for the acceleration of war programmes. The war prisoners would be enslaved to donate their blood for the wounded soldiers and dig pits for the death camps. Women would be used in particular for the sexual gratification of army men and for the production of babies as an instrument of war.

Some of the events of war

1. Gang Rape and murder;
2. Burning of places of worship and libraries and of culture and civilization;
3. Bombarding on important places;
4. Destruction of archeological statues; and
5. Attacking political leaders and killing them;
6. Creating terror by secret killing and killing mercilessly by mutilation of limbs and important body organs;

7. Using explosives to kill in public places;
8. Total annihilation of minority race;
9. Open use of swords and weapons to wipe out the adversaries for ethnic cleansing;
10. Killing of writers, journalists and eminent persons of opposing race.

When the civilization of a nation undergoes a transformation, the interim period is followed by a great holocaust, which is more frightening, coercive, and painful. Some methods applied in different countries in the bygone medieval period for the Transformation of Civilizations may be enumerated in this connection. In the present day world these methods are unmistakably followed in some countries and in case of obstruction it is followed in a different form without any deflection of its spirit.

17. Means of Transformatory Actions (Ethnic Cleansing)

Modern tools can't provide the solution to the present ideological crisis in human societies especially in the Islamic world, unless they are in agreement with the ultimate aims of Islamic civilizations.

– Global Islamic Movement

When a civilization encounters another civilization with all its distinct characteristics and objectives, the two collide each other with their wings of culture and perspectives like two thunder clouds with all their forces. The centre of that collision is the transformatory point, which causes change in the shape of two civilizations as it happens in the case of a collision of divergent clouds that give the shape of thunder, lightning, storm and down stream. The followings are some of the procedures followed by the invading race to dominate over the targeted feebler society or race. The procedures were followed in the medieval period and are being followed with some modifications in the present day wars. Implementation of these procedures cannot be avoided, if not with its full swing, in the future wars meant for the Transformation of civilizations.

Ethnic Cleansing

Ethnic cleansing is a combination of killing, terror, rape, impregnation and conversion etc., an attempt for the extinction of a race from its motherland and is the final stage of escalation of Transformation of Civilizations. This is the fundamental concept or the basic idea of a warrior race to expedite the transformatory apprehensions in the clash of civilizations. This plays a vital role as the action plan to wipe out the weaker race from the surface of the soil where it exists. Its root is embedded in the "theory of evolution" which signifies that a weaker creature that lacks the capacity of self-defence cannot exist. The present world basically exists on the theory of the "Survival of the fittest". This theory en-mass leads to the theory of "Transformation of Civilizations".

Ways and Means of Transformation of Civilizations

(a) Throat slitting

This is exclusively considered as a religious part of Islam. In this process a man slits the throat of the victim and leaves it to die in utter agony. This is an easy and inexpensive process to exterminate a man to die in gasping. However barbarous this method may be, this system well known as "Halal" also has its significance in killing millions of animals everyday throughout the world for meat. Throat-slitting is also accepted to intensify the Islamic observations. In many cases girls going to school without hijab or women moving outside without burqa are also put to death by throat-slitting even though the country is not under Islamic subjugation. Presently the people of Euro-America came across the throat-slitting policy of Muslims after their soldiers have been found dead in the soil of Northern Iraq by this religious process of killing.

(b) Roasting

In the medieval period this method was invariably followed by Muslim Sultans to create terror among the victimized race. As a result religious conversion to Islam became easy and the flow was rapid. According to this system a huge cauldron filled with oil is set on the hearth. When the oil ferments the man is thrown into it, roasted in the boiled oil and dies in utter agony. The frightened audiences either accept instant conversion or flee from the kingdom.

In another similar method the victim is seated on a thick iron plate or sheet in a burning hearth. Then boiled water or fire-hot sand is poured over his body. The victim dies fluttered.

(c) Sawing

According to this process the victim is put in a cage and exhibited round the town to frighten the targeted society and to propagate his execution by sawing. Then he is put between two pillars tightly and immovably interposed. Sawing starts from the midmost part of his head to divide the victim's body into two pieces.

(d) Cogging

The victim who is reluctant to be converted is made to roll over one of the two cogged wheels which are tightly fixed face to face each between two posts. Then the wheel is made to move by wielding its handle in round shape. The victim is immediately ripped into two pieces.

Sawing and bifurcating by the cogging wheel was invariably used to terrify, subdue and convert the Sikhs of Punjab who were ever ready to sacrifice their lives but not to surrender their religion. They were the chief protectors of the Hindus. In course of time the Sikhs turned out into a warring race to defend Indian religion and culture.

(e) Burning

In this method the victim is hanged upside down with his legs tightly fastened to the branch of a tree. Fire is lit from below. In the case of mass burning long rafters are hovered over two pillars at their two ends. Victims are hanged on the rafter with their legs tightly fixed with the rope. Dried grass and straw are piled below and fire is lighted.

Snatching away the children from their parents and throwing them into burning flames without any hesitation was also a system largely followed to create terror and convert people in the medieval period. Rather it was done with a self-satisfaction that the executor performed a religious duty by reducing the number of heathens from this world. It was prevailing as a system of terror. Combustible garments inserted with inflammable sulphuric powder were given to the victims to clad. Then he was set on fire.

(f) Slaughtering

In this method the victim is imprisoned in an iron cage and is moved around the town to disseminate information about his execution and to create terror among the people. Then he is brought to the place of execution. In the presence of the surrounded crowd the executioner raises his sword and detaches the head from the body with a stroke. Slaughtering is the common process of killing a person like an animal.

(g) Lashing

This is a very dreadful process to create terror among the infidels. Even women and children are not spared from whipping. This causes profuse bloodshed and leads to faint and ultimate death. Lashing is considered to be the most terrific step as it dishonors a person and demoralizes the infidel and sparks a constant feeling of fear, which remains squeezed in his gene for generation.

(h) Bifurcation

This is generally done in the case of enemies' children. By hovering inversely to a baby the killers tug its two legs in opposite direction and kill the victim by tearing the body.

(i) Sealing

Through this process the victim is persuaded to embrace the religion of the persecutor; on his denial to get converted, a wall is raised encircling him. Its upper part is constructed like a tomb. At last the ridge of the bastion is sealed to let the victim die suffocated.

(j) Closed door killing

This process is generally applied to women who are not pliable to the executioners. They are confined in a locked room.

No food or water is served to them. Being forbidden from the fundamental needs of life they die out of hunger and thirst in that cursed cell. Sealing causes instant death whereas in killing by gasping the victim takes a few days to die in hunger and thirst.

(k) Down thrusting

This is a very horrendous act followed for some decades in India while it was under Islamic dominion. According to this process, the selected beautiful women are collocated as war booty and are kept in the ground floor of a multi-storyed mansion (popularly known as "Imambaras"). These wretched women are stored there naked or with transparent slim clothes. After day-fall the warriors or military officers congregate there and each of them carry his chosen woman into the rooms upstairs. Huge and long pipes are fixed in the upper part of the building with its terminus leading to the adjacent river where a flat rock is targeted just below the water surface suiting to the end of the pipe. Through out the night the woman is copulated and after the rape is over, before the daybreak, the wretched woman is squeezed in to the pipe with her head downwards and pushed to slip through the pipe and smash her head violently over the rock. Being crushed to death her corpse floats over the water and sails away in the river stream. Nobody is there to give protection to these wretched women or protest against such cruelty.

Although the above instances are the mediaeval practices, these are still alive and unmistakably followed today with slight variations. Owing to the invention and use of sophisticated weapons the methods of persecution and the methods of frightening and killing slightly differ. But the nature of cruelty is infallibly the same or more. Even new methods of cruelty have been innovated to clamp down on the opponents. Some such instances may be contemplated.

(l) Blood Sucking

Sucking the prisoners' blood through the syringe to torture and weaken them is another inhuman act clandestine to martial law and military tradition. To torture and demoralize a person or a nation the believers can go to such an extent to commit such crimes whereas the Holy Scripture describes that the body of an unbeliever is purely impure and combustible. These prisoners are forcibly used as regular blood donors. Very often profuse blood sucking makes prisoners die.

(m) Head drilling

Hot sanguinary iron rod is used for searing the midmost part of the forehead where a tip of sandal paste is streaked or skull of a victim as a symbol of torture. Gouging the eyes of the victim and leaving him to die in pain is another method followed since long. One is tempted to do all these heinous acts only in the name of that religion which impels man to hate a man.

(n) Hacking and earthling

Cutting one hand and the opposite leg of a victim is a traditional religious mandatory punishment. Religious commandment to bring the law in to individual authority and commitment of such cruel deeds are not considered as cruel. Generally women who are considered guilty for disobedience, committing adultery or in major cases defying invitation for copulation are buried waist deep or breast in a pit and stoned to death. Such punishments are rampant even today.

(o) Stabbing

To Throw the babies high up and catch them penetrated through the bayonet of a gun is a very common sight in an area affected with national transformation. Snatching away milk fed babies from their mothers and throwing them under the tank is also a very common scene in the present day torturing centres. After the victims being trodden by the tank, disfigured beyond identity, oil is poured over the dead body and the mother is asked to light the fire.

Knife is a nice weapon to accelerate the process of ethnic cleansing to make the transformation of civilization a great success, especially when it is in the hands of Mujahids. Chopper is the shortened shape of sword, the Islamic religious emblem that is very dear to Islamic youths. Islam as a satisfactory performance does not sanction killing without torture. Machete is the best weapon to make an animal bleed to death with torture. In a communal riot stricken area the knives blaze around like dragonflies in the warm sky. As Halal is a sacred duty for every Muslim, it is found in dozens in every family.

(p) Disemboweling

The transformatory apprehension of civilization has generated another new system "disemboweling". According to this system the soldiers at war disembowel the pregnancy of a conceived women of the adversary race by directly shooting or by ripping the womb. The intension is to kill the embryo of the rival race from its very conception. The disemboweling is implemented as a weapon of ethnic cleansing and such method of torture is followed even today.

(q) Killing by torture

Killers in their action seem more dreadful than ferocious beasts. One can't expect from a man to have derived pleasure by killing a man or by torturing him mercilessly. Religious frenzy or fanaticism relevant to "Transformatory Apprehensions" generates a peculiar type of distinct sentiments that creates more havoc and more startling news.

An incident may be cited in this regard. Towards 1950 a Bengali girl (a girl from Bangladesh who had taken refuge in India) was given in marriage to a gentleman. After the marital grandeur was over, the bride was accompanied to her bedroom to meet the groom in the nuptial night. Both were happy to meet each other. The girl talked to her new mate with a calm and amusing voice. Every thing was normal. But no sooner had she seen her husband in a sexual pose she fainted. The nig' t was over. Nights succeeded nights. Whenever she sees her husband in a pose of cohabitation she immediately gets fainted. The husband was a scrupulous gentleman. Without thinking ill of her he carried her to the medical hospital for psychotherapy. After a long enquiry the riddle was unravelled.

"In the pre-Independent India communal riot in Bangladesh was launched by the "Direct Action Day" order of Mohammed Ali Jinnah, the founder of Pakistan. The armed Muslim assailants slaughtered non-Muslim civilians in a preplanned way. This girl accompanied by her refugee family members rushed towards South for a place of safety. All her family members except herself and her elder sister fell down on the way at the firing and stabbing from the rear. The two sisters could save themselves from the point of gun and bayonet and ran away. Suddenly they saw a Muslim Mujahid chasing them. Because she was too young she could escape herself but her sister fell a prey to that Mujahid. He forcibly caught hold of her elder sister, tugged off her Sari and raped her in the clear observation of the girl who was shivering out of fear and peeping, hiding behind a nearby tree. The jehadi fighter, after he quenched his carnal thirst, raised his rifle and penetrated the bayonet into her vagina and ground the bayonet with his fists. Then he kicked her with a thundering laughter and left the place. The girl witnessed the instant death of her sister in utter agony."

When the girl sees her excited husband ready for marital union, suddenly the memory of the bayonet comes to her mind. The recollection of the plight of her sister rushes to her memory and immediately she gets fainted out of fear of the apparent penetration of the bayonet. After having a long days' treatment she got rid of her fear and was restored to her normal position. (Verbal evidence collected from Bengali refugees who fled from Bangladesh at the time of partition of India)

During the Kargil war between Pakistan and India, the dead bodies of six Indian soldiers were handed over to India by Pakistan. It was seen that the vital parts of the bodies were so severely hacked and stabbed that it was beyond recognition. The penis and testicles of the soldiers were cut off and their eyes were gouged out while they were alive. In the Kashmir part of India some victims were found having a hole made on the pit of their chest and the liver taken out from inside by pious Mujahids.

Laxman Dev (Banda Vairagi or Banda Singh) of India is a name that heads the torturing list of human history. He was once a king and later he became an ascetic. On the call of Guru Govind Singh he returned to the kingdom fold and fought bravely. Unfortunately he was defeated, nabbed and was presented before the Sultan.

He was promised a nice luxurious future along with the restoration of his kingdom on the condition that he should change his faith and embrace Islam. He spurned the proposal. He was tied tightly to a post and was made blind by penetrating burning iron rods through his eyes.

The next day he was again promised a nice future with the release from imprisonment. But on his denial to change the faith his tongue was cut off. Again the next day he was assured freedom with the restoration of his kingdom. Still then he restrained himself from all these temptations. The angry authority placed his son before him, beheaded him and squeezed the flesh of his son into his mouth and again asked him to change his faith. Still he denied. Then the followers of the faith disfigured his whole body and killed him.

Although this is an incident of 18th century, the occurrences of such incidents are alive even today. Such incidents of torture to death imposed on the infidels have been observed as religious operations since the time of Prophet Mohammed. Mohammed himself had initiated such steps preparatory for conversion in to Islam. Once, by order of Mohammed a man named Thumama bin Uthal was nabbed by his cavaliers and brought to his presence. Mohammed asked him "Thumama! What do you want? "(Whether you will change your faith or not?) Thumama said – "If you would kill me, then I shall remain grateful to you. If you want money, then tell me how much would you want?" Mohammed went back without any reply. Thumama was left tied to the post. Next day he came to Thumama and asked the same question. Thumama's reply was the same as the earlier one. On the third day when Mohammed came to Thumama and put the same question, Thumama gladly consented that he has not only changed his faith, he has accepted Mohammed as the paramount authority in his life.

Machete, dagger, etc., are the best weapons in a civil war affected country to torture a victim up to death. Religious fanatics regarding the treatment for tortured killing make no difference in gender. In Rwandan areas women are entirely disrobed; all their belongings are taken off and then starts the treatment of machete after rape. Their legs are hacked below the knee and two hands are cut into pieces below two elbows in spite of their request to gun them down and bless them with an instant death. They are thrown on the roadside in this condition with their kids vainly looking on with eyes full of tears. With a painful survival of two or three days they die in utter agony and are often eaten by stray dogs.

In another cruel method of persecution the victim's leg is tightened behind a truck with a long rope with the victim's face downwards. Then the truck starts to move. The victim is dragged on the road by the moving vehicle and suffers a miserable death.

Presently the young generation of Palestine is suffering from Post Traumatic Stress Disorder (PTSD). The symptoms of disorder that includes thumb sucking, crying, clinging to parents, nightmares, bed-wetting, poor appetites, slim sleeping patterns, short attention spans, aggression towards siblings or parents, etc. Palestine Television shows non-stop images of 'Intifada' or uprising against Israel including close-up views of bodies after they have been ripped apart by bullets, gun battles, funerals and grieving relatives is exacerbating the situation.

The footage shows an eleven-year boy Mohammed Aldorra who became the symbol of Intifada. The death of this young Palestinian boy, whose widely televised death by Israel gun-firing has developed the symptoms of PTSD. The footage shows Aldorra cowering in terror next to his father who is signaling for help from behind the concrete wall where they are trapped, then being struck by bullets and finally lying slumped across his wounded father's lap.

There are many events to denote the ways of persecution made by the stronger race on the weaker to wipe them out for the occupation and use of their land, property and women. In medieval India an invader Babar took much interest to pile up the skulls of the beheaded infidels .It was a great pleasure for him to see the piles of skulls up to tower height. Women unwilling to cohabit with the oppressor were ordered to be buried knee deep or breast deep and were stoned to death.

(r) Mutilation of limbs

Cutting the penis and allowing the victims to die in excruciating pain or remain impotent forever with a censured and humiliated life is another way of punishment to the victim of an adversarial race. This is another heinous way of demoralizing the enemy. In the Mohammedan attack against the non-Muslims there are numerous instances of mutilation of male genital organs, and piling them up to a visible height is a common occurrence. Cutting off the breast of non-Muslim women and the penis of non-Muslim men are also common events prevailing in many Islamic countries or the countries which were under Islamic invasion. The breast is slashed to dishonour the women folk of an adversarial race and penis of a male is sheared as the most successful step to close down the birth progress of rival groups. Dr. Taslima Nasrin, the revolutionary exiled woman novelist of Bangladesh has given some thrilling and spine-chilling instances of such cursed gentlemen in her masterpiece Lajja (Shame). The border police of Bangladesh are specially instructed to break the backbones and pound the ribs of Chakma Buddhists, Christian tribals and Bengali Hindus to make them invalid for life. The cutting of one leg and its opposite hand, mutilation of tongue, the gouging of eyes, the tagging of nails with pincers allowing the victims to die with intolerable pain are included in this category. Generally Kafirs or non-Muslims are made impotent by mutilating their penis in Islamic majority countries to slow down their racial multiplication. Many of them were castrated and used as eunuchs.

(s) Unilateral Marriage through Exogamy and Birth Proliferation through Polygamy

Unilateral marriage of a group or society with the women folk of rival groups accounts for hastening the transformatory apprehension and ethnic cleansing of a nation. Such matrimonial alliances are intentionally made in a preplanned manner by the aggressive force to increase their population. On the other hand this system of marriage affects the population growth of the bridal race in the reverse.

Unilateral marriage generally takes place by coaxing. If a society gives unilateral freedom or sanction of free sex to its women folk, then the adversarial society takes its opportunity and increases its population that provokes ethnic cleansing either by coaxing or by force. This method is largely followed in the Euro-American countries and in India. The marriage of Arabian settlers in Euro-America to white ladies in abundance, the paradoxical marriage system of Muslim youths to Hindu girls in India and the forcible marriage attempt of victorious alien rulers to indigenous girls supports this point of unilateral marriage.

Islam allows Muslim males to marry non-Islamic women. It allows polygamy and exogamy for Muslim males but strictly adheres to monogamy for women. There is no religious sanction of Muslim girls to marry outside Islam. The marriage of Lisa Halaby to the king of Jordan was highly appreciated by the Muslims. She changed her Christian religion and became a Muslim queen. Even she was given an Islamic name, Noor, after she got converted to Islam. On the contrary there is not a visible example of non-Muslim youth married to a Muslim girl unhurriedly, gracefully and unfrowned. Farukh Abdullah, the Chief Minister inherited of Jammu and Kashmir married a British Christian lady. No objection. His son, a Member of Parliament married to a Hindu girl of Kashmir. No objection. But when his daughter married to a young Hindu Parliamentarian of India there was a tsunami of objection and threatening. Neither the Chief Minister father nor the Parliamentarian brother attended the ceremony.

Islamic Policy of Grow and Get

(Synonym of British Policy of "Divide and Rule")

This is the most important and dreadful of policies to escalate the process of Transformation of civilizations. This was quite unknown to the rest of the world and, if it was known it was not yet seriously taken that human beings have been being used by Islam as the most important weapon of war since the advent of Islam. A plane is generally used as a carrier of passengers and goods in space. But recently it was be used as a weapon to destroy the World Trade Centre and kill thousands. An army is deployed in the battlefield to handle weapons and kill enemy forces. But Islam can make best use of human beings as a weapon of war. The definition of war has been changed with its relevance from battlefield to the field of popular election. By heavy birth proliferation a race (a) can win a popular election though vote politics (b) a war through deployment of man power and (c) control its adversarial compatriot group or political parties through conveyance of mass opinion and pull it from backward. Birth proliferation brings benefit to the proliferating nation in many ways. Mass public opinion compelled the U.S.S.R to retreat its army from Afghanistan. Islam through birth proliferation is determined to win 'India, Pakistan and Bangladesh. The same would be the fate of the U.S.A and European countries. No capital is needed to invest or no labour is needed to produce children. Birth proliferation is the easiest and cheapest of processes.

Rape for pregnancy, unhurried coition with prolific women, polygamy, etc., are some ways to enhance the birth rate. An example can be quoted of Mohammed Yasin Mohammed of Malaysia, who had 47 children out of four wives. Those children produced 168 grand children, 251 great grand children and 17 great great grand children. All 483 descendants had gathered in the religious celebration of Eid ul Fitre in last December 2002 in Kuala Lumpur.

There is a good heaven for those who embrace Islam. A man is authorized to be the husband of as many wives as he can. It is learnt that the king of Bhawalpur of Pakistan had 390 wives. Among them were some British and Anglo-Indians. Proper account of his children is not known.

In the yer 1947 India was divided into India and Pakistan. The kingdom of Junagarh came into the territory of India owing to its Hindu majority. But the Muslim king opted for Pakistan. He had hundreds of dogs and wives. He was more interested for his pets. In the midst of communal tension he hurriedly started for Pakistan. He embarked the plane with all his dogs and wives. But the communal tension was so severe that hurriedly he asked the pilot to start the plane leaving some of his wives and children in Junagarh.

Islam's policy of "Grow and Get" is a more profiteering policy than the "Divide and Rule" policy sponsored by the British government. In course of time the whole world would come under the banner of Islam as long as its policy of birth proliferation continues unabated and unobstructed. Birth control and family planning policy, homosexual marriage, etc., followed by the Western countries is extinctive of their civilizations and on the contrary it helps to accelerate the expansion of Islam.

During the medieval period more number of death of soldiers of enemy force was counted as a mark of victory. During the last century death of more number of civilians from the opposition side was counted as the victory. But in the 21st century the notion of defeat and victory would get a total change. In this century the number of birth in a rival society or enemy race and growth of enemy population would conclude not only the fate of a nation but also the future of a civilization.

(t) Demolition of Holy Places

The demolition of holy places such as synagogues, churches etc., demoralizes and frightens the inhabitants, unleash their faith and flee from that land. The I.S.I of Pakistan has planned and attempted to decimate the churches and kill the Christian devotees by bombing on these Churches and temples. Bombardments on Euro-American Embassies situated in different countries also come under this category.

(u) Kidnapping

Kidnapping of men and women is a very common practice in an Islam majority area. The kidnapping of women for rape and occasionally for marriage is a common occurrence. If an appreciable lady became the choice of a Muslim youth, it takes no time to abduct her by the masquerading Muslim gangs to molest against her wishes. The kidnapping of men to kill them simply with the allegations that they were involved in spying or in some anti-Islamic activities are very common incidents in Islamic countries.

(v) Conversion

Conversion is a fundamental weapon for the Transformation of Civilizations. History reveals that the majority of conversions takes place by threat, coaxing, oppression, force and by all possible measures of torture that can be exerted upon the converted race. Out of the two most convert-sick religions conversion to Christianity started after the death of Jesus Christ and it hastened possibly after 300 A.D. But in Islam it started from the very starting point of Islam and mostly by the blade of the sword and by the Prophet himself. By conversion executant nations bastardize a race by exterminating its socio-cultural and religious identity. The converted race becomes a lackey in gross subservience to the oppressor nation which converted them. The next generations of the converted race introduce themselves as the unstinted inheritants of the converters and try to convert others into the converters' religion with unquestioning obedience. Thus continues the process of Transformation of Civilizations.

(w) Rape and Impregnation

In the present warfare rape, though done clandestinely, is considered as an established weapon of war. But to rape the women folk of the defeated race is a very common, rightous and religious practice of Islam since its inception.

In India, physical sanctity is given supreme honour and every sort of physical protection is accorded to women from their childhood up to their old age and death. After the advent of Islam there was a great change in the social structure of India. When the Indian warriors apprehended certain defeat and death at the hands of Muslim invaders, they killed their women folk by poisoning or slaying them before going to the battlefield. After the war was over, when the victorious Mujahids of Islam entered the town, they found only corpses of women. Nevertheless they did not spare the dead bodies and raped them. This heinous act impelled the Indian women to resort to Sati or Jauhar Brat or the committing of suicide in multitudes by jumping into the flames of pyre.

Rape is used as a weapon of terror and dishonour to the vanquished race. In the Pakistan- Bangladesh war Muslim youths kidnapped non- Muslim girls and raped them as a very common practice of post-war practice. In this situation the "father was forced to rape his daughter and the son was forced to rape his mother and the brother was forced to rape his sister at the point of the gun. Everybody knows the story of a 14 year old girl who was raped by 12 soldiers and killed together with her one day old baby."

Rape is treated as an instrument of ethnic cleansing. Apart from disrespect to the vanquished group, rape is used to exterminate the adversarial race from its very foundation. Hence in modern warfare the strong victorious race molests the women folk of the defeated race systematically until they become pregnant. The aim is to animate the embryos of their own breed in the womb of the women of the defeated race and force the women to become the mothers of the babies of their shame. During the Bosnian war in the year 1992-94 the Serbs raped the Bosnian women and impregnated them in thousands. In the 1971 war, the Pakistani soldiers raped the Bengali women in thousands until they became pregnant.

As Mother Teresa, the lady of Nobel Prize fame, was opposed to abortion, only very few victims could be aborted. Almost 18,000 of the impregnated women gave birth to illicit children fathered by Pak soldiers. Towards the year 1987 these unclaimed youths of Bangladesh born of that barbaric act, fathered by Pakistani soldiers, were called back by the I.S.I. of Pakistan to be deployed in the war against the U.S.S.R. After the disintegration of the U.S.S.R they were sent to Kashmir with arms and ammunitions to segregate it from India.

The system of keeping slave girls in harems prevalent in the medieval period has been manifested as today's rape camps in military cantonments with no variation except the change of name. The women who were no further considered eligible to be used in the harems were sold in the markets. But in modern times death camps where the women who were infertile in rape camps are shifted to death camps. The last decade of the last century was marked with such rape camps and death camps in the integrated land of the former-Yugoslavian state. In the rape camps women in thousands were regularly raped up to pregnancy to give birth to children as a symbol of transformatory escalation of civilization relevant to ethnic cleansing.

Thus rape has its repercussion in winning battles, accumulating wealth, conquering land and winning in popular elections.

(x) *Infiltration and migration*

People make attempt to migrate from their homeland to contiguous flourishing countries to earn their bread. Those host countries also require labourers for their construction work or nation building purpose. Hence they barter each other's possession i.e., manual labour for remuneration and facilities for settlement.

Migration is also very often succeeded by infiltration. Wage earners from Africa and Asian countries particularly Muslims rushed to the U.S.A and other European countries in millions. Millions of Bangladeshi Muslim infiltrators came to India through its long stretched border and gratified the need of the minority vote-hankering politicians. Infiltration to Euro-America is made through mountain tracks, river and sea routes. Once the infiltrators reach the land they start their nation-building plan from their own perspective.

(y) *Alienated Nationalism*

In the changing situation a civilian automatically feels himself as an alien national in his own country. The whole society feels the loneliness of alienation. Gradually the feeling of depression and the feeling of repudiated life engrave on his mind. One begins to feel that all his family is under the mercy of another society which is stronger, dominant, formidable and more horrendous. The survival of his society is under the mercy of the dominant race. His life is a life of exposition-exposed to looting, raping and killing. He is permitted by a superior race to live in the world and is subject to death when his exitence is no more required. Out of impoverishment, lack of means of livelihood and utter humiliation he thinks that the best way to escape from all sorrows, pains and mental agony is to commit suicide. Than the rapid commitment of suicide developes in that degenerated society and it transgresses its limit of control. The government takes a sigh of relief observing this self-destructive ction of the dying race and thinking that its plan is being worked out without any effort.

(z) Explosion

This is the most modern amuriition to destroy enriched races and nations. Although the nuclear bomb was used in the Second World War against Japan, the USA or the allied power did not intend to destroy the Shinto race. Last two world wars were the wars of defeat and victory based on commercial expansion and show of one's supremacy in the field of modern technology. But the Transformational explosion that is being done in the Third World War is quite different. Today the idea of explosion basically means to destroy the civilization or the race of a nation from its very root.

The explosives used and to be used in the Third World War are not as much the same as that were used in the last World Wars. Its area of application is very limited but its process is spontaneous. Self-suicide bombardment is a vivid example of such explosion. Here attempt is made to destroy a particular race or nation. Rajiv Gandhi is perhaps the first prominent national leader to be the target of suicide bomber. But the intention of the suicide bomber was not for any ethnic cleansing. His assassination was purely on political ground like that of Abraham Lincoln, Mr Kenedy and Anwar Sadat. But the plane bomb used to demolish the World Trade Centre of the USA, death of Princess Diana in car accident in Paris and the suicidal attempt to shatter the Indian Parliament House etc are meant for ethnic cleansing and for the acceleration of Transformation of Civilizations. In future this human bombs would exceed all other lethal weapons in the field of use. It would come out as the most horrendous weapon in the hands of man. Man would use men as instruments to kill men.

Phases of Ethnic Cleansing

First Phase

Debilitations of weaker community and strength and vigour of stronger community form the means of ethnic cleansing in the first phase. In the first phase of ethnic cleansing a community of a society or the social life of country loses its balance of power, organized life-style and enduring capacity. The people of that community or society become haughty, showy, luxury-seeking, pleasure-loving, disunited, tender in mind and body, delinquent, lazy, womanish, cowardly, extremely selfish and isolated lovers. They are least concerned about their society or even their community.

On the other hand it so happens that other community of that society or the social life of that country becomes more invincible, formidable, invasive, strongly organized and united. The civilian becomes more tenacious, diligent, hard in gesticulation and intoning and gregarious. They remain ever interested to develop their own community and want to confine their life with in their community dimension.

In such a situation if a country or society which comprises of many communities the people who belong to the community with the former characteristics become the targeted race or victimized community of the latter. When the communal balance dwindles, the aggressive community exploits the impeccable community. Thus starts the clash of civilizations that activates the process of Ethnic Cleansing relevant to the Transformation of Civilizations.

Second Phase

This is the revealing portion of Transformation, which perpetuates as a series of cold war or pseudo war between the two communities or between communities. During this period the stronger community intensifies its strength feeding on its counterpart targeted community as parasites considering it to be its adversarial race.

The following are the significances of the second phase of Ethnic Cleansing that accelerates the metamorphosis of the degenerated or down-trodden targeted society's civilization by the stronger invasive community.

(a) Conversion of an indigenous citizen into an alien faith

(b) Carnage of indigenous citizens by aliens with minor or no reaction at all.

(c) Unilateral display of love, romance and philandering by the youths of stronger minorities with the girls of the weaker majority class.

(d) Unilateral or forced marriage of indigenous women to aliens.

(e) Molestation and impregnation of ethnic women by aliens without any reaction.

(f) Framing of secularism oriented constitution, which is not obvious in its definition of nationalism.

(g) Fraudulent description of the constitution of a nation which defines that all are equal before the law but in practice its implementation is discriminatory, anti-majority, anti-national and opposed to the national mainstream.

(h) Decadence of ethnic majority by the implementation of discriminatory law.

(i) Decrease in the population of indigenous citizens by migration or birth control.

(j) Increase in the number of infiltrators with dominant characteristics.

(k) Turning of ethnic civilians into refugees in their own country.

(l) Recognition and nationalization of an alien culture with its expensive stream of dissemination.

(m) Unobstructed capacity of anti-nationals of a country to continue perennial civil war.

(n) Upper hand of foreign powers and their interference in the internal administration of a country.

(o) Over-lordship of minorities with exceptional rights as super class citizens.

(p) Actions of ruling class that favours the annihilation of ethnic race.

Third Phase

After the actions of the Second Phase comes to perfection and reaches its climax, then starts the third phase of Ethnic Cleansing. This escalates the catastrophe of a degenerated community or society owing to its large-scale conversion, murder and expulsion from the native land. This is the concluding stage of Transformation of Civilizations that consecrates an alien civilization in the pit of an ethnic civilization declaring one civilization victorious and the other vanquished.

The following are the significances of the Third phase of Ethnic Cleansing that gives shape to an alien civilization over another ancient or old civilization. Instances are quoted from the occurrences that took place in Pakistan and Bangladesh.

(a) Shifting of Ethnic population

Apart from killing in multitude the shifting of ethnic population also hastens the action of Transformation of Civilizations. An instance from Bangladesh may be quoted in this regard. In the year 1947 the northern part of Mymensingh (Bangladesh) had nearly 90% Christian population of converted Garo Tribes. After the brutal persecution in the year 1964 and 1971 these Garo Christians were displaced in a sustained manner from Bangladesh to its frontier province of India. By the year 1979, the Garo Christian population in North Mymensingh (Bangladesh) dwindled to zero. In the mean while Muslims from other thickly populated areas of Bangladesh and those who were expelled from Myanmar came and occupied the land of expelled Christian Garo tribes.

(b) Sex-driven terror

Outraging the modesty of women folk is a better way to dominate and destroy a race than launching a war against it. Rape by victorious society does not need any risk, responsibility, pain or expenditure. Hence the Muslims of Bangladesh have resorted to this as a better way to exterminate the Hindus. They disembowel the pregnant Hindu women by knifing their abdomen. They even gang rape the women until their death. Such demonic acts they do in front of the victim's husbands, sons and fathers. Such behaviour is permissible in Islam. The raping of Kafir women is praise worthy and is not considered sinful in Islam. They tore out the genital organs of Hindu males in front of the victim's wives, children, mothers and sisters.

A pretty Hindu girl cannot marry at her own will in Bangladesh. When a Muslim youth marks a Hindu girl suitable to be accepted, he proceeds with his company to the girl's house. Instantly he informs her family members about the confirmation of the marriage. The helpless girl marries the Muslim youth against her sweet will. Such kind of marriages is rampant throughout Bangladesh. This is not different than rape.

The condition of Hindus in the villages of Bangladesh is worse than that of the African slaves of 18th century. Without any provocation Muslims abduct Hindu women whenever and wherever they like and gangrape them at regular intervals. Their family members are threatened not to lodge any complaint at the police station. If by chance and out of rage anybody informs the police, the police briefs that the girl covariates with the Muslim youth on her own will. If the informer is the victim herself, the police officials detain the girl for medical examination and rape the girl in the precinct of the police station. After the heinous act is over the authorities typically say them to leave Bangladesh soon and go to India because the Malayun (the filthy worms of Islamic hell) have no place in Bangladesh. Police protection is completely denied to minorities in Muslim countries all over the world.

If any objection rises from the Hindu side, the Muslims burn the men alive and chop off the breasts of women and insert red-hot iron into their vagina.

A scene of ethnic cleansing may best be illustrated in the eyes of no less a witness than a British businessman Mr.Sanders who left East Pakistan on April 2, 1971 enroute to the U.K. He is an eyewitness of the sadistic sex-driven and brutal tortures of young women living at Rocky Hall of Dacca University. This occurrence took place in the year 1971 when the acts of

Transformation of Civilizations took place in the middle of Bangladesh by wiping out non-Muslim minorities on the point of gun and bayonet, as a part of Jehad.

"............ about 350 to 400 Pakistani troops attacked the Rockey Hall. They entered all the rooms lodging the girls and dragged them out, tearing off their clothing one by one as they were being pulled and manhandled.

"There was panic and shrieks could be heard. Saris, skirts, Salwars were ripped and flung aside. Next blouses, kameezes and brassieres were torn off and the girls were physical lifted by their breasts or hair-some, held upside down.

"As they tried to cover their shame with their hands, the troops kicked them with their fists, some even bayoneted the delicate private parts, blood trickling therein.

"Next came the raping. The girls were pinned down to the floor face upwards; legs mercilessly pulled apart and fully stretched-then finally the brutal act of raping.

"The girls cried, shrieked and struggled, but the beastly soldiers went on raping. Blood ran as 10 or 12 beasts raped each girl successively one after another. Most of the girls fell unconscious as the troops departed after satisfying their devilish lust.

"The girls were in such a condition that they could not even cover up their bodies.

"They were so badly mutilated – breasts bitten off, private parts torn by the forced thrust of the fist and kicking of the boots and throats throttled whenever there was any resistance.

"It was at this juncture that 50 brave girls jumped to their death from the Hall instead of falling into the hands of the barbarians.

"Particularly pathetic was the fate of a 12-year old girl who had come to see one of the students in the college. This juvenile breathed her last as a brutal Pathan sepoy assaulted her. The girl gave a pitiful shriek and never came to her senses, but the brute went on fornicating her till he reached his climax and then he gave a final kick with his boots on her pubic region. By then the girl had died. Blood was flowing from her lap.

"The worst came when some Pathans resorted to sodomy with the grown up girls. They simply swooned due to pain. Most of their rectums got torn and blood ran profusely. Still the devils did not leave them alone.

"The assault upon the Rockey Hall happens to be one of a dozen similar brutalities known to have been committed on women and children by the Punjabi and Pathan troops in Dacca". (S.K.Bhatacharya, Genocide in East Pakistan/ Bangladesh, 27)"

(c) Authorized Rape

In this context people of the stronger nation take it their privilege, predilection or a religious duty to molest the women of weaker race. Hence they use the women of the vanquished or intimidated race to mitigate their carnal desire.

In Bangladesh the constant fear of kidnapping for rape prevents Hindu girls from going school. They confine themselves round the clock only in their homes. In several villages Hindu girls hardly stay constantly in a particular place for fear of being spotted by Muslim rapists. They move from village to village and stay near their relatives.

There are villages in Bangladesh where women are raped regardless of their age at regular intervals. Even the babies are not spared. In some villages Hindus leave their homes in the evening and conceal themselves in the nearby ponds, forests and bushes..

In the littoral villages Muslim youths lift from schools as many girls as required, carry them to the river bank and gang rape them in the trawler for days together. No police come for an enquiry. In many villages Muslim youths lay their hands on the Hindu girls in the street, squeeze their breasts without any reservation, pull the ears of Hindu boys and kick them out without any provocation.

In many villages middle aged Muslims enter into the house and kidnap the female members including the pair of mother and daughter, rape them for several days. If the spinster becomes pregnant, she is compelled for a Nikah (Islamic matrimonial negotiation) with the rapist, which is nothing but an illusion. The wretched women are sold to somebody or are compelled for prostitution.

Muslims advertise that harassed Hindus may contact them for help. But when the victims approach them for help they are again victimized. If the complainant is a woman she is raped. Hence terrified and frustrated Hindus don't need to complain.

Rapists in the villages move freely like lords. They don't flee or hide themselves. They rape the Hindu women of their choice at regular intervals. Very often they ask for money in exchange of raping their spotted girls of Hindu families. Nevertheless they commit treachery. They abduct the girl.

(d) Projected Program

Ethnic cleansing can best be illustrated from one instance that occurred at the time of the partition of India. Sheikhpura is a small town, which comprised a population of 20 thousand. 80% of them were non-Muslims, the Hindus. It was declared by radio on August, 17, 1947, just two days after partition, that Seikhpura belongs to Pakistan.

As Pakistan was made only on communal ground, the Government of Pakistan started a campaign for ethnic cleansing of the non-Muslims and accordingly Sheikhpura was a target. Having consulted with the local S.P. Mirza Mohammed Bakr, the District Collector of Sheikhpura declared 144 and announced that non-Muslims would not leave Seikhpura without the permission of the Govt. Meanwhile the Beloch force and Muslim marauders were assembled there to inaugurate the massacre. The Government declared curfew in Seikhpura on August 24, 1947 at 2.00 P.M., which was only meant for the non-Muslims. Then started a march of the armed force followed by Muslim leaders and Mujahids harnessed with choppers and machetes stridently shouting "Allah O Akber". Jehad (Islamic holy war) started by the Mujahids (religious fighters) against the unarmed Kafirs (non-Muslim civilians) in Krishna Nagar, Akal Garh and Ram Nagar. After 24 hours of the holy war, the incessant carnage, the whole of about 16,000 people that constituted the 80% of the total population were turned into piles of corpses. Nobody was there to cry for the victims except the Prime Minister of India, JawaharLal Nehru, who came four days after with the Prime Minister of Pakistan Liaqat Ali Khan to witness the holocaust.

After the partition millions of non-Muslim Hindus repatriated to India and took refuge in Gilgit, Baltistan, Mirpur, Bhimbar, Muzaffarpur, etc., which formed a part of Kashmir province of India. Mohammed Ali Jinnah with a determination to capture Kashmir from India declared Jehad. Pakistani armed Mujahids without a moment's hesitation launched Jehad against the (Kafir) non-Muslim Hindus. Incessant killing and looting followed it. As it was customary, it followed the pillage of gold ornaments and valuable utensils by the religious fighters. The ethnic cleansing of the non-Muslims in the name of Jehad helped Pakistan to earn enormous chattel and material wealth.

The Nehru family was always compassionate towards Muslims. He was pressurized to defend Kashmir. Hence he sent the Indian army to the Kashmir province and consigned Mohammed Seikh Abdullah, the then ruler of Kashmir, to direct the Indian army to free the occupied regions of India from the clutches of Pakistan. Md.Seikh Abdullah was a staunch Islamic fundamentalist. He was reluctant to continue the rescue operation because those occupied parts were heavily crowded with Hindu refugees. He apprehended non-Muslim majority in Kashmir if those areas were liberated from Pakistani occupation. After 10 days of rescue operation he ordered a cease-fire. Muslim Mujahids encircled the area and fell upon the unarmed kafir refugees. The road leading to India was closed by the order of Md. Ali Jinnah. The minority Hindu refugees had no other way to escape. The Muslim Mujahids pounced upon them and started killing and looting. It was found that at the end of November, 1947 almost the whole of 95,000 non-Muslims were killed according to the principle of Jehad. Presently it is under the subjugation of Pakistan by the name of Azad Kashmir. This occupied province has become the breeding ground of Islamic terrorists.

(e) Consequence of Ethnic Cleansing

Attempt for an ethnic cleansing has its serious consequences. History has not recorded the ethnic cleansing of past centuries to witness the formation of the Gulf Countries and other Islamic states in the Middle East and East Asia. The same is the case of Afghanistan of ancient India. To make India a secular country it was needed to kill 80 million people during the period 1000 to 1525 A.D. The Belgian Historian Koenraad Elst says, perhaps this is the largest ever massacre history has recorded and that was made by Muslim invaders in a country. The formation of Pakistan witnessed a massacre of millions of Hindus within a month. To Islamise Kashmir Muslims killed 2 million Hindus just after the partition of India in the year 1947. Even after this issue, simply to keep Kashmir as an integral part of India 61,000 civilians in addition to 6,000 army men have sacrificed their lives at the hands of terrorists. Bangladesh is formed on the graves of 3 million Hindus of East Pakistan.

In the Pak-Bangladesh war of 1971 some 98000 Pak soldiers were deployed in Bangladesh to suppress the rebellion of the freedom movement. The barbarous soldiers killed more than 3 million unarmed civilians within the duration of almost 15 days and molested the Bangladeshi women.

(f) Repudiated and wretched life of inferiority

Man like any other animal wants shelter and food, love and affection, consolation and hope, Dearth of these requirements lead to a down trodden life, a life of monotony, melancholy and gloom. A life permeated with grief and dishonour ends before time. The Hindus of Bangladesh and Pakistan are in such a perishing condition whose wealth is ever exposed to loot, women are ever exposed to rape, the men are ever exposed to gun and life, ever exposed to dishonour. It is natural that the society is exposed to extinction.

The reason for the Hindus of Bangladesh to remain dumbfounded is that the government of Bangladesh has totally disarmed the Hindu folk and on the other hand it has deployed Bangladesh rifles to clamp down any possible provocation.

On the other hand weapons, particularly the sword is the religious emblem of Islam, which is invariably found in every Muslim house. Light provocations make them come out with all their armaments. If the environment is under tension for any other reason, they tranquilize their mind only by retaliating Hindus whom they consider their enemies, only for the reason that they are Kafirs, non-Muslims. They are liable to be slaughtered and their women, to be raped and mustered for prostitution. There is no way for Hindus even by name to dishonour or provoke the Muslims of Bangladesh and Pakistan.

Muslims always pose with a religious notion that their society must exclusively be their own. They don't want a single non-Muslim, a heinous Kafir, a worm of hell, to exist in their society. Ethnic cleansing of a non-Muslim race from the surface of the world is their born motto. Nobody trains a tiger to pounce upon a deer nor teaches a fowl to catch a bird. Moreover Muslims never allow a minority race to exist in their homeland. So if they are outraged for some other reasons, they take revenge on the Hindus. When the cosmonaut of the U.S.A put his footprint on the moon, the Muslims in Pakistan and Bangladesh fell on the innocent Hindus with their swords and raped their women and looted their property on the pretext that the U.S.A defiled the moon. In the year 1992 when the Indians demolished an Islamic structure built upon a Hindu temple in India, the Muslims attacked the Hindus in Bangladesh and Pakistan. They killed the Hindus in thousands, looted their property and raped Hindu women all over Bangladesh. Thousands of Hindu temples all over Bangladesh and Pakistan were pulverized. In Bhola (Bangladesh) the Muslims disrobed hundreds of non-Muslim women and carried them in a procession stark naked. The women had not a single thread of clothing on their body. A Minister of Bangladesh regretted for not being informed earlier to see and enjoy the fun.

It was another incident that took place in the year 1992 when some Hindus forcibly demolished the Islamic structure constructed over a temple in the Uttar Pradesh province of India. In retaliation many ancient Hindu monuments of Hindu heritage were destroyed in Pakistan and Bangladesh, which were the two ancient Hindu provinces of undivided India. The massacre of unarmed and innocent Hindus in those two countries followed this demolition. During this incident a woman with her milk-fed baby was thrown into flames of fire in a moor in the midst of a vindictive cheering crowd. The family members of the deceased women lodged a complaint at the police station. Apprehending legal complexities, the indicted youths came to the victim's house and forced for a compromise. On reluctance, they were threatened with retaliation. The Hindus had no other way. The religious law narrates that if the victim pardons and the accused repents of his crime, then there is no need for prosecution. The dreadful criminals were exonerated.

(g) Shifting of possessions

During the interim period of Transformation of Civilizations all the belongings of a vanquished community or society come under the clutch of a victorious community or society. All the movable and immovable property of the individuals or community as a whole of a down-graded race automatically come under the dominance of the stronger race that establishes its victory over its adversarial race or society or civilization.

Hence the accumulated wealth of a man, whatever may be his status, no matter whether it is movable or immovable, is subject to transfer from his hand or from the ownership of his decayed community to the hands of the individuals or the community of the stronger race. Even the womenfolk also become an source of entertainment and enjoyment of the stronger race.

The property or wealth shifts from a race to its hostile race without any effort or with little effort in this final stage of Transformation of Civilizations.

One cannot feel the brunt of Ethnic Cleansing when it is at its primary stage of the first phase. So in the first and second phase, if a man of a stronger race filches the property of the targeted or victimized race, the man is indicted and prosecuted as culpable or offensive. But during the final stage of Transformation of Civilization or the 3rd phase of Ethnic Cleansing the individual or community of the victimized race counts little to his property. He gives more importance to his life's security than his material wealth. The exchange value of the property of the victimized race comes down almost to zero, which the owner shares for a penny or for no price. His entire attempt concentrates only on how to flee from that surrounding to save his life.

Some 60 years ago when there was no active function of the banking system in India, the people of rural areas in Pakistan and Bangladesh saved their monetary assets in coins and through gold ornaments and mostly used to bury them under earth for safety from theft. When they came to the final stage of ethnic cleansing they began to flee from their home, home village and homeland. They had only what they had clad. They crossed thousands of kms. to take shelter and reached the dense forests of the southern provinces of India, which were thronged with tigers and elephants. Government of India ascertained these places for their rehabilitation. The great landlords of Pakistan and Bangladesh were found cleaning the forests and tilling the land with ploughs, milking buffalos, reaping and harvesting the crops with their own hands. What they had with them of their motherland was the memory of their past.

All the non-Muslims and Christian European countries and the U.S.A are presently under the stream of Ist phase of Ethnic Cleansing. The whole of India except Kashmir, Nepal, the Philippines and many African countries are presently under the experiment of the second stage of Ethnic Cleansing. Jammu and Kashmir province of India, Chechnya of Russia, etc., are under the final stage of the process of Ethnic Cleansing.

(h) *Development of Suicidal tendency and enhancement of suicide*

The development of suicidal tendency becomes inevitable when a man reaches the stage of the third phase of Ethnic Cleansing. When a man or a community is left jobless, penniless, homeless and landless, then he or the community finds no other way except fleeing from that place to find out his destination elsewhere. But where is he to go? If all the doors of opportunity are closed to him, he comes out to the foreground either to kill or to be killed. Such feelings have driven many youths in Algeria, Palestine, Afghanistan and Pakistan to become extremists or terrorists. Such a situation gave rise to the Naxalites, the P.W.G members in India. If the gear reverses the people find no other way except committing suicide. The alternative is to face any of the inevitable coercions of Transformation of Civilizations. The third way is to face death after endless persecution.

In the last 80s Israel expelled some 460 Palestinians from its occupied territory alleging them to have been involved in subversive activities. All those Palestinians expelled from their homeland spent months together under the open sky. The Muslim countries including the contiguous Lebanon did not come for their rescue for fear of Israel's ire. Among those wretched Palestinians were many doctors, engineers, lawyers, teachers, administrative officers and politicians including women and children. Gradually they perished. Presently there is a tug of war between the Jews and Muslims precipitating the process of Ethnic Cleansing relevant to Transformation of Civilizations.

Truth is some thing, which is above all eruditions and imaginations. It is above the miracle and fantasy. Truth is the practical expression of infallible calculation based on the evidences of past history and incidents of the present world. We must prepare ourselves to welcome the insurmountable law of Truth and hence the law of Transformation of Civilizations. Even if we do not welcome it, spontaneously it would come to our doorstep. Yes, see, here it is!

(18) Glimpses of Transformation of Civilisations

First Phase

As described earlier, almost all the non-Islamic European countries, the USA and other Christian Nations that have inculeated secularism in their constitution and boast themselves as civilians of secular country with Islam as minority community of their society are under the process of First Phase of Transformation of Civilizations. Ballistic missiles and other lethal weapons forming as major protective war instruments cannot save a country from the danger of this transformational attack. Transformation of Civilizations is exclusively related to civil war. Birth proliferation, abduction of women of majority community and impregnation, birth control of majority community on their own interest, marriage policy exogamy resorted by minority community and simultaneously increasing in the number of minority race are the chief sources of Transformation of Civilizations of a country by the society of the minority community.

All the democratic secular countries like India, Philippines and Sectarian countries like Nepal, European countries like England and France etc. come under this category. Though Indian is in a severe position of this phase and it has also tasted the brunt of third phase like the former USSR and Sudan, other European countries like England and France etc. have not felt the fervour of Transformation of Civilizations because thery are at the beginning stage of first phase.

Second Phase

Process of Formation of a State within a State accordiing to the Law of Transformation of Civilizations

(Based on the Transformational Visibilities in Kashmir, from 1320-2020)

Kashmir bears the testimony of how a fully ethnic Hindu majority province of ancient Bharat Varsha or the present disintegrated India was turned out into a Hindu minority province in a long struggle for existence through seven hundred years of invasion according to the law of Transformation of Civilizations and how it got truncated from its original terrain to turn out into an Islamic nation through a planned process of struggle to gratify the great Transformation.

As a noble chunk of its motherland India, Kashmir has advocated and preached the principles of non-violence for 2,500 years. For its noble panorama it is known worldwide as the "Paradise on earth". But soon after the advent of Islam in this land, it became a land of bloody massacre and its natives became the victims of foreign invaders. Gradually there came about a great change in the proportion of its population and the natives were turned into a minor community.

This has now become a place of tug-of-war on the question of occupation between India, its motherland and Pakistan which vanguards to occupy it on behalf of Gobal Islamic Movement. Pakistan was also a part of India since its historical exitence in the map of world culture as Aryavart or Vedic Bharat Varsh. It was formed in the year 1947 as a result of 700 years of Islamic invasion against India. Now Kashmir, a beautiful terrain of India, has been vandalised by Pakistan according to the principle of Global Islamic Invasion. Situated on the foothills of the Himalayan mountain range it is well known as the "Heaven on Earth" for its unforgettable natural panorama.

For the first time it came to the notice of Islam in the year 1320. A Muslim invader named Dulacha who came from Turkey started a series of plunder and persecution. As a traditional practice of Islamic invasion he mercilessly killed thousands of people, plundered all the wealth, set fire to the houses, turned the women and children into slaves and converted the rest to Islam.

Sultan Sikandar (1389-1413) who was noted as "the iconoclast" pulverized all the Hindu temples of Kashmir and imposed Jiziya tax on non-Muslims. He started a perennial stream of Hindu carnage and Islamic terrorism. He converted millions of Kashmiri people to Islam. It was only in his tenure that Hindus became a minority community in Kashmir. The pile shaped mark in the midmost part of "Dal Lake" kown as 'But Mazar' or the pile of Hindu Kafirs " bears the testimony of non-Islamic carnage till to-day. It was only in 1820 that the emperor Ranjit Singh conquered Kashmir and annexed Kashmir with his Kingdom.

When the British left India in the year 1947 Kashmir was again left in jeopardy. India was partitioned into India and Pakistan. The King of Kashmir like all other independent estates was privileged either to annex his kingdom with India or with Pakistan or remain independent.

Mohamed Ali Jinnah, the founder of Islamic Pakistan, pressurized the Hindu king of Jammu and Kashmir through the then British Governor General Mount Batten to annex Kashmir with Pakistan. On his failure to convince the king, he ordered the Muslims of Pakistan to exterminate the Hindus of Kashmir. The link road between Kashmir and the rest of India was stretched through Pakistan. Hence after the segregation of Pakistan all communication links between India and Kashmir through Pakistan were closed by the order of Jinnah. Kashmir was completely secluded from the outer world, emergency supply system was disrupted and Jinnah ordered his Muslim marauders to slaughter the Hindus. Then continued the barbarous, unilateral holocaust, plunder and rape of Hindu women. There was no way to escape to take shelter, or to save one's life. On 24 and 25 of October 1947 the Muslim religious fighters in the valley of Kashmir massacred millions of helpless Hindus. Even pregnant women and nurses in the hospitals were not spared by the Islamic sword.

The majority of soldiers of the Kashmir army were Muslims. When Mohammed Ali Jinnah ordered to assault the people of Kashmir, the Muslim soldiers left the army of Kashmir with all the weapons and joined the Pakistani soldiers to fight against Kashmir. Terrorist groups were formed over-night in Pakistan. After a few days of militant training they were sent to the field to fight against Kashmir and plunder the wealth of the non-Muslims. They were conveniently led to infiltrate into Kashmir across the Jhelum river. Hundreds of boats were deployed to carry these ferocious Mujahids to reach the soil of Kashmir. The distressed cry of raped women, the adversity of orphaned children and murdering of blood stained people made the environment pitiable. In the districts of Jhelum, Sialkote and Rawalpindi of Pakistan where the populations of non-Muslims were 15 to 20%, carnage was rampant there up to their complete extinction. The slaughter of non-Muslims in the town of Mirpur, Bhimber, Kotli, Rajouri, Punch, etc., of Jammu was extremely horrendous.

Apart from this unilateral carnage made by the Islamic militants, the Islamic Mujahids got a chance to plunder so much wealth and so many women to rape that they could not reach Srinagar, the capital of Kashmir, on time. Such instances are hardly seen in the military history of the world where there is no army to protect the town and resist the advancement of the invaders. Instead, there was enormous wealth to be plundered and women to be molested that resisted the advancement of the enemy. Some regular markets were opened in Pakistan to sell captured Hindu women as slave girls.

When the Muslims assaulted on the non-Muslims being backed by the administrative power block of Islamic bigotry, the non-Muslims were collocated in multi-storied buildings as refugees. They saw in full view the kidnapping of their women folk and plundering of their property. The killing of non-Muslims with poison-stained sword and snatching money was a common scene. When the rest of the riot-stricken people moved towards India they were denied to depart as a mark of ostensible secular policy of Jinnah. They were determined to go and embarked on the train. Out of two trains carrying refugees, one stopped at Chalisa and the other at Kamol station near Lahore. All the refugees in the train were killed in the compartments. Two trains with corpses only reached Amritsar. About 95,000 non-Muslims were killed in Bhimbar, Baltistan, Mirpur and Gilgit Division of Kashmir. But at that time the total death toll was approximately 500000 non-Muslims.

78,114 square km. area of Kashmir is presently under the control of Pakistan. Terrorists have attacked more than 2300 times on the security force of India. More than half a million civilians have suffered barbaric death since 1947 but the number has been officially limited to about 10 thousand.

The administrative situation of a Muslim-dominated state changes compared to the other provinces of a country. In Jamu and Kashmir, the post of Chief Minister has been exclusively held by Muslims since the Independence of India. Many dreadful terrorists indicted of murder and other subversive activities are regularly set free by order of an enquiry committee on the Independence Days and Republic Days. The number of such acquitted terrorists in Kashmir is not less than 7 thousand. In an affected province there is no security of judicial authorities that decrees to punish a criminal. Here the case of honorable justice Neelakanth Ganju comes to light. He passed the death sentence against Maqbul Batt who had his hand in killing the ambassador in England R.H. Mahatre. A few days after his execution, Ganju became a target of terrorists. His dead body was found lying near a drain for days. Nobody dared come to receive it for fear of the terrorists.

Besides the expansion of Islamic education hundreds of mosques were raised over-night in Kashmir in the name of religious preaching. Most powerful mikes are used in the mosques for Ajan. It is estimated that 1,000 mosques have been constructed in each decade since 1970. Anti-national and provocative speeches are delivered through these instruments.

Attempts are made to imbibe the Government Officers into Islamic thoughts. After Mohamed Seikh Abdullah came to power in 1975 he allowed the reading of Namaz 5 times in the offices during the office hours. By the instigation of Mullahs, Govt. servants of Jammu and Kashmir began to trim their beard. After transforming Kashmir, the Global Islamic Movement is on the way to swallow Jammu.

This is the fate of Kashmir, which was once the noblest of Hindu kingdoms for ages. Presently this is a Muslim-dominated state. Almost all the public representatives of the state assembly and the members of the Parliament are Muslims. Government is indifferent to rescue the non-Muslim minority from the worst situation. Some Chief Ministers, out of their Islamic ethos, are linked with the secessionist groups of Kashmir. The majority of police are Muslims. The army is powerless to react under the heavy pressure of the government. National politicians come down to discuss with the secessionist and the militant groups for a solution of the national problem. Government takes every care for the security and health of the militant leaders.

The Muslim militants of Kashmir or the Mujahiddins of Islamic Jehad send threatening letters to the non-Muslims of Kashmir to leave their homes and go away. "Because Kashmir is the land of Allah it is only the Muslims who can stay. Non-Muslims are forbidden to stay here. On their unwilling or denial to leave the place their business establishments will be blasted, their children will be persecuted and they will be gunned down."

Apart from these threats the letters are complemented by the details of victims, where their children are reading, what their grown up daughters are doing, where and how much their landed property is etc. It is natural that anybody who reads this letter gets terrified and feverish. Threatening orders to leave Kashmir are passed through thousands of mikes hanged at the top of mosques. Out of fear of the terrorists or the Mujahiddins, Muslim owners of business enterprises and landlords expel their non-Muslim employees from their services. Next moment they start the carnage of non-Muslims in broad day-light. Non-Muslims flee without turning their face to take shelter in the refugee camps.

Reign of terrorism with its reign of terror in affected Kashmir

When a country directly comes under the perimeter of Transformation of Civilization or when it comes under the operational field of the third face of Ethnic Cleansing, the persecution of the minority becomes the law of the land. No Government of the constitutional authority, no force of humanitarian value comes for rescue. No journalist of international repute gets success to depict the blatant and vivid picture of the real situation. The following are some horrendous instances of Kashmir, which generally take place in any place that comes under the third phase of ethnic cleansing.

B.L.Sarma, a native of Ompura of Badgam district, is a worker of Sher-e-Kashmir Medical Institute. He is a handsome young man of 29. Like all others he had also come to this world to enjoy its varieties. The colourful dream of marriage was also imminent. But his one crime was that he was born in a non-Muslim family of Kashmir. In this unilateral communal riot he could feel the heat of terrorism all around him and apprehended danger to life. All his dreams were dispelled in utter despair. Determined to leave the land for safety he packed all his utensils to set out with his old mother in search of an asylum. It was April 19, 1990. He had the plan to leave the place the next day. But he did not know that fortune's disposal for him was different. All on a sudden he found some terrorists entered into his house. His palpitation began to count fast. The Mujahids pounced upon him. His old mother screamed supplicant voice- "This is my only son, sirs. Persecute me in whatever way you like. You kill me. But please save him. There is nobody else in this world to help me except him." The prayer of the old lady could not change the heart of the religious fighters. They made a hole in the skull of the victim. Blood began to flow profusely. They dragged him out of the house and tore his cloth to strand a rope They tied him to the trunk of a tree. Then started incessant beating by cudgel and iron rod. The wretched victim went on telling – "Kill me at once, please don't torture me."

The victim had no knowledge that it is the sacred duty of an Islamic religious fighter to kill a non-Muslim by torture. The old mother was sobbingly observing the torture of her only son till he turned into a corpse.

Another incident of April 13, 1990, Sarbananda Kaul of Bijbehera of Anant Nag district was an eminent non-Islamic scholar of the Quran and Islam. Also he was a regular reader of the Quran. At that time he was translating this Islamic scripture. He was also a noted teacher of that locality. This foolish scholar did not have the idea that his life-burner would be put off according to the theory of the Quran. When the call of Jehad was trumpeted for non-Muslims to leave Kashmir, his fleeing relatives requested him to leave Kashmir with them. But the 67 year old Kaul had deep faith over his numerous Muslim friends, students and known persons. "Is there no value of my perseverance of so many years?"- he exclaimed. The learned Kaul did not evaluate his non-Islamic personal image in the balance of the Quranic Jehad.

Unexpectedly on that day 4-armed Muslim Mujahids intruded into his house. Kaul only looked them with open mouth in wonder. They told Kaul that he has to go to certain place to answer some questions. His family members requested them to instantly ask him the questions. But the Mujahids were adamant on their stand. Finding no other way Kaul walked ahead, being followed by his 27years old son Birendra Kaul. He was an engineer in TELCO. The four-gunned men followed them. Father and son walked like two sheep being carried to the abattoir. The old Kaul had a suitcase in his hand. The Mujahids warned the females to take off their ornaments from their body. All the ornaments of his family were preserved in it. While the Kauls were going on the way being flanked by the Mujahids, nobody resisted their journey.

After two days of painful anxiety the dead bodies of the two were found. The flame of candle holed the midmost part of the forehead of both father and the son. Both were given intolerable torture. Bones of limbs were pounded, cut into pieces. Tufts of hair from their head were forcibly pulled off. Their eyes were gouged out and sockets were filled with chilly powder. Seeing the dead bodies of her husband and the only son the old lady Kaul fell down on the floor. It was her last sleep.

Such a black day came in the life of B.K.Ganju. In a cold morning he found his name in the hit list of non-Muslims stuck on the wall of the nearby mosque. No sooner had he known this, he and his wife became very worried. Their mind began to panick like that of a terrified deer. They only thought over where to go and whom to report. The first problem was how they should come out of their house. They thought to report it to the police. But to them the police is also an agent of terrorists. As soon as they would report, the news would reach the terrorists. Then their punishment would be very severe. His wife served him food, but he could not eat. Night came, but they could not sleep. Both of them spent the whole night with eyes open. Fear disturbed their mind. A little sound made them feel that somebody was knocking at the door. They began to weep. What is the fault of Mr. Ganju that he would be killed ? The next night also they could not sleep. The telephone rang. Mr. Ganju went to pick up the receiver but declined to touch it for fear of the terrorists.

On the third day at 9.00 o'clock there was the sound of somebody knocking at the door. Mrs. Ganju replied from inside that her husband is not at home. He has gone to the office. "We have got some urgent work with him. It is not the time to go to office" came the reply from outside in a rude voice. Mrs. Ganju could not open the door.

A little later Mrs. Ganju saw outside through the window. Nobody was seen. She took a sigh of relief. But what would they do ? How many days would they be confined to the house? She raised the phone to report to the police and to the office of Mr. Ganju. Soon there was the sound of a detonation to break an old door from the side of her neighbour. Mrs. Ganju asked her husband to jump into the roof and hide himself in a tin box. Then two terrible looking Muslim youths entered the house. One having a Kalasnikov and the other a pistol in his hand. They began to search every corner of the house. No whereabouts of Mr. Ganju was found. They saw a room with locked doors. They asked Mrs. Ganju to open the room. There was the key with her. The two became very angry. They broke open the door and searched every nook and corner of the room but in vain. "The rat has been hidden some where, but how long?" They commented.

Within a few seconds they got the information of Ganju from the neighbour. They rushed on to the roof. Mrs. Ganju simply kept looking on at the heart-rending scene. Her limbs did not work. She could not speak. She began to count the seconds to see her husband's plight. Then she could hear the terrific booming of the Kalasmikov. Blood began to drip from the cracks of the roof. Mr. Ganju slept in the roof forever. The religious fighters of Islam did not turn their face to see Mrs.Ganju who was lying half head.

An Islamic servant does not spare the life of his non-Muslim master when he avails of a chance. Here was an affluent man named Ashok Bajaj with a good carpet business in Kashmir. It was in March 26, 1990; his two Muslim servants called upon their master to their house with some pretension. They killed him there and disfigured his body by savagely cutting his limbs. His wife was informed to come and carry the dead body. Mrs. Usha Bajaj, wife of this millionaire Ashok Bajaj, ran to the refugee camp with her seven daughters and stayed there with her father who had taken shelter there earlier.

Ashok Kumar was a young man of 30 of Srinagar. It was an incident that took place early on February 24, 1990 when he was destined to go to the other world. But it was quite unexpected. He had gone marketing where three Muslim youths surrounded him. Before he could ask anything, bullets were fired from their pistols. Fluttered in excruciating pain he appealed for rescue with an outburst cry. To quench their demonic thirst the three Mujahids began to dance around Ashok Kumar. Blood soaked Ashok requested them to kill him instantly and save him from pain. His entire request was in vain. The Quran reiterated to kill the enemy miring him in utter pain. Hence the sdistic fun of pain cannot be enjoyed if the victim is given the chance to die instantly. After a little while the police van was seen coming towards the spot. The terrorists fired Ashok Kumar at his chest and belly. In the density of heavy snowfall his dead body was silenced.

Pandit Brajnath Gowswamy of Haldibada Tahasil was forcibly carried away from his small cottage by the Jehadi fighters to inflict a religious treatment on him. After torturing him for a long time they mended his mouth and hanged him on a tree upside down. Even after he died in severe pain with a sealed mouth his dead body was not allowed to be let down from the tree. When it was detected that a non-Muslim night watcher had cut the rope and brought down the corpse he was threatened to death.

Out of fear he slipped to Jammu. After some days when he returned to Kashmir, he became a target of the Islamic sword.

An Intelligence Officer T.K.Rajdan was on his way in a car. The Mujahids stopped him on the way and gunned him down. They took him to the nearby mosque, searched his pockets and then threw away his dead body. His family members were so much terrified that they could not dare to perform his funeral ceremony.

Mr.K.L.Ganju was a veteran professor of Agriculture University of Sapar. He was fully aware of the burning situation of Kashmir and the fleeing of non-Muslims from the land. He had an unshakable belief that he had many Muslim friends who are very friendly and amusing. But to the travesty of luck this wretched fellow had not contemplated on the intrinsic ideology of Jehad.

May 2, 1990 came in the life of Dr Ganju as the day of doom. Dr K.L.Ganju, his wife professor Mrs. Pran Jatta and one of his cousins were dining at 9.00 P.M. All on a sudden entered into his house four Muslim youths with guns and pistols in their hands. They ordered the Ganju family to accompany them. Mr. and Mrs. Ganju were dumb-founded on hearing this unexpected and unpleasant order. But there was no time to take any decision. Those three walked ahead with the Mujahids but could not dare to ask them where they are led. Their known persons on the way also went unwittingly. Even no body came up to report to the police.

The place of killing of these three was a mosque situated on the bank of Jhelum. At first Professor Ganju was gunned down from very near. Due to some unknown reason his dead body was not thrown into the river for some days. A bullet struck Ganju's cousin but however he could escape by throwing himself into the river. Now came the time of Mrs. Ganju in rotation to witness the sexual gratification of the religious fighters. She was tortured in an extremely barbarious manner. After the Mujahids raped her one by one, they cut her breasts and threw them to be eaten by dogs. She was tied to a stone and was thrown into the river. Her body was traced after six days.

When the Mujahids were dragging Chamanlal Pandit of Bandgam district of Kashmir to slaughter him, his five-year-old daughter weeping told the Mujahids. "Please leave my father." His wife was looking on at this heart-rendering scene with eyes full of tears. The hard core religious youths told her daughter, "We swear in the name of Allah, we shall send back your father to you." True to their promise they severely tortured Chamanlal, killed him mercilessly and sent back the dead body to his house.

It was another incident of February 12,1990, the execution day of Maqbul Batt. Batt was a dreaded Islamic Mujahid who was entangled in the murder of R.H.Mahatre, an Indian envoy stationed in England. The terrorists were in search of a victim to celebrate the execution day. This day was quite inauspicious to Mr.Bhan, a well-posted Intelligence Officer of Kashmir, who was targeted by the terrorists. The trained militant Mujahids knew that this Officer was now in a bullet proof Jacket. Mr. Bhan was also unhurriedly moving as he was fully alert about the chaotic situation. To trap the victim Mr.Bhan, the terrorists just passed by him 2/3 times. When they were confirmed that the victim is now within the purview of their operation, the terrorists came from the rear and placed the pistol on Bhan's neck facing it upwards and triggered. The pellet came out bursting through the head and the mouth. Bhan fell down on the ground in a pool of blood. The execution day of Maqbul Batt was celebrated."

Pakistan's Independence Day was celebrated in the same manner on August 14, 1993. On that day the Muslim Mujahids stopped a bus on the way carrying 42 passengers from Kistabada to Jammu. All the Muslim passengers were asked to descend from the vehicle. There were only 16 non-Muslim passengers left in the bus. After moving a little distance they again stopped the bus in a turning and gunned down all the 16 passengers. The Independence Day of Pakistan was celebrated.

In his book "The Man Eaters of Kumaon" the world famous hunter Jim Corbett has mentioned that while hunting a man-eater he has given every chance to the target to escape. Only once he killed a man-eater while it was asleep. He has expressed his regret in the book for having killed a sleeping tiger committing it to be an inhuman act. But such type of killing of non-Muslim children, men, and women is a day-to-day affair in a Muslim-dominated land. It is also considered and emboldened as a sacred and religious duty, a way to achieve Islamic Paradise.

The Murder of the working Secretary of "All India Kashmir Pandit Conference" Mr.Ashok Kaji was also no less inhuman and barbarous. First, all his bones were broken by severely beating him. Blood began to bleed profusely. Nobody came to his rescue though this barbaric incident was happening in broad daylight. Kaji was painfully telling, "Please don't inflict me more pain. Kill me at once." But it is the sacred duty of a Muslim

Mujahid to kill a non-Muslim by torture. It was only when the sound of a police van was heard, the militants kindly showered bullets on the Kaji and left the place.

Lasa Kaul, the Director of T.V., was triggered on February, 12, 1990 on his way home. His only crime was that all that he produced in the T.V. was un-Islamic.

Apart from non-Muslims, these militants also victimized many Muslims who opposed such kind of atrocities of terrorists. According to the Quran a Muslim who is not true to Islam is also punishable like non-Muslims. It is anti-Islamic for a Muslim to accept a non-Islamic Government. A woman without a burka and a girl without a hijab are also severely punished. A bomb connected with the bodies of Mohammed Akbar and Sailuddinand was blasted. Their fault was that they were servants of an Anti-Islamic Government.

Satis Tiku is a well-known name in the Kashmir valley as a social worker. But as a non-Islamic being his social service is not countable in a Muslim majority society. It was the morning of February2,1990.Two Muslim youths came to meet Satish Tiku in his house. Observing their suspicious tendency Satis Tiku's sister informed them of his absence. They left the place . But when Satish Tiku came to know that his sister has sent them back by telling lies he scolded her not to be over-suspicious and came out of his house to find them out. Just before reaching the road he was caught in the eyes of the hunters. All on a sudden the guns in the hands of the Mujahids began to bang. Blood stained Satis Tiku instantaneously fell there forever.

This is an incident of February 1990. This took place in the district of Bad gam. Tejkrishna Rajdan, aged about 30, was working in Punjab. He came to Kashmir on leave to spend some days with his family members. While on the way he saw his Muslim friend. Both embarked on the bus bound to Lal Chowk. The bus as usual stopped on the way. Some passengers came down and some got into it. Suddenly there occurred some unprecedented incident. The old Muslim friend of Rajdan struck out a pistol from his pocket and fired aiming at his non-Muslim friend. Not being satisfied with such a religious deed he asked the crowd to kick up the dead body and drag it out of the bus.

People dragged it to the nearby mosque and kept it hanging for exhibition till the police came.

Murder and massacres are common phenomena in Kashmir. Almost every day some 25 to 30 innocent civilians are killed in cold blood during the last decade of the last millennium. An instance in the village of Champurari of Doda district may be cited. It was in January 1998 when some militants came to this village and forced the male members to come out of their house and stand in a row on the road. Then the militants gunned them down in the presence of their wives and children and disappeared as usual.

It is also seen that security force nab the dreaded terrorists in exchange of their life nd put them in prison but political conspirators of appeasement set them free in hundreds in occasions of National Days.

It is learnt that the leaders of Jamat e Islami only appoint fundamentalist Muslims in police service. These Muslims forcibly convert Hindus into Muslims. Muslims killd the mahant of Keshabnath temple smashing him by the gun butt on his head. His crime ws that he was reluctant to accept Islam.

Few years ao a Muslim abducted the wife of a Kashmiri Pandit. His husband brought a warrant under section 100 of CRPC to rescue his wife but failed in his attempt. The police did not bring her to the magistrate. The reason was that she had got converted into Islam.

Everybody from a 2 months old baby to a 90-year-old man has become the victim of the militants. According to the statement of the social worker Lavo Bhati, Muslim Youths rape the daughters and daughters-in-law of aristocratic families in front of their sons, brothers and relatives. After the raped women have lost their senses their blood is sucked through the syringe. Their limbs are hacked and breasts cut into pieces. Little children are snatched off from the lap of their mother and are killed by pulling their legs in opposite directions and thrown to the dogs. They tattoo on their breasts "Victory to Pakistan", etc., without caring for the agony. The intention behind such deeds is to create terror in the minds of non-Muslims that would enable them to leave the place helping the Muslims to extend the Islamic imperialism. All that was done in Kashmir against the non-Muslims was in the name of Allah.

There is another incident that took place in June25, 04. The militants from South Kashmir kidnapped at gunpoint Senior Engineer of IRCON Sudhir kumar of Pulwama district of South Kashmir with his brother. Nobody could know their whereabouts. The next day the two brothers were found plunged in a field. Their hands were tied with rope and throats were slit.

There are instances of pulling out of liver by ripping the chest and hacking flesh from the body. The explosion of bombs, the tearing of the national flag, the demolition of temples, the delivery of explosive speeches (like 'Kafirs'! Leave Kashmir and get out leaving your wealth, your girls and young daughters for us") are the day-to-day affairs in Kashmir.

Transformation of Civilizations by Islamic militancy or the Jehadi fighters was intensified in the year 1990 when more than 350000 Kashmir Pandits and Sikh Hindus were forced to evacuate the valley. This year saw the killing of more than 1200 Kashmir Pandits and Sikhs in three hands of Muslim militants. No human right commission or any leader of International fame came forward to speak against this butchery. The Muslim youths of Kashmir valley got appointment in different government jobs. Those jobs that remained vacant after the Hindus left the valley were also filled in by the Muslim youths. Not even a single Hindu was qualified to get appointment in Kashmir.

After the non-Muslims leave the land their houses are occupied by the Muslims and the vacant jobs are filled-up by the Mujahids. Nothing is impossible for Allah. He is very kind to His followers. Along with this process of ethnic cleansing of Hindus, Islamisation of Kashmir is also in its quick progress. Instances of throat slitting, beheading and gunning down and acid attack on women for not having covered their body by burqa are also seen in abundance in Kashmir, a province under a secular Hindu majority government of India. The Muslim women in Kashmir valley are asked to produce more children and are allured to be awarded for proliferation. Besides they are asked to have sex with the terrorists. As a result the growth of Islamic population in the Muslim majority area of Kashmir during the last twenty years grew to 94% whereas in the Hindu majority area of Jammu the percentage of population growth is limited to 43%. Women are asked to go under Burka and not to be interested in study. Any defiance of it results in shearing of the nose or the distortion of the face by pouring acid or gunning down by bullet.

Foreign militants are advised that country chicken and women are abundantly and cheaply available in Kashmir. This tempts them to rush to Kashmir to enjoy houry, (the most beautiful women available in Islamic heaven after death). Hence soon after their arrival they enter a house and ask for chicken and women. They forcibly rape women either young or old without any discrimination even in front of their male members. Its resistance leads them to inhuman torture and death. After the Hindus fled from the hill now it is the turn of the Muslim family who are the worst sufferers at the hands of the militants.

Thus the soil of Kashmir has witnessed the killing of 1500000 unarmed impeccable citizens, since 1985, at the hands of the Jehadi fighters of Pakistan, the outrider of Global Islamic Movement, to escalate the process of ethnic cleansing in India, the largest democratic nation of the world, which is at present the greatest target of Transformation of Civilizations.

Instruments of Global Islamic Movement to synthasize Kashmir into a separate country : Kashmir Liberation Movement

The rulers of Pakistan formed this organization to segregate Kashmir from India. In the year 1989 its name was changed into Kashmir Liberation Alliance. Its allied organizations are Al Jammu Kashmir Muslim Conference, Jamat-e-Islami, Olema-e-Islam, Azad Kashmir, Jammu Kashmir Liberation League, Azad Muslim Conference, etc. Jammu and Kashmir Liberation Front (J.K.L.F.) is an outcome of these organizations. The proposals that Kashmir Liberation Alliance passed in November 4,1990 are:

(i) To try explicitly for plebiscite in Kashmir and prepare to face all kinds of difficulties.

(ii) To spurn the proposal to distribute Kashmir between the two countries and to fight for an integrated Kashmir on behalf of Pakistan.

(iii) To disseminate world wide that the Kashmir problem is an internal problem of India, where the Government itself transgresses human Rights.

(iv) To animate the flow of revolution in Kashmir for its freedom and to provide all sorts of assistance to the Mujahids and to give them the honour of martyrs in their death.

(v) To exterminate Hindus from the land of Kashmir by implementing Shariat law and imposing Islam.

(vi) To disseminate through Inter Islamic Organizations that Kashmir is an Islamic state.

It is also narrated that it is purely Islamic and religious. To oppose it is to oppose Islam.

This Islamic Alliance had sent a team of representative to America. This team met the Secretary General of the U.N.O and the Human Rights Commission authorities of the U.N.O. They demanded justice and independence for Kashmir. They also launched a strike before the Head Office of U.N.O. demanding that Kashmir is part and parcel of Pakistan. The press and American electronic media also disseminated the interview of the representatives.

All Party Hurriat Conference

It is a federal body to which several political and non-political organizations, nearly all from the valley, are affiliated. It is recognized by the Organization of Islamic Conference, an International Islamic Institution, as a representative body and participates in its deliberations as an observer. From time to time the government of India has allowed its representatives to travel abroad to attend the OIC meetings. This gives this Institution an International status. It offers itself to be a party and proposes "tripartite talks on Kashmir " for the solution of the problem.

Hurriat does not recognize the state of Jammu and Kashmir as an integral part of India.

Laskar-e-Toiba

This is a dreaded Islamic Jehadi Organisation to convert not only Kashmir but the whole of India into an Islamic land. This institution is universally known as L-e-T and is involved in lethal explosions and heads in the Jihadi list.

Apart from implementing its subversive activities in 36 key towns of India, LeT has also extended its activities to Allahabad, Patna, Thane,Bangalore, Chennai, Udaypur, Khandwa, etc. Pakistani militant organizations also supply weapons to their Indian counterparts besides running narcotics trades and fake note transactions to escalate holy war Jehad in Jammu and Kashmir. It has aimed at destroying Indian refineries and petrol depots to disrupt Indian Economy.

Jais-e-Mohammed

This organization has planned to perpetuate terrorist activities in Ayodhya and other prominent cities besides enlisting the names of some national bigwigs for assassination. This organization has earned more than one billion rupees through narcotics and drug trade. Fake currencies of higher denomination are being printed in Pakistan and dispatched through Nepal to substantiate such organizations and create havoc in India.

Pakistan has released hundreds of its militants imprisoned in different prisons and dispatched them to India and other European countries to create destabilization and spread terrorism.

ISI of Pakistan

This is the chief patron of all the subversive activities committed in Jammu and Kashmir. There are more than 20 thousand Kashmiri youths who are trained at handling most sophisticated lethal weapons. Permanent training camps are stationed at Gohat, Larkana, Sangli, Sargodha, Muri, Sialkot, Lahore etc. It is redundant to mention that almost all the Islamic countries including Iran are actively observing the progress of Islamization of Kashmir. Osama bin Laden is the key patron behind this scene.

There are almost 60000 militants stationed at the Indo-Pak border to infiltrate into India. Having obstructed from the Kashmir border by the Indian army to enter into India, the terrorists now infiltrate through the border of Jammu, Gujrat, Rajastan, Punjab and Bangladesh. More than twenty million infiltrators have been staying in India.

The I.S.I. of Pakistan works out the following plans through Islamic fundamentalists–

a) to turn out Kashmir valley into an Islamic State.

b) to expel the nationalists of Kashmir who have allegiance to India.

c) to plunder the central aid at the point of the gun.

d) to get the jobs of Hindus of Kashmir by expelling them from the land through terror and force.

e) to keep the provincial administration under their control.

f) to occupy all jobs of central Government without any interview, examination and requisite qualification.

There are other militant organizations with a determination to segregate Kashmir from India and declare it an Islamic state. Some of them are–

Jamat-e-Islami, Kashmir Muslim Liberation Front, Islamic students League, Dukhtran-e-Milat, Mahaj-e-Azad, Muslim United Front, Ikhwan-ul-Muslimeen, Hizbul Mujahiddin, Mujahiddin Party, Al-Umar Mujahiddin, Muslim Janbaj Force, Al Baqaraq, Alla Tigers, Al Jehadia, Mahaj-e-Azadi, Islamic Jamat-e-tulba, J.K.L.F., Inqilabi Front, "Hizbulla, Pasdaran-e- Islami, Islamic Students' League, Operation Balakot, Al Mustafa Liberation Tigers, Zia Tigers, Al Jihad, Hit Squad, Pak Commando Force, Kashmir Freedom Party, Guerilla Commando, Al Khomenei, Hizab Islami, Freedom Movement, Zinna Tigers, National Muslim United front, Students' Jamiat,Forces of Muslim Fidayeen,All Amr Mujahiddin, Gods Panther,Jihad police commandos,Majlis Ittihad Muslimee,Jamat Yaran Islam etc.

The present population of Kashmir is 8.2 million. The population of Muslims is 7.19 million, forming 87.8 per cent of the total population of the province. After an exhaustive Jehad launched by the Global Islamic Movement in Kashmir, now it has turned out to be an Islamic majority state in an Islamic minority nation that is "India that is Bharat".

Kashmir on 2020 according to the assessment of Transformation of Civilizations

The fervour of civilization Transformation in Kashmir is so pungent that one can hardly hope about Kashmir's existence as an integral part of India towards 2020. Presently one can witness the metamorphosis of the existing ethnic society in Kashmir and the vulnerability of its traditional culture. Transformation of a civilization into another according to this law can be clearly marked in Jammu and Kashmir. Social and cultural deteriorations are the two basic symbols of the transformation of a civilization. Sexual persecution, physical violence and political harassment or lack of political will to give protection to the ethnic community, etc., are the basic factors for the deterioration of a society. Regarding the physical violence there does not seem to have a single day that is not soaked with the blood of Transformational victims. Regarding sex in a disciplined society it is commended. But in a distorted society it is demanded. In this situation, the father of a chosen girl is threatened to death if he disagrees to act according to the dictates of a militant to hand over his daughter to gratify the illigetimate sex drive of his companions. Such incidents are innumerable in Kashmir. Gouging out the eyes, chopping the ears, nose and tongue of the women by terrorists are still rampant in Kashmir valley. The life style of the people of Kashmir is gradually coming into the clutch of militants.

Third Phase

Process of Formation of a State from a State According to the Theory of Transformation of Civilizations

(Bangladesh, Relevant to its Developments During the Period from 1971 to 2020)

This country bears the testimony of how a Muslim majority land turns out into a monolithic Islamic country gradually and systematically according to the law of Transformation of Civilizations deeimating the non-Muslim minority population from 50% to below 5%.) The law bears the testimony of the past history of Perso-Iran, the present history of Indo-Pakistan and future expectations of Indo Kashmir and all other countries including Euro-America which are put on the cauldron of Transformation of Civilizations pertaining to the theory of the survival of the fittest, struggle for existence and theory of evolution.

Bengal, an ancient abode of Hindu Civilization and a nice province of ancient India, was divided on the line of communal population into East Bengal and West Bengal, which formed parts of Pakistan and India respectively in the year 1947.

The Muslims of Pakistan started violating the political and human rights of the Hindu minorities in accordance with the definite plan of Pakistan to convert them into Islam. In 1965 Pakistan introduced the "Enemy Property Act," declaring Hindus and non-Muslims as enemies and imposed the law, which favoured the Muslims to loot the property of the Hindus. East Pakistan (Bangladesh) started persecuting the Hindus by plundering their property and kidnapping Hindu women as if it was their right. In an Islamic state it becomes their right to persecute the minorities in every possible way. The Hindus were deprived of their right to dignity and freedom. The importance of their witness in the court is counted as zero even when Muslims rape Hindu girls in broad daylight.

In the year 1971, during the "Bangladesh Liberation Movement" the Hindus joined their hands with the Muslims of Bangladesh with a hope to form a separate secular country according to the assurances given to them by the Muslims.

According to the religious order of the Quran when a non-Muslim is in war against a Muslim, other Muslims would not side with the non-Muslims to help them to fight against Muslims. So when the Pakistani army came to suppress the rebellion at Dhaka in Bangladesh they confronted the Indian army. The war that was to be fought between West Pakistan and East Pakistan changed into a war between Pakistan and India or a war between Muslims and non-Muslims.

Taking the advantage of the confusing situation the Muslims of East Pakistan too joined hands with the Muslims of West Pakistan and began to slaughter the Hindus. This violence followed the massacre of unarmed Hindus, which created a world record. Many international authorities of history asserted this barbaric incident as the highest pogrom in the history of human civilization. Thousands of children were born as a result of rape. Tens of thousands of Hindu women were abducted and raped, converted to Islam and sold as sex slaves in other Islamic countries. At the end it was found that 3 million Hindus of Bangladesh were killed in the war besides a death toll of 17000 Indian soldiers. An Independent Bangladesh was formed over the graves of such a lofty pile of Hindu corpses.

The Independence of Bangladesh marked a series of vendetta. Anarchy and destabilization became the significance of this independent country. But one thing was constant in this entire chaotic situation. It was Hindu baiting. Constant looting of property of the Hindus, constant killing of the Hindus and constant raping of Hindu women became a consensus in Bangladesh since 1971.

In accordance with the Islamic law, police protection is totally denied to the minorities. This has resulted in an all-pervasive harassment and physical violence of the Hindu Buddhist women folk. The Hindus had no choice but to keep silence. The intensity of mass rape of Hindu women and looting their assets generated a psychological depression and fear in the Hindus that made them leave the country escalating the Transformation of Civilizations through ethnic cleansing.

Political party members also play zest with the Hindus as their pastime entertainment. Very often the leaders of Bangladesh National Party (B.N.P) come and caution the Hindus about the possible kidnapping of their daughters by the hooligans of opposition parties. To escape from the apprehended danger of abduction, they advise the Hindus to leave the village for the time being leaving the lands under their custody. Out of fear of being dishnoured the Hindus flee from their village for some days. On their return they find that all their belongings have been occupied by the leaders of Awami

League as well as the Bangladesh National Party according to the law of "Vested Property Act" which is exclusively framed to forfeit the property of the Hindus.

In the field of politics, non-Muslims are treated as puppet voters. Out of 8 million voters only 1 million could cast their votes and it was also under their threatening direction.

Almost all the indigenous Hindus of Bangladesh who were once noted as landlords have now become ciphers. A Hindu farmer has to offer a major share of his harvest to Muslim mafias of the village in Bangladesh. On his remaining absent from home for some days all his landed property is forfeited under this "Vested Property Act."

In villages Muslims act as police for the Hindus. They can detain a Hindu, interrogate him, can grope his pockets, search his body in a nasty way and snatch his valuables without any reason. They can lay their hands on Hindu girls without any hesitation. What is generally shown at the religious performance of Hindus in Bangladesh is only an eye-wash. The Hindus are asked to make a show of it and are photographed by Muslims for its dissemination.

After being dishonored and swaggered by the Muslim youths when the Hindus reach the bus stand or Railway station they find their fowlers waiting there before hand to snatch away all their belongings and their pretty-looking daughters. The Hindus embark on the vehicle empty handed leaving behind their girls in the hands of those who were preemptively prepared to rape them.

The miseries of Hindus do not come to the notice of the world at large because if any agent of international level or any foreigner comes to know about a Bangladesh Hindu, the Muslim bodyguards, who are no less horrendous for these humble creatures, escort him. Out of fear and coercion the Hindus cannot express their miseries to any Human Right Activists. The true picture of their miseries remains unrevealed in Bangladesh.

The plight of the Hindus in Bangladesh can best be illustrated from a recent incident that took place in Gazipur town, 30 kms from Dhaka, the capital of Bangladesh, on July 4,

2003. A Hindu school student Rajib was waving the cricket trophy, which slipped off from his hand and broke into pieces. His teammates became so angry that they battered him with iron rod and wooden stick until the teenager Rajib bled to death. The police arrested some teenagers but none was there available for immediate comment.

Abstaining from all walks of life the Hindus neither can study, nor run a business, nor marry on their own will, nor get any employment. They cannot have free movement in the streets. As a whole they have lost their rights and hopes to live. All government jobs and means of livelihood are denied to minorities. No passport is issued to the minority Hindus to go to any foreign country to earn their livelihood. In he military, in the public sector and in other fields of employment the Hindus' presence is totally zero.

After the 8th parliamentary election in Bangladesh the Muslims are determined to declare Bangladesh a monolithic Islamic country. So the only way to gratify their will is to expel or kill Bangladeshi non –Muslims. The best and the easiest means to expel or convert them is to rape their women folk and loot their property. Since 1947 there is not a single day when a Hindu has not been persecuted or murdered or his women folk molested. Nearly 5 million Hindus, Buddhists and Christian refugees crossed over to India absolutely penniless during the years 1947 to 1957.During 1957 to 1970, close up the gap 4 million Hindus came to India as refugees. Most of them crossed over the border in a clandestine manner and the key reason for the departure was torture, rape, loot and shooting.

The Muslims of Pakistan and Bangladesh harmonize with the Hindus as Indians. Muslims all over the world that Hindus are exclusively Indians. They should belong to India only. Amazingly this feeling is not rebounded by the government of India. On the contrary the strong Islamic lobby owing to their racial solidarity and minority privileges profoundly influences the government of India. The media agencies are anti-pathetic towards these Hindu refugees. The United nations High commissioner for Refugees is also callous to recognize their refugee status due to their mild protests and the indifference of the government of India, the last abode of Hindus in the world. Being harassed and disappointed, looted and dishonored, the Bangladeshi Hindus are left to lie under the open sky and die unnoticed.

Bangladesh, which was an abode of the Hindus with their 100% population for thousands of years as the descendants of the Vedic Aryans, was changed into an Islam majority country after 700 years of Islamic invasion of India. In the year 1947, nearly one million Hindus and Sikhs were killed in West Pakistan, resulting in the fleeing of 6.5 million refugees to India. In the year 1950, nearly half a million Hindus were slaughtered in East Pakistan. This led to another exodus of 4.5 million Hindus. Next came one of the biggest genocide in recorded history. In the year 1971, three million Hindus were butchered and two hundred thousand women were raped and murdered in cold blood in East Pakistan.

In the year 1947, there were 13 million Hindus in Bangladesh constituting 28 % of the total population. In 1981, this population came down to 9.5 million. In the census of 1951 the Hindu population was 22.5% in Bangladesh. But in 1991 this percentage came down to 10.5%.Today the population of Hindus in Bangladesh is below 7%.

After the annihilation of the existing 1.5 million minority Hindus through utter monotony, melancholy, gloom and dumb-founded life under heavy persecution by the valiant members of the Global Islamic Movement and the utter negligence of the Hindu majority democratic country of India and estranged by the Human Rights Commissions and missions of the U.N.O, it would declare itself a monolithic Islamic country like Iran, like Iraq towards the end of the second decade of 21st century.

Role of Bangladesh as an Islamic Nation

Bangladesh has produced the largst number of migrants, infiltrators and refugees in the world. Moreover this country hs the reputation to produce more children who automatically hatch out, grow up and try to migrate for their livelihood.

Largest number of them come to India stealthily by crossing the Indo-Bangladesh border and merges themselves in the great ocean of Islamic minority community. The government of Bangladesh also has considered it to be the best way to control its explosive population. As Islam declares birth control by any means unlawful and anti-Islamic, government is helpless to resort such measures like abortion or. other means of family planning. There are almost 25 to 30 million infiltrators in India who have exclusively come from Bangladesh. As each Islamic youth is an international citizen he can migrate from India as well as from Bangladesh to other lalmlc and non-Islamic countries. Girls of poor Islamic countries are exported to rich Islamic countries as slave girls and brides. Bangladeshi women folk innumerably migrate to India. Boys in large numbers go to non-Islamic countries in general as wage earners, migrants, refugees and jehadi fighters or terrorists. Presently their chief target is India, the only largest non-lalamic Hindu country of the world,

Bangladesh has been the most protected asylum for Islamic terrorists. Some aggressive Islamic groups are getting organized in Bangladesh. Fundamental political parties like Jamat e Islami back many of them Jamat e Islami is presently in power in alliance with the Bangladesh National Party. There are seven aggressive groups In Bangladesh who have their political bases in the parliament like Jamat e Islami, Nizam e Islami etc. Bangladesh was succeeding towards Pakistan before the 11/9 events. But Its fervor cooled loon when the USA became more aggressive against the Islamic world after the demolition of the World Trade Centre.

Bangladesh has been turned out as the safest heaven for Islamic terrorists after the USA army over flooded Pakistan and Afghanistan. The terrorists established their Asian center of Islamic activities in Bangladesh. Begum Khalida Zia remains less concerned about their activities. The militants of Bangladesh aim at bringing a change in the present system of administration in Bangladesh and introduce a Taliban type of government, which would solve all the economic, political and social problems according to the law of Shariat.

They also express their view that the government system of Islamic countries who support the Christian Westerners should be changed. According to information from Bangladesh, ISI of Pakistan is the chief financer to these militants. It is known that'in the year 2003 the militants of Bangladesh received more than 50 million dollars from ISI of Pakistan. There are three reasons why Khalida Zia supports these terrorist organizations.

First, she wants to curb the growing strength of Awami League, her opponent party by the help of th ese militants. These militants are the only groups who can overpower the Awami League. Secondly the Islamic fraternity between Pakistan and Bangladesh urges to establish the militant network to smash their nearest. common enemy India. Besides the government in power thinks that inflow of financial aid is possible only through militancy whether the inflow may be in the name of tourism or aid to madrassas. Besides Bangladesh has taken the step to feed militancy keeping an eye on India, For Bangladesh India is a great power that may endanger the integrity of Bangladesh Hence it thinks of encountering the super power of Indian hegemony by feeding the Islamic militancy.

Today Bangladesh, an Islamic province on the Chest of ancient India has no less contribution for the enhancement of the strength oj. secessionist groups like ULFA, BODO, and NSCN in India. The ISI of Pakistan has also revived its contact with Jehadi fighters of Bangladesh to open an Eastern front in India.

In the last centuries ethnic cleansing has gifted global Islamism many lands in different parts of the world. It gave Pakistan and Bangladesh in India, Afghanistan in Aryavarta, Iran in ancient Persia, Egypt in ancient Misser, Bosnia in Yugoslavia and many other lands in the former U.S.S.R. In the current century apparently the ethnic cleansing may present a vast country "India" to globallslamism. The process of action is so rapid that it is going to be materialized with in 15 to 20 years, even though Hindus in India would not have converted themselves into a race of minority by that time. Presently Euro American countries are put on same cauldron.

19. Role of Global Islamic Movement for the Transformation of Civilizations

It is not Islam that should be modernized; it is the modern age that should be Islamised.

– Global Islamic Movement

Constituents of Global Islamic Movement

(a) Organization of Islamic Conference (OIC)

The Organization of Islamic Conference (OIC) came into being on May 1971 at Rabat. Under the banner of this conference the Heads of states of Islamic countries unite to discuss on their common problems relevant to Islamic solidarity, strength, security, economic issues, etc. This is the Islamic counterpart of the United Nations Organization (U.N.O), which is thought to be the organization of non-Muslim nations to gratify their own interests against the fundamental interests of Muslims. In other words, the UNO is synonymous to the OIC. It holds its meetings every three years. The second meet was held at Lahore in 1974 and at Mecca on January 1981. It consists of more than 52 Islamic member states. The O.I.C has some special committees to fulfill their Islamic goals. One of them is the Al-Qods committee. It was founded in 1975. Its aim is to implement the resolutions made by the O.I.C on the liberation issue of Bait-ul-Muqaddas, the temple at Jerusalem. This is the holiest place of more than one billion Muslim believers of the world. The following are some of the activities of the OIC -

a) To promote Islamic solidarity

b) To strengthen the struggle of all Muslims with a view to safeguard their dignity, independence and national rights.

c) To strengthen the state policies of Arab countries and of Iran and follow a similar strength in the region.

d) To set out an Islamic resolution on the issue of the Persian gulf security and withdrawal of the foreign forces from the region.

e) To condemn military relations with Israel or any move that threatens the security of Islamic States.

f) To strengthen the position of Syria and Lebanon in confronting the Jews.

g) To familiarize the Arab people with the current way of thinking and create a better understanding between the Arab and Iranian people.

h) To investigate ways to establish the Arab Iranian common market.

i) To investigate ways of setting up air and sea transportation facilities between Iran and Arab countries particularly those in the Persian gulf region.

The USA leads the Western world with an invincible army force to universalize European civilization and to modernize the backward nations envisaging plans and programmes through an internationalized institution the "United Nations Organizations". In a similar way Muslim world has formed a parallel institution for the promotion of Islamic interest and human values according to Islam in the name of "Global Islamic Movement". The Global Islamic Movement (G.I.M) represents the Muslim world and encounters the United Nations Organizations (U.N.O) that represents the Western World. The Red Cross of the UNO is synonymous with the Red Crescent of GMO. Like the USA, Iran leads the Islamic world with a self-sacrificing strong religious army in the name of Mujahiddins, the Jehadi fighters to universalize Islamic civilization and to Islamise the backward nations and non-Islamic countries envisaging its plans and projects through this unified Islamic organization, the Organization of Islamic conference. This Organization interferes in the internal affairs of all non-Islamic countries of the world to promote the interest of Islam and the Muslim minorities of those countries.

In the VIII th summit of the O.I.C held at Tehran in 9 – 11 December, 97, some 55 Muslim Heads of state and top officials of the O.I.C. member countries participated to discuss the common problems that Muslim societies have to face. This Tehran declaration called on the O.I.C secretariat to encourage women's participation in the activities related to the O.I.C. Like the European common market it also called for the establishment of an Islamic common market in a bid to strengthen Islamic solidarity and encourage the advancement of the Muslim world within the context of world trade. There was also a proposal to set an Islamic International Tribunal and interaction sessions among the members of the Parliaments in Muslim countries to encounter the International Tribunal of the UNO. In this conference discussion was also held on Bosnia, Palestine, Afghanistan and Kashmir.

(b) Pilgrimage to Mecca

An Islamic nation has a good system to inspire and unify the Muslims of the whole world irrespective of nation, gender or colour to swamp them in the Islamic code of conduct. That is the Islamic system of pilgrimage to Mecca. According to this system every Muslim from every corner of the world is entitled to visit Mecca, the centre of Islamic pilgrimage, at least once in his life. To carry out this sacred duty Muslims from different countries of the world assemble here, exchange their thoughts, confirm their Islamic solidarity and universal Islamic brotherhood. After their pilgrimage festivity is over they return to their respective homelands with an Islamic bent of mind and with a determination to turn their respective countries into an Islamic nation called Dar-ul-Islam.

During their visit to Mecca they move in unison (circuits) around the Kaaba. The great annual congregation on the planet earth is held in the month of Dhul-Hi-Jjah, the 12th month of the Islamic lunar calendar. The wonderful unity of millions of people of every colour, language and race clad in the simplest of garb, the Ehram and standing shoulder to shoulder towards the holy Kaaba is really a miraculous illustration of global Islamic solidarity. This wonderful unity is a doctrine of practice of faith transformed to action.

According to the Islamic liturgy every pilgrim has to wear, or clad with, Ehram, an unstitched white dress, which even the fashion-conscious man has to wear one day in his journey. The throng of pilgrims, starting on different days and from different countries converges at Mecca; the most sacred and inviolable place where no Muslim, whatever the language, colour or nationality, is a stranger and where the visitor and dweller have equal rights. At the return journey the brainwashed travellers try to arrive at their respective homelands with the idea to preach and propagate international Islamic brotherhood.

Though the confluence at Mecca every year is a traditional system of Islam, its religious motive has been seasoned with the global Islamisation and launching of Jehad against the enemy i.e. the non-Muslims. The militant Islamic movement has initiated its communal influence since 1995. The International Islamic brotherhood has now been directed to stand as a solid entity and raise the sword of Islam to convert the world into a world of Islam with Mecca as the holiest epicentre of the Islamic world.

(c) Jehad, a globally applicable instrument, in a new trend

There was a constant Jehad between Iraq and Iran from 1980 to 1987 where 0.6 million people from both sides died and more than 7 million were injured. In Syria, Islamic Sunni Brother-hood fought against President Asad of Syria and was crushed by the Government mercilessly.

In the later period Muslims realized that in the Jehadi war between Islamic nations none except Muslims only suffer and the Western countries get their benefits with profits by selling arms and ammunitions to the belligerent Islamic states. This conscience stuck to the Islamic mind after the Iraq- America war. Thereafter they diverted their concentration towards first three points. First, they must wage war against the non-Muslims and non-Muslim dominated governments by helping the Islamic warriors of that country, as it happens in India (in the province of Kashmir); the Israel, the Philippines, etc.

Secondly they must continue war against the secular government in Islamic majority countries to turn the country into Dar-ul-Islam. This war or Jehad is fought between fundamentalist Muslims and secular Muslims as we see in Turkey, Syria, Algeria, Egypt, etc.

Thirdly Muslims must fight only against the non-Islamic entities like communist Russia and Christian Serbs to free the Islamic majority territories from the clutches of Russia and other communist countries.

Last but not the least is their incessant Jehad against the European Christians in the form of demographic attack and conversion of European Christians into Muslims and pulverise the hegemony of the USA.

This is the position and process of present Islamic Jehad. The aim is to globalize Islam. The Globalization of Islam means to make the whole world devoid of a single non-Muslim civilian. The Islamic thought-wave has its final destination on the U.S.A; whose defeat would decide and declare the final victory of Islam over the world, concluding the Transformation of Civilizations.

As a result of Islamic renaissance Muslims now feel that they are in no way inferior to the Euro-American Christians. On the contrary, they are privileged to Islamise the whole world and to stand against injustice done to the Muslims by the Christians world wide. They feel that in whichever corner of the world they are, they are one. That is why when a blind Islamic clergy man who was born in Egypt was indicted for explosion in the USA's World Trade Centre thousands of Muslims in Cape Town, capital of South Africa, started anti-American and anti-Zionist demonstrations to release him from imprisonment. In the last USA –Iraq war of March 2003, when the USA attacked Iraq and imprisoned Saddam Hussain, Indian Muslims declared to repudiate American beverage and Philippino Muslims burnt the effigies of American President George Bush. The Muslims of all the Islamic and Euro-American countries raised a strong protest against the suzerainity of the USA. This protest on the other hand established universal Islamic brotherhood with a determination to challenge the hegemonism of Euro-American super power.

Muslims worldwide organize 'Qods Day' rally on the last Friday of the holy fasting month of Ramadan in protest against the occupation of Israel. Participants every year revolt against the occupation of Arab and Palestinian lands particularly the city of Bait ul Muqaddas (Jerusalem).

The Muslim world has also prepared a plan to confront the Western cultural invasion. In pursuing this goal it has proposed to work on the following points.

(a) Propagation of Islamic culture among the Muslims and the Islamic society (b) Improving co-operation among the Muslims and consolidate Muslim unity (c) Introduction of Islamic thought and behaviour through presentation in an acceptable and appropriate manner to the existing cultures and people in the world (d) Using innovative and contemporary methods for presenting Islamic thoughts in different languages (e) Avoiding intolerance and bigotry in presenting Islamic thoughts. Their core assumption is as follows:

> "Solutions to human problems only exist in Islam. Human equality, kindness, mercy and salvation are fundamental Islamic principles. According to the Islamic scholars Marxism has collapsed worldwide and capitalism is paralyzed. Hence Islam, with its comprehensive principles and distinguishable perspectives will be the principal choice of the world and to turn out the world into a Muslim world, the kingdom of Allah."

Even the tide of globalization, which is a weapon in the hands of Westerners to capture and crush different cultures on the surface of the planet earth, will be futile to captivate Islamic civilization. Rather at the climax of cultural interaction both Islam and Christianity will find each standing against the other with a motive to exercise one's suzeiranity over the other. In the tide of globalization all the non-Westernized cultures will be swept away except Islam. Islam has become alert since the ringing of the warning bell that informs about the coming of the cultural invasion. For long they have attempted to keep their religion and society safe.

The Globalization policy sponsored by the Euro-Americans will not have any effect on Islam because its foundation is deep-rooted. It is embedded on some human instinct that is gratified religiously and culturally and that gratification will not be available with the amenities that globalization provides. The Globalization sponsored by the Western powers is nothing but cheap availability of luxury amenities and war ammunitions.

Unambiguously, globalization has its effect to some extent on the outward behavior or activities of Muslim society like the issue of Fatwa in Iran in favour of Women to lead congregational prayers for female worshippers, women having the right and privilege to contest in the presidential elections in some Islamic countries, etc.

Another globalised Islamic institution Hizbulla (Hizb-Allah) was established in June 1996 with its first session held in Tehran. Presiding over the conference the Islamic spiritual leader Ayatollah Ali Khomenei said that this organization would reach all continents and all countries of the world for the propagation of Islam, for the expansion of Islam and for the subversion of anti-Islams. Hizb Allah would act as a standard-bearer for the Islamic revolution throughout the world to launch a new wave of attack on US targets around the world.

There is another international Islamic institution "World Islamic Front for Jehad against Jews and Crusaders". The name itself denotes that this organization is destined to exterminate the Jews and Christians from the surface of the earth. This organization appeals to all the Islamic militant terrorists to unite and stand under one global organization to fight for the cause of Islam and Allah.

To combat in the field of Jehad, fighters from Ethiopia, Somalia, Eritrea, Kenya and Uganda are getting training in all types of subversive activities, violence and assassination. Thereafter they are sent to neighbouring countries, which are chosen as targets for intensive activities. Due to Saudi Arabia's policy of neutrality under the pressure of America, Arabian Mujahids get militant terrorist training in Afghanistan and Pakistan.

Hizab Allah of Lebanan, Pasdaran of Iran, National Islamic front of Sudan, SIUP of Somalia, Islamic Republic Organization of Kenya, Islamic Front of Ethiopia, Islamic Jehad of Eritrea, etc., have come under the one roof of Global Islamic Movement to fight against their enemies.

(d) Islamic Ummah

Every independent country has a national thinking and national characteristics that shape the culture, language, education system, etc., of that country. That is why despite all sorts of cordiality, bilateral and multilateral relations and common marketing system between France, Germany, Italy and England, etc., they differ from each other in language, culture, political and administrative system. But the Islamic segment is a different one. The Muslims who live in Canada, the United States, Europe and other parts of the world are part of the Islamic Ummah and are exactly the same as those who live in Islamic countries like Iran, Iraq or Palestine. A Muslim in the USA is always Islam thought-provoking. He has always an intention in mind to expand the Islamic culture and language in the USA. He takes the beef or hamburger in a hotel if he is satisfied that the animal killed for the purpose is slaughtered in an Islamic way. A French Muslim fights in the French court to allow his daughter to go to school with Islamic attire instead of her school uniform. When the Bosnian Muslim refugees are in need of aid, Indian Muslim film actor, with a national reputation visits the foreign countries appealing to the tycoons for financial help for the war-affected Bosnians. He never bothers about the adversities of earthquake striken, flood and cyclone hit people of his own country. To free Kashmir from the dominion of India a British Muslim leaves his mother and motherland forever, gets Jehadi training in Pakistan, fights against India and dies at New Delhi. On asking about the inclination of a Muslim youth of Kargil whether he is in support of Pakistan or India, without a moment's hesitation he replies that he is at the receiving end to get the Fatwa (religion order) from his religious dictator of Iran. It signifies that if the Iranian religious leader would inform him to fight against India, without any hesitation he would jump out with weapons to launch a civil war. This is Ummah, the Islamic brotherhood.

The Indian born British author Salman Rushdie faced a death sentence by the father of Iranian Islamic revolution Ayatullah Ruholla Khomeini. The government of Iran slackened the fatwa after his death. Some Jehadi groups vowed to renovate the religious order by raising a fund collected from selling their own blood. It was not patronized directly by the government of Iran. But when the United States of America frowned at Osama Bin Laden for his suspected conviction in the American embassy bombardment, America again became the eyesore of Muslims. To harmonize the Osama's incident, Iran's revolutionary guards again declared that the 1989 decree sentencing the British Author Salman Rushdie to death still stands and called on Iran's leadership to act on it. This elite military unit asked the republic to use diplomatic means to support the rights of Muslims and of the World's disenfranchised people to assure the historical decree of Iran not to be forgotten.

Islamic brotherhood is so intensified and rampant that whenever an insignificant incident hurts the Islamic sentiment, people rush out for protest clamouring Allah Ho Akbar and "Islam in danger."

There was a "World Muslim Youth Conference" held on July 22nd, 2000 at Tehran that lasted for 9 days. The young men assembled from different corners of the world had raised some proposals. One proposal was to start a separate media instead of the present Western controlled media which creates a very wrong notion about Islam in the minds of both Muslims and non-Muslims. According to them Christians and Western countries systematically have perpetuated a cultural invasion particularly against Islam through the media controlled by them. Iran was requested to lead the way and help other countries to launch an Islamic Network through which Muslims world be able to freely communicate with each other and be less dependent on the Western controlled media.

In the conference much emphasis was laid on Islamic unity that is above all the sectarian groups. To strengthen the idea it was exemplified that during the crusades when Christians conquered Bait-ul-Muqaddas, Jerusalem, they killed all the Muslims irrespective of their denominational variations. Hence Muslims (a) should prioritize their unity,(b) they should safeguard their religious identity and(c) they should take practical steps against Western disseminations.

(e) Exhortations of Mohammed through Quran and Allah

> *"The day will surely come when unbelievers will wish that they were Muslims".*
>
> *(Prophet Mohammed* in Quran, 15/11)

Mohammed is the only religious figure in the history of the world, who could erect a society formed with one people, one nation and one race. We find one in all and all in one in the society framed by Mohammed. This is his exclusive contribution to the human race. He very wisely made the worship of one God, the Allah, compulsory among his followers and installed himself as the only mediator (Prophet) between Allah and his followers, the common Muslims. By this befitting idea he created such a religious environment where the sayings of Mohammed, the sayings of Allah and the sayings of the Quran became one and the same.

A systematic contemplation of the Quran reveals that attempt has been made to brainwash the Muslims by making repeated exhortations to obey God, the only God Allah, the Almighty and ever merciful and his Prophet Mohammed while simultaneously illustrating the sexual pleasures of Paradise and the horrors of hell.

Mohammed, the founder of Islamic way of approach to non-Muslims

During his primary stage of Prophethood Mohammed was very lenient in his behaviour. He did not impose any body to accept Islam. But no sooner he became victorious and powerful he inserted a special way of approach for the spread of Islam. This is the Islamic way of approach and Islamic rulers have been imitating it since generations whenever they get a powerful position to challenge their non-Islamic counterparts.

With a destination of Islamising the neighboring states of Asia and Europe Mohammed sent message of peace to the ruling authorities. In a letter he wrote to Caesar, the king of Rome to abandon Christianity and accept Islam. In his letter claiming himself as the last Prophet of Allah, the almighty Mohammed described "O king of Rome! I invite you to accept Islam (That Allah is the only God, He has no equal and Mohammed is his Prophet), if you embrace Islam, Allah will assure you protection from all evils and impediments. Your riches and influence will be doubled If you become a convert But If you disagree to renounce Christianity and accept Islam then you will be held responsible for your sin and for the sins committed by your subjects (To repudiate an invitation to accept Islam is a sin and its only reward is death). Allah is merciful and wise.

Mohammed sent the next letter to the king of Iran. "O King! I write this letter in the name of Allah, the most benevolent and merciful, I testify that Allah is the only Lord, He is matchless and incomparable. I am his Prophet. O king of Persia! I invite you by His order to accept Islam with free mind end open heart, *I warn the entire human race that Allah has sent me as his Prophet for all the people of the world. Let the irreligious Kafirs (non-Muslims) listen His message clearly.* O king! Keep yourself free from all sorts of dangers that you have to face for not having accepted Islam. If you don't accept my invitation, you will be held responsible for your sins and sins of your race for not accepting Islam. The king of Iran was arrogant and wanted to imprison Mohammed. But within a very short period his son who ascended the throne of Iran and embrassed Islam assassinated him. On his instigation, the Governor of Yemen embraced Islam with all his friends and relatives and immediately informed Mohammed about his conversion.

Mohammed sent the third letter to the king Nazzasi of Albania. In the same atonement Mohammed wrote the letter to the king. The Christian king was surprised and terrified on hearing the contents of the letter. He knew the strength and desires of Mohammed. But he was very clever. He applied his presence of mind and very tactfully escaped from the frowning of Mohammed. He pleased Mohamed by gratifying his passions. Earlier he had given shelter to Muslim refugees He immediately ordered to bring a box made of trunk and inserted the letter in it. Then he told that as long as the letter of Mohammed is safe in the box, his kingdom is safe from invasion of Mohammed.

He hosted the messenger of Mohammed, the messenger of Allah with utmost hospitality. He sent an amount of 1000 pounds, five pairs of precious clothes and two most beautiful women. Mohammed was pleased with these gifts. He kept the lady Maria for his entertainment and presented the other to one of his companions.

Mohammed's fourth letter of invitation to accept Islam was written to the king of Egypt. In every of his letters there was an inkling to the target to accept either of the two- Islam or the consequence of not accepting it.

The fifth letter of Mohammed was written to the king of Bahrain. The subject mater was the same as before. The king of Bahrain instantly embraced Islam along with all his subjects except some obstinate Jews who opposed Mohammed and his Islam. The king of Bahrain reported their defiance to Mohammed and asked him to take action against the Jews. Soon Islam began to spread like wild fire.

Mohammed, the chief architect and proponent of Jehad

> *"The sword" says Mohammed "is the key of heaven and of hell: a drop of blood shed in the cause of God, a night spent in arms, is of more avail than two months of fasting and prayer; whoever fails in battle, his sins are forgiven.*
>
> – Decline and fall of Roman Empire,
> Edward Gibbon, Page 240.

The deeds of Prophet Mohammed and his followers became ideals to be followed and imitated by all Muslims in later years. The broad pattern of crimes got fermented with the religious war in the name of Jehad. Islam undertook to raid in order to (a) invade the lands of non Muslims (b) kill the rest of men and women folk with their children during or after the wars are over where they got victories. (c) keep the surviving beautiful girls in their harem as slave girls or impregnate them in rape camps. Their only aim is to produce Muslim children using the womb of non-Muslim mothers and thereby increase their population) (d) pulverize the non-Islamic places of worship and study centres and build mosques in these places.

This is exactly the pattern of Jehad, to perform all these Islamic activities Allah has revealed the Muslims in the Quran and Mohammed himself has worked out during his lifetime. Hadis, the complimentary religious book of Islam, also elaborates to do or work out all such activities in the name of Jehad, in the name of Islam and in the name of Allah. Traditionally the Muslim kings or Sultans have sincerely followed these Islamic orders and the Mullahs have been inspiring their people to work out the revelations of the Quran.

During his lifetime Prophet Mohammed raided Jews and defeated them in every field of battle. His procedure of fighting against the non-Muslims was entirely new and hence it brought him victory. First he libeled and demarked every non-Muslim as his enemy. He is the first man to introduce guerilla war. He launched war at mid night when all were asleep and far from any war-provoking situation. Raid accompanied plunder, conflagration and rape that stupefied the unarmed and unprepared humble citizens to surrender, get converted and become immediate followers of the Prophet to get the booty and slave girls. All the Jews who were taken as prisoners by Mohammed were beheaded in cold blood. The raid undertaken by the Prophet and the methods followed by him became the guidelines for successive Sultans, Kings and later Governments. So what the terrorists or Jehadi fighters are doing today are the ideals or examples set before them by Mohammed and described in the Quran.

The instinct of Islam to exterminate the non-Muslims is latent in its fundamental concept. Before Mohammed's revelation as a prophet, there were varieties of religious followers in Arab including the Jews and Pagans. After the consecration of Islam Mohammed expressed his desire to bring all the people of Arabia into the fold of Islam. Hence narrating his plan he told his followers not to force anybody to accept Islam. Let the non-believers be given a chance either to accept Islam or the sword of Islam. Accordingly those who did not accept Islam were put to death. In due course the whole of the Arabian Peninsula came under the fold of Islam.

After the Paradise and hell there comes Lord Allah (there is no God but Allah) and Mohammed, the only prophet to stimulate the Jehadi sentiment of Muslims through the precepts of the Quran. Jehad is the Islamic ideology for a perpetual war against non-Muslims. All his statements are obviously embroidered in the Quran with the denotation that non-Muslims are subject to death in an Islam dominated land. Then their next alternative is to leave the land for the safety and security of their lives without any delay (50/36).

No time is ascertained to launch Jehad against an infidel (retaliatory war against non Muslims). Be it a pitch dark night with the snoring Kafirs in dream or the most abortive day time, the non believers are never free from the schemes of Allah (7/97-99).

The Quranic order to plunder the non-Muslims' property, to distribute it among the Muslim war partners and to reserve 1/5th of the booty exclusively as Allah's share is a very cunningly planned scheme to attract the non-Muslims to embrace Islam and launch Jehad against their immediate infidel relatives and other non-Muslim infidels (69/20-21).

Verily Allah himself has impelled Mohammed to persuade his followers to continue a perennial fight against the infidels. He has described Mohammed the ratio of proportionate strength between Muslims and non-Muslims as 1:10 respectively. Allah has also spurred Mohammed that as the non-Muslims lack intelligence in fighting, 100 Muslims can easily bring 1000 infidels under their control (8/65).

> Allah has also challenged Mohammed's Prophethood for his not having taken any attempt to kill the non-Muslim captives. So long as Mohammed has not killed his captives he can't claim to be a Prophet. Here Allah confirmed the Prophet as a killer of Kafirs and authorized Mohammed to kill the non-Muslims as a sacred part of his duty as a Prophet. Here lies the seed of Jehad, the never ending religious war against non-Muslims.

Mohammed is the only religious preacher in history who interlaced religious prayer with war. He made his followers to be ever surveilant for their safety and security. Prayer and sword go side by side with Islam. According to Mohammed all are not required to go for prayer in the routinely prayer time (4/102).

Similarly all are not required to go for war. While the war is in promulgation some must remain present in the Mosque for connotation of the ethics of Islam related to Jehad. Those who returned from the war should be informed about the perspectives of Islam (9/122).

Hence presently Jehadi psyche plays a very important and inevitable part from the mosques to the Islamic society in general and guerilla war field in particular. Islam exemplifies the following conclusions that (a) a Muslim must be a religious body of Islam (b) he must possesses a warring attitude (c) He must possess a sense of hatred towards the non Muslims (d) and in favourable circumstances he must show his religious vigour. (e) He must think about his attainment of Paradise and abstention from hell.

Allah proclaimed killing the infidels by Muslims as rightful and religious. Allah is ever unkind and cruel towards the non-Muslims who are unquestionably His creation. He is repeatedly praised in the Quran as wise, forgiving, quixotic, kind-hearted, tremendous, omnipotent, etc.

One single sentence from the Quran or from the mouth of Mohammed is sufficient to comprehend the distinction of Islam and the duty of a Muslim. Mohammed is quoted to have said in the scripture. "If you are a true follower of Allah, you have to continue Jehad for the sake of Allah. If you repudiate Jehad and remain satisfied only with growing plants, you would be looked down upon by Allah and you will not be recognized by Him until you have not returned to your own religion and declared Jehad (uncompromising war against the non-Muslim enemies)."

Non-Muslim women, the chief target of Jehadi war for the expansion of Islam

> *The apostle sanctified the license of embracing the female captives as their wives or concubines and the enjoyment of wealth and beauty was a feeble type of joys of Paradise prepared for the valiant martyrs of the faith.*
>
> – Decline and fall of Roman Empire, *Edward Gibbon*

Mohammed made Jehad more horrible by combining it with sex. When war infects from battlefield to town and villages, then the encounter of military men with common women is a consensus. Then women who are quite impeccable and unarmed come in to the perimeter of Islamic war mathematics. These non-Muslim women are treated as slave girls and are permitted by the Quran to be sexually enjoyed by the Muslims in an indiscriminate manner. This licence has been granted to all Muslims since the time of the Prophet. When a non-Muslim woman, whether she is married or a spinster, becomes captive, she immediately comes under the authority of a Muslim to be used and entertained by him according to his sweet will and pleasure (54/24).

So the only rule of war they observed without fail is to fall upon the helpless civil population after a battle had been won. Women are their prize and booty, their premium. Mohammed introduced rape as a weapon of war. In the year 1971 Pakistani soldiers killed thousands of infidel women. The most charming among them were held to be raped in the military cantonments. Their garments were taken off from them and kept them stark naked in apprehension of committing suicide with the help of their garments., This is only one among hundreds of such instances one can get from the Indian Islamic history. Allah-ud-din Khiliji's irresistible attempt to marry the Queen of Mewar followed a horrendous bloody battle that gave rise to the self-immolatory custom of the women folk in India. When the women folk apprehended that the defeat of their male members against Muslims is certain and that this would lead them to be gang raped, they committed suicide by taking poison. But when it was found that even their dead bodies are not spared from this heinous act they resorted to the Jouhar Brat (Commitment of suicide by voluntarily jumping down into the burning pyre) to escape from this corporeal stalemate.

However Jehadi psyche has its deep root in the orgy of pillage and captivity of non-Muslim women. Hence as long as there are womenfolk in non-Islamic society in any corner of the world and as long as there is abundant wealth in the hands of non-Muslim companies or persons or in the mines underneath the land under occupation of non-Muslims in any part of the world, there is Jehad with its wagon of accessories.

Mohammed did not show any respect even by name to the non-Muslim women folk. The Quran records the exhortation of Allah to Prophet Mohammed in this regard.

"Oh Prophet! Lo! We have made lawful unto thee thy wives unto whom thou hast paid dowries, and those whom thy right hand possesses of those whom Allah hath given thee as spoils of war" (33/50).

While there is religious war between Muslims and non-Muslims, non-Muslim women are particularly targeted by the Muslim folk. Amazingly there is provision for entrance of non-Muslim women in to the Islamic society but there is no way for their exit.

The Quran has asserted women as tilth (cultivable land) for Muslims. A Muslim master can use his women who are in his hand as he can use his land. He can use the land at any time he likes. (2/223).

Mohammed, the formiddable vower to extinguish the Christians and the Jews

Both Mohammed and Islam are particularly retaliatory towards Christians and Jews. In course of all attempts for conversion into Islam when the infidels would be stupefied they would find no other way than leaning towards Islam. Hence the generous Prophet predicts – "The day will surely come when the unbelievers will wish that they were Muslims" (Ch.15 verse 11).

Mohammed has reiterated in the Quran the view of Allah on Christianity and Jews. To quote Him, "Fight against those of the books (of Christianity and Jews) who don't believe in Allah and don't forbid what Allah has forbidden and don't obey Islam until they are dishonoured and pay Jeziya tax in their own hand (S 9/?9)".

Mohammed again says – "We have provoked the fire of detachment and contempt among them (The Christians) and this would continue up to the Day of Judgment. Allah would teach them about their actions. (S 5/14)."

Mohammed found Christianity as the key rival of Islam. So he unhurriedly narrated and convinced his followers and others who were his contemporary that Islam compared to Christianity is far better as a religion and as a society. Even he did not spare the pictures that depict the cross. He obliterated them (541/836).

Mohammed, as Prophet of Allah, disbelieves many theories of the holy Bible and clarifies on Christianity. He rebuffs the theory of the Trinity as described in the holy Bible. According to the theory of the Trinity as mentioned in the Bible, the Father, the Son and the holy Spirit is one and inseparable. Here Mohammed contends that the Biblical statement on the Trinity is not acceptable. Allah is the only Father (father of all Prophets including Jesus) and Jesus is his son, Gabriel is the soul, (4/171).

He also rebuffs the Resurrection theory of Jesus as is described in the Bible. Regarding this incident Mohammed mentions that Lord Allah had picked up his son Jesus with him. Yesus who was crucified was not real Jesus. A spurious Yesus was hanged on the cross and was crucified (4/157-158).

Comparing to Mary, the holy mother of Jesus, with Fatima, the great emancipator of man-kind Prophet Mohammed says "Mary was the lady of women of her time but my daughter Fatima is the lady of women of all times from the beginning to the end".

There is no mention of Mohammed or Allah in the holy Bible. But Bibilical liturgy has got its proper place in the Quran.

The miraculous birth of Prophet Jesus is described in the holy Quran, which contains a sura (chapter 19) titled 'Mary', where it is described – Oh Mary! Allah has chosen you and purified you above the women of the worlds (3:41)

Christians do not accept Allah as the father of Jesus. But however Muslims admit this legendary tale and confess that Allah has purified Mary.

Nevertheless in many ways Muslims evaluate Fatima as a better and superior being than Mary. According to them Fatima lived a full social life and perfectly performed the roles of a wife, a daughter and a mother, roles that Mary was not destined to fulfil. Therefore it becomes clear that the distinction of Mary applies to her position among women of her ages to come.

The third distinction which places Fatima above Mary is her being the mother of Imam Hussein (AS) and Hassan (AS), the leaders of the youths of paradise who were certainly superior to Jesus, who, despite his merits was not sent by Allah to serve as a model to mankind. Jesus, it is said, did not marry and even if he did, his progeny was not chosen for the leadership of mankind.

Fatima gave birth to eleven Imams. The last one of them was Imam Mahdi. When he will appear again, he will lead the prayer in Bayt ul Muqaddas (Jerusalem) as the XIIth infallible successor of Prophet Mohammed. According to Islam, Mary's son Prophet Jesus will not appear but he will pray behind Imam Mehdi and act as his lieutenant in the world government of peace.

Mohammed had a sense of extreme hatred for both Christians and Jews. So Allah angrily passed Mohammed an order that the Christians and the Jews (non believers among the people of the Book) shall be burnt for ever in the fire of hell because they are the vilest of all creatures. (Ch, 98 verse 8).

Prophet Mohammed himself swears "I will throw out Christians and Jews from Arab peninsula and will not allow any one to live there except Muslims. He again reiterates "If I remain alive, then God willing, I will turn out all Jews and Christians from the Arabian Peninsula."

This Arhat-e-Nababi (saying of Prophet) describes why the Muslims attempt for an ethnic cleansing whenever they get the upper hand.

"That he should continue fighting against the non-believers or non- Muslims (He who believes Allah as the only God and Mohammed the only Prophet of Allah is a believer) and he should always be unkind and harsh towards a non-Muslim (1X/123). A Muslim should not accept a non-Muslim to be his friend (IV/144). Non-Muslims in general and Jews and Christians in particular are not meant for a friend of Muslims. If any Muslim accepts them as his friend he will become perverted. Allah never shows the way to perverted Muslims (V/51).

Allah has strictly advised the Muslims to make friendship only with Muslims. According to Allah, the creator of the whole universe, only hatred emanates from the face of non-Muslims. What they have concealed in their heart is extremely dangerous (111/118). Allah deprived the Jews from their due share for their misconduct and creation of unnecessary impediments in the way of Allah (IV/160). Non-Muslims are the stark enemies of Muslims (IV/101).

Allah swears that he himself would frighten the non-Muslims. Then the Muslims, the followers of Allah, behead them and root out their fingers (VIII/12).

Let the believers spend the assets of non-Muslims. Only the non-Muslims will be thronged into the infinite hell (VIII/30).

After the lapse of the sacred months let the Muslims wherever they find non-Muslims, captivate them. If the non-Muslims change their heart and keep faith in Allah alone, then only they are liable for liberation (1X/5).

Let the Muslims fight against the non-Muslims and be harsh with them. The ultimate abode of nonbelievers is hell alone (1X/73). The non-Muslims and idolators are bound to resort to the flames of hell. They are the worst of the created beings. The non-Muslims are subject to take boiling drink and rest in the painful doom (X/15).

Let the Muslims take the unbelievers, the non-Muslims, in chain for exposure to the hell fire. He would be given the food that is served to sinners only (LX1X/30-37). The doom of hell is destined for them who don't believe in Allah. The end of their itinerary is hell (67/6).

The only food for the non-Muslims is the Zaqqum fruit that grows only in hell. It seems like boiled water and molten brass in the belly of the sinner. "Tug him in to the midst of hell and pour boiled water over his head" (64/43-50).

Allah has exclusively and emphatically narrated in the Quran that he who says that Jesus is a Messiah and the son of Mary, is a disbeliever. The Quran has described about Jesus himself quoting to the Jews that Allah is his Lord and the Lord of the Jews. Jesus himself has told that Allah has prohibited their entry into Paradise who impeach that they are equal to Allah. Their tenement is only in fire.

The following provisions are made for the non-believers of Islam that distinguishes them from the beloved believers of Allah. These sayings expose the real intention of Islam and that provokes Muslims to fight against non-Muslims (the unbelievers, Kafirs and the enemies of Islam)

(1) We shall say, 'lay hold of him. Burn him in the fire of hell, then fasten him with a chain 70 cubits long, for he did not believe in Allah.(69:30-33)

(2) Lo! Those who disbelieve our revelations, we shall expose them to fire. As often their skins are consumed we shall exchange them for fresh skins that they may test the torment. (4:56)

(3) Garments of fire have been prepared for unbelievers. Scalding water shall be poured upon their heads, melting their skins and that which is in their bellies. They shall be lashed with red hot iron.(22:19-21)

(4) Lo! Ye and that which ye worship besides Allah are fuel of hell. (21;9-8)

(5) Allah has cursed the un-believers and proposed for them a brazing hell (33:60)

(6) Unbelievers are enemies of Allah and they will be roasted in hell (4:14)

(7) I shall cast terror into the hearts of the infidels, strike off their heads........(8:12)

(8) Believers! Make war on the infidels who dwell around you. (9:123)

(9) Slay the idol worshippers wherever you find them. Arrest them, besiege them, and lie in ambush everywhere for them...(9:5)

(10) ......award Allah's enemies, the fire. Therein is their immortal home(41:28).

"These twins (believers and nonbelievers) are two opponents who contend about their Lord. But as for those who disbelieve, garments of fire will be cut out for them; boiling fluid will be poured down on their heads".

The Islamic Lord then continues – "After pouring down the fluid, all their disbeliefs which are stored in their bellies and skins will get melted. Hooked sharp iron rod is kept reserved for them. If they come again with grief and in a suppliant tone, then they will be expelled with the help of the iron rod with the rebuffing "taste the dooms of burning". (XXII/19-22)"

There are uncountable censured words for non Muslims like– "Lo ! we have prepared for disbelievers manacles and carcasses and a raging fire". (LXXVI/4)

Mohammed advised his followers to confirm their friendship only among themselves (i.e, only among Muslims). He had no faith, no interest and no compassion for non-Muslims. He always suspected and spurned non-Muslims. So he expressed the feeling of Allah before his fellowmen that they must prepare even to abandon their fathers and brothers if they see that their siblings are trying to mingle with non-Muslims. (9:14)

Mohammed in general was very much interested in murder. But he had an important role in exterminating the Jews. He made several attempts to bring the Jews into his fold but he failed in his mission to convert them (2/100). On the contrary the Jews underestimated Mohammed as a Prophet. Once when Mohammed asked the Jews to contribute for Islam, the Jews, out of joke, told him that perhaps Allah is a poor creature. Otherwise Mohammed would not have begged for him (3/181).

The Jews wanted that Mohammed should be killed or at least the Muslims should be expelled from Medina. So Mohammed turned against the Jews.

Mohammed shall be ever remembered as a veteran warrior. He had a mastermind to detect the debilities of his enemies and strike unmistakably at the exact spot. Once he started an expedition against a Jews' tribe. He had a handful of soldiers to fight against the strong Jewish army. Mohammed's followers entreated him not to launch the war against the Jews, as they are more in number, well equipped and comparatively stronger than the Islamic army. But to Mohammed, a war against the Jews was a game of entertainment. He exhorted his fighters that he is well aware of the Jews' psyche. Though the Jews are stronger, more in number and well equipped, they lack unity. They are divided into many groups. When a group of Jews are slaughtered by another group of Jews, then the other groups simply enjoy the sight without any reaction. They are more interested in infighting than fighting against their enemies. Lack of unity among the Jews is the best weapon in the hands of Islam to defeat them and kill them, the Prophet reiterated. Hence there is no question of defeat in a fight against the Jews. (59/11.12,13). What Mohammed told was a feat of practical thinking.

As to his expectation the Jews fought bravely but were miserably defeated. In the later period Islam fought and extended its empire following the direction of Mohammed. He formed the structure of an expansive society, which is strongly founded on a distinctive Islamic unity with a military discipline. On one occasion he murdered the entire male folk of a Jewish tribe, the Beni Quraizah and sold the women folk and children into slavery. (S33:26).

Mohammed had taken some merciless and cruel steps in the name of religion that shows the power of Islam and creates instant favour for the Quran and Islam.

One such case is that of a lady poet of Medina, daughter of Marwan. She wrote a poem where she warned the tribes of Medina against the Prophet." Do you expect good from him after the killing of your chiefs, like a hungry man waiting for the cooking broth?"-She wrote. When the Prophet heard this he said to his followers –"Who will rid me off Marwan's daughter?" A follower named Umayr, eager to prove his loyalty to Islam offered to assassinate her. This he did that very night while the victim was asleep with her youngest baby on her breast. The prophet thanked him and told him-: You have helped Allah and his apostle. "The message went home and the people of the husband of Asma instead of resorting to retaliation became Muslims because they saw the power of Islam.

If a woman is found guilty of adultery, her only punishment is to put her to death by earthing her up to her waist or chest then pelting her with stones. Mohammed the prophet first introduced this system in the sacred religion of Islam. He allowed his followers to kill an adulterous woman in his presence although she herself had disclosed the act to Mohammed and asked for expiation.

At Medina 700 Jews were dragged in chains to the market place of the city, they descended alive into the grave prepared for their execution and burial and the apostle beheld with an inflexibl eye the slaughter of his helpless enemies. Chaiber was the seat of Jews power in Arabia. The chief of the tribe was tortured, in the presence of Mohammed, to force a confession of his hidden treasure.

Mohammed invaded a Jewish race, Bani Al-Nadir, and defeated them in a staunch battle. Unlike as was done previously, he did not distribute the plundered wealth of this race. He kept the whole booty with him to meet his private expenses and to purchase war equipment. A Jew called Kinana Ibn Ali al Huquiq was a leader of a Jewish tribe. The followers of Mohammed captured his fort. The man had concealed that he had a little amount of gold with him. When Mohammed was informed about it, he called for him and tortured him by putting burning coals on his chest. He died fluttered.

After the battle of Badr a Jew called Uqba was taken captive by the Prophet to be executed. He asked Mohammed in a supplicant tone about the future safety of his wife and children. Mohammed assured him to provide hell fire to them.

In the year 627 Mohammed attacked the Jews of Qureja and imprisoned them. Then they were dragged in chain to the main market and all but one of the 800 Jews were beheaded and buried in the grave. The only man who consented to embrace Islam was unleashed. The same massacre of Jews was repeated after two years in 629 in the Khyber war. He himself beheaded the imprisoned Jews with his Sword.

Allah encouraged slavery. The plundering of non-Muslim's property and its distribution among the Muslims, the acquisition of women as war booty, raping them and selling them in the market and keeping them as slaves – all these were given religious dignity in Islam. The slaves had the only right in life, that they should worship no other God but Allah. In exchange, Allah promised not to punish them. (550/850).

Mohammed is the only Prophet who gave the idea of rapid conversion by inciting the convert to kill his immediate kinsmen with his own hand. He exalts, "Even if your father is not a Muslim, kill him instantly." So in a family no sooner had a man got converted to Islam, than all his family members are immediately declared as non-Muslims or Kafirs and come under the category of those persons who are destined to be killed. So when a non-Muslim father is not privileged to escape from the Islamic sword of his son, then what about others? The conversion and killing of those who depreciate conversion goes side by side in Islam. The very law is applied to the non-Muslims of a country or region where Muslims are in majority.

Mohammed dictates through the Quran that the Arabs are the only real Muslims of first class while all other Muslims converted by conquest and their children throughout the world are inferior and second grade Muslims. As wished by Allah they must exist under Arab's supremacy as their superior first class Muslims. Mohammed has left one billion Mohammedans behind him within a span of 1400 years. The Quran has dissolved into Islam. The Islamic sword is and will be as it was 1400 years ago. The use of missile is no more needed; it has proved to be a useless weapon. Islam has been inherited with two more exclusive weapons. One is oil reserves and the other is birth proliferation. The Islamic sword is still glittering.

(f) Jiziya (A tax over non-Muslims for their Conditional Survival) and Islamic Code of Imposition on Christians and Jews

Mohammed had nourished the idea of imposition of a tax in the name of Jiziya that was extremely beneficial for the safety and expansion of Islam. Jiziya is imposed in a country where there are Christians and Jews in majority and the administration is under Islam. Imposition of this tax kept the non-Muslim group or society (meaning Christians and Jews) as an under-estimated race, inferior society consisting of second class citizens who are destined to stay ever oppressed and exploited. As a token of exploitation they are required to pay the tax in humiliation.

Because Christians and Jews are non-Muslims, they are marked as infidels. To the Muslims, the Jews and Christians are people of little faith. All the infidels living under the Islamic rule are supposed to pay this special tax called the Jiziya. This indicates their acceptance of Islam as the superior religion. The Jews and Christians are required to pay Jiziya simply for their survival in an Islamic country as "Jimmis" being the people of the book (meaning the Bible with both Testaments). They are granted mercy to live in Islamic country as second class citizens by paying the Jiziya.

Regarding the Jiziya or poll tax Mohammed says – "Fight those who don't profess the true faith till they pay Jiziya with the hand of humility (Quran IX/29)". For the payment of the tax Christians and Jews (Jimmis) are required to come on foot and give it to the Muslim receiver who should be seated and place his hand over the palm of the Jimmi standing in front of him and receive the commutation fees.

Though there are very few Christians and Jews remaining in Islamic countries like Iran, Pakistan, and Algeria they are not required to pay the commutation money due to the heavy impact of American and Western power force over them. But when America, England France, Germany, etc., are now put in the Islamic cauldron, the fate of Christian minorities in Islamic countries can be clearly imagined. Explosion in Churches, the kidnapping and killing of Europeans and Americans in different countries of the world have become rampant since the beginning of this first decade. There is a slow and steady process of conversion and Islamisation of America and other European countries. Time is the Supreme Judge to decree the names of the nations which are enlisted to pay Jiziya which is a reality in the present, was a reality in the past and, according to the laws of action that modifies the repetition of history, which will be a reality in the near future, most probably towards 2015.

Apart from this payment the Christians and Jews have to live and lead an inferior life, which is obviously described the pitiable life of second-class citizens. The Christians and Jews in a Muslim-dominated country must follow the following twenty points of disabilities.

Code of Imposition on Christians, Jews and other non-Muslims for their conditional survival

1. No Christian or Jew can build up a Church or a Synagogue in the Dar-ul- Islam (land under Islamic rule).
2. They can't repair any old place of worship, which have been destroyed by the Muslims.
3. They can't prevent or deny any Muslim traveller if he likes to stay in their church or synagogue.
4. A Christian or Jew is bound to host a Muslim if he wants to stay in their house. The term of this staying may be extended to an indefinite period if the honourable Muslim guest falls ill.
5. They are not to harbour any hostility to give aid and comfort their hostile elements.
6. The Christians and Jews should not prevent anyone of them from getting converted to Islam.
7. The Christians and Jews are required to show due respect to every Muslim.
8. They should not name themselves with Islamic names. (Before conversion to Islam).

9. The Christians and Jews should not ride a horse with saddle and bridle.
10. They should not keep any weapons with them.
11. The Christians and Jews cannot wear signet rings or seals on their finger.
12. They can't sell liquor or drink wine openly.
13. The Christians can't use Islamic dress. To pose with Islamic dress is exclusively meant only for the Muslims.
14. The Christians and Jews must allow Muslims to participate in their private meetings and functions. There must be a Muslim member in the managing committee of a Christian institution.
15. The Christians and Jews should wear such kind of dress so as to distinguish themselves from a Muslim. Their dressing style must indicate their inferiority of appearance before a Muslim.
16. Christian customs and usages should not be propagated amongst the Muslim society.
17. A Christian or a Jew can't build a house near a Muslim's house as his neighbour.
18. The dead body of a Christian or a Jew is called Marhoom and that of a Muslim is called Anjahani. A marhoom cannot be brought near the graveyards of Muslims.
19. The Christians and Jews cannot mourn their dead loudly, nor can they observe their religious practices publicly.
20. Because the Christians and Jews are inferior creatures as compared to Muslims, they can't keep Muslim slaves with them.

To test the veracity of this Islamic imposition on non-Islamic minority countries one can visit Bangladesh, the former East Pakistan, where the minority Hindus live a life of the most heinous of citizens. The fate of the Hindu and Christian minorities in Pakistan is beyond imagination.

20. Islamic Social Metamorphosis of Affetecd Nations
(During the period of Transformation of Civilizations)

Definition of social metamorphosis– As mentioned earlier, the Third World War will be a global civil war. The first tangible step of that global civil war is the socio-cultural invasion by a stronger nation over a nation which is weaker or less defensive in its socio-cultural affinity. Presently Islam has come out as the strongest nation (Dear readers should bear in mind that a Muslim community in a non-Islamic country is a nation within a nation) in all aspects in almost all the non-Islamic countries or nations of the world. It does not matter whether their minority status in a nation like England or the USA is a microscopic or clearly visible minority. They are the most defensive and the strongest minority flourishing with their religious discipline, fast-growing population and stark xenophobic attitude with a totalitarian, aggressive life-style. Such an aggressive life style in the Muslim community developed after the great Islamic renaissance. Where ever they stay in any corner of the world their socio-cultural environment spreads in all directions defending their strong ethos. This is the Islamic socio-cultural invasion as the strongest minority in a non-Islamic majority country that would give rise to a civil war at the end of their perfection when it naturally hurts the religious sentiments of the majority community. The non-Islamic community everywhere in the world is socio-culturally not as defensive as Islam. Hence unwittingly Islam ramifies its ever-spreading culture in a majority society (i.e., a nation where Islam is considered a minority society). The majority society undergoes a great change. The first change it feels is with its (national) religious population. This religious population (of majority society) is its socio-cultural population, which the majority society feels is very feeble. Religious secularism is the venom that ruins the brain of the majority people of a non-Islamic majority society. It makes them defenceless. This is the reason why a majority society gradually undergoes a state of social change under the influence of the strongest minority community. Gradually it loses its national life style as a majority community. This is the social metamorphosis of an affected nation.

Definition of affected nation

From the Islamic point of view a country is divided into two parts. A non-Islamic country or the country which is under the process of Islamization, is called Dar-ul-Harab. A country that has been Islamised or an Islamic country is called Dar-ul- Islam. There is hardly any country in the world, which is beyond the reach of the Muslims or the Islamic purview of conversion. All the non-Islamic nations which are meant to be Islamised or under the process of Islamisation are called the affected nations. The feeling of alienation, mutual distrust, apprehension of fear and insecurity to life will become the general characteristics of an affected nation.

> Hence all the non-Islamic countries of the world are affected nations. Among them the USA and all the European Christian nations are key targets. The non-Islamic state Israel tops the targeted list.

The U.S.A and other prominent European Christian countries have already been under this Jehadi trap and the different presumptions show that the Islamization of the U.S.A and the Christian countries is so deep-rooted and centripetal that this Muslim minority community accompanied with the Afro-Americans could dare to raise a strong revolt against the Government of the USA and its allied powers. The programme of assault on the USA and its allies has been done in such an organized and disciplined manner that its result is only accountable for the Transformation of Civilizations. The Islamic law is very smoothly and cunningly truncating the socio-cultural fetters of the non-Islamic nations (where the Muslims form a minority community) with the help of its secular-minded political leaders. When the majority community would get alerted in defence of their socio-cultural identity, then it would give rise to friction. This friction is very often called the communal riot. In a massive state this is called communal war. When this communal war simultaneously takes place in almost all the non-Islamic secular countries of the world it will be termed as the "Global Civil War".

Some critics may argue that Islamic nations should also be defined as the most affected nations owing to their sufferings at the hands of the Euro-American countries. The Jews and other Christian adversaries also mercilessly persecute the Muslims.

This argument is not relevant to this issue. During the course of Transformation of Civilizations, Islamic civilization is the single largest civilization in the world that is expanding its dominion over all other civilizations. One script, one Prophet, one single indelible and unchangeable ideology controls the whole of Islamic civilization and Islamic nationalism. To define it briefly, Islamic nationalism, Islamic culture and Islamic civilization are one and indivisible. Hence Islam is the single largest nation in the world compared to all other nations. It means that everywhere in the world, in all the Islamic and non-Islamic countries, Islam nationalism is one and inseparable. But it is not the same in case of any other nationalism. Regarding the issues of nationalism France differs from England, and the USA differs from Germany though all of them are Christian nations. Their culture, language and social life style differ from one another. The Hindus in India are westernized to some extent but their culture is Hindu. Their language is Indian. Non-Islamic countries differ in culture, language and civilization from one another. But Islam is one in every sphere of life throughout the world. Hence only Islam is in the way of victory over all other civilizations. Though the USA is strong in military affairs, it can easily be brought into the subjugation of Islam, as soon as its national Christian population can be brought to a lower stage than Islam. The oil reserves of former communist USSR are now in the hands of Islamic nations. Here the authority or the ownership shifted and not the place of reserves. Transfer of power, position and wealth (both earthly and mineral) even without war is possible if the ownership shifts. It is possible exclusively through the Transformation of Civilizations.

Islamic Scenario in an Affected Nation

Non-Islamic societies lack two basic characteristics to face the Islamic onslaught in way of their social deterioration caused by Islamic aggression. They are (a) lack of awareness of social security, (b) lack of integrated defensive force.

(a)Lack of awareness of social security: This is the basic reason for the downfall of non-Islamic infrastructure. The government formed by secular democracy rules majority of the non-Islamic population of the world. A secular government concentrates on religious neutral materialism as the key source of its social upliftment. A society that recognizes secular materialism as the key source of its social development can hardly withstand in the civil war for existence against the society, which doesn't recognize irreligious materialism as its main source of enrichment. Accordingly non-Muslim society with its technological character faces the traumas related to materialistic life that weakens the national strength or immunity.

The working population of a country destined to flourish by materialism is generally divided into two major groups. One, the employed group completely having become mechanized devotes its whole time in the job profession for monetary gain and does not take any interest for it's sociable benefit. On the other hand the unemployed group, the majority of which languishes under less remuneration or no remuneration. The hard working group with a meager income, which is insufficient for it's daily livelihood, always fights for its survival leads a desperate life with the apprehension of a dark future. Gradually majority of them get frustrated and take shelter of evil means like theft, murder, addiction etc and become a burden to the society.

In a secular democratic society the bureaucrats who belong to the former group out of their selfish mentality never bother for their social security. The frustrated and unemployed group remains far away from thinking about its social security owing to its excruciating mental agony based on insufficient means of livelihood.

Hence both the groups who constitute the whole population of secular democratic society don't petrify themselves to face the tide of civil war. As the civil war is concerned to social security and military is concerned to national security, the military cannot afford its skill for a social secular protection as it is constituted by the conscription of the people of both the majority and minority class. Hence an invitation to military interference unmistakably leads to the segregation of National Defense Force. Incessant civil war is inevitable in a secular democratic country or a non-Muslim majority country where Muslims form a stronger minority. Here it should be remembered that a Muslim is never secular democratic because secular democracy is an alien and un-Islamic thought.

Communism is a parasitical philosophy, which feeds on secularism and secular democracy. The moment secular democracy fades away from a country the mist of communism automatically vanishes. Communism has no place in Islam. The relation between Communism and Islam is same as the relation between a mongoose and a snake. During the Islamic revolution in Iran the communist party of Iran rendered its full service to Ayatollah Khomeini against the king of Iran. After the revolution was over Khomeini declared communism an out law. He arrested the leaders, killed many of them and crushed communism.

(b) Lack of integrated defence force: Democratic secular country invites another chaotic situation to its integrated system. That is lack of integrated defensive force to protect its national integrity. When a particular community heads to be religiously or communally stronger than other communities, automatically it leads to establish its separate social identity. Such tendency of the community impels to be separated from all other communities and form a social or national life of its own, which causes a great national disintegration or partition of the nation.

Such communal feeling of former USSR military force brought great disaster in the army while it was involved in war against Afghanistan. Consequently the greatest empire of the communist world demolished into pieces in the year 1992. The same feeling of alienation of Islamic soldiers of Kashmir made them to leave the Kashmiri regiment of king Hari Singh and join with the Pakistani army. They carried away with them the weapons from the Kashmiri regiment and fought against India where the day before they were its citizens. Iran, under the former Shahenshah Rejah Pehlhavi Arya Meher was a secular country with Islamic majority. But when the people became religiously fanatic they revolted and dethroned the king and turned Iran into an Islamic country.

In a recent event the world witnessed how Islam spread its dragon hood and swallowed the USSR and occupied the oil reserves remaining under its soil. During the process of Islamization of Euro-America and other affected nations the following incidents are feasible, particularly when the Islamic minority confronts non-Islamic majority with a 40:60 ratio.

Non-Muslims in an Islam-dominated land are considered and treated as enemies. Hence their property will be declared as enemies' property under a special act named "Enemies' Property Act". Soon after the declaration this will be confiscated from them and would be distributed among the needy Muslims.

Here communism differs a little, relevant to the distribution of property. They seize the property from 'haves' and distribute it among the 'haven'ts. But the Muslims seize the property from the non-Muslims either by plundering or by robbery and distribute it among themselves.

Even in the riot-stricken areas Muslim youths come to request the people to donate their blood for the healing of their wounded soldiers. Fear is also a mother of generosity. When some young men come forward to donate blood and lie on the make shift bed, needles are inserted into the vein and the draining of blood continues until their death.

The Kafirs of the affected nations will not be spared from public lashing by the civil transformers for any conviction or fornication. The public lashing of women is no more an excuse. This causes profuse bleeding, loss of sense and at last, instant death. Public lashing and stoning to death very often occur in cases of pre-marital love affairs.

Love affairs before marriage are anti-Islamic and severe punishment is reserved for those who are nabbed in this incident. Even throat slashing and gunning down is no more considered unjustifiable if married women are found in illicit relations with male persons.

The Americans practically had no knowledge of fear. This word was confined only to their dictionary till 11.9.2001. After the fall of first Islamic thunderbolt on the World Trade Centre they began to think about it. This brunt will be further followed not by any tenable retaliatory attempt against the USA, but by the constant kidnapping and rape, sexual attack, sexual slavery, etc. Forcible marriage and marriage by coaxing to Euro-American ladies by Muslim youths will be rampant. The kidnapping and raping of Kafir women is praised in Islam and is not considered sinful. The more handsome an affected nation's ladies are, the more is the chance of gang-rape by Islamic religious warriors.

When the transformatory action has already been started in the affected nations, a change in its social life-style is inevitable. The women of the affected nations would be compelled to haunt under Burka, a black body-covering from top to toe. One can find British ladies walk wearing the burka in England. The girls in France are found going to school under the hijab, an Islamic headscarf. British Muslim women have ceased to intermingle among their male co-workers in the office and interlace with male members in cabarets, clubs or butleries.

The girls of the affected nations cannot walk freely with dignity in those provinces where Islam is in dominance. If a Muslim youth passes any comment on her even in some vulgar sense, she can't claim her right to impeach against him. A Muslim has a Jehadi right to vex a virgin. (2/235).

If any body wants to know how women would be exactly treated in a Muslim-dominant nation, he must see the movie "Not Without My Daughter" which is based on a true story of an American lady married to an Iranian. The husband deceitfully took her and her daughter to Iran and made a slave out of her.

The groups like gays and lesbians will be severely punished or will be gunned down in public. The Marriage of homosexual couples in the church, reciprocal divorce system, contract marriages, etc., will be a dream. No free movement of a spinster with her boy friend will be found on the highway. A slight peep of a part of a limb underneath the burka will cause disaster. In many cases such instances provoked fundamentalists to hack the legs no matter how a womn would sustain herself.

A girl of an affected nation cannot marry a youth at her sweet will. Her un-fettered life will be contracted into a small fraction of a confined family where she may have to spend her days with the other 2 or 3 co-wives of her husband. Unlike the present Euro-America she cannot leave her husband for another. In an Islamised world she has to attend to the call of her polygamous thick-bearded husband even against her complete reluctance owing to her illness or any physical inconvenience. She can be expelled from her husband's house without any prior intimation or any court's decree. Divorce has become easier by using the short message service media. One can divorce his wife on the very day of the marriage. The Muslim husband is the final authority and is above the court of law to pass the decree of divorce. There is no appellate court against a Muslim husband who wants to divorce his wife. The best friend of a Euro-American Muslim lady is her co-wife with whom alone she can move through the streets, not for the sake of any entertainment but simply to visit her siblings with her husband's permission. She has no right over her womb to conceive a particular number of children in it. It is the wish of her husband to ascertain the number. It is her pious duty only to look after her children that her husband blesses her with even after being divorced by him without having any legal maintenance. Even if she is divorced contrary to her wish, she cannot be financially supported either on behalf of the court, or by her former husband.

The affected nations of Islamic fervour would be compelled to create funds for the maintenance of Muslim divorcees. After tree utterances of "Talaq", the divorce is completed and a wife has no right to stay in that house. Even if the husband wants to retain his divorced partner, he cannot accept her directly. The divorcee has to approach some body other than her former husband to spend some nights with her as her bedmate. She has to satisfy him in cohabitation. After the man is fully satisfied with her and allows her to go, she may, with his permission again come back to her (first) husband who had divorced her. As long as the second one is not satisfied to leave her or divorce her, she has no privilege to meet her divorcer. So very often young ladies choose an old man as their second husband to get a quick divorce.

Another turning point in the social life is the diminishing of women's value in society. The Euro-American system where women are given more privileges than men, would turn a volt face. In Western countries 80% females divorce their male counterparts. But when the storm of Transformation of Civilizations begins, this phenomenon would undergo a long change. Males in Euro-America would attain full privilege to exercise the right of divorce. On the contrary women folk would be entirely divested from such rights. Sexual monopoly, the enjoyment of plundered wealth (women are considered a part of the wealth of men) and the allurement of after-life in Paradise would doubly encourage men to get converted into Islam.

In the revised footage of slavery non-Muslim girls and women of the affected nations and Euro-America would be the only target. They would be invariably treated as slave girls. The Quran has permitted the Muslim males to sexually enjoy the slave woman in an indiscriminate manner. This privilege has been consigned to all Muslims right from Mohammed up to date.

Here slave does not mean any inferior or backward group or class who are mentally undeveloped and physically strong. The word 'slave' is used here particularly for girls who are brought as captives or who belong to the vanquished non-Muslim society or who are inferior in strength to pull on together with the Muslims. When non-Muslims form the minority group or become weaker before the Muslim community, soon their women folk would be stigmatized as captive women or slave girls. Captive women, whether married or unmarried, are the objects of sexual gratification by the Muslims as a religious sanction given by Allah. (S 4:24).

Apart from some slave girls Prophet Mohammed had 11 wives. The majority of them were war widows of vanquished races. At the age of 53 he married a girl of 10, named Ayesha. He was stimulated by Allah to cohabit with the married non-Muslim women who were treated as the spoils of war.(S 33:50)

A systematic destruction of churches and temples has already been started in the different affected nations of the world. This system is going to be realized in all the affected nations in the coming years as a direct humiliation to Euro-America. The Euro-American countries, which were the main propagators of Christianity, will face the doom of their global project in their own homeland. Religious practices will be banned and jobs and sanction of trade licence would be stopped. There would be no legal redresses. According to the religious stance, Muslim officers would always remain in favour of Muslim police while encountering the case of non- Muslims.

In the Muslim dominated provinces of the affected nations, police protection would be denied to a non-Muslim. Physical violence will be a consensus in the Western landscape and particularly in the case of kidnapping pretty-looking non-Muslim girls. During this period the aged parents of Euro-America would see their daughters getting gang raped by the religious Islamic fighters.

Although the Quran has forbidden Muslims to befriend Christians and Jews and marked them off as the arch enemy of Islam, Allah has never discouraged his followers to cohabit with the enemies' women folk on the contrary. He has vehemently encouraged them to sexually ravage the women as a farmer tills his land with a plough as and when he wishes.

The foetus would be brought out of the wombs of non-Muslim pregnant women directly by slitting their wombs with knives. Babies and children would also be beheaded. Severed heads will be pressed up on the breasts of their mother for feeding. The Kafir ladies of the affected nations would see their children thrown into the air and caught through bayonets.

Muslims at times would infiltrate into the non-Muslim dominated villages and introduce themselves as members of some social organization meant for fighting against the persecution inflicted by the Muslims. But they are no different than the masquerading robbers who show their real nature just after they get success in spreading their hypocritical net. They first ascertain the location and number of handsome girls and women and plan how to lift them. Next, they ascertain the standard of living of the inhabitants. Then they utilize each chance of sacking the women folk. After having raped them, they unleash them for a ransom. They are privileged to do this by the dictates of the holy book along with an assurance of enjoying the same sexual life in Paradise. In no time they change their colour and collect money from the non-Muslims towards contribution for their charitable organization to fight against the Muslims. This is their process of exploitation and extortion of non-Muslim families in Muslim-dominated areas or provinces morally and financially.

A lady in Euro-America cannot work as a model. She cannot lead a life style of the noted film star Elizabeth Taylor who married seven husbands on eight occasions. She cannot enjoy free movements or free living. A wife, if she becomes sick may have the apprehension of being immediately replaced by another co-wife for her husband who can very rightfully divorce her to save his money from her treatment, no matter how much love she bears for him. Beauty queen contests would be a memory of the past. Blood-soaked dead bodies of beauty queens would be found on the way while they are on the journey when the racial proportion of Muslims in Euro-America would reach the height of 40% of the total population.

Where splashing of acid on the face of women who go unveiled is a consensus, what would not be the fate of women who goes freely smoking and drinking? American women who have succeeded in fighting to have equal rights will be bound to lose half of their full right as a citizen if they come under the Shariat rule. Four women would be required to prove the veracity of an incident where two males are sufficient as witnesses for the same case.

In an affected nation like Euro-America women's education will be confined to madrassas or up to their attainment of puberty. The confinement of her knowledge in learning Arabic language, the only language comprehensible to Allah, and the recitation of the Quranic verses or Ayats are sufficient for her to lead an ideal family life. It is beyond imagination to allow a male doctor to attend to a sick woman patient. You will find little girls lying with slit throats on the roadside in all the affected nations for their only crime that they went to school without hijabs or were accompanied by their boy friend.

The daily routine of a woman will be entirely scheduled according to the transformed custom. In America a lady will be deprived of even killing a cock for her domestic consumption. Only the male members of her family are privileged to slaughter an animal or a bird for cooking purposes. On their instantaneous absence at home she has to go up to 7 consecutive neighbours next to her door to find a male. If she fails in spite of her attempt to get a male she is privileged to slash the (throat of the) cock but under the pretext of a male. For such action she must keep hold of a pipe in front of her, which symbolizes the male organ, and then only she may start killing the bird.

The second decade of this century would find the people of the USA and European countries taking their meal sitting round on the floor instead of lounging at the dining table. They would sit around a plate served with foodstuff and partake concertedly from that plate instead of eating separately and independently according to their own choice. One tumbler is sufficient to quench the thirst of scores of people each one touching his mouth to sip the water one after another. Spoons and sticks used as dining utensils would be declared useless as these are the prohibited parts of the Islamic dining system.

Free style French kissing is an imagination and natural kissing is impossible. The kissing crazy American ladies will shiver in agony when they find their dear boy friends (boy friend is also a word of dictionary in an Islamic U.S.A.) with a thick bearded cheek. The family discipline of a Christian America will find a volt-face in an Islamised U.S.A. The celebration of festivals like the Valentine's Day, the day of love, and other similar festivals would unilaterally disappear.

In a Transformational situation a Muslim criminal rarely gets arrested. There are two reasons. First, if the ruling party is non-Muslim dominated; it would favour the criminal for his self-interest in getting minority votes. If the ruling party is a Muslim dominated party, the convict gets a religious favour. For a Muslim, to help a non-Muslim against the interest of a Muslim, is anti-Islamic. Euro-Americans would be amazed to find out that the dreaded terrorists and criminals who are imprisoned for years together for their horrendous acts would be unleashed with unqualified apology as soon as the government of that province formed with a majority of Muslim members would come to power.

The feeling of alienation, mutual distrust, apprehension of fear and insecurity to life will become the national character of the affected nations. A wave of alienation in the minds of Euro-Americans would rise towards the beginning of the second decade. The Westerners would be alienated from many opportunities which they had been enjoying unobstructed since their domination. This feeling of alienation would engross their mind until they become converted to Islam or leave the land forever.

Individual alienation would lead to national and international alienation. A Westerner would be startled when he would come to know that the word "Goodnight", "Bye Bye" have been replaced by Sabba Katir, "Good Morning Mr!" by Issalam Aaleikum, "May God bless you" by Khuda Hafiz, etc., and these alien words are spoken by a large number of his compatriot Euro-Americans. A company officer with his tonsured head covered with a turban and bearded face would be found offering Namaz by closing the door of the office room at regular intervals. When questioned about their Western mother tongue, a large number of Euro-Americans would be found replying in Perso-Arabic instead of in English or French or German.

Islam is averse to painting, music, photography and poetry. Flamboyant arts, statues, etc., which have enlivened the life stream of Euro-America's nationalism, would be dispelled soon after the process of Transformation gets escalated in this soil. Like all other citizens of the affected nations the Euro-Americans would also be identified either as Euro-American Muslims or as Euro-American Christians. Presently the West is well acquainted as the Christian West, imbibed with the Christian Civilization. The very word "Christian Civilization" of the West will gradually become indistinct in course of the cultural invasion of Islam and would be stored in the pages of the history of Europe.

From the linguistic point of view another significant change in the coming decade would be the change of meaning and the definition of some words like "race". At present the word 'race' signifies Blacks and Whites according to Euro-American terminology. But henceforth race would be defined on communal ground as the Christian race and Muslim race, symbolizing the Cross and the Crescent respectively.

The nice national nomenclature of Euro-Americans would entirely cease. The names like Ronald, Bill, George, Alexander, Vladimir, Harry, Tom, Dick, John, Martin, William, Mary, Huntington, Diana, Alexander, Charles, Elizabeth, Victoria, etc., would be soon replaced by the pleasing Ali, Taslimuddin, Fazlul, Akhtar, Sirkaband, Akbar, Rehaman, Tazuddin, Jawahar, Nazma, Jehangir, Fatima, Mufti, etc., all with a prefix or suffix of Mohammed, Begum, Seikh, Sayed, etc.

After the first national life in the land of the U.S.A by the Red Indians and the second national life led by the Europeans in the brand name of American national life, now the present national life of America is going to be usurped by the Islamic national life, which is rapidly advancing and dominating world wide.

There would be another revolutionary change in the social life of all the affected nations of the world including Euro-America. The birth rate of the Muslim minority would get an unexpected high rise owing to their religious ideology, which simultaneously encourages early marriage and birth proliferation. The Muslims in almost all the non-Islamic secular countries get the privilege to marry before the age limit ascertained by the constitution of their respective secular nations according to their special right of religious minority. Generally in rural and even in urban areas Muslim boys marry soon after they attain puberty, almost at the age of 14/15. Poverty never remains as a hindrance in the way of their marriage or breeding. This helps to form a luxuriant, strong and populous group in their respective non-Islamic nations paving them the way to become the majority community of that country and dismantle the non-Islamic infrastructure of that land simultaneously pulverizing its non-Islamic civilization.

Recently the USA, under duress, has given access to Islamic religious emblems in postage. Towards the middle of the second decade of this century no more pictures of George Washington, the founding father of American nationalism, or Abraham Lincoln, the great emancipator of slaves, be found in the postal stamps of the U.S.A. Euro American common postal stamps and the postal stamps of all the affected nations will bear the pictures of bare landscapes and the portrait of the sacred mosque of Arabia signifying Islam. Similarly Euro-American currencies will be printed with the pictures of Mecca and Medina. Coins will be engraved with mosques and in Arabic language, the language of global Islamism. This process is rampant.

In Islam, pigs are the most heinous of beasts. In course of Islamisation of the affected countries the pigs gradually would disappear. White pigs may not face the same fate because the Turks, though Muslims, are habituated to pork-eating. Notably Turkey is a pork-exporting country. Coming under the reformative impact of Kemal Pasha, European Muslims will not so easily forbid the pork; though the rearing of pig is strictly prohibited in all other Islamic countries. The meat of donkey is permitted in Quran. Hence the meat of donkey can replace pork and the rearing of donkey will be introduced in place of pig as a new system of domestication in the USA.

The present system of abattoirs will be entirely replaced from the whole of Europe and the USA by the Islamic system of "halal" during 2020. No true Muslim would take the meat of the animals killed in the ordinary way. In the majority of slaughter houses of the world Muslims work as butchers. To satisfy the larger community by providing them exclusively halal meat, the authorities would make provisions to slaughter the animals according to the Islamic system, that is, by cutting their throat with a sharp knife and letting them die in excruciating pain. The slitting of throat is the only way to slaughter the meat breed animals. Hunting is strictly prohibited for the preparation of meat. In many cases knives and machetes will replace missiles and rockets. These will be used in plenty mostly to slit the throats of animals and human beings besides stabbing.

The printing of calendars with any human face will be considered a great offence. Printing the pictures showing the sensual parts of women in calendars for advertisement will be out of question. The modeling, beauty queen contest and the film industry are day-dreams in an Islam dominated society.

No living thing will be photographed. The taking of photograph is considered irreligious in Islam. Video shooting at a marriage function is a criminal offence. The police are authorized to tear a photo into pieces or disfigure it in a photo studio if he finds that the photo is larger than the size of a passport. They are also entitled and authorized to act as religious police. They are not as secular as the Scotland Yard police. The Islamic Police can innocently rebuff a non-Islamic citizen and can impose any sort of atrocity against their women folk. The Radio Shariat would replace the American Broadcasting Corporation and the British Broadcasting Corporation. Singing melodious songs or having recorded music cassettes is considered as a serious offence. Pop singers and dancers and actors like Madonna, Michel Jackson, etc., would be the target of the sword or bullet. They are the most heinous and villainous creatures in an Islamic kingdom.

A highly expensive budget would be inculcated in the national budget speculation in all the Euro-American countries. This budget would be exclusively for their internal security or civil security. During the second decade of this century every individual of Euro-America and the other affected nations will be required to maintain security guards. The USA's Defence Force would exert most of its time and energy to safeguard its people within the country. The European countries would also face the same fate. The metro lines, railway stations, national and international airports, parks, dam projects, auditoriums, etc., would be put under heavy security. The maintenance of internal security would be a great burden on its national exchequer.

Euro-America and the other affected nations would lose their credibility in maintaining secrecy. The maintenance of secrecy is a must in the field of scientific research work, defence force, and general administration. As a Muslim youth is devoted to his own race and global Islamic solidarity rather than the interest of his non-Islamised nation, he cannot provide any convenient access to the non-Islamic society of his own nation to prosper against Islam.

When a Muslim is the citizen of any one of the 12 member countries of the European Economic Committee, inevitably he is a member of the European community according to the great Maastricht Treaty. He can sense all the national affairs of a common European banking and currency system, foreign policy and common security, European citizenship, limits of power, the Parliament of Europe, the commission of Europe, administration of justice and domestic affairs, solidarity fund, new fields and about the social policy. All the principles accorded in the Maastricht Treaty for the knitting of the European countries, the Western European countries, would be materialized from the Muslim point of view. Any deviation of it would lead to unending chaos and the realization of it would lead to the Islamisation of Europe.

The celebration of festivals like the Valentine's Day, the day of love and other similar festivities would be baffled under suspicion and apprehension of danger. The New Year's Day that is celebrated on every first day of January would be shifted to the Islamic New Year's Day of Muharram.

Pre-communal secret killings relevant to civil war would be rampant during the period of Transformation. The great architects of Euro-American culture, Science, Music, the Arts, etc., would be assassinated in broad daylight to the utter helplessness of the present Westerners as the majority of judicial authorities, administrative officers and elected politicians would have belonged to Muslims. There are even evidences of Muslim army men gunning down their non- Muslim army officers in the military camps in the Muslim minority countries showing some or other reasons. There is no question of deployment of non-Muslims in the army in a Muslim majority country.

Night clubs, cabarets and other centres of entertainment would no more be in vision. An attempt of firing by militants at the nightclubs in different parts of the country would caution the people not to go there and the managing authorities would automatically close down the business.

The Euro-American dress code has its own distinctions. Their hairstyle and wearing of upper and lower garments, use of coat, suit, tie, shoes, etc., have been followed not only by the British common wealth countries but also by almost all the developed countries of the world including the underdeveloped African countries, the communist countries, Buddhist lands and other affected nations. This clothing style is worldwide considered as modern, secular and irreligious. But Islam has its own dress-code to suit its religion and culture. Islam has everything religious and culture-oriented up to the shaving of one's pubic hair and the circumcision of the genital organ.

The system of "Khatna" or cutting the outer skin of the penis that covers the organ is the old traditional system of te Jews, which had been inherited by both Islam and Christianity. Even Lord Jesus and his followers Peter etc., had undergone this ritual as staunch followers of Judaism. It is only Paul who, in order to bring reformation in Christianity and make this religion universal brought some changes both in ethics and in the system. He abolished the Sunnat (system) or Khatna from Christianity. But still it is inevitable in Islam. After the Islamisation of Euro-America and the other affected nations, people will have to rush to hospitals and stand in queue to cut carefully the soft skin cover of their penis and they would see that their male babies get their skin cut soon after their birth. Both male and female should see to it that their public hair must always be clean-shaven. They have to spare their time once every day or at least thrice a week to shave their private parts. Some herbal ointments are also in use, which keeps that part completely safe from hair sprout. You cannot urinate like the animals do. After you are converted to Islam, you cannot simply shake the organ and insert it into its own place. Soon after your urination is over, you have to wash it with clean water. If you have not stored water with you while you are on the way then you have to resort to an alternate solution. Keep hold of a small stone in your pocket. After urination is over, take the stone and rub your organ with it. It is as good as washing by water, according to Islam.

Even if you have embraced Islam, it is immaterial whether you have accepted it out of fear or pleasure; you are not safe from Islamic humility if you don't observe meticulously the Islamic tenets. Suppose you wrote a poem in praise of George Washington or Abraham Lincoln out of reverence for their contribution to nation-building. No sooner are you detected of having written this poem, you are declared an apostate for your un-Islamic writing. As a Muslim you are authorized to write praising none but Allah and his Prophet. No Wordsworth, no Byron, no Shelly, no Eliot, Tagore or Hess, nobody is praiseworthy for his voluminous literary writings. All are the itinerants of hell as their subject matter is not related to Islam, in praise of Mohammed and Allah. They are all apostates. Your wife and children of love no more belong to you the next moment you are declared an apostate. You cannot claim that they belong to you nor can they also claim that you belong to them. You lost every right of your being the paramount authority over them even including the right of talaq or divorce. After all you are no more a Muslim then, nor even a Christian, your former position. Thereafter your most favourite friend is "death".

Your children are not allowed to fly kites. It is abandoned in Islam. If a mother laughs aloud she is subject to be beaten (A small display of jaw is unlawful). Similarly you cannot find an arbiter in an Islamised America. In an Islamic country a Muslim can't act as an arbiter to stand impartially between a Muslim and a non-Muslim party.

Your hobby of keeping a Dalmatian, Alsatian, Labrador, Afghan, Gray Hound or even a poodle would be a fool's errand. Species of these dogs would disappear from Euro-America and the other affected nations. However you can have pet cats because these are found in plenty in Mecca.

As a consequence of Transformation, some unprecedented changes may occur in the social life of Euro-America. Christians would be forced to leave the areas, regions or states where they become a minority. They have to take refuge in other parts of Euro-America where they are in majority. Westerners would be amazed to find that the dreaded terrorists and criminals of horrendous acts imprisoned for years together would be released with unqualified apology as soon as the government of that province formed with a Muslim majority would come to power.

Towards the end of the second decade refugee camps would be rampant in all the affected nations.. Euro-American Christians in a Muslim-dominated area would be the key targets of Jehadi fighters. They would take refuge in the makeshift camps in Euro-America. The Government of Euro-America will be pressurized both by the Muslims and by the Afro-Americans to amend the constitution so as to suit the minorities to maintain their special status and privileges.

There would be the debut of suicide bombers among the Islamic Jehadi fighters in every corner of the Euro-American countries and other affected nations. After the ramification of these self-killers in Euro-America, terror would diffuse in all the non-Islamic countries of the world.

The kidnapping of women for molestation and men as hostage and the killing would be a day-to-day affair in all the Euro-American countries. The kidnapping of Euro-Americans in different Islamic countries would be a consensus. The Euro-Americans' journey into the Islamic majority countries or the countries dominated by Muslims would be jeopardized.

The Euro Americans in different Islamic countries would get a dreadful set-back with severe loss of human lives. They would be compelled to retreat to their respective countries.

Gradually the Muslim-dominated areas would demand for a plebiscite. The demand for an Islamic homeland will be the next issue. It is tantamount to the demand of an independent Islamic state. The formation of a state within a state where a man can take refugee in his homeland is one of the peculiar characteristics of the period of Transformation of Civilizations.

The most important change in Euro-America will be the replacement of American and British English by Arabic. The Quran will replace the Holy Bible and International Terrorism network would replace Information Technology (I.T).

5

Conclusion

(a) An Ultimate Ultimatum

When the community or the country as a whole reaches the third stage of ethnic cleansing, all will be in the same boat. A man may be the President of a state for a record period or the Prime Minister of a nation for a long term. Another may be very learned in a number of subjects. Still another may be a Nobel laureate of wonderful inventions useful for mankind. It may be that one is a noted social worker or philanthropist of international fame and vast fortunes, while another is a capable administrative officer of a state. There may be world-class crickters and hockey-players and Olympic champions of world record. We may find many skillful engineers and physicians, learned professors of international repute and academic abilities and achievements. Saints and sadhus may mingle with sincners and the riff-raff of this world. There will be people from every walk of life trying to be busy with their particular aims and purposes in this transitory world of ours. Whoever they are, whatever their station in life, none can finally escape the terrible and inevitable pangs of Ethnic Cleansing. All are bound to come down to the level and rank of street beggars with begging bowls in their hands (if their society undergoes a transformational experiment under the pressure of the coercive race of an alien civilization). When a society reaches the third phase of Ethnic Cleansing, all its citizens become bound to face its cruel and inescapable catastrophe.

(b) An Eye Opener?

The process of Global Civil War is on. This Civil war is basically an internal war. When it is simultaneously fought in all the nations of the world, then it is called the "Global Civil War". Hence its fervour cannot be felt or realized as in the former two World Wars. It may so happen that the war may end up without any hue and cry. It does not require a high sounding bombardment or such types of dissemination. The war has already begun in those countries that have given access to infiltration, conversion, high rate of infant breeding, unilateral marriages, etc. The Global Civil War will end when the Transformation of Civilizations is over.

To confront the Global Civil War, a nation must produce religiously and culturally determined civilians who would risk their lives for the protection of their respective national civilizations, which are an entity of culture, religion, language and motherland. The projection of secularism, particularly as professed in India is suicidal and violently detrimental for nation-building. The USA and European countries, though strong enough to confront its enemies in external war fields, don't seem to have prompted to confront the Global Civil War, the War that starts from within.

The religion that can inspire its followers best to proceed as civil warriors brings victory to the nation. Even if a man is more imbibed with the national feeling and national pride which is deeply rooted in his mind and body, he can hardly stand before a religious civil warrior who is more formidable than any nationalist. Religious nationalism combined with military aspiration and determination of racial animosity generates vigorous force and tremendous bravery in the followers than civic nationals. The Quran is the only religious scripture in the world, which creates religious nationalism, imparts militant aspirations and determines racial xenophobia. It is getting ready for a civil war in every corner of the world against the non-Muslims and exclusively in the Euro-American soil with all its needful equipment.

The Global Islamic Movement has started its initiatives for its victory in the greatest Transformation of Civilizations of this millennium. It is possible only when Euro-America and the affected nations come under the subjugation of Islam. The defensive force of Euro American culture with its modern civilization is on the verge of encountering a horrendous brunt of Islamic force. According to a speculation the Christian population of the U.S.A and Europe will come down nearly to form the minority group towards 2015. Then there would be the realization of the fervour of Transformation of Civilizations in Euro-America. All gulf countries have started the final preparations of war against the strongest formidable fort of non-Islamic nations, the Euro-American entity, vibrating the spirit of Transformation of Civilizations. After the second phase of Ethnic Cleansing in the Euro-American countries is over, the entire Gulf countries would sever all their bilateral and multilateral agreements according to their Islamic principles as dictated in the Quran. (2/225)."

"It is inundated to say that a subversive Islamic success against a non-islamic country anywhere in the world accounts for the subversive success of Islam against the whole of affected nations. Death of a Christian or a Jew or a Hindu in any part of the world signifies the decrease of a number amongst the defensive force of affected nations. The situation is vice-versa in the case of Islam."

The Clash of civilization necessitates war in all its shapes-civil war, cold war and external war. The civil war is followed by communal riots and internal holocaust. Cold war spreads like wild fire that oxidizes whatever it finds in its precincts. It also spreads like cancer, which expands secretly and reveals itself at the final stage. Successful immigration, infiltration, conversion, birth proliferation, etc., are the weapons of cold war. Islam has most successfully conducted the exercise of all these war weapons all over the world for confrontation against its enemies. Jehad is extremely prompt in all the aspects of war.

Generally everybody poses an illusive childish idea that a war to be fought must take place somewhere in a land which is away from his sweet home. Such expectations and speculations were true to some extent in the case of the last two World Wars. But regarding the ensuing Global Civil War its antecedents are quite different.

It is time for all the people of the world to face the great devastation of the impending Global Civil War. This Civil War would conflagrate around our sweet homes setting it ablaze, churning all of us as its participants in spite of our reluctance, hesitation and fear to participate in it.

The duration of the war may be some 10 to 15 years. But if the stipulated programme of the war delays due to the insufficiency of human weapons or for some other reasons, it may be extended to another 5 to 10 years, i.e, up to 2030 instead of 2020, but the Global Civil War is inevitable to consign the Transformation of Civilizations a great success.

The Expansion of imperialism presently means to win over a civilization. Islam has cherished to expand its imperialism only by winning over the modern civilization, the Western civilization, which exclusively means the Euro-American Christian civilization.

The Collision or clash of two civilizations would naturally and inevitably generate communal commotion, which will perpetuate an incessant flow of blood until the force of collision subsides.

The Great Transformation of Civilizations would prove which society is the fittest for survival. During this process the unfit societies in their struggle for existence would be extinct with their respective civilizations, leaving behind them some millions of orphans and molested widows, all but converted to the religion of the victorious dominant society.

Bibliography

Abbasi, S.M. Madani : *Family of the Holy Prophet,* Adam Publishers and Distributors, New Delhi.

Abbusi, S.M. Madami : *Riyadh-us-Saleheer,* Vol. I & II: Kitab Bhaban, New Delhi.

Abdullah-Al-Mamun Suhrawardy: *The Saying of Prophet Mohammed.* (No Publication Mentioned).

Afzal Hussain: *Sachha Deen,* Markaj Muktaba Islami, Delhi.

Ahmad Ilyas : *The Social Contract and the Islamic State,* Kitab Bhawan, New Delhi.

Ahmad, Hazrat Mirza *Bashirud-Din-Mahmud,* Mirza Washim Ahmad, Nazir Dawat-O-Tabligh, Qadian (India).

Ali, Syed Ameer : *The Spirit of Islam,* Kitab Bhawan, New Delhi.

Arab, A Short History (Hindi) (Author's name not mentioned), Prabhakar Sahityalok, Rani Katara, Lucknow.

Bhattacharya, S.K. : *Ganocide in East Pakistan/Bangladesh,* A.Ghosh, 5720, W. Little York, 216,Houston, Texas, USA.

Budayauni, M. Tayyib Bakhsh : *Sirat-un-Nabi,* Kitab Bhawan, New Delhi.

Bulandshari, Maulana Muhammed Ashiq : *The Wives of Prophet Mohammed,* Islamic Book Service, New Delhi.

Census Report of 2001, Government of India.

Dard, Maulavi A.R. : *The Hadith,* Book Depot, Latif-O-Ishaat, Qadian, Punjab.

Dehlvi Maulana Mohamed Saeed: *Isabella,* Saeed International, New Delhi.

Effendi Shoghi : *Call to Nations,* Bahai World Cetre, Universal House of Justice.

Ghosh, A : *The Koran and Kafir* (Islam and Infidel), A.Ghosh, 5720, W. Little York Suit, #216, Hauston, Texas-7709, USA.

Goel, Sitaram : *Hindu Society Under Siege,* Voice of India, New Delhi.

Gopal, Ram : *Bisawabyapi Islami Atankabad aur Bharat* (Hindi): Hindu Writers Forum, Delhi.

Guhathakurta, S : *Hindu Republic of Bie Bango,* Published by the Author, 16, Marcus Lane, Calcutta.

Hamidullah, Muhammad: *Battlefields of the Prophet Muhammad,* Kitab Bhawan, New Delhi.

Hassan, Masud-ul : *Hadrat Ali Murtada,* Kitab Bhawan, New Delhi.

Hathurani Maulana A.M. : *Names for Muslim Children,* Adam Publishers and Distributors, Delhi.

Idris, Gaafr Sheika : *The Process of Islamization,* Muslim Students' Association of the USA.

Illahi, Maulana Mohammed Ashiq : *The Daughter of Prophet Mohammed,* Islamic Book Service, New Delhi.

Khairabadi, Mail: *Islami Shariat,* Markaji Muktaba Islami, Delhi.

Khan, Muhammad Muhsin : *Sahib Al Bukhari,* Vol. I-IX, Kitab Bhawan, New Delhi.

Madhok, Balraj : *Kashmir Ka Sach,* Akhil Bharati, Delhi.

Malik, Fida Hussain: *Wives of Holy Prophet,* Adam Publishers and Distributers, Delhi.

Maududi, S.Abul A'la : *Jihad in Islam,* Islamic Publication Limited, Lahore, Pakistan.

Maududi, Sayyid Abul A'la : *Towards Understanding Islam,* Markaji Muktaba Islami Publishers, Delhi.

Mutahhari, Ayatullah : *A Discourse on the Islamic Republic,* Islamic Propagation Organisation (Tehran).

Naqavi, Dr. Ali Mohammed : *Islam and Nationalism,* Islamic Propagation Organisation, Tehran, Islamic Republic of Iran.

Pickshall, M. and Jallendhari Mohammed: *Al Quran-al-Hakim,* Kutub Khana Ishayat-ul-Islam, Delhi.

Shaikh, Anwar : *Islam, the Arab National Movement,* Principality Publishers, P.O. Box 918, Cardiff, Great Britain, CF2, 4YP

Sheshadri, H.V. : *The Tragic Story of Partition,* Jagaran Prakashan, Bangalore.

Siddiqi, Abdul Hamid: *Sahih Muslim:* Vol. I-IV, Kitab Bhawan, New Delhi.

Singh, Basudev : *Manabata Ka Shatru Islam* (Hindi), Shaktisena Publications, 15, Marcus Lane, Calcutta.

Tarjuma Quran Shariff, Ratan and Co., 16, Daryaganj, New Delhi.

Thanvi, Maulana Ashraf Ali : *Answer to Modernism,* Publishers and Distributers, Delhi.

Tirmizi, Imam Abu Isa: *Shamail-e-Tirmizi,* Kitab Bhawan, New Delhi.

Yusufali, Abdullah : *The Holy Quran* Vol. I-II, Kutub Khana Ishayat-ul-Islam, Delhi.

Index